Beijing

Recent Titles in Contemporary World Cities

Tokyo: Geography, History, and Culture
Louis G. Perez

Beijing

GEOGRAPHY, HISTORY, AND CULTURE

Qian Guo

Contemporary World Cities

An Imprint of ABC-CLIO, LLC
Santa Barbara, California • Denver, Colorado

Library of Congress Cataloging-in-Publication Data

Names: Guo, Qian (Geography teacher) author.
Title: Beijing : geography, history, and culture / Qian Guo.
Description: First edition. | Santa Barbara : ABC-CLIO, 2020. | Series:
  Contemporary world cities | Includes bibliographical references and
  index. |
Identifiers: LCCN 2019050091 (print) | LCCN 2019050092 (ebook) | ISBN
  9781440868047 (hardcover) | ISBN 9781440868054 (ebook)
Subjects: LCSH: Beijing (China)
Classification: LCC DS795 .G85 2020 (print) | LCC DS795 (ebook) | DDC
  951/.156—dc23
LC record available at https://lccn.loc.gov/2019050091
LC ebook record available at https://lccn.loc.gov/2019050092

ISBN: 978-1-4408-6804-7 (print)
        978-1-4408-6805-4 (ebook)

24 23 22 21 20   1 2 3 4 5

This book is also available as an eBook.

ABC-CLIO
An Imprint of ABC-CLIO, LLC

ABC-CLIO, LLC
147 Castilian Drive
Santa Barbara, California 93117
www.abc-clio.com

This book is printed on acid-free paper ∞

Manufactured in the United States of America

Contents

Series Foreword

In William Shakespeare's *The Tragedy of Coriolanus*, the character Sicinius poses the question, "What is the city but the people?"[1] According to the United Nations, our global cities are made up of more than half of the people in the world, with a projection that 60 percent of the world's population will be living in urban centers by 2030.[2] But diving deeper than population statistics, Sicinius was right—the heart of a city is not in its architecture or green spaces, nor is it in its stores, restaurants, Wall Streets, or red-light districts. The heart of a city is found in the people that live there, their diversity and unity, and the strong heartbeat that makes the city unique and loved by visitors and natives alike.

What is it like to live in these global centers, the main hubs of countries and regions, where industries thrive, immigrants settle, and traditions evolve? The *Contemporary World Cities* series examines the world's major urban centers—from Tokyo to Mexico City, Beijing to London, and Moscow to Paris. Each volume focuses on one major global city, incorporating information on the host country, but honing in on the urban center itself. Volumes begin with a preface and chronology of major events that have occurred in the city, followed by chapters covering the following topics:

- Location
- People
- History
- Politics
- Economy
- Environment and Sustainability
- Local Crime and Violence
- Security Issues

- Natural Hazards and Emergency Management
- Culture and Lifestyle
- The City in Pop Culture
- The Future

Chapters can be read on their own or one after another, with information suitable for researchers, general readers, and even travelers. "Did you know...?" sidebar boxes are scattered throughout the text, providing readers with intriguing fun facts about culture, taboos, and the "unwritten" rules of the city, such as how to properly order food from a street vendor to breaking down how the subway system *really* works. Chapters are accompanied by "Life in the City" inset boxes, memoir-styled interviews with people who have lived or visited each city, including exchange students and natives. These anecdotes include stories about culture shock, typical daily customs, and life in the city during major world events.

Contemporary World Cities allows readers to fully immerse themselves in another culture by gaining a better understanding of the culture, history, and society that make up the urban nerve centers of countries.

NOTES

1. William Shakespeare. *The Tragedy of Coriolanus.* Act 3, Scene 1. http://shakespeare.mit.edu/coriolanus/coriolanus.3.1.html.

2. "The World's Cities in 2016 Data Booklet." United Nations, 2016, page ii. https://www.un.org/en/development/desa/population/publications/pdf/urbanization/the_worlds_cities_in_2016_data_booklet.pdf.

Preface

Beijing in the twenty-first century stands out as the window for outsiders to look into China and the stage for the Chinese to showcase their country to the world.

Beijing is the capital of the People's Republic of China (PRC) and has been the capital of unified China for much of the last seven and a half centuries. It must be "the model of all places," a goal that is dictated by the central, instead of the municipal, government and that is to be achieved with no national resources spared.

Beijing is an ancient city in one of the oldest civilizations, with origins dating back three thousand years. Its prominence arose during the late imperial period and has sustained since as a result of environmental changes and geopolitical reconfigurations in East Asia. Therefore, Beijing is the best witness and bearer of profound political, economic, and cultural transformations in recent Chinese history.

Beijing is a megacity with a population of 21.5 million in 2018. It is the second-largest city in China after Shanghai (24.2 million) and one of the four government-designated megacities along with Shanghai, Shenzhen, and Guangzhou. Together with Shanghai, Chongqing, and Tianjin, Beijing is also one of the four centrally administered municipalities.

Beijing's long-standing capital status has made it a leading center for cultural institutions and the new economy. It has the largest number of universities and colleges, corporate headquarters, and unicorns—that is, privately held firms with market valuation exceeding USD 1 billion—and the greatest concentration of venture capital among all Chinese cities.

There are Chinese cities that rival Beijing in either historical heritage or economic might, but none can match Beijing in both regards. Xian and Luoyang, venerable ancient capital cities, do not come close to Beijing in economic and political prowess today. Shanghai and Shenzhen, also megacities and economic powerhouses, did not attain distinction until modern times.

WORLD RECORDS

Beijing holds a number of world records. First, it has seven UNESCO World Heritage Sites (the Forbidden City, the Temple of Heaven, the Summer Palace, the Great Wall, the Ming Tombs, the Peking Man Site at Zhoukoudian, and the Grand Canal). Second, it is acknowledged that Beihai Park is the oldest royal garden (eleventh century), the Forbidden City is the largest royal palace complex, and the Ming Tombs is the best-preserved royal burial site with the largest number of emperor's tombs. Third, Tiananmen Square is the largest central city square with 440,000 square meters (108.7 acres). Fourth, Beijing is the first city to host both Summer (2008) and Winter (2022) Olympic Games.

This is an opportune time to keep a close eye on Beijing, as it is undergoing unparalleled socioeconomic and spatial transformations. Beijing is endeavoring to reaffirm its role as the national center of politics, culture, international exchanges, and technological innovations. At the same time, noncapital functions are being dispersed from the city's urban core. Beijing's municipal government has relocated to Tongzhou, a brand-new capital subcenter in the eastern suburbs. A special district to the south of Beijing, the Xiongan New Area, is being developed as the new home for manufacturing, wholesale and logistics, and higher education as well as their respective workforces relocating from Beijing.

Beijing: Geography, History, and Culture is intended to serve high school and college undergraduate students as well as others who need a comprehensive introduction to Beijing. The twelve chapters cover a wide range of topics and the most important aspects of the city, including the natural

BEIJING OR PEKING

Beijing is the official romanization of the capital city of the People's Republic of China (PRC); it means the "northern (*bei*) capital (*jing*)." *Peking*, the historical romanization of *Beijing*, derived from what French missionaries transcribed as *Pékin*, based on how Nankinese (the dialect of Nanjing area), the official tongue of the time, pronounced *Bei-Jing* in the seventeenth century. In the 1950s, the PRC adopted a new romanization system, *hanyu pinyin*, in which *Beijing* replaced *Peking*. *Beijing* became the standard name internationally after the United Nations adopted hanyu pinyin in 1979 for transliterating Chinese names. However, *Peking* has been kept in the names of some historical brands and institutions, such as Peking roast duck and Peking University.

setting (chapter 1), demographic characteristics (chapter 2), a survey of pre-PRC history (chapter 3), politics and governance during the PRC era (chapter 4), the capital status and economic development (chapter 5), major environmental challenges and coping strategies (chapter 6), public safety and crime prevention (chapter 7), terrorist threats and security measures (chapter 8), natural hazards and mitigation (chapter 9), culture and life-style (chapter 10), creation and consumption of pop culture (chapter 11), and an overview of major trends and challenges in the future (chapter 12).

I would like to thank my friends and family for their support, especially those who contributed to the "Life in the City" insets. I am grateful to my beloved Beth, Galen, and Ethan, who tolerated my lack of attention to them while working on the book. Ms. Kaitlin Ciarmiello, editor of this book series, provided me with support, guidance, and patience. I would also like to thank the copy editor, Lisa Crowder, for her outstanding work.

Having been born and raised in Beijing, I see this book project as an emotional journey as much as an intellectual endeavor. It is also a tribute to my late father, who was named "born in Beijing" and who first intro-duced me to the many wonders of the city.

Chronology

ca. 700,000–200,000 BCE
Early humans (*Homo erectus pekinensis*), known as Peking Man, reside in limestone caves in the Zhoukoudian area.

ca. 18,000 BCE
Modern humans (*Homo sapiens*), known as Upper Cave Man, live in the caves of hilltops in the Zhoukoudian area.

ca. 10,000–2000 BCE
Neolithic societies are present in the modern Beijing area.

1045 BCE
Beijing is founded as the city of Ji. It becomes the capital of Ji, a vassal state of the Zhou Dynasty (1046–256 BCE).

865 BCE
Yan's verifiable chronicles begin.

ca. Seventh century BCE
Yan conquers Ji and moves its capital to the city of Ji, at the site of today's central Beijing.

697 BCE
Yan moves its capital south because of raids by nomads.

657 BCE
Yan moves its capital back to the city of Ji.

475–222 BCE
Yan contends for hegemony during the Warring States period.

226 BCE
Qin conquers Yan and destroys the city of Ji.

222 BCE
The Qin Dynasty rebuilds the city of Ji and makes it the seat of the Guang-yang Commandery (*jun*).

215 BCE
Qin Shihuangdi (the founding emperor of Qin, 259–210 BCE) reaches the city of Ji on his fourth tour of the newly unified empire.

206 BCE–8 CE
The city of Ji alternates between the vassal capital and commandery seat during the Western Han Dynasty (206 BCE–9 CE).

9–220
The city of Ji remains a commandery seat during the Xin Regime (9–25 CE) and Eastern Han Dynasty (25–220 CE).

220–581
The city of Ji frequently changes hands among warlords and nomadic groups and functions as a key regional center during the Northern and Southern Dynasties period.

250
Liu Jing, a regional governor, commences a flood control and irrigation project that significantly mitigates natural hazards and improves agriculture for the next nine centuries.

307
Construction of the first Buddhist monastery in the Beijing area, Tanze Temple, starts on Tanze Hills, 30 kilometers (18 miles) west of today's central Beijing.

352
Murong Jun, a warlord of nomadic Xianbei origin, declares himself emperor of "Former Yan" (337–370) and selects the city of Ji as his capital.

607
The city of Ji becomes the seat of the Zhuo Commandery during the Sui Dynasty (581–618).

608
The completion of the Yongji Canal, part of the canal projects under Sui Emperor Yangdi (569–618), connects the capital of Luoyang with the city of Ji.

618
The city of Ji becomes the city of Youzhou during the Tang Dynasty (618–907) as the seat of Youzhou (You Province).

696

Fayuan Temple, then called Minzhong Temple, is built in commemoration of the troops who died during the Tang Dynasty's Korean campaign. It now houses the Chinese Academy of Buddhism and the largest Buddhist library in China.

742

Tang Emperor Xuanzong (685–762) converts provinces (*zhou*) to commanderies (*jun*), through which the city of Youzhou becomes the seat of the Fanyang Commandery.

755

An Lushan, a former court minion and Fanyang military governor, launches a major revolt against the Tang Dynasty.

758

Fanyang becomes Youzhou again as commanderies (*jun*) are converted back to provinces (*zhou*).

936

A warlord with Central Asian origin surrenders Youzhou and fifteen other provinces to the Khitan Liao Dynasty (916–1125). Liao names the city Nanjing ("Southern Capital") or Yanjing ("Capital of Yan").

979

Song (960–1279) is defeated by Liao at the Gaoliang River near Nanjing, which commences two and a half centuries of nomadic rule in northern China.

996

The first mosque is built in the southern suburbs of Nanjing, in today's Oxen Street Muslim community.

1123

Nanjing is sacked by the Jurchen Jin Dynasty (1115–1234) and is returned to Song as the seat of Yanshan Fu (province).

1125

The Jin army attacks and retakes the city, renaming it Yanjing.

1149

The usurper Wanyan Liang announces a plan to move the capital to Yanjing and renames it Zhongdu ("Middle Capital").

1153

The Jin capital officially relocates to Zhongdu, marking the historical beginning of Beijing as a dynastic capital.

1192

The Lugou Bridge ("Marco Polo Bridge") over the Yongding River, 15 kilometers (9.3 miles) to the south of Jin Zhongdu, is completed after three years of construction.

1215

Mongols, led by Genghis Khan, sack Zhongdu after a yearlong siege and rename it Yanjing.

1264

Kublai Khan, a grandson of Genghis Khan and the governor of China proper, renames the city Zhongdu and designates it as a provisional capital of the Mongol Empire.

1267

Kublai Khan commissions a new imperial capital city to the northeast of Zhongdu.

1272

Kublai Khan designates the new imperial city as the capital of the Yuan Dynasty (1271–1368) and names it Dadu ("Grand Capital"), also known in Mongolian as Khanbaliq ("Khan's City"). It is the first time in history that Beijing is the capital of a unified China.

1275

Marco Polo arrives in Dadu with his father and uncle.

1279–1293

The Grand Canal is completed under the supervision of Guo Shoujing (1231–1316), connecting Beijing to southern China.

1283, January 9

Wen Tianxiang is executed in Dadu. As a chancellor of the Southern Song Dynasty (1127–1279), he is considered a patriot and poet in Chinese history.

1285

Construction of the imperial capital is officially completed.

1285–1294

Four hundred thousand to five hundred thousand new residents move into the new city of Dadu, many of whom are from Zhongdu (the old city).

Late 1200s

Coal is widely used as a supplement to firewood for heating and refining pig iron.

Early to mid-1300s

Work persists to repair and reinforce the earthen city walls.

1359

Barbicans are added to the eleven city gates.

1368, January 23

Zhu Yuanzhang founds the Ming Dynasty (1368–1644), with its capital in Nanjing.

1368, September

The Ming army sacks Dadu and destroys the royal palaces. The city is renamed Beiping ("Northern Peace"). To strengthen its defense, a brick-layer is added to the city's earthen walls, and a new wall is built 2.8 kilometers (1.73 miles) to the south of Dadu's northern wall.

1370

Zhu Di, a ten-year-old prince, is conferred Prince of Yan, with appanage in Beiping.

1380

Zhu Di arrives in Beiping to reign as Prince of Yan.

1399, August 6

Zhu Di launches a rebellion from Beiping against the new emperor (also his nephew).

1399, October

The court's five hundred thousand–strong army lays an unsuccessful siege on Beiping.

1400, May

The court's six hundred thousand–strong army lays a second unsuccessful siege on Beiping.

1403, January

Zhu Di prevails during the civil war and ascends to the crown as Emperor Yongle (1403–1424). Beiping becomes the subsidiary capital and is renamed Beijing ("Northern Capital") for the first time in history. Beijing and its environs become the Shuntian Fu, the capital district.

1403

Emperor Yongle commissions Yongle Dadian (Great Canon of the Yongle Era, or Yongle Canon).

1406

Emperor Yongle commissions the construction of royal palaces in Beijing, which sets the city's perimeters and grid pattern that remain to this day.

1408

Yongle Canon is completed and becomes the largest known encyclopedia in the world with 11,095 volumes.

1409
Emperor Yongle's tomb construction starts in the western hills, the first of the thirteen emperor's tombs to be built in the area.

1420
Emperor Yongle announces his decision to move the main capital to Beijing and to make Nanjing the subsidiary capital.

1421
The court officially opens in Beijing.

1425
Emperor Xuande (1425–1435) starts the process of moving the capital back to Nanjing.

1436
The construction of gate towers starts over all nine city gates.

1441
Emperor Zhengtong (1435–1449) halts moving the capital back to Nanjing and reaffirms Beijing as the capital.

1445
The work to cover the entire city wall with bricks begins.

1449, September 1
Oirat Mongols defeat a five hundred thousand–strong Ming army and capture Emperor Zhengtong at Fort Tumu (in today's Hebei Province).

1449, November
The siege on Beijing by Oirat Mongols is repelled at the city walls under the leadership of Yu Qian, a deputy minister of war, who has installed a new emperor, Emperor Jingtai.

1457
A court coup d'état deposes Emperor Jingtai and resurrects former emperor Zhengtong, now crowned as Emperor Tianshun; Yu Qian is killed during the coup.

Mid-1400s
Beijing's fuel source begins to switch from wood to coal because of deforestation in the surrounding highlands of the city. The growing dependency on coal from Beijing's environs leads to severe environmental deterioration.

1461, August 7
General Cao Qin and his troops of Mongol and Han descent carry out a daylong insurrection in Beijing in reaction to ongoing purges by Emperor

Tianshun. This event marks the last time during the Ming Dynasty that Mongols play an important role in Ming court affairs.

1531
The construction of temples of the earth, sun, and moon reframes Beijing in a Daoist eight-diagram layout.

1550
Tatar Mongols advance on Beijing but retreat within days after raiding the environs and signing a trade treaty with Ming.

1553
Emperor Jiajing (1507–1567) orders construction of an outer wall to enhance the defense against the Mongols. Only the southern section of the proposed outer wall is completed, however, which gives the walled city of Beijing a unique 凸shape.

1564
Barbicans are added to the seven gates of the outer wall.

1601
The Jesuit priest Matteo Ricci (1552–1610) arrives in Beijing and becomes the first European to enter the Forbidden City upon the invitation of Emperor Wanli.

1605
Emperor Wanli (1563–1620) permits Ricci to build the Southern Cathedral (Nantang), the first Catholic church in the city.

1626, May 30
A huge explosion in the southwestern corner of the Inner City, at the location of a munition and weapons depot, kills between several hundred and twenty thousand people and causes widespread property damage, including damage to the Forbidden City. The incident is known as Wanggongchang Explosion (the Great Tianqi Explosion). The cause of the explosion is still debated.

1629
The semisedentary hunting-fishing Manchus breach the Great Wall and lay siege on Beijing under the leadership of Huang Taiji (also known as Abahai) for months. They also trick the Ming court to execute Yuan Chonghuan, the Ming general who has led a successful defense.

1643
A plague pandemic hits Beijing, claiming around two hundred thousand lives.

1644, April 25
Rebel forces led by Li Zicheng take over Beijing. The Ming emperor Chong-zhen hangs himself on Coal Hill behind the Forbidden City.

1644, May 27
Li Zicheng suffers a major defeat at the hands of former Ming forces and Manchus near the Shanhaiguan Pass of the Great Wall.

1644, June 3
Li Zicheng is crowned as the emperor of the Shun Dynasty and flees the city the next day; in all, he has occupied Beijing for forty-one days.

1644, June 6
Manchus capture Beijing and declare it the capital of the Qing Dynasty (1644–1911). Balking traditional practice, Manchus assume the Forbidden City instead of destroying it.

1648
The court starts the process of displacing civilians in the Inner City with the troops of the Eight Banners.

1650
The first Catholic cathedral (South Cathedral) is completed under the supervision of Johann Adam Schall von Bell, a German Jesuit and astronomer who came to Beijing in 1623.

1671
The court issues an edict to ban opera theaters and other entertainment establishments in the Inner City.

1679, September 2
A magnitude 8.0 earthquake strikes near Beijing, causing 45,500 deaths and widespread damage in the capital and its environs.

1698, August
Emperor Kangxi confers a new name, Yongding He ("Ever-Definite River"), to Hun He ("Muddy River"), the largest river in Beijing and its environs after the completion of large-scale and successful flood mitigation projects.

1709
Construction commences on Yuanmingyuan (known in the West as "the Old Summer Palace"), which includes three adjacent imperial gardens.

1729
The first foreign language (Latin) school opens in Beijing.

1747

Giuseppe Castiglione and Michel Benoist, Jesuits serving in the court, begin architectural designs for the European gardens in Yuanmingyuan, which are completed in 1783.

1762

An imperial edict is issued to prohibit bannermen from frequenting bars and theaters.

1763

Cao Xueqin, author of *Dream of the Red Chamber*, one of the four Chinese classic novels, dies in Beijing.

1770

The major construction on Yuanmingyuan is completed.

1781

The city's population reaches 776,242, prompting the court to restrict new immigration.

1787

Siku quanshu (Complete Library in the Four Branches of Literature) is completed and becomes the world's longest series of books at the time.

1793, August 21

The first British diplomatic mission to China, the Macartney Embassy, reaches Beijing. It is received by Emperor Qianlong in Chengde on September 14.

1803, April 11

An assassin attacks Emperor Jiaqing's entourage inside the Forbidden City.

1813, September 15

Over two hundred followers of the White Lotus Sect launch an attack on the Forbidden City and reach the inner court before being repelled.

1860, September 21

Anglo-French forces defeat the Qing army in the Battle of Baliqiao (Palikao), east of Beijing, during the Second Opium War.

1860, October 13

Anglo-French forces enter Beijing.

1860, October 18

Anglo-French forces set Yuanmingyuan aflame.

1861, November 8
The two empress dowagers seize power in a court coup d'état after the death of Emperor Xianfeng. One of them, Cixi, eventually becomes the de facto ruler of China until her death in 1908.

1864, August
The American Congregational Church establishes the Yu Ying School, the first Christian missionary school in Beijing.

1865
The first railroad track in China, 500 meters (1,640 feet) long, is built outside the Xuanwumen Gate by a British merchant, but it is ordered to be dismantled soon thereafter.

1883, July 20
Electrical power lines are set up between Tianjin and Tongzhou.

1888
Reconstruction is complete for a royal garden destroyed during the Second Opium War using funds for the imperial navy. The rebuilt garden is renamed Yiheyuan and is known in the West as the Summer Palace.

1895, May 2
Kang Youwei and Liang Qichao lead over 1,300 scholars to file a royal petition for political reforms.

1898, June 11
Emperor Guangxu proclaims political reform, which is known as Wuxu Reform or the One Hundred Days' Reform.

1898, July 3
Peking University is founded and will go on to be considered "the Harvard University of China."

1898, September 21
Empress Dowager Cixi carries out a coup to stop reforms. Emperor Guangxu is placed under house arrest, and six of the reformist leaders are arrested and executed.

1900
The Boxer Rebellion, an antiforeigner populist movement, results in a fifty-five-day siege on the Legation Quarter and intervention by allied forces from eight countries. The court flees, and the allied forces occupy the capital.

1901, September 7
The Boxer Protocol is signed at the Spanish Legation, which incurs an indemnity of 450 million taels of fine silver, which are equal to USD 333

million in 1901, over a course of thirty-nine years and permits foreign military presence in China.

1902
Two railroad stations are built on the east and west sides of the Zhengyangmen Gate (Qianmen).

1903, January 19
Ketteler-Denkmal, a masonry memorial gate (*paifang*), is erected at the location where German ambassador Clemens von Ketteler was assassinated by the Qing troops during the Boxer Rebellion. It is abolished after World War I.

1904, January 2
Beijing installs its first telephone exchange.

1905, August 20
The first daily newspaper for women in China, the *Beijing Women's Daily*, is published.

1906
The first civilian electric power company starts operation.

1908
The Capital Running Water Stock Corporation is founded with funding from selling shares to the Chinese public.

1908, November 14
Emperor Guangxu dies, and Empress Dowager Cixi dies twenty-one hours later.

1908, December 2
Aisin Gioro Puyi (1906–1967) is crowned as Emperor Xuantong of the Qing Dynasty. He is to become "the Last Emperor" in Chinese history.

1909
The Imperial Beijing-Zhangjiakou Railway starts operation as the first railroad in China built without foreign investment.

1911, June
The Central Postal Office is inaugurated.

1912, February 12
In the aftermath of the 1911 Xinhai Revolution, Empress Dowager Longyu signs the abdication agreement on behalf of five-year-old Emperor Xuantong, effectively ending both the Qing Dynasty and China's imperial era.

1912, March 3
A mutiny takes place by troops loyal to Yuan Shikai, who uses it as excuse for refusing to relocate to Nanjing and to recognize it as the national capital.

1912, March 10
Yuan Shikai is sworn in as the provisional president of the Republic of China (ROC) and retains Beijing as the national capital.

1912, August 25
Kuomintang (KMT, the Chinese Nationalist Party) is founded at the Huguang Guild Hall.

1912, August 27
The Beijing Library, the predecessor of the National Library of China, opens to public after three years of preparation.

1913, October 10
Yuan Shikai is sworn in as the president of the Republic of China in the Forbidden City.

1915
Infrastructure modernization takes place throughout the city. Tiananmen Square is created after demolishing the barbican of the Zhengyangmen Gate.

1915, May 9
Yuan's government is forced to sign unequal treaties with Japan, which ignites massive nationwide protests. The ROC government designates the day as the National Day of Shame.

1915, December 12
Yuan Shikai is crowned as emperor of the Empire of China.

1916, March 23
Yuan Shikai abdicates and resumes the presidency of the ROC. He dies on June 6.

1917, July 1
Zhang Xun, a warlord and Qing loyalist, carries out a coup to restore the Qing Dynasty. The so-called Manchu Restoration lasts for twelve days.

1917, September
The Rockefeller Foundation opens the Peking Union Medical College at the former mansion of Prince Yu.

1919, May 4
College students protest in Tiananmen Square in response to the treatment of China by the Allied Powers during negotiations of the Treaty of

Versailles. It comes to be known as the May Fourth Movement and marks the advent of China's student social activism and political modernization.

1921
Evidence of proto-humans is first discovered in the limestone caves in Dragon Bone Hill of Zhoukoudian.

1923, June 26
For unknown causes, a fire in the Forbidden City destroys 130 structures and the treasures in them.

1924, November 5
Warlord Feng Yuxiang takes control of the ROC provisional government after a coup and forces the abdicated Qing court out of the Forbidden City, where it had resided since 1912.

1924, December 31
Sun Zhongshan, the founder of the ROC, arrives in Beijing to broker reconciliations among various political factions.

1925, March 12
Sun Zhongshan dies of cancer and is entombed at the Temple of Azure Clouds in Fragrant Hills.

1926, March 18
A large number of demonstrators gather in front of Tiananmen Gate and march on government offices, demanding the abolishment of unequal international treaties. Soldiers open fire, killing dozens and wounding many more. The incident comes to be known as the March 18 Massacre.

1927, April 28
Li Dazhao, a founder of the Chinese Communist Party (CCP) and a college professor, is executed by a warlord.

1928, June 20
Beijing is renamed Beiping by the new ROC government under Kuomintang (KMT), which has moved the national capital to Nanjing after triumphing in its Northern Expedition.

1929, December 2
The first intact skull of Peking Man is excavated in Dragon Bone Hill of Zhoukoudian.

1930
Beiping is downgraded to a municipality of Hebei Province, but it is then elevated to a centrally administered municipality.

1933
Selected historical and cultural artifacts from the Palace Museum in the Forbidden City are transported to Shanghai to avoid potential seizure by the Japanese.

1935, December 9
Student-led mass protests break out, demanding the Chinese government actively resist Japanese aggression. The event comes to be known as December 9th Movement.

1937, July 7
Clashes between the Chinese and Japanese troops near Lugou Bridge (Marco Polo Bridge) lead to nationwide resistance to the Japanese invasion.

1937, October
Beiping is renamed Beijing by the Japanese-controlled puppet government.

1940, May
The city ruins of Liao and Jin are excavated.

1941, December 8
The fossils of Peking Man are shipped out of Beijing under the escort of U.S. Marines but disappear when the convoy is intercepted by the Japanese.

1945, August
Chinese forces liberate Beijing and rename it Beiping.

1946, December 24
An alleged sexual assault of a college student by a U.S. Marine causes nationwide protests.

1949, January 31
Communist forces take over Beiping without major combat, hence preserving many of the historical relics in the city.

1949, September 8
The CCP and its political allies decide to select Peiping as the capital of the People's Republic of China and rename the city Beijing.

1949, October 1
The Central People's Government of the PRC is officially established, followed by celebratory activities of three hundred thousand people and a military parade in Tiananmen Square.

1950, March 30
All six major dredging projects of the city's sewer and drainage systems are completed.

1951, August
The Judge Advocate Section of Beijing's Military Central Committee convicts and sentences to death Antonio Riva, an Italian, and Ruichi Yamaguchi, a Japanese, as ringleaders of a plot to assassinate the PRC's top leaders.

1952
Seven new colleges are formed as existing colleges and universities are restructured.

1952
Demolition of the city gates begins for traffic improvement.

1953
Five new colleges are formed.

1953, June 30
Beijing's population reaches 2.7 million based on the first population census of the PRC.

1954
Three new colleges are formed.

1955
Four new colleges are formed.

1956
Six new colleges are formed.

1956–1958
Beijing's administrative perimeters take shape after several adjacent counties come under Beijing's jurisdiction.

1956–1958
Systematic demolition of the Outer City walls and about half of the Inner City walls begins.

1958
Five more colleges are formed, adding to the growing list of colleges and universities in Beijing.

1958–1965
The city walls are systematically demolished to make way for modern transportation infrastructure.

1959
Ten landmark buildings are completed in commemoration of the PRC's tenth anniversary, and Tiananmen Square is expanded from 110,000 square meters to 400,000 square meters, the largest public square in the world at the time.

1960
Beijing undergoes administrative realignment, which creates eight urban districts and nine rural counties.

1960, September
Miyun Reservoir is completed as the largest reservoir in North China and a major water supply source for Beijing.

1964, June 30
The second population census shows Beijing's population at 7.6 million, of which 58 percent are urban.

1964
Three new colleges are formed.

1965
Systematic demolition of the remaining Inner City walls for subway construction takes place.

1966–1968
The Great Proletarian Cultural Revolution breaks out in Beijing, with mass rallies of the Red Guards in Tiananmen Square. It quickly descends into ten-year-long chaos.

1966, August 24
Preeminent novelist and playwright Lao She commits suicide.

1967
A new district, Shijingshan, is incorporated to become the home of the Capital Iron and Steel Corporation.

1967, October 17
Puyi, the last emperor of China, dies of cancer.

1969, October
The first urban subway in China is completed.

1971, September 13
Marshall Lin Biao, the second-highest PRC leader, dies in a plane crash in Mongolia after a political fallout with Mao Zedong, the paramount leader of the PRC.

1972, February 21
U.S. president Richard Nixon arrives in Beijing and meets with Mao Zedong.

1974, October
The first modern overpass is constructed at the site of the Jianguomen Gate near the new diplomatic quarter.

1976, April
The first public protest during the PRC era takes place in Tiananmen Square and ends with a government crackdown.

1976, September 9
Mao Zedong, founder of the PRC, dies at the age of eighty-two.

1976, October 6
Leaders of the radical wing of the CCP, dubbed "the Gang of Four," are purged, marking the end of the Great Proletarian Cultural Revolution.

1977, July 31
Deng Xiaoping appears at an international soccer match to proclaim his resumption of power and the commencement of economic reform.

1977, August 29
The Chairman Mao Zedong Memorial Hall is completed in Tiananmen Square.

1978, December
"The policy of reform and opening up" is announced at the CCP's Third Plenum of the 11th Congress.

1979
The short-lived political liberalization of Beijing Spring gives birth to the Democracy Wall, which is removed after a few months. Its high-profile advocate, Wei Jingsheng, is convicted of leaking state secrets and sentenced to fifteen years in prison.

1980
A new district, Yanshan, is established to accommodate the behemoth Yanshan Petrochemical Corporation.

1981, September 27
The first Beijing International Marathon is held.

1983, September 23
Construction starts on the new Beijing Library, which will be 140,000 square meters (1.5 million square feet).

1984, September 19
Phase 2 of the city's subway project is completed.

1987
Beijing selects city flowers (chrysanthemum and Chinese rose) and city trees (Chinese scholar tree and oriental arborvitae).

1987, October 6
The new Beijing Library opens to the public.

1987, December 10
Construction starts on the first segregated expressway in China, the Beijing-Tianjin-Tanggu (port) Expressway.

1988, May 10
The State Council approves the Beijing New Technological Development Experiment Zone with a planned area of 100 square kilometers (38.6 square miles).

1988, June 29
The Relic Park of Yuanmingyuan opens to the public.

1989, May
Beijing is nearly paralyzed by large-scale demonstrations led by college students.

1989, June 4
The military clashes with demonstrators in and around Tiananmen Square, resulting in a large number of casualties and enactment of martial law.

1990, January
The State Council ends martial law in most areas of Beijing.

1990, September 22
Beijing hosts the Eleventh Asian Games, the first time such games are held in China.

1990, November 6
The Fourth National Census concludes that Beijing's population has exceeded ten million.

1993, September 23
Beijing loses to Sydney in its bid to host the 2000 Summer Olympics at the International Olympics Committee meeting.

1994
The forty-eight-kilometer (thirty miles) Third Ring Road qualifies as an expressway with a designed speed limit of eighty kilometers per hour (fifty miles per hour).

1995, April 27
Chen Xitong, Beijing's CCP secretary and a member of the CCP Politburo, is removed from office amid corruption scandals after the suicide of a deputy mayor, Wang Baosen.

1995, May 1
Beijing implements a five-day work week.

1995, September
Beijing hosts the Fourth World Conference on Women with forty-seven thousand participants, the largest-ever gathering of government and NGO representatives at a United Nations conference.

1996
Pilot programs are implemented for domestic waste sorting.

1997, February 14
A high-ranking North Korean official escapes into the South Korean embassy and applies for political asylum.

1997, February 28
Deng Xiaoping dies at the age of ninety-three.

1997, March 7
Two bombs are detonated on buses, killing five and injuring many more. The East Turkestan Islamic Movement (ETIM) claims responsibility.

1997, June 27
A major explosion kills nine and injures thirty-nine at a chemical facility in Tongxian, east of central Beijing.

1997, June 30
Celebrations break out in Beijing and throughout China on Hong Kong's return to Chinese sovereignty.

1997, July 8
The first air-conditioned bus starts operation in Beijing.

1998, October 28
A Chinese airliner from Beijing to Kunming is hijacked to Taiwan, the last time such a hijack takes place.

1999, April 25
Followers of Falun Gong, considered either as a spiritual movement or as a cult, carry out two large sit-in protests, which lead to a government ban of Falun Gong on July 22.

1999, May 8
Massive protests break out against the U.S. bombing of the Chinese Embassy to Yugoslavia in Belgrade during NATO operations. Protestors amass outside the U.S. Embassy and pelt it with rocks and other objects.

1999, October 1
A large parade is held in Tiananmen Square to celebrate the PRC's fiftieth anniversary, the first time such parades had been held since 1984.

1999, November 15
The Chinese and U.S. governments sign a bilateral agreement over China's ascension to the World Trade Organization (WTO).

2000, November 1
The Fifth National Census reveals Beijing's permanent resident population is 13.8 million.

2001, January 1
Baidu, a leading Chinese internet search company, is founded in Beijing.

2001, January 23
Several Falun Gong followers self-immolate in Tiananmen Square.

2001, June
The Fourth Ring Road is completed as an expressway with a total length of 65.3 kilometers (40.6 miles).

2001, July 13
Beijing wins the bid to host the XXIX (29th) Summer Olympiad.

2002, June 16
Twelve people die in an arson at an internet bar in Haidian District.

2002, July 24
Liu Xiaoqing, a prominent actress, is arrested for tax evasion.

2003
In the spring, Beijing is stricken by an outbreak of severe acute respiratory syndrome (SARS), which results in 2,521 reported cases and 193 deaths.

2003, November 1
The entire 98 kilometers (61 miles) of the Fifth Ring Road is open to traffic, but many drivers shun it due to high tolls.

2004, February 5
A stampede causes thirty-seven deaths and fifteen injuries at a Lantern Festival in Miyun County.

2004
The China Open, a professional tennis tournament, is held for the first time.

2005
Two PRC citizens, Wo Weihan and Guo Wanjun, are arrested under charges of spying for Taiwan. They are subsequently sentenced to death and executed in 2008.

2005, April 29
The heads of the Chinese Communist Party and Chinese Nationalist Party meet for the first time since 1946.

2006, May 10
Yikatong, an integrated circuit card (ICC), replaces all traditional public transit cards that had been used for sixty-nine years.

2006, November 4–5
The Beijing Summit of the Forum on China-Africa Cooperation (FOCAC) is attended by heads of state or high-ranking officials from forty-eight African countries.

2008, February 29
Terminal 3 of the Beijing Capital International Airport opens as the largest single-building terminal in the world.

2008, August 1
The Beijing-Tianjin intercity railway starts operation as the first high-speed rail service in China with a top speed of 350 kilometers (217 miles) per hour.

2008, August 8–24
The XXIX (29th) Summer Olympiad is held in Beijing.

2008, August 9
A man attacks two American tourists at the Drum Tower, killing one and wounding the other as well as their guide before committing suicide.

2009, February 9
Illegal fireworks set ablaze and destroy a nearly completed skyscraper next to the China Central Television building.

2009, June 23
Liu Xiaobo, a signatory of Charter 08, is arrested on charges of "inciting subversion of state power." He is later awarded the 2010 Nobel Peace Prize.

2009, September
The 187-kilometer (116 miles) Sixth Ring Road opens to traffic.

2009, October 1
Mass celebrations, including a military parade, are held in commemoration of the sixtieth anniversary of the PRC.

2009
The authorities promote waste sorting among public entities. By the end of the year, 30 percent of the city's neighborhoods are covered by one hundred demonstration sorting stations.

2010, April
Beijing starts closed-off management for communities at the urban-rural interface to control transient population.

2010, July 1
The four districts in Beijing's urban core (Dongcheng, Xicheng, Xuanwu, and Chongwen) are consolidated into the Dongcheng and Xicheng Districts.

2010, November 1
The Sixth National Census shows Beijing's permanent resident population is 19.6 million.

2012
The Beijing Municipal Government announces it will establish an administrative subcenter in the Tongzhou District.

2012, March 1
The Beijing Domestic Waste Management Regulations are implemented.

2012, July 21
The strongest rainstorm in sixty-one years causes at least seventy-nine deaths, major flooding, and widespread property damage.

2012, November 15
Xi Jinping is elected the CCP's general secretary and chairman of the Central Military Commission.

2013, March 14
The National People's Congress elects Xi Jinping as the PRC president.

2013, October 28
An SUV plows through pedestrians, killing two and injuring dozens, in Tiananmen Square before crashing in front of the Tiananmen Gate and catching fire amid explosions. All three people inside, from the same Uyghur family, die. The Turkistan Islamic Party claims responsibility.

2014, February 8
Beijing and Zhangjiakou submit a joint bid for the 2022 Twenty-Fourth Winter Olympics.

2014, March 26
Several students from Peking University found Ofo, starting a period of fierce competition among bike-sharing startups, including Mobike.

2014, October
Asia Infrastructure Investment Bank (AIIB) is founded in Beijing with twenty-two member countries.

2014, November 5–11
The APEC Summit is held in a suburban resort (Yanxihu).

2014, November 20
The State Council issues new city classifications based on a five-tier system. Beijing is in the top tier as one of the megacities—a city with more than ten million residents.

2014, December 26
Construction starts on the Beijing Daxing International Airport (PKX).

2014, December 27
The south–north water diversion project reaches Beijing.

2015
The groundbreaking ceremony is held for the administrative subcenter in the Tongzhou District as part of Beijing's decentralization process.

2015, July 31
The International Olympic Committee (IOC) announces that Beijing and Zhangjiakou will cohost the 2022 Winter Olympics, making Beijing the first city in the world to host both Summer and Winter Olympics.

2015, September 3
A massive military parade commemorates the seventieth anniversary of Victory over Japan Day of World War II.

2016
The 1,000-kilometer (621 miles) Seventh Ring Road is completed, but only 38 kilometers of the road are within Beijing.

2016, October 30
The air quality index (AQI) is over one hundred in the morning, but a cold wave comes through in the afternoon with strong winds that brings the AQI down to below twenty.

2017, March 18
The last large coal-firing power plant in Beijing goes off-line but has to come back online in late 2018 due to high prices and short supply of natural gas.

2017, April 1
The Xiongan New Area is established to promote regional integration among Beijing, Tianjin, and Hebei Province (Jing-Jin-Ji).

2017, August 1
Beijing begins housing programs to assist the needs of low-income residents. Homes with joint property rights are paid for and owned by the buyer and the government, with the buyer having full user right.

2017, September 27
The State Council responds to Beijing's 2016–2035 Master Plan by emphasizing capping the city's population at twenty-three million.

2017, November 18
An apartment complex in southern Daxing District catches fire, killing nineteen people, mostly migrant workers and their families. The authorities begin to demolish entrenched "urban villages" in the aftermath of the tragedy.

2018, July 26
A man detonates an improvised explosive device (IED) outside the U.S. Embassy, injuring only himself.

2018, August 21
A tip hotline is opened for citizens to file complaints against misconduct by rental intermediary businesses.

2018, September 21
The Double First Class University Plan is announced with eight of the thirty-six Class A universities located in Beijing.

2018, November–December
The China Animal Disease Control Center reports African swine fever cases in the suburbs.

2018, December 28
The State Council officially approves the Master Plan for Xiongan New Area, Hebei Province (2018–2035), commencing rapid development of the Xiongan New Area.

2018
By the end of the year, 2,300 public entities participate in compulsory waste sorting.

2019, January 7–10
North Korean leader Kim Jong-un visits Beijing.

2019, January 8
A maintenance worker attacks pupils in an elementary school, wounding twenty.

2019, January 11
The capital subcenter officially opens for business.

2019, April 25–27
Beijing hosts the Second Belt and Road Forum for International Cooperation.

2019, April 29
The 2019 Beijing International Horticultural Exposition opens as an A1 exposition on a 503-hectare park.

2019, April 30
A large rally is held in the Great Hall of the People commemorating the centennial anniversary of the May Fourth Movement.

2019, May 13
Beijing Daxing International Airport conducts trial takeoffs and landings in advance of the planned September opening.

2019, July 20
Over one hundred thousand applicants have applied for Point-Based Household Registration by the deadline, and six thousand will be granted permanent household registered status.

2019, July
By the end of July, Beijing has over 7,800 5G base stations and will exceed 10,000 by the end of the year.

2019, September
Preparations are underway for the PRC's seventieth anniversary on October 1, including parade rehearsals, a no-fly zone for the six urban districts, strict postal inspections, and an air raid drill outside of the Fifth Ring Road.

2019, October 1
Massive celebration is held in Tiananmen Square, featuring a large military parade and evening fireworks, in commemoration of the seventieth anniversary of the PRC.

2019, November 12
Two patients from Inner Mongolia are confirmed to have plague after more than a week of testing and treatment in quarantine.

2019, November 25
The Beijing Municipal Ecology and Environment Bureau reports that the average concentration of PM2.5 was 41 micrograms per cubic meter for the first ten months, which represents a decrease of 16.3 percent year-on-year.

CHINA

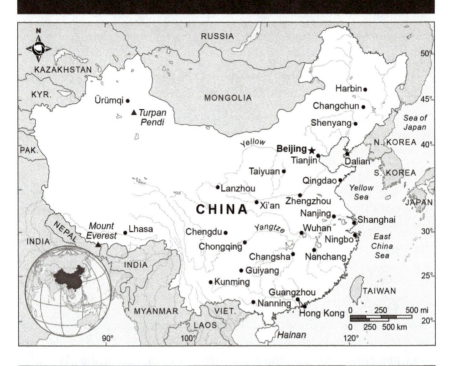

CITY STREET MAP OF BEIJING

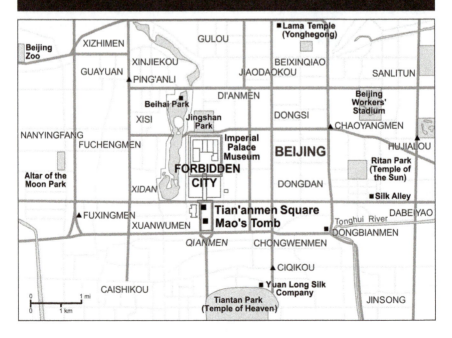

1

Location

A city is intrinsically connected to its natural environment and bears the imprints of the latitude and longitude location, climate (long-term average weather conditions), and topography (landform configurations). Nature's influence on a city changes over time along with changes in population, lifestyle, technology, and economy. A city's quality of life and sustainability largely depend on how its development fits in its natural environment.

Beijing (39°54′ N, 116°23′ E) is located in the mid-latitude temperate climate zone and near the east coast of Eurasia. It has the typical East Asia (temperate) monsoon climate, which covers much of East Asia, including Eastern China, Japan, and the Korean Peninsula. This climate is characterized by cold, very dry winters and warm, wet summers in comparison to other types of temperate climates. It is the result of the great land-sea contrast between Eurasia, the largest continent, and the Pacific, the largest ocean, in the world.

Beijing is similar to some American cities of comparable latitude locations, such as Chicago, New York City, and Philadelphia, in terms of average annual and seasonal temperatures (Table 1.1). However, a closer examination reveals important differences between Beijing and its U. S. counterparts: Beijing has slightly colder winters and warmer summers and has significantly less precipitation. Between 1982 and 2012, Beijing had an average annual precipitation of 610 mm (24 inches), which is within the 400–800 mm (16–32 inches) range of annual precipitation for semi-humid climates; its precipitation has great seasonal variations, however, concentrating in the summer and leaving the winter exceedingly dry (Table 1.1). Between October 23, 2017, and March 16, 2018, for example, Beijing registered the longest period on record, 145 days, with no verifiable precipitation.

Climate data also show that Beijing's annual precipitation fluctuated greatly over time with intermittent wetter and drier periods. Between 1978 and 2016, for example, the annual precipitation ranged from a low of 266.9 millimeters (10.5 inches) in 1999 to a high of 813.2 millimeters (32 inches) in 1994, with average annual precipitation of 547.4 millimeters (21.6 inches). In recent years, the annual precipitation has shown a slight uptick: the 2018 annual precipitation was 575.5 millimeters (22.66 inches), slightly more than that in 2017 (540.7 mm).

Beijing has four distinct seasons. In winter, high-pressure systems develop and situate in Siberia and generate north–northwest prevailing winds, covering much of East Asia with cold and dry weather. Intense cold waves regularly break through the barriers of warmer air masses and rush down south, plunging East Asia, including Beijing, into deep freeze for days. In summer, the Eurasian heartland heats up quickly, and the resultant low pressures near the land surface create an enormous "vacuum" that "sucks in" the warm and moist air masses from the Pacific Ocean. South–southeast prevailing winds in the summer bring about three-quarters of the annual precipitation to Eastern China.

Beijing's spring and autumn are relatively short. Spring may not be as pleasant as elsewhere despite the warm-up and return of green foliage; it is windy and dry with recurrent sand and dust storms and drastic temperature fluctuations. Autumn is the best season of the year in Beijing. Starting

DID YOU KNOW?

SEASONAL CLOTHING

Beijing has four distinct seasons. The summer, usually from late May to mid-September, calls for light and comfortable clothes that can be easily washed and dried, such as T-shirts, cargo pants, and shorts. The winter, usually from mid-November to late March, requires a winter jacket or down garment, thermal shirts and pants, and a hat, scarf, and gloves. Spring (late March to late May) and autumn (mid-September to mid-November) are relatively brief and are best served by sturdy, warm, and washable clothes, such as a comfortable jacket, a heavier sweater, or a casual coat. For most visitors, it may suffice to bring a pair of comfortable waterproof shoes for walking and moderate climbing. Sandals are good for warmer seasons, and hiking boots are useful if one expects to be in rugged terrains. Travelers will find most merchandise in ample supply in China and comparable in price and quality to U.S. stores.

Table 1.1   Climate Comparison of Beijing, Chicago, New York City, and Philadelphia (1982–2012)

City	January Average Temperature	July Average Temperature	Temperature Difference January vs. July	Average Annual Precipitation	Precipitation Difference January vs. July
Beijing (39°54'N)	24.8°F (−4.0°C)	79.3°F (26.3°C)	54.5°F (30.3°C)	24.0 inches (610 mm)	7.6 inches (192 mm)
Chicago (41°51'N)	23.0°F (−5.0°C)	74.3°F (23.5°C)	51.3°F (28.5°C)	36.1 inches (918 mm)	2.4 inches (62 mm)
New York City (40°42'N)	30.9°F (−0.6°C)	76.1°F (24.5°C)	45.2°F (25.1°C)	45.0 inches (1,144 mm)	1.2 inch (29 mm)
Philadelphia (39°57'N)	31.6°F (−0.2°C)	76.8°F (24.9°C)	45.2°F (25.1°C)	43.8 inches (1,113 mm)	1.6 inches (40 mm)

Source: "Climate Data for Cities Worldwide." CLIMATE-DATA.ORG. https://en.climate-data.org.

in late August or early September, the air clears up precipitously, and every rain brings refreshing coolness; the interlude of residual summer heat and looming winter chill continues until November, when the fall foliage finally fades and the city readies itself to brace the first cold waves from Siberia.

The descriptions of Beijing's climate can be oversimplistic because they usually focus on the climatic conditions in the urban area of the city. The size and topography of Beijing make its climate pattern more complex. A Chinese municipality conventionally consists of the central city and a number of surrounding counties, which makes the municipal administrative area much larger than its built area, where most residents reside. Beijing, for example, has a total area of 16,410 square kilometers (6,336 square miles) in comparison to the 302 square miles of New York City, 234 square miles for Chicago, and 142 square miles for Philadelphia. More than 60 percent of Beijing's municipal territory, however, consists of rural areas dominated by mountains (above 600 meters) and hills (between 100 and 600 meters), which have significantly higher precipitation and lower average temperature than the flat areas where the historical urban core, or what people identify as Beijing, is located.

Topography is another key feature of the physical landscape, and Beijing's topographic conditions dictated factors in the city's site selection and physical layout. The People's Republic of China consists of three great topographic steps from the west to the east: the Tibetan Plateau, with an average elevation above 4,000 meters (13,000 feet); the mountains, plateaus, and basins, with an average elevation between 1,000 and 2,000 meters (3,300–6,600 feet); and eastern plains and river valleys, with an average elevation below 500 meters (1,640 feet). Beijing is located on the third topographic step, on the northern end of North China Plain.

Beijing is situated on an alluvial plain known as the Beijing Plain and is sheltered on the west and northwest by the Taihang Mountains and on the north and northeast by the Yanshan Mountains. These two mountain ranges mark the boundary between the second and third topographic steps; they also demarcate the semihumid climate in the North China Plain to the east and semiarid climate in the Mongolian and Loess Plateaus to the west. The Beijing Plain inclines gently from the west and northwest to the south and southeast and merges into the expanse of the North China Plain in the south. Urban settlement has always been located on the Beijing Plain, which gives visitors and residents alike the impression that the city is flat, although only about one-third of the territory of the Beijing Municipality is on flat land with an average elevation of 43.5 meters (143 feet). The other two-thirds consist of low mountains, ranging from 1,000 to 1,500 meters (3,300–5,000 feet), and their foothills.

Beijing's topographic setting resembles a south-facing concave. Sheltered on the west, north, and northeast against wintry weather, Beijing opens up to the vast expanse of the North China Plain and is embraced by the sunshine and warm air from the south. It must not have been lost on the ancient Chinese that such a setting emulates the most ideal scenarios of feng shui, or Chinese geomancy, for human settlement. It also caught the attention and imagination of contemporary scholars from both China and overseas. Hou Renzhi (1911–2013), one of China's preeminent scholars on Beijing's historical geography, recalled how he was mesmerized by the "bay-like" setting of Beijing (then called "Peiping") Plain, flanked by mountains on three sides, when he traveled to Beijing from the south in 1931. He soon discovered that nearly a quarter century earlier the American geologist Bailey Willis (1857–1949) had marveled over the same geographical setting and coined the term "Bay of Peking" in describing the unique physical layout of Beijing.

Hydrological conditions distinguish Beijing from other major cities because it is neither at a port nor on a large river. Numerous rivers from the mountains sculpted the Beijing Plain through constant alluvial activities, such as substantial sediment deposition, course change, and stream capturing. Rivers such as the Yongding, Chaobai, Wenyu, Daqing, and Ji Canal infused and replenished the groundwater that was the main water source for human activities on the Beijing Plain. Among them, Yongding is the longest, with 189 kilometers (114 miles) of its entire 747-kilometer (464 miles) course running through western Beijing. Originating from the Loess Plateau, the Yongding River has been both a curse and a blessing for the Beijing Plain and the evolution of the city of Beijing. On the one hand, frequent flooding and course change made it dangerous to settle along the river's banks. On the other hand, the river brought substantial sediments from the Loess Plateau that helped shape the Beijing Plain, enriching its soils and providing ample replenishment of the large aquifers.

The ancient city builders and settlers selected a low ridge between the Yongding and Chaobai Rivers to lessen the impact of the flooding hazard while taking advantage of the abundant groundwater resources. It was not until the 1950s, however, that systematic flood mitigation projects finally stopped the Yongding River from flooding Beijing. In modern times, climate change and the overdraft of water in the upper streams have caused the Yongding River to frequently run dry in the Beijing environs. Visitors to the Luguo (Marco Polo) Bridge, a famous historical river crossing on Yongding River, may only see a parched ditch over which the 830-year-old bridge crosses.

Historically, aquifers were the most important source of water supply on the Beijing Plain. Therefore, the site selection for early Beijing was

mainly determined by groundwater availability. The earliest urban settlement on the Beijing Plain was at the groundwater overflow zone of what
Willis referred to as the "artesian zone" of the Bay of Peking. Along this
artesian zone, good quality water was available from either groundwater
(wells) or nearby marshes or bogs in ancient riverbeds. The city of Beijing
has remained at the same hydrological location since its conception three
thousand years ago. Changes in groundwater conditions did result in a
minor site shift of the capital's center to the immediate northwest at the
beginning of the Yuan Dynasty (1271–1368) to make more plentiful water
sources, such as lakes and marshland, more accessible to the new capital.

The native vegetation in Beijing was broadleaf deciduous forest composed of oaks and pines. As in other parts of Eastern China, however,
intensive sedentary agricultural activities and deforestation have completely transformed native soils and vegetations in the Beijing environs.
Isolated areas at high elevations may still have pockets of native plants and
soils. Patches of spectacular alpine meadows can still be found on some of
the tallest peaks, usually slightly above 2,000 meters (6,561 feet), in the
Beijing environs, such as the Beijing Baihuashan ("flower mountains")
National Nature Reserve of Biodiversity.

The ideal layout of Chinese cities is outlined in detail in *Kao Gong Ji*
("Book of Artificers" or "Records of Trades"), a classic on science and technology completed in the late Western Han Dynasty (206 BCE–24 CE). As
the foremost guide for city design and building in ancient China, *Kao Gong
Ji* prescribes an ideal city layout as being a checkerboard pattern with nine
subdivisions based on the land survey at the time, *jingtian zhi* (the well-
field system). The subdivisions are delineated by nine vertical and nine
horizontal thoroughfare axes. It dictates that the city should have a north–
south orientation, be built on flatland and near water, and be walled for
protection; efforts should be made to open main gates, doors, and windows
to the south. For an imperial capital, the royal palaces and other key structures must be on a central axis with markets behind them; ancestral temples must be to the left and divine altars to the right of the palaces.

Beijing's physical setting is ideal for building a Chinese imperial capital.
The unobstructed and sizable Beijing Plain provided plenty of space for the
physical layout of a large city, and the configuration of the Bay of Peking
would give the capital both a natural shelter, aptly described by some as a
"dragon's chair," and adequate water supply from the abundant aquifers
and artesian wells. Other famed ancient Chinese capitals may have
obtained some aspects of the ideal capital design outlined in *Kao Gong Ji*
but were constrained by both their physical setting and technological
know-how at the time to fully realize the ideal layout. For example, the
capital of the Western Han Dynasty (206 BCE–24 CE), Changan (near
today's Xian), had the royal palace in the southern part of the city because

of its higher elevation. The northern part of Changan was a low-lying area close to the Wei River and was where the markets and communities of the commoners were located. The eastern capital of the Tang Dynasty (618–907), Luoyang, had a grid layout, but the Luo River imposed an insurmountable obstacle for a central axis. Even the first capital of the Ming Dynasty (1368–1644), Nanjing, had an irregular shape due to the impact of the Yangzi (Yangtze) River.

It was only on the expanses of the Beijing Plain, flanked by sheltering mountains on three sides, that the ingenious urban designers and builders of ancient China were able to fully attain the heavenly matrimony between the unique and salient natural environment and the highest form of an imperial capital. The Yuan Dynasty's Beijing (Dadu), completed in 1285, adopted the nine-square layout proscribed in *Kao Gong Ji* for the first time in Chinese history. The succeeding Ming Dynasty modified the perimeters of the Yuan Beijing and placed the royal palaces at the geometric center of the capital, a layout that the last imperial dynasty, Qing (1644–1911), largely inherited. Indeed, it was in the unparalleled natural embrace of the Bay of Peking that the highest form of the Chinese capital city was achieved.

EXPERIENCING BEIJING THROUGH THE SENSES

LIFE
IN THE
CITY

I was brought to Beijing as a newborn and have been back there a number of times since then. Three things stand out in my memories of the city.

First, Beijing was so crowded everywhere and all the time. The streets were filled with people, bikes, and cars and taxis beeping at each other like crazy. Crowds were pushing and shoving on and off buses and subway trains. I was also amused by large groups of people in Tiantan (the Temple of Heaven) doing exercises in unbelievable unison.

Second, I was overwhelmed by the foods and people's obsession with them. There were so many eateries and so much food every time we had meals either in restaurants or at home. My relatives urged me to eat more and put food on my plate. I did become fond of the foods there, from Peking roast duck to noodles served in hole-in-the-wall places. I would ask for some American fast food when I felt homesick, and I enjoyed KFC—I swear they use different chicken and spices because KFC in China just tasted better, especially the spicy chicken sandwiches. My favorite snack was the sugar-coated haws on a thin bamboo stick. It was such a delicious treat that thinking about it now makes my mouth water.

Third, Beijing relates to me with very specific sensory cues. The smell in the air was the most distinct reminder of the place to me, though I could not pinpoint what it was and where it came from. Was it the smell of motor vehicle exhaust? Was it the Chinese cigarettes that every man appeared to be smoking? Was it from all the cooking?

In the fall of 2018, a big wildfire sent sooty smoke to our area (San Francisco Bay Area), forcing school closures and cancellations of outdoor activities. When I finally ventured outside, a light bulb went on in my head. Wow, this is the smell, the smell of Beijing! It was the smell of polluted air that brought back all the fun memories. I felt almost nostalgic when I learned air quality was getting better in Beijing. I have long associated the smell of complicated, unclean air with the oversized and ancient city. Would it still be the same place if the smell were gone?

—Galen Guo

2

People

When China officially launched economic reform in 1978, 17.9 percent of its population lived and worked in cities. Four decades later, in 2018, Chinese cities were home to 59.6 percent of the population. In comparison, it took the United States twice as long to reach the same level of urbanization (1860–1940). Beijing is at the forefront of China's breathtaking urbanization. With a total population of 21.54 million in 2018, it is the second-largest Chinese city after Shanghai. It is a Chinese megacity with 86.5 percent of its 21.5 million residents in 2018 registered as urban residents. Population changes provide a unique perspective on Beijing's development and a cautionary tale on the relationship between population governance and sustainable urban development.

HISTORICAL CHANGES AND MODERN GROWTH

Beijing's population change has been directly related to the city's functions, and it has undergone several drastically different historical periods, including the frontier city era (1100 BCE–1153 CE), the imperial capital era (1153–1911), the Republican era (1911–1949), and the PRC era (1949–present).

Historical Changes

As a frontier city on the periphery of China's agricultural heartland, Beijing's urban population rarely exceeded 200,000 and appears to have fluctuated greatly due to wars and environmental changes. At the end of the Tang Dynasty (618–907), the population in Beijing and its environs dwindled because of protracted conflicts among the warlords, but it rebounded after the Khitan Liao Dynasty (907–1127) made the city one of the regional capitals in 938 CE, reaching about 150,000 by the end of Liao.

The Jurchen Jin Dynasty (1115–1234) relocated its main capital to Beijing in 1153. Although only having unified northern China, the Jin Dynasty did usher in the era of Beijing as an imperial capital. As the capital, Beijing's population began to undergo phenomenal growth, approaching one million people in the early fourteenth century during the Mongol Yuan Dynasty (1271–1368). Both the Ming (1368–1644) and Qing (1644–1911) Dynasties implemented strict rules to curb Beijing's population, including strict control over residential registration, repatriation of migrants, the compulsory departure of retired or dismissed officials and their families, and the dispersal of some of the nobilities from the city. Such measures were in part responsible for capping Beijing's population at under two million during the entire late imperial era.

During the early Republican era, Beijing's population underwent a surge from an influx of the rural poor, mainly from the adjacent Hebei Province. Beijing's population growth became stagnant, however, due to the loss of its capital status (1928–1949) and lack of economic growth as well as Japanese occupation and the Chinese civil war. Beijing's population was about two million in 1948.

Modern Growth

In 1949, Beijing became the capital of the People's Republic of China (PRC). Since then, it has experienced tremendous ebb and flow of population change, which can be divided into five phases.

During phase 1 (1949–1960), Beijing underwent phenomenal growth, and its population skyrocketed from about 2 million to 7.4 million. Such a drastic increase came from four main sources. First, the central government agencies brought in hundreds of thousands of new employees from all over the country. Second, in 1958, Beijing annexed nine surrounding counties, which added 2.7 million people to the city's population. Third, the rate of the population's natural increase (the difference between natural births and deaths in a year) remained high during this period and hit a record in 1957 as the entire country underwent a baby boom. Fourth, the government's Great Leap Forward campaign, which promoted drastic industrialization and urbanization, started in 1958, inducing more than 700,000 workers to Beijing.

During phase 2 (1961–1976), the overall population change in Beijing was stagnant due to two traumatic events in modern Chinese history. First, the Three Years of Difficulty (1959–1961), known as the Great Chinese Famine in the West, was caused by failed government policies, natural disasters, and a fallout with the Soviet Union. Second, the Cultural Revolution (1966–1976), a decade of intense political turmoil, crippled the society and exerted tremendous human tolls. During this phase, the government restricted immigration and carried out reversed urbanization, which led to the permanent or temperate exodus of many Beijing residents.

During phase 3 (1977–1994), the early stage of reform saw steady population growth as rural residents moved to cities in search of work and a better life, which more than offset the effects of low natural increase rate as the result of strict family planning known as the *one-child policy*. Most of these newcomers did not have *household registration* status, i.e., they did not have legal residential status in Beijing and, therefore, did not qualify for welfare and benefits that household-registered residents were entitled to. Beijing's population increased at an annual average rate of 160,000, and the total population grew from 8.6 million in 1977 to 11.3 million in 1994.

During phase 4 (1995–2000), deepening reform accelerated the population influx to coastal regions and major cities. Beijing's population grew from 12.5 million in 1995 to 13.6 million in 2000, which translated into an average annual increase of 220,000. Most of this increase was driven by immigration, as the rate of natural increase remained extremely low.

Phase 5 (2001–2015) was a period of explosive population growth. Beijing's population jumped from 13.9 million in 2001 to 21.7 million in 2015, with an average annual increase of 560,000. A construction boom and the rapid growth of the service sector made Beijing a favored destination for people who were pushed out of impoverished small towns and villages and pulled into major cities.

Economic reform has been responsible for Beijing's rapid population growth in the last four decades (Table 2.1). In recent years, Beijing authorities have implemented policies in an effort to slow down population growth and reduce congestion, overcrowding, and pollution. These policies along with skyrocketing living expenses may have combined to cause an abrupt stop of population growth. The city's permanent resident population, that is, people who live in the city for at least six months of the calendar year, edged up by merely 16,000 from 2015 to 2016 and decreased by 22,000 from 2016 to 2017 and 165,000 from 2017 to 2018. This was the first time that Beijing had experienced population declines in two consecutive years.

Table 2.1   Population Change in Beijing, 1978–2018

Year	Permanent Resident Population (million)	Percentage Increase over Previous Year (%)	Permanent Non-Household Registered Population (million)	Percentage Increase over Previous Year (%)
1978	8.7		0.2	
1979	9.0	2.9	0.3	21.6
1980	9.0	0.8	0.2	−29.8
1981	9.2	1.6	0.2	−1.1
1982	9.4	1.7	0.2	−6.5
1983	9.5	1.6	0.2	−2.3
1984	9.7	1.6	0.2	17.9
1985	9.8	1.7	0.2	16.7
1986	10.3	4.8	0.6	145.9
1987	10.5	1.8	0.6	3.9
1988	10.6	1.3	0.6	1.4
1989	10.8	1.3	0.5	−9.9
1990	10.9	1.0	0.5	−0.2
1991	10.9	0.7	0.5	1.3
1992	11.0	0.7	0.6	4.8
1993	11.1	0.9	0.6	6.5
1994	11.3	1.2	0.6	3.9
1995	12.5	11.2	1.8	186.1
1996	12.6	0.7	1.8	0.5
1997	12.4	−1.5	1.5	−15.0
1998	12.5	0.5	1.5	−0.3
1999	12.6	0.9	1.6	2.1
2000	13.6	8.5	2.6	62.7
2001	13.9	1.6	2.6	2.6
2002	14.2	2.8	2.9	9.2
2003	14.6	2.3	3.1	7.2
2004	14.9	2.5	3.3	7.2
2005	15.4	3.0	3.6	8.3
2006	16.0	4.1	4.0	12.9
2007	16.8	4.7	4.6	14.7
2008	17.7	5.7	5.4	16.9

(continued)

Table 2.1   (continued)

Year	Permanent Resident Population (million)	Percentage Increase over Previous Year (%)	Permanent Non-Household Registered Population (million)	Percentage Increase over Previous Year (%)
2009	18.6	5.0	6.1	13.5
2010	19.6	5.5	7.0	14.7
2011	20.2	2.9	7.4	5.3
2012	20.7	2.5	7.7	4.3
2013	21.1	2.2	8.0	3.7
2014	21.5	1.7	8.2	2.0
2015	21.7	0.9	8.2	0.5
2016	21.7	0.1	8.1	−1.8
2017	21.7	−0.1	7.9	−1.6
2018	21.5	−0.8	7.6	−3.7

Source: "Population and Employment." 2019 Annual Statistical Information (in Chinese). http://tjj.beijing.gov.cn/tjsj/ndtjzl/2018ndtjzl_6949/rkyjy_6680/201902/t20190220_417100.html.

What is more remarkable is that a significant portion of the migrant population, classified as the "permanent non-household registered population," decreased at a faster rate: it went up by a mere 50,000 from 2015 to 2016 and decreased by 132,000 from 2016 to 2017 and almost 300,000 from 2017 to 2018! It remains to be seen whether these demographic trends will continue in Beijing.

IMMIGRATION AND "MOBILE POPULATION"

Beijing as the national capital has been a leading destination for bureaucrats, intellectuals, merchants, refugees, and other migrants. Population control is a key aspect of governance, and various measures have been adopted. The most effective of these measures is the household registration system called *hukou*, which keeps official records on each household and is a de facto residential permit system. The hukou system became even more stringent in the late 1950s when it became the prerequisite for employment and government rationing, effectively halting population mobility in the pre-reform era. Economic reform opened the flood gate for population mobility, especially after the ration system was abolished in the

A slum near Beijing's central business district, where migrant workers live, labor, and raise their families. (Grace0612/Dreamstime.com)

early 1990s, and Beijing became a top destination for immigration. Beijing's non-household registered residents, that is, those who live in the city for at least six months without hukou, reached 7.65 million in 2018, or about one-third of Beijing's total permanent resident population. In addition, there is the so-called mobile population that is not included in official surveys but may number in the millions in Beijing at any given time.

In an effort to slow down explosive population growth, the Beijing Municipal Government has set the goal of capping Beijing's permanent resident population at twenty-three million by the year 2020. In achieving this goal, some think tanks and media outlets have called for optimizing Beijing's population by reducing the so-called *low-end population*, that is, migrants who are poor and low-skilled. The term low-end population in official documents was quickly removed after a public uproar, but it is obvious that the authorities are targeting immigrants and have tried to push out migrant workers by abolishing their slum-like residential areas along the urban-rural interface, causing great tension. The tension reached a climax on November 18, 2017, when a building fire broke out in an illegally constructed multiuse building located near the South Sixth Ring Road. The building had three hundred low-rent, squalid rooms that housed over four hundred migrant workers and their families in the upper floors. The fire and ensuing explosion killed nineteen and injured many more.

In the aftermath of the fire, the government carried out a massive safety inspection campaign that targeted migrant communities within the Fifth Ring Road. Building owners were required to bring their properties up to the city's fire and building codes within a short time. A failure to do so meant their properties would be condemned and set aside for demolition. One of the campaign's goals was to push out the low-end population. It was estimated that over two hundred thousand temporary residents were displaced by the campaign. The authorities claimed that the campaign was supported by Beijing's "native" residents nearly uniformly. However, the consequences of this campaign were at best a double-edged sword, as the low-end population is the main source of cheap labor, especially for the booming fast-delivery business that Beijing and other large cities increasingly depend on.

DENSITY AND DISTRIBUTION

The population density for Beijing proper was 1,324 people per square kilometer (3,429 per square mile) in 2016, which was much lower than that of other world cities. For example, for the same year, Tokyo's population density per square kilometer was 2,627 (6,804 per square mile), London's was 5,590 (14,477 per square mile), New York City's was 10,742 (27,807 per square mile), and Paris's was 21,500 (55,673 per square mile). However, Beijing's surprisingly low population density is misleading because it is based on the population of the entire city proper, which includes large surrounding rural and suburban areas. Within Beijing proper, population distribution is highly uneven and exhibits a gradient decrease from the center of the city outward in a concentric zone pattern, roughly corresponding to the six ring roads (beltways) that encircle Beijing. The sixteen districts of the city are divided into four primary function zones based on their level of urbanization and development priorities. These zones also reflect Beijing's geographical pattern of population density.

Zone 1, *the core capital function zone*, which can be referred to as the capital core, includes the two urban districts that roughly cover the area within the historical city walls along which the Second Ring Road runs. Its population density exceeds 23,400 per square kilometer (60,606 per square mile), which is comparable to the crowded urban cores in such other world cities as Tokyo, London, New York City, and Paris.

Zone 2, *the expanded urban function zone*, includes the other four urban districts sprawling between the Second and Sixth Ring Roads. This zone has been the fastest growing in terms of population and commercial development and has an average density of about 8,000 residents per square kilometer (20,720 per square mile).

Zones 1 and 2 constitute the urban core of Beijing with the city's six officially classified urban districts. Beijing's urban core accounts for only 8 percent of the land in the city proper but about 60 percent of the city's permanent resident population.

Zone 3, *the new urban development zone*, consists of the five districts encircling Beijing's urban core. Its population density ranges from 1,000 to 1,600 per square kilometer (2,590–4,144 per square mile). Home to most of the new and rapidly growing outer suburbs, the flat land in the south and east of the city proper is where much of the future growth will be.

Zone 4, *the ecological conservation development zone*, has the remaining five districts in the mountainous west and north of the city proper. It has a low population density of 200–400 per square kilometer (518–1,036 per square mile). As its name indicates, this zone will remain sparsely populated and restricted of commercial development.

The Beijing Municipal Government, through planning and other regulatory measures, has tried to alleviate congestion and overcrowding in zone 1 by encouraging suburban development in zones 2 and 3. The effort has had some success. Data shows that between 2000 and 2012, the average annual population growth in zone 1 was a meager 0.2 percent, while the population growth rate was 4.1 percent in zone 2, 5.95 percent in zone 3, and 1.2 percent in zone 4.

It should be noted that most immigrants in Beijing, as in other cities, are forced to crowd into substandard housing in slums and squatters concentrated along the urban fringe. In 2015, for example, 65 percent of those who do not have Beijing hukou resided between the Fourth and Sixth Ring Roads. Their communities are often neglected and suffer from high crime rates, gang violence, and organized crime. The lack of basic public services, such as waste disposal, has led to a public sanitation crisis that in turn endangers both the slum dwellers and the entire city.

ETHNIC DIVERSITY

As a frontier city, Beijing was a hub of economic and cultural exchange among hunting, nomadic, and sedentary societies. As the imperial capital, Beijing became the mecca of East Asia, where soldiers, merchants, farmers, and nomads from all corners of the world converged. Ethnic diversity remains a deeply embedded heritage and a distinguishing characteristic of Beijing in comparison to other leading Chinese cities. Every one of Beijing's sixteen districts has more than thirty of the fifty-five officially recognized minority nationality groups, and the two fastest-growing districts in zone 2, Chaoyang and Haidian, have all of them.

Based on the 2010 population census, 96 percent of Beijing's population is Han Chinese, the ethnic majority in China. The Man (Manchu) and the

Hui (Chinese Muslims) account for more than 80 percent of the minority population, each with about a quarter million people. As members of the ruling ethnic group of the Qing Dynasty, many Manchus disguised their identity after the dynasty ended to avoid reprisals. In recent years, however, there has been a surge among Manchus to reclaim their ethnic status. Ancestors of the Hui people were from Persia and the Middle East and arrived in Beijing in large numbers during the Yuan Dynasty. Other notable ethnic groups include Mongols, Koreans, Tujia, Zhuang, and Miao (Hmong).

Beijing's ethnic minorities are spatially dispersed throughout the city, though about 60 percent of them reside in the six urban districts (zones 1 and 2). There are numerous ethnic enclaves in the suburban and rural districts, including five ethnic minority townships and 157 administrative villages in Beijing proper. Most of these ethnic enclaves belong to minority groups that have had a historical presence in Beijing, such as the Manchus, the Hui, and the Mongols. In contrast, the only ethnic enclave in the urban core is the Oxen Street (Niujie) district, which the Hui have maintained for centuries because of their religion and lifestyle. Recent urban renewal projects have displaced some of the Hui population in the Oxen Street district, but the mosques and renowned halal eateries have helped retain the Hui's distinct cultural landscape.

VITAL STATISTICS

In comparison to China's national average, Beijing has lower birth and death rates, a lower infant mortality rate, a more balanced sex ratio, longer life expectancy, smaller household size, an aging population, and higher education attainment (Table 2.2). Beijing's vital statistics are similar to those in developed societies, reflecting the effects of the high living standards that the city's residents enjoy.

The low rate of natural increase can be attributed to China's one-child policy, the official family planning policy introduced in 1979 that required each married couple to have no more than one child. Minority nationality groups were exempt from this policy and, as a result, tend to have younger populations. A 2018 population survey showed that 12.4 percent of Beijing's ethnic minority groups were zero to fourteen years of age, which was nearly 4 percent higher than the city's average. The de facto law officially ended in 2015, but this has failed to generate any spike in the birth rate. To the contrary, residents appear to be less likely to have children, with the birth rate dipping to 8.24 per 1,000 residents in 2018. While young yuppies and DINKs (couples with a double income and no kids) have a similar lifestyle to their counterparts in New York City or Tokyo, rural migrant workers are increasingly unwilling to have more kids because of the high costs and uncertainty of raising children in big cities such as Beijing.

Table 2.2 Vital Statistics for Beijing and China's National Average, 2016

	BR%	DR%	Sex Ratio (Female= 100)	Household Size	Life Expectancy at Birth	Newborn Death Rate%	Dependent Population%	Illiteracy Rate%
National Average	12.9	7.1	105	3.1	76.3	5.40	37.9	5.28
Beijing	9.3	5.2	106*	2.6	82.0	2.21	29.2	1.56

Source: Various tables in "population" of China Statistical Yearbook. 2017. http://www.stats.gov.cn/tjsj/ndsj/2017/indexeh.htm. "Beijing's Life Expectancy Rises to 82.15 Years." *China Daily*, July 12, 2018. http://www.chinadaily.com.cn/a/201807/12/WS5b4714d5a310796df4df6160.html.

* The non-household registered population, which is disproportionately from rural and small town areas and more traditional, demonstrates a higher birth rate and sex ratio. For example, the sex ratio for Beijing's household registered population was 100 in 2016, and for the non-household registered population, which accounted for 30% of Beijing's total population, it was 117 in the same year and was higher than the United Nations' 102–107 normal range. Gender preference in family planning was clearly a factor.

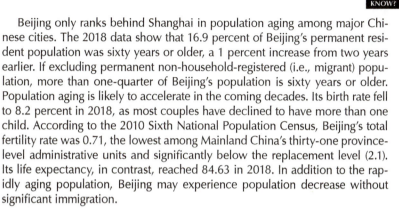

An Aging City

Beijing only ranks behind Shanghai in population aging among major Chinese cities. The 2018 data show that 16.9 percent of Beijing's permanent resident population was sixty years or older, a 1 percent increase from two years earlier. If excluding permanent non-household-registered (i.e., migrant) population, more than one-quarter of Beijing's population is sixty years or older. Population aging is likely to accelerate in the coming decades. Its birth rate fell to 8.2 percent in 2018, as most couples have declined to have more than one child. According to the 2010 Sixth National Population Census, Beijing's total fertility rate was 0.71, the lowest among Mainland China's thirty-one province-level administrative units and significantly below the replacement level (2.1). Its life expectancy, in contrast, reached 84.63 in 2018. In addition to the rapidly aging population, Beijing may experience population decrease without significant immigration.

At the same time, aging has become an escalating demographic challenge, especially in China's large cities. By the late 1990s, Beijing had already reached the United Nations' benchmark for an aging population: at least 8 percent of its population was sixty-five years of age or older. The 2010 population census showed that 8.7 percent of the city's population was seniors, and the ratio jumped to 9.2 percent in 2012. The rapidly aging population has been driven by the decrease in the birth rate exacerbated by several decades of the one-child policy and an increase in life expectancy due to substantially improved living standards.

The aging population puts growing pressure on infrastructure and services, especially in the already crowded urban core, where there is a large concentration of native residents who tend to be older. There is a surging need for assisted living and nursing home facilities, as the retiring baby boomers are coming to terms with the fact that they could not and should not depend on their children to take care of them. Retirement communities and senior services are thriving to capitalize in the new business opportunity, but most of them are located in the suburbs, where it is less expensive for business operations that require plenty of space. It is, therefore, conceivable that retirees have an incentive to move to the suburbs.

The population challenges facing Beijing are similar to those confronting other megacities in China and the world. While the target population of twenty-three million for year 2020 is arbitrary, Beijing's long-term population strategy appears to ride on decentralization of noncapital functions, which is designed to improve environmental conditions and quality of life. In addition to Beijing's new capital subcenter, the Xiongan New

Area is a more ambitious and groundbreaking undertaking that will have a direct impact on Beijing's population and change the city's economic and social conditions in the years to come. In the meantime, Beijing's population growth will continue to slow due to low fertility and a decline in immigration, and the aging population will grow and add to the momentum toward population suburbanization.

 LIFE IN THE CITY

MAKING MY WAY IN BEIJING

I am from a small town in Henan Province—I'd call myself a country bumpkin. I had dreamed of coming to Beijing, and my first impressions did not disappoint: the streets were so wide and clean, the buses were so long and smooth, the skyscrapers were so tall and shiny, and the people were so handsome and fashionable. The most overwhelming experience I had in Beijing was the Victory Day Parade on September 3, 2015. Areas around Tiananmen Square, including where I lived back then, were all sealed off two days before the parade, and I almost went hungry because I forgot to stock up enough food. Despite the hassle, once the parade started, we all got on the roof of the house and had a glimpse of it. I felt a sense of national pride as I was overwhelmed by the loud flyovers of aircrafts and columns of military vehicles.

Quickly my awe turned to anguish when reality struck. I got a menial job that paid so poorly that I barely had enough money to eat three meals a day. Fortunately, I had several friends for mutual support, and a friend from Beijing managed to find a place for us to stay for free. I was ashamed to ask for money from my family, so I had to tough it out. The agony lasted for a year, during which time I had thought of giving up and returning home, where I knew wouldn't have any career opportunities for me.

Things began to look up when I finally got a different, better-paying job as a leasing agent. I did not like the job, but the better pay allowed me to survive and search for other opportunities. I then got a job at company specializing in financial software development, and I quickly moved up to be a project manager. My career success made me more marketable, and over a year ago, I became the IT services manager at a large asset management company. I am doing well: good pay, a lot of responsibility, and no overtime. I have been enjoying the worldly experience in Beijing.

Looking back, it was worth the hardship for me to come to Beijing. Had I stayed closer to home, I definitely would not have had the career opportunities and exposure to the big, exciting world. I am so grateful to my family and friends who have supported my endeavors in Beijing. I need to continue to improve and upgrade myself to prepare for any drastic changes, as the ongoing Sino-American trade war casts a long shadow on the financial sector, arousing a lot of uncertainties.

—Yanan

3

History

Beijing projects two images to many people: an ancient city and the perpetual capital of China. Both are essentially accurate. In 2015, great fanfare commemorated the 3,060th anniversary of the city's founding during the apex of the Bronze Age in East Asia. Beijing has been the capital of unified China since Kublai Khan (1215–1294) of the Mongol Empire declared it the Grand Capital (Dadu) of the Yuan Dynasty (1271–1368) in 1272, with only two brief interruptions (1368–1403 and 1928–1949).

A more careful historical probe, however, reveals that Beijing was on the periphery of the Chinese civilization geographically and socioeconomically during its first two millennia. It was an important Chinese frontier city as a military outpost and a hub of exchange between nomadic and sedentary agricultural realms. It was not, however, a center of Chinese economy, politics, or high culture. Beijing's fortune changed after the eleventh century, when long-term environmental changes resulted in geopolitical reconfigurations in East Asia. Beijing first emerged as the leading city of the northern regions and then as the political and cultural center of all of China. Beijing would never relinquish its capital status for the remainder of China's imperial era.

Historically, Chinese cities did not constitute an independent administrative level. A city was a region's economic and cultural center that was walled for protection and governed by the county where it was located; it might have had a unique name or simply been referred to as the city of a specific administrative division. The imperial capital was first and foremost the home of the monarch, and the court was directly in charge of all its affairs and domain, such as the royal palaces, government offices, and the city walls and gates. The rest of the capital was governed by counties with administrative territories in the city. These counties were under the jurisdiction of a capital district (usually prefecture-level, commonly referred to as *fu*), which included a number of counties and a large hinterland surrounding the walled city.

Beijing bore various names in its three thousand years of history and did not get the name Beijing (Northern Capital) until the beginning of the 1400s (Table 3.1). For the purpose of clarity, the historical overview uses *Beijing*, preceded by a periodic name when necessary, to describe the walled city and its immediate vicinities and *Beijing and its environs* to refer to the city and its surrounding areas. Beijing proper, on the other hand, delineates the city's modern municipal peripheries.

The overview of Beijing's history is divided into four eras: (1) the era of the frontier city; (2) the era of functional transition, the Liao and Jin Dynasties; (3) the era of the imperial capital, the Yuan, Ming, and Qing Dynasties; and (4) the Republican era, the Republic of China (ROC). Development during the People's Republic of China (PRC) is covered in detail in other subject-specific chapters. Each of the four eras is further divided into several periods. These eras and periods provide a chronological context for major events and changes that contributed to Beijing's rise on the national and international stages as well as the city's evolution in urban design and functions.

BEIJING AS A FRONTIER CITY

The Chinese narrative about Beijing's history usually starts with the Peking Man (*Homo erectus pekinensis*), whose fossilized skulls and other bone fragments were discovered in southwestern Beijing proper in the 1920s. Scientific consensus has concluded, however, that there is no direct lineage between these hominids from a half million years ago and modern humans. Nevertheless, Beijing and its environs continued to be home to archaic and modern *H. sapiens*.

There is increasing archeological evidence that Beijing and its environs were integral to the dawn of Chinese civilization during Neolithic times (ca. 5000–ca. 6000 BCE). Settlements were thriving with emerging crop cultivation and animal husbandry on the area's warm, humid plains. Legend has it that the Battle of Banquan, one of three epic tribal wars during the time of Three Sovereigns and Five Emperors, took place near the Lower Banquan Villages in northwestern Beijing proper about 4,500–5,000 years ago. According to the *Records of the Grand Historian* (ca. 95 BCE) by the

Table 3.1   Historical Names of Beijing

Time Period	City Name	Dynastic and Jurisdiction Status
Prehistorical era (ca. 2000–1000 BCE)	Youdu (Place of the North)	A town built by descendants of the legendary Yellow Emperor in Youzhou (Land of the North), one of the twelve regions of ancient China.
Eleventh century–476 BCE (Zhou Dynasty: Spring and Autumn Periods)	Ji	Seat of Ji, a vassal state; later taken over by Yan, a nearby vassal state.
476–221 BCE (Zhou Dynasty: Warring States Period)	Ji; also known as Yan or Yandu (Capital of Yan) after Ji was conquered by Yan	Seat of Yan, a vassal state.
221–206 BCE (Qin Dynasty)		Seat of Guangyang Commandery under the Qin Dynasty.
202–80 BCE		Seat of the vassal state Yan under the Western Han Dynasty.
80–73 BCE		Seat of Youzhou Commandery under the Western Han Dynasty.
73 BCE–25 CE		Seat of the vassal state Guangyang under the Western Han Dynasty.
25–265	Ji* *The city was sometimes referred to by the respective commandery or province names, for which it was the governing seat, e.g., "Youzhou" or "Guangyang"	Seat of the provincial governor of Youzhou (25–96) and Guangyang Commandery under the Eastern Han Dynasty.
265–319		Seat of the vassal state Yan under the Western Jin Dynasty.
319–583		Seat of Youzhou Commandery during the Northern and Southern Dynasties era.
583–607		Youzhou Commandery abolished by the Sui Dynasty.
607–618		Seat of Zhuo Commandery in the Sui Dynasty.
618–730		Seat of Youzhou Commandery and Youzhou military governorship (718–730), under the Tang Dynasty.
730–759	Youzhou	Seat of the Youzhou (930–742) and Fanyang (742–755) military governorships.

(continued)

Table 3.1   (continued)

Time Period	City Name	Dynastic and Jurisdiction Status
759–763	Yanjing	Capital of An Lushan's "Great Yan" during the An Lushan Rebellion (755–763).
763–938	Youzhou	Seat of the Youzhou and Lulong military governorships of the Tang Dynasty and during the Five Dynasties (907–979).
938–1123	Nanjing (Southern Capital, 938–1012) or Yanjing (Capital of Yan, 1012–1123)	The subsidiary capital of the Liao Dynasty for the south.
1123–1125	Yanshanfu	Ruled by the Northern Song Dynasty.
1125–1153	Yanjing	Ruled by the Jin Dynasty.
1153–1215	Zhongdu (Middle Capital)	Capital of the Jin Dynasty.
1215–1264	Yanjing	Ruled by the Mongol Khanate.
1264–1272	Zhongdu (Middle Capital)	
1272–1368	Dadu (Grand Capital), also known as Khanbaliq or Cambaluc (the Khan's City)	Winter capital of the Yuan Dynasty.
1368–1403	Beiping (Peace in the North)	Seat of the Yan Princedom under the Ming Dynasty.
1403–1911	Beijing (Northern Capital), Shuntianfu (Capital District)	Capital for the Ming and Qing Dynasties.
1912–1928	Beijing	Capital of the Republic of China (ROC).
1928–1937	Beiping	Special Municipality of ROC.
1937–1945	Beijing	Under Japanese occupation.
1945–1949	Beiping	Municipality of ROC.
1949–Present	Beijing	Capital of the People's Republic of China (PRC).

Source: "History of Beijing." *China Daily*, December 12, 2012. http://www .chinadaily.com.cn/beijing/2012-12/09/content_15998473.htm.
"Beijing's Historical Evolution." Douban, January 22, 2018. https://site.douban .com/216685/widget/notes/14258731/note/654442689/ (in Chinese).

THE MYSTERY OF PEKING MAN FOSSILS

DID YOU KNOW?

Excavations in the 1920s and 1930s at Zhoukoudian yielded six skulls and over two hundred other bone fragments belonging to the Peking Man (*Homo erectus pekinensis*). In September 1941, as hostilities between Japan and the United States became increasingly imminent, the fossils, which had been stored at the Union Medical College in Beijing, were packed up and escorted by U.S. Marines to Camp Holcomb at Qinhuangdao, from where they would be sent to the United States for safekeeping (at the American Museum of Natural History in New York City). The two crates containing the fossils arrived at Qinhuangdao on the morning of December 8, 1941, hours after the Japanese attack on Pearl Harbor. The fossils then vanished, despite various attempts since then to locate them. Speculations, rumors, and fraudulent claims abound, but so far the fate of the invaluable fossils remains a mystery.

---

greatest Chinese historian, Sima Qian (ca. 145–ca. 86 BCE), Huangdi (the Yellow Emperor), whom the Chinese consider as their common ancestor, defeated his rival, Yandi (the Flame Emperor), but then made peace and joined forces with him. The Chinese believe that the battle led to unification among sedentary agricultural tribes and gave birth to the Chinese nation. The name *you*, which means "tranquil and secluded," came into use for Beijing and its environs during this time because of the region's northeastern peripheral location vis-à-vis the emerging heartland of Chinese civilization.

Shang–Western Zhou Period
(ca. Eleventh–Eighth Centuries BCE)

There are no known concurrent historical accounts for Beijing during the legendary Xia Dynasty (ca. 2070–ca. 1600 BCE) and much of the Shang Dynasty (ca. 1600–1046 BCE). Inscriptions on Shang oracle bones point to several subordinate primeval states in Beijing and its environs by late Shang (beginning of the eleventh century BCE). One of them, "Yan," had contacts with Shang through trade and marriage. The other was "Ji," a name that might have derived from a local Asteraceae herb, purportedly ruled by descendants of the Yellow Emperor.

Beijing and its environs were at a strategic location during this period. Due to a much warmer and more humid climate than today, the North China Plain was dominated by impassable swamps and marshland. The only viable north–south route trekked along the eastern foothills of the

Taihang Mountains and diverged to the northwest and northeast near today's Beijing; it was the interregional transportation linkage that allowed Ji and Yan to thrive.

According to the *Records of the Grand Historian*, after overthrowing the Shang, the early kings of the Zhou Dynasty (1046–256 BCE) endorsed Ji's status as a subordinate and conferred a new vassal to a kin and loyal supporter, once again under the name Yan. Archeological excavations in the late 1950s uncovered bronzeware from early Zhou showing inscriptions that confirmed these events and pinpointed the state of Yan's original seat at a village called Liulihe in southwestern Beijing proper, only a few miles to the southeast of the Peking Man site. More speculative studies place the seat of the state of Ji at an ancient earthen mount, the Hill of Ji, in modern Beijing, though this conclusion has solicited reputable dissentions. Called Jicheng (City of Ji), the protocity was to become the geographical anchor of Beijing for the next two millennia. In 1995, a monument was erected on the presumed site of the Hill of Ji to commemorate the beginning of Beijing. Both Yan and Ji became widely used and interchangeable names or aliases for Beijing ever since.

Spring and Autumn Period (770–476 BCE)

There is a gap in both written records and material evidence between the Western Zhou Dynasty (1045–771 BCE) and the Spring and Autumn period of the Eastern Zhou Dynasty (770–221 BCE), and, as a result, it is not clear as to what transpired in Beijing and its environs between the eleventh and eighth centuries BCE. When historical chronicles resumed, there was no longer any mention of the state of Ji, and Jicheng (Beijing) was now the seat of the state of Yan. It appeared that sometime during this time gap, Yan conquered Ji and took over its capital. It is speculated that Yan's original seat, built at a major crossing of the Yongding River, might have suffered from frequent flooding and river course changes. Situated in a higher elevation, Yan Beijing (Jicheng) was much less vulnerable to flood hazards while still enjoying steady water supply from bogs and springs along an abandoned course of the Yongding River. The secured water supply was a key site advantage that gave rise to and sustained ancient Yan Beijing for the next two millennia. Today, four small lakes next to the Beijing Western Railroad Station, called Lotus Pool, are the remnants of a once vital water source for ancient Beijing.

During the late Shang and Zhou periods, the climate in East Asia became drier and cooler, which pushed the boundary between nomadic and sedentary agricultures southward. The state of Yan, situated in the north end of the heartland of sedentary agricultural economy, began to feel the pressure from nomadic tribes from the north and had to move its capital to the south at the end of the seventh century BCE. Four decades later (657 BCE), however, the duke of Yan led a series of successful campaigns that led to reclaiming Jicheng, and made Yan a formidable contender for hegemony among the vassal states.

Warring States Period (473–221 BCE)

By the beginning of the Warring States period, Yan had emerged as one of the seven powerful feudal states, with territories that extended to the Yellow River in the south and to the Yalu River along today's Sino-Korean border. Yan Beijing (Jicheng) became a bulwark of defense and a hub of exchange between realms of sedentary agricultural and nomadic societies. Yan built walled fortifications across its northern and southern boundaries to fend off invaders from the nomadic north and rivals from the south. Yan's culture was heavily influenced by nomadic cultures and was known for its fearless knights-errant.

Toward the end of the Warring States, the state of Qin rose to be the dominant power as its army marched invincibly across the land. In 227 BCE, as the Qin army began to amass along Yan's southern borders, the crown prince of Yan and Jing Ke, a renowned knight-errant, plotted the assassination of the king of Qin in Yan Beijing (Jicheng). Although the feeble attempt failed, it would become an epic in Chinese history and culture. The king of Qin, on the other hand, would go on to unify China and become its first emperor, Qin Shihuangdi (r. 221–210 BCE). In 226 BCE, Yan Beijing fell to the invading Qin army and was subsequently destroyed. The Qin Dynasty (221–206 BCE) tore down Yan's southern walls but kept the northern walls as part of the Great Wall of Qin.

Qin–Han Period (221 BCE–220 CE)

In 221 BCE, Qin Shihuangdi abolished the vassal system and implemented a national administrative hierarchy of commanderies (prefectures) and counties. Qin Beijing retained its name (Jicheng) and became the seat of the Guangyang Commandery, marking the beginning of Beijing as a regional administrative center.

The Qin Dynasty was also able to build a nationwide expressway network in its short lifespan, which allowed it to strengthen its grip on the newly conquered land. The expressway approaching from the south diverged into three routes at Qin Beijing: one due east to northeast to the northeast plains, one due north through the Yanshan Mountains to the

Mongolian Plateau, and one to the northwest through the Taihang Mountains to the northern Loess Plateau. Qin Beijing solidified its position as the leading hub of trade and transportation in the northeastern frontier and a key defense outpost of the Qin empire against nomadic incursions.

During the Western Han Dynasty (206 BCE–8 CE), royal vassals and a commandery-county system coexisted. Despite frequent changes, frontier regions were dominated by vassals, and Han Beijing (Jicheng) was the capital of the vassal of Yan during much of Western Han. During the Eastern Han Dynasty (25–220 CE), a three-layered zhou (province), jun (commandery), and xian (county) administrative system was implemented, and Han Beijing became the seat of the provincial governorship of Youzhou.

Throughout the entire Han period (206 BCE–220 CE), the climate was warm and humid in the northern interior. The Han Dynasty's economic and political core was in the middle and lower Yellow River area, and the valley of the Wei River, a tributary of the Yellow River, was the pivot of the empire. The Han Chinese mainly had to contend with the Xiongnu, a nomadic people who had formed a confederation, on the semiarid grasslands along the middle Yellow River valley, especially in the areas to the south of Yellow River Loop (hetao). Han Beijing remained a provincial, albeit important, city of the northeastern frontier, but there are few details in the written records about its urban life.

First Intermediate Period (220–581)

The three-and-a-half centuries following the end of Eastern Han Dynasty were a time of tremendous chaos across northern China. Beijing (Jicheng) was hotly contested by warlords. Before and during the period of Three Kingdoms (Sanguo, 220–280), Beijing was the staging center for Chinese expeditions into the northeast against marauding Tungus tribal coalitions, especially Wuhuan and Xianbei. During the Western Jin Dynasty (265–316), the climate in East Asia had become cooler and drier, devastating the steppe grassland and forcing nomadic groups to move south and settle along the Chinese northern frontier. Referred to as *hu* (barbarians) in ancient China, these peoples had diverse ethnic, economic, and geographical origins.

The War of Eight Princes (291–306) caused the collapse of the economy and social order in northern China. Amid the turmoil, nomadic groups revolted, causing prolonged war, pillaging, famine, and genocide during the so-called Revolt of the Five Barbarians (wuhu luanhua, 304–316). Millions of refugees fled south, marking the beginning of a southward shift of the Chinese population and economic center. During this chaotic time,

Beijing was under the control of various ethnic factions and warlords and remained a regional administrative center.

Sui–Tang Period (581–907)

After the first intermediate period, China entered yet another period of unification during the Sui Dynasty (581–618) and much of the Tang Dynasty (618–907). While northern China struggled to recover, the lower Yangzi River valley emerged as the economic and population centers of China. At the same time, centuries of human disasters and climate change forced nomadic groups to move east and adapt to the new more humid environment. Tang Beijing, also called Youzhou Cheng (the city of Youzhou), became the most important center of the northeastern frontier, from which expeditions were launched into the steppes and the northeast.

Supplying these large military operations became a strategic challenge for China. As a coping strategy, Emperor Yangdi (569–618) of the Sui Dynasty constructed canal networks to connect Luoyang, the capital, with the Yangzi River Delta to the south and Sui Beijing (Jicheng) to the north. From Sui Beijing, nearly one million troops were amassed to launch three failed campaigns against Goguryeo, an emerging power based in the northeast plains and the Korean Peninsula. Emperor Taizong (598–649) of the Tang Dynasty (618–907) also used Tang Beijing (Youzhou) as the forward base to launch an expedition into the Korean Peninsula (644). Upon his return the next year, Emperor Taizong ordered a temple built in Tang Beijing to commemorate the war dead, which became the first Buddhist temple within the city of Beijing upon its eventual completion in 696 (today's Fayuan Temple).

These expeditions drained the national treasury and caused many casualties. It was a direct cause of the collapse of the Sui Dynasty, and it took decades for the Tang Dynasty to finally conquer Goguryeo. There was, and still is, geopolitical imperative behind this ostensive obsession of Chinese rulers to control the northeast plains and the Korean Peninsula. The region's geography and resources could foster the rapid rise of a regional power that was bound to expand southward. Once the invaders breached the Great Wall, there were few barriers on the vast North China Plain to slow down and repel them. The ancient Chinese were keenly aware of this geostrategic vulnerability and tried to preempt any potential threats rising from the northeast. Failure to hold the line at Beijing, on the other hand, has repeatedly proven disastrous to China's national security.

As nomadic groups continued to encroach into Tang territories, the Tang Dynasty devised a two-pronged strategy: the subjugated nomadic groups were settled as a defense buffer, and ten military governorships, each leading a large military garrison district, were formed along the frontier. Tang Beijing (Youzhou) became the seat of the largest garrison district, Fanyang, with a standing army of ninety thousand, an indication that the geopolitical threat to China proper was shifting from the northwest to the northeast.

The second half of the Tang Dynasty was characterized as being fragmented politically and in decline economically. An Lushan, a once-favored court minion of Persian Turkic origin, became the military governor of Fanyang and two other garrison districts in the northeast. Worried that he was losing the court's support, An revolted in 755, leading an army of 150,000 westward to attack Changan, the Tang capital, near today's city of Xian. The rebellion devolved into a protracted civil war that continued for eight years, devastating China and marking the turning point of Chinese civilization. For the rest of the Tang Dynasty, Beijing was repeatedly destroyed and rebuilt as the military governors, who were de facto warlords, waged wars against each other. Meanwhile, barbarian groups from the north began to overrun the border regions. The downfall of Tang (907) marked the changing geopolitical configuration in East Asia, which would reshape Beijing's fate and China's destiny in the ensuing centuries.

Second Intermediate Period (907–979)

The chaotic period of the so-called Five Dynasties and Ten States (907–960) followed the end of the Tang Dynasty, when regional warlords and barbarian groups contended with each other in northern China. One of them, the Khitans, founded the Liao Dynasty (907–1125) and controlled a vast empire from the Mongolian Steppes to the northeast forests. In 936, a military governor, Shi Jingtang, proclaimed himself emperor of Later Jin Dynasty and pleaded for support from the Khitan Liao Dynasty (916–1125). In return, Shi ceded to Liao sixteen zhous (commanderies), including Youzhou, along the Chinese northern frontier.

Liao's control of the traditional Chinese frontier indicated a fundamental transformation of some nomadic groups from marauders to occupiers in China. They inevitably adopted, at least in part, the Chinese culture while struggling to retain their heritage. During this transitional period, Beijing's indispensable function shifted from a Chinese frontier hub to a capital of great and contrasting cultural realms of sedentary agriculture, nomadic pastoralism, and mixed hunting-farming economy.

BEIJING AS THE IMPERIAL CAPITAL

The Song Dynasty (960–1279) is regarded by some as the apex of Chinese civilization in terms of its highly developed economy and sophisticated technology. It never regained control of its northern frontier, however, and as a result, it remained under strategic threat from the rising powers in the north. At the same time, it was the barbarians who endeavored to establish sustainable governance of the sedentary agricultural regions while retaining in control of their homeland. It was their success in building and sustaining empires encompassing diverse economic and cultural realms that would change the course of history in East Asia and the fate of Beijing forever.

Beijing's Transition during the Liao and Jin Periods (916–1234)

The Khitans of the Liao Dynasty recognized that it must adopt Chinese-style laws and governing infrastructure to establish effective control over the newly conquered Chinese regions. Liao rulers enlisted the services of a large number of Chinese literati (shi dafu), men who were schooled in Confucian doctrines and comprised the core of imperial China's bureaucracy. The Liao Dynasty set up four auxiliary capitals, or regional administrative centers, to govern its vast and diverse territories based on their economic and cultural conditions. Beijing, near the southern border of Liao, became the center for governing the traditionally Chinese agricultural areas. The city was officially named Nanjing (Southern Capital) in 938 but was also referred to as Yanjing (Capital of the Yan Area).

Liao Beijing (Nanjing) was the largest of all Liao cities and the major revenue source for Liao. The new capital was built where the ancient city of Beijing had stood and was not much larger, with a perimeter of about 23 kilometers (14 miles). While the square layout and south-facing main gates reflected Chinese influence, the eastern gate of the city was the only official entry, reflecting the Khitans' sun worship heritage. The civilian quarters retained much of the Tang layout of walled neighborhoods (fang). At its prime, Liao Beijing had twenty-six fang and nearly three hundred thousand residents.

Meanwhile, the Song Dynasty (960–1279) emerged from the civil war. In an effort to regain control of the northern frontier, in 979, Emperor Taizong (939–997) hastily launched a large northern expedition. The Song army was resoundingly defeated in the Battle of Gaoliang River, a tributary of the Yongding River to the northwest of Liao Beijing. The Chinese were not to regain control of Beijing until the army of Ming (1368–1644) retook it near four centuries later.

Liao and Song eventually reached a peace treaty in 1004, which sustained peace between the two powers for more than a century. In the meantime, environmental degradation in the northern interior, due to both long-range climate change and unsustainable human activities, had forced the Chinese population and economic centers to move south, while nomadic societies migrated east. Conflicts inevitably arose from such great geopolitical reconfigurations. A seminomadic, semisedentary Tungus people, known as the Jurchens, emerged from the northeastern plains and toppled Liao after a series of joint campaigns with Song. The Jurchens founded the Jin Dynasty in 1122 and took over Liao Beijing (Nanjing) the same year. Beijing was returned to Song and became the seat for Yanshan Fu, but Jin retook the city three years later and renamed it Yanjing.

In 1151, a top court official, Wanyan Liang, assassinated the Jin emperor and usurped the crown. In 1153, Wanyan Liang moved the Jin capital to Beijing (Yanjing) and renamed it Zhongdu (Central Capital). Despite court intrigues, the real reason for Jin to move its capital to Beijing was geopolitical. Beijing presented a superior strategic position to command over realms of sedentary agriculture to the south, nomadic pastoralism to the north and northwest, and the mixed hunting-farming economy to the northeast. From Beijing (Zhongdu), Jin rulers aspired to unify China with their homeland. As the Jin court became more sinicized, it distanced itself from its roots in the steppes by, for example, compiling official chronicles and reducing the number of Nabo, or field headquarters, from four to two. Nabo was the mobile command center of nomadic societies such as the Khitans and the Jurchens that was also employed as a deterrence showcase to potential challengers. At the end of the twelfth century, the Jin Dynasty even built a thousand miles of walls along its northern borders to defend against the emerging Mongols.

Wanyan Liang mobilized several hundred thousand soldiers and twice as many civilian laborers to build Jin Beijing (Zhongdu). He drew his blueprint for the new capital based on the design of Kaifeng (Bianjing), Northern Song's capital that the Jurchens had sacked in 1126. The Song royal palaces in Kaifeng were systematically dismantled so that their building materials could be used for the new royal palaces in Jin Beijing, which was nearly twice as big as Liao Beijing. The royal palaces were situated at the center of the city with civic services and altars aligned symmetrically on their sides, following the principles for urban design outlined in *Kao Gong Ji* (The Artificers' Records).

The Jin Dynasty refurbished and expanded canals in and around Beijing to secure water sources for both urban consumption and commercial navigation. The canal networks contributed to the prosperity of many port cities along the canals, including Tongzhou, to the east of Jin Beijing. The population and economy grew rapidly in Beijing and its environs. Jin Beijing grew from a regional administrative and military town to a capital city of converging government bureaucracy, civil society, economic consumption, and high culture on par with Hangzhou (Linan), the capital of the Southern Song Dynasty (1127–1279).

Peace and prosperity did not last for the Jurchens, however. By the early 1200s, the Mongols led by Genghis Khan had begun their epic conquests through Eurasia. In 1214, Genghis Khan attacked Jin Beijing (Zhongdu) and sacked the city after eleven months of siege. The royal palaces were set ablaze by both the defenders and attackers, and the fire raged for more than a month, completely ravaging the capital city that had existed for merely sixty-three years. Ironically, some of the royal resorts, built outside the walled city, survived and still exist as popular parks today, such as Beihai (North Sea), Taoranting (Joyful Pavilion), and Diaoyutai (Fishing Terrace).

Yuan Period (1272–1368)

As they swept through Eurasia in the thirteenth century, the Mongols came into contact with diverse civilizations. The outcome of these interactions, random as they might have been, deeply affected regional economies and cultures. In 1251, Kublai Khan, a grandson of Genghis Khan and brother of reigning leader Möngke Khan, was appointed to govern the newly conquered Chinese regions. He became immersed in Chinese culture and surrounded himself with Chinese literati. He was receptive of the idea that the Mongols must adapt to the Chinese culture rather than eradicating it to achieve sustainable rule over China. Kublai emerged victorious from a brutal succession war (1260–1264) but became alienated from many Mongol elites, who resented his embrace of the Chinese way of life. As the Mongol Empire splintered into several Khanates, Kublai's domain shrunk to China proper, Tibet, and the eastern Mongolian Plateau. In 1271, Kublai Khan officially renamed his Khanate "Yuan Dynasty" (1271–1368). Between this year and 1275, Marco Polo reached Shangdu, also known as Xanadu, which meant the "upper capital," where he was received by Kublai Khan.

Kublai Khan realized that he needed a capital city that would allow him to control and govern the different realms of his empire. His advisers persuaded him to select Beijing as the main capital because of its imposing position to China proper and easy access to the Mongolian Plateau. During his visit to Beijing in 1264, Kublai Khan lodged in a former Jin royal resort (today's Beihai Park) to the immediate northeast of Jin Beijing. He was so enchanted by the natural setting around Taiye Lake (Great Liquid Pond) that he decreed the new capital be built in the area. The man who was charged with this task was one of Kublai's favorite advisers, Liu Bingzhong (1216–1274), a Han Chinese who was the chief planner and architect of Shangdu (1252–1254).

The center of Jin Beijing had been in ruins since the royal palaces were burned down in 1215, though the rest of the city was densely populated.

The site for the new capital presented a clean slate for construction. More importantly, the traditional water sources for Beijing, Lotus River and Lotus Pool, could no longer adequately supply a bigger city, but the new site had ample surface and groundwater supply fed by several rivers, as shown by Taiye Lake.

Construction started in 1267. The new capital's rectangular layout was defined by walls of pounded earth mixed with reeds and lumber. The walls measured 28.6 kilometers (17.8 miles) in total length, and the walled city had nearly 50 square kilometers (19 square miles) in total area, almost three times the size of Jin Beijing. Liu's design of Yuan Beijing reflected influence of both the model city layout outlined in Kao Gong Ji and Mongol customs. First, in aligning with the cosmic forces, a central axis and a central point were set to guide the spatial arrangements of key buildings. The royal compound was located on the central-south side of the city, with the imperial court on the front and royal residence to the back. A large marketplace was allocated to the north–northwest of the city near the major canal terminus. Altars and temples for ancestral worship were located on the east side of the central axis, and those for earth and harvest sacrificial rituals were placed on the west side.

The city was dissected by nine north–south thoroughfares and nine east–west ones, as dictated by the "supreme number principle" in Kao Gong Ji. There were three gates each on the south, east, and west walls but only two on the north wall. According to Daoist cosmology, the north corresponds to Kan, one of the eight astrological symbols that embodies dangerous traps. It is said that Liu, an expert of Daoist cosmology, remedied the problem by not having the middle gate on the north wall to prevent sinister spirits from entering the city and directly approaching the royal palaces. The gate arrangement was later inherited by the Ming and Qing Dynasties. The gates were given names drawn from Chinese classics on nature and man. The sparsely populated northern part of the city was walled in and slated for future development.

In 1272, Kublai Khan proclaimed Beijing "Dadu" (Grand Capital), known as Daidu or Khanbaliq to the Mongols, of the Yuan Dynasty. In 1274, Kublai Khan officially opened his court in Beijing. Liu Bingzhong passed away in Xanadu the same year and did not live to see this completed masterpiece. By 1285, much of the imperial complex was completed.

Upon completion, Yuan Beijing (Dadu) was sparsely populated. The court encouraged the rich and powerful to relocate from Jin Beijing, now known as the "old city," by providing land grants of 8 mu (1 mu = 0.165 acre) per family for approved family residences. Within a decade, more than four hundred thousand people had moved into the new city. The policy might have had enduring effects on the socioeconomic geography of

Yuan Beijing by segregating the well-to-do from the common folks, who did not qualify for the land grant and continued to cluster in the old city.

It is important to note that Kublai and successive Yuan emperors maintained a two-capital system between Shangdu (also known as Xanadu, the summer capital) and Dadu (the winter capital). The purpose of this system was to make sure that the Yuan court controlled, in both physical presence and governing efficiency, the Mongolian steppes and the vast, newly conquered China proper. Yuan emperors would open court in yurts for emergent matters when they were en route to one capital or the other.

The challenge of supplying the capital persisted through interregional shipping of food and other materials, only this was more daunting because Yuan Beijing was significantly larger and more populated than its predecessors, Jin Beijing (Zhongdu) and Liao Beijing (Nanjing or Yanjing). One of Liu's disciples, Guo Shoujing (1231–1316), was charged with improving water supply and navigation for the capital. He was instrumental in rerouting and expanding the canal networks. In 1283, the Jing-Hang (Beijing–Hangzhou) Grand Canal was completed, linking Yuan Beijing (Dadu) directly to Hangzhou in the productive Yangzi River Delta and shortening the Sui Dynasty canal routes by about three hundred miles. The completion of the Beijing–Tongzhou section of the Grand Canal made strategic supplies from the Yangzi River Delta directly to Yuan Beijing (Dadu) faster, cheaper, and in much larger bulk shipments. Kublai Khan was so thrilled to see the loaded vessels anchoring right outside the Imperial City that he conferred the name Tonghui (benefits from connections) to the Beijing–Tongzhou canal. Today, the Tonghui Canal flows near Beijing's central business district (CBD) and booming eastern suburbs, but it is more of a historical reminder rather than the vital transportation link that it once was.

It would be erroneous to assume that Yuan Beijing was a typical Chinese capital city. In a scene from an Italian American television miniseries, *Marco Polo* (1982–1983), Kublai Khan wants to have a last ride with Marco Polo, who came to bid farewell to the elderly emperor. Having difficulty mounting his horse, Kublai bemoans both his frailty and the waning nomadic tradition in his court. In the background, one sees yurts and large meadows on the grounds of the Forbidden City. Yuan Beijing was a capital city that amalgamated elements of Chinese, Mongol, and other cultures and displayed a religious landscape mosaic with numerous Lamarist monasteries, Daoist and Buddhist temples, and Islamic mosques, showing the Mongols' openness to cultural diversity. While Liu Bingzhong, a Chinese, was the chief planner of Yuan Beijing (Dadu), the architect for the royal palaces was a Persian, Yeheidie'erding (Amir al-Din). Ethnic diversity in Kublai's court certainly did not stop there: his prime minister Sengge (?–1291) was a Tibetan, and his imperial chief for finance and taxation, Ahmad Fanakati (?–1282), was a Muslim from the Fergana Basin in today's Uzbekistan.

The Mongols' reverence for water left an enduring imprint on Beijing with the incorporation of water elements. Royal palaces were built around the expanded Taiye Lake, which became known as the "three seas": the southern sea, the central sea, and the northern sea. The inner chambers and living quarters were built in styles found in Mongolia or Central Asia and were not cordoned off from the front court, which was a requirement for classic Chinese royal palaces. The walls and palaces were painted white, a color that the Mongols favored but considered taboo in the Chinese tradition. There were also many eclectic features, such as royal halls covered with animal hides and glass, bathhouses, structures with white walls and white glass tile roofs, and wide meadows between palaces.

The grandeur and scale of Yuan Beijing astounded the Venetian traveler Marco Polo, who visited the newly completed capital in the 1280s. His accounts of Dadu (Taidu), known also for its Mongol Turkic name, Khanbaliq (Cambaluc), left vivid and detailed descriptions that were unmatched in any other historical texts and thus are worth a lengthy quote:

> As regards the size of this (new) city you must know that it has a compass of 24 miles, for each side of it hath a length of 6 miles, and it is four-square. And it is all walled round with walls of earth which have a thickness of full ten paces at bottom, and a height of more than 10 paces; but they are not so thick at top, for they diminish in thickness as they rise, so that at top they are only about 3 paces thick. And they are provided throughout with loop-holed battlements, which are all whitewashed.
>
> There are 12 gates, and over each gate there is a great and handsome palace, so that there are on each side of the square three gates and five palaces; for (I ought to mention) there is at each angle also a great and handsome palace. In those palaces are vast halls in which are kept the arms of the city garrison.
>
> The streets are so straight and wide that you can see right along them from end to end and from one gate to the other. And up and down the city there are beautiful palaces, and many great and fine hostelries, and fine houses in great numbers. (All the plots of ground on which the houses of the city are built are four-square, and laid out with straight lines; all the plots being occupied by great and spacious palaces, with courts and gardens of proportionate size. All these plots were assigned to different heads of families. Each square plot is encompassed by handsome streets for traffic; and thus the whole city is arranged in squares just like a chess-board, and disposed in a manner so perfect and masterly that it is impossible to give a description that should do it justice.)[1]

Yuan Beijing showcased cutting-edge urban design and infrastructure of the time. A series of surface channels and culverts followed the northwest–southeast natural gradient, providing a sophisticated drainage system to manage runoff and mitigate flooding. The surface channels were covered with stone slabs where they intersected with streets. There were stone slab culverts on city walls reinforced on the sides and the bottom by iron ingots. This effective drainage system was retained by the Ming and Qing Dynasties and remained effective until the city walls were demolished.

Coal became widely used in Yuan Beijing in the late 1200s. The swelling population and robust economy incurred great demand for fuel for cooking and heating. Coal was a timely and plentiful substitute for the dwindling forests in the western mountains and hills. The government sanctioned and directly partook in coal mining; there were trading markets and storage facilities for coal in the city, where a gate on the west wall was dedicated to coal transportation. Some have argued that Beijing could not have been sustainable as a large capital city had coal not been available as the alternative energy source. Inefficient use of coal, however, sowed the seeds for a slew of environmental problems in times to come.

The residential design of Yuan Beijing aimed at much greater openness and mobility in comparison to traditional Chinese urban neighborhoods. During the Tang and Song Dynasties, urban residential areas consisted of walled subdivisions with controlled entryways (fang). In contrast, residential neighborhoods in Yuan Beijing, still called fang, were subdivided by major avenues and streets instead of walls. The entryways were effectively eliminated, and residential dwellings became visible and accessible from streets and alleyways. There were three classes of passageways: the boulevards measured about 37 meters (121 feet) wide, the streets measured about 18 meters (59 feet) wide, and the neighborhood lanes, called *hutong*, measured about 9 meters (29 feet) wide. Until recently, the name hutong was believed to have originated from a Mongolian word meaning "water well," as the nomads congregated at water sources. The latest research, however, appears to reveal a more complex, non-Mongol origin. Nevertheless, many neighborhood lanes maintained water wells as a measure of fire prevention.

One of the most important traditional Chinese residential dwellings, the courtyard house, dates back to the tenth century BCE. It evolved through time and eventually settled on a quadrangle form called *siheyuan*. A distinct and mature form of siheyuan became popular in Yuan Beijing as the rich and famous moved their homesteads to the new capital. The typical Yuan Beijing siheyuan consisted of four sections of rooms in a north–south orientation, which by design creates a central courtyard. Siheyuan was widely adopted in Yuan Beijing in part because its rectangular form and north–south orientation conformed to both feng shui requirements and the capital's checkerboard layout. Its configuration also accommodated the familial order and reinforced the privacy and security of the extended family. While the imperial palaces and gardens occupied the visual and geometric center of Yuan Beijing, the web of hutong and the blocks of siheyuan seamlessly filled in the city's checkerboard layout and bestowed upon it a unique and uniform landscape.

Yuan Beijing was a major commercial center of not only the Yuan Dynasty but also the world. By the early fourteenth century, the capital city's annual tax revenue had reached over one hundred thousand silver pieces, much of which came from trade, both domestic and international, more than the entire empire's tax revenue, except for that from the Henan Province and Yangzi Delta. Marco Polo, himself a merchant, recorded the capital's economic prosperity driven by domestic and international trade:

> You must know that the city of Cambaluc hath such a multitude of houses, and such a vast population inside the walls and outside, that it seems quite past all possibility. There is a suburb outside each of the gates, which are twelve in number; and these suburbs are so great that they contain more people than the city itself (for the suburb of one gate spreads in width till it meets the suburb of the next, whilst they extend in length some three or four miles). In those suburbs lodge the foreign merchants and travelers, of whom there are always great numbers who have come to bring presents to the Emperor, or to sell articles at Court, or because the city affords so good a mart to attract traders. (There are in each of the suburbs, to a distance of a mile from the city, numerous fine hostelries for the lodgment of merchants from different parts of the world, and a special hostelry is assigned to each description of people, as if we should say there is one for the Lombards, another for the Germans, and a third for the Frenchmen.) And thus there are as many good houses outside of the city as inside, without counting those that belong to the great lords and barons, which are very numerous.
>
> . . .
>
> As a sample, I tell you, no day in the year passes that there do not enter the city 1000 cart-loads of silk alone, from which are made quantities of cloth of silk and gold, and of other goods. And this is not to be wondered at; for in all the countries round about there is no flax, so that everything has to be made of silk. It is true, indeed, that in some parts of the country there is cotton and hemp, but not sufficient for their wants. This, however, is not of much consequence, because silk is so abundant and cheap, and is a more valuable substance than either flax or cotton.
>
> Round about this great city of Cambaluc there are some 200 other cities at various distances, from which traders come to sell their goods and buy others for their lords; and all find means to make their sales and purchases, so that the traffic of the city is passing great.[2]

Although the Yuan Dynasty lasted for merely a century, Yuan Beijing left an enduring legacy as a planned imperial capital. Yuan Beijing struck a remarkable balance between Chinese urban tradition and nomadic cultures. It made breakthroughs in urban design, land use planning, infrastructure, and management. For the first time in history, Beijing was a world class city with robust trade and commerce as well as cultural exchange. Although limited physical evidence of Yuan Beijing remains today, the city inherited and integrated many important attributes from the Grand Capital, such as the central axis, the symmetrical layout, the residential design, and the canal transportation system.

Perhaps more importantly, Beijing's ascension as the national capital during the Yuan Dynasty was the culmination of transformation in East Asia since the early fourth century, when long-range climatic changes and environmental degradation in the western interior started driving Chinese population south and nomadic groups east. In addition, eastward extension of the coastline around the Bo Sea in the previous two millennia had created a flat coastal passage between the northeast forests and the North China Plain. The highly contested geopolitical front line shifted to the east. Beijing emerged with much greater geopolitical significance than its former role as a regional military outpost and transportation hub: it was now the center for commanding the entirety of East Asia.

Ming Dynasty Period (1368–1644)

The Yuan Dynasty's relative short reign could be largely attributed to its endless court intrigue and discriminatory ethnic policies. The latter divided the population into four classes, with the Mongols on top, followed by "color-eyed" people who had Central and Western Asian ancestries. Northern Chinese were classified as being higher than southern Chinese, who were the last to be conquered. By the mid-fourteenth century, the Yuan Dynasty was confronted with a series of natural and human disasters, such as heavy taxation, large-scale flooding along the Yellow River, and bubonic plague. The court's poor response to these disasters caused widespread unrest and open rebellions. The largest revolt, the Red Turban (Hongjin), started in the Yangzi River Delta area, and the faction led by Zhu Yuanzhang eventually emerged victorious after defeating other rebel forces and unifying most of southern China. Zhu then launched a northern expedition and sacked Yuan Beijing in 1368. In the same year, he was enthroned as Emperor Hongwu of the Ming Dynasty (1368–1644) and chose Jinling, on the Yangzi River, as his capital, renaming it Nanjing (Southern Capital). Yuan Beijing (Dadu) was renamed Beiping (Northern Peace).

Emperor Hongwu had seriously considered choosing a capital located farther north, driven by his ambition of consolidating control over the entire former Yuan realm. He finally chose Nanjing because it was located in the Yangzi River Delta, his power base and China's most advanced economic region. His decision made economic sense, but it circumvented the geopolitical threat posed by the remnants of Yuan, which had fled to the

Mongolian Plateau but had not given up on resurrecting its empire. In response, the Ming Dynasty set up more than twenty principalities along the northern frontier supported by military garrisons. In 1370, Beijing (Beiping) became the seat of the prince of Yan, Zhu Di (1360–1424), the fourth son of Emperor Hongwu. The Yan Principality became the most powerful among its peers because of its paramount geostrategic importance. Losing control of Beiping would be disastrous to Han Chinese rule and expose the entire China proper, as the fate of the Song Dynasty had shown.

Emperor Hongwu died in 1398, and the throne was passed to his imperial grandson. The new emperor attempted to reclaim power from the powerful princes (mostly his uncles) by demoting or exiling a number of them. Zhu Di, the prince of Yan, revolted with the support that he had cultivated in his three-decade reign in his principality. After three years of bloody war, Zhu Di overthrew his nephew and declared himself emperor of Ming (Emperor Yongle) in 1402. Emperor Yongle is best known for his two great achievements during his twenty-one-year reign: the Yongle Canon, which was the large encyclopedia in Chinese history and perhaps the earliest in the world (1408), and seven large-scale seafaring expeditions (1405–1433), the so-called treasure voyages, led by court eunuch and Chinese Muslim Zheng He. His third, and equally important, achievement was the relocation of the Ming capital from Nanjing to Beijing and the reconstruction of Beijing in the configuration and grandeur that we can still see today.

Fierce court debate over capital selection started immediately after Emperor Yongle's ascension to (or usurpation of) the throne. In 1403, as a transitional maneuver, Emperor Yongle elevated Beiping (Northern Peace) to xingzai (a de facto capital during an imperial excursion) and renamed it Beijing (Northern Capital). This was the first time in history that the city was named Beijing. Construction of royal palaces started in 1406 and completed fourteen years later (1420). Emperor Yongle officially moved the capital from Nanjing to Beijing in 1421, though he had started his own royal tomb construction in the hills northwest of Beijing in 1409, showing his determination in relocating the capital to the crowd of somewhat reluctant literati.

There are still debates as to why Ming relocated its capital to Beijing. Some argue that Emperor Yongle wanted to retreat to his power base after having usurped the crown; others insist that he chose Beijing as the capital because he understood the geopolitics. The latter is a more plausible explanation for his insistence in moving the capital to Beijing. As the prince of Yan, Emperor Yongle led a number of expeditions into the steppes in pursuit of the remnants of the Yuan Dynasty. As the emperor, he launched five more expeditions from Beijing and died during the last one. Emperor

Yongle must have been keenly aware that China's security could only be guaranteed with control over the northern steppes and forests, where threats to China proper arose, and Beijing was the command center for such a monumental mission.

After Emperor Yongle passed away in 1424, it became clear that the Ming Dynasty did not have the ability to eradicate the threat from the Mongols, and the ambition of a multirealm empire began to fade away. As a result, Beijing as the capital appeared to make no sense, as it was vulnerable to Mongol incursions and costly to maintain. The next emperor considered moving the capital back to Nanjing, but the proposed relocation was halted by a series of earthquakes in Nanjing during his extremely short reign (September 7, 1424–May 29, 1425). Succeeding emperors and the bureaucracy eventually came to recognize that having Beijing as the capital would allow the court to mobilize resources against Mongol incursions most effectively. The capital on the frontier would also prevent the military garrisons from becoming too powerful and ambitious, as in the cases of the An Lushan Rebellion (755–763) and the insurgency led by the prince of Yan (Emperor Yongle) only a generation before.

By the early Ming Dynasty, Beijing had become dependent on supplies from the Yangzi Delta. During the late Yuan Dynasty, sections of the Grand Canal became clogged up, and canal shipping was supplanted by sea transportation. Failing to secure sea transportation routes, however, the Ming Dynasty dredged and expanded the Grand Canal. The Ming court carried out large-scale settlement programs in Beijing and its environs that were implemented with incentives, including free land, farming tools, and tax relief to boost the local economy. A large number of cashiered soldiers, transients, and ex-convicts were also settled.

After the downfall of the Yuan Dynasty, Beijing underwent a major transformation. Upon taking over the Yuan capital, the Ming army abandoned the northern third of the city because of both defense concerns and compliance to classic rites, which required a city's perimeter to be no more than one-third the size of the capital (Nanjing). The contraction of Ming Beijing (Peiping) cost the city two gates, one on the eastern wall and one on the western wall. A new northern wall was built about 2.5 kilometers (1.5 miles) south of Yuan Beijing's northern wall. The construction was carried out in such haste that the new wall simply encased any building structures along its way, as revealed by the demolition of Beijing's city walls in the 1950s and 1960s.

The Yuan royal palaces were immediately torn down, which was a common Chinese practice to erase any symbolism of the previous rulers. The Ming official overseeing the demolition described the grandeur and scale of the Yuan royal complexes with phrases such as "heavenly" and "unprecedented" as they were being razed to the ground. Some elements or concepts of Yuan Beijing were retained, as they conformed to traditional Chinese urban design, including the central axis, the checkerboard street pattern, and the eastern and western city walls. Ming Beijing also inherited benefits from Yuan Beijing's development, including a reliable and plentiful water supply, the relatively low risk for flooding, and vital supplies from the Yangzi Delta through the Grand Canal. Once construction for the new capital started in 1406, however, crucial differences began to surface between Yuan Beijing (Dadu) and Ming Beijing.

First, there were further adjustments to the city perimeters. In 1419, the southern wall was moved about one kilometer (0.6 miles) farther south, positioning the Forbidden City at the center of the city. This adjustment also gave Ming Beijing a more squarish shape, with the east–west length about 1.24 times the north–south length, conforming to the Chinese cosmological ideal of "round heaven and square earth." Yuan Beijing's southern wall then became the foundation of Changan Avenue, a key east–west thoroughfare. The new city walls of Ming Beijing totaled 22.5 kilometers (14 miles).

Second, a new central axis was set roughly 150 meters (492 feet) to the east of Yuan Beijing's central axis and became the new baseline of the capital city. A man-made hill behind the new Forbidden City became the new geographical center of Ming Beijing. Known as Coal Hill or Longevity Hill during the Ming Dynasty, this man-made earthen mount was built on the site of the central hall of the Yuan royal palaces, a design aimed at disrupting the feng shui of the Yuan Dynasty by suppressing its heavenly endowed energy flow.

Third, the Ming Forbidden City was in strict conformity to the principles outlined in Kao Gong Ji. Emperor Yongle adopted the same blueprint that his father, Emperor Hongwu, had for Nanjing's royal palaces, and the new Forbidden City became the absolute geographical and functional center of Ming Beijing. Its arrangements were intended to emulate the Daoist unity of heaven and human and the Confucian doctrine of propriety. All key structures of the royal palaces were positioned on the central axis, with lesser buildings on either side as a display of balance and order. The formal residential quarters for the emperor mirrored Chinese celestial cognition, as the emperor claimed to be the son of heaven (tianzi). The celestial vault included three enclosures: the Purple Forbidden, the Supreme Palace, and the Heavenly Market. Among them, the Purple Forbidden enclosure in the middle was regarded as the residence of the celestial emperor, hence the name for the entire royal palace compound, the (Purple) Forbidden City. The front section of the Forbidden City paralleled the Supreme Palace enclosure and was used to hold court and major ceremonies.

The market, heavenly or earthly, should ideally be on the north (back) side of the Forbidden City. In Ming and Qing Beijing, however, the location of the main market took an exception to this rule. During the Yuan Dynasty, Beijing's main marketplace was around the Grand Canal terminus behind the palaces. During the Ming Dynasty, however, trade and commerce shifted to the South City (the Outer City), where there was direct access to the docks of the refurbished section of the Grand Canal (Tonghui Canal). There were specialized trade spots for draft animals, ceramics, rice, coal, firewood, and so on, as well as labor markets. Some streets and hutong still bear the market names today, for example, Avenue of Horse and Mule Market and Firewood Hutong, among others, even though the markets themselves are long gone.

Fourth, there were substantial upgrades to the city's defense system. Ming Beijing rebuilt and reinforced Beijing's fortification. Between 1436 and 1439, gate towers and barbicans were added to all nine gates. The elaborate barbican ("urn city") consisted of an archery tower, sluice, and auxiliary walls running perpendicularly to the main city wall. Corner towers were constructed on the turning points of the city walls. The moats were dredged, and their banks were reinforced with stones and bricks; all wooden bridges over the moats were upgraded to stone bridges. Yuan Beijing's city walls were of rammed earth, except for the sections near the gates, and were prone to damage from summer downpours. Troops had to be mobilized to plant reeds near the city to provide materials for reed rows, which were used to cover the walls during the rainy season. In 1445, a 1-meter-thick (3.5 feet) brick layer was added to Ming Beijing's city walls, which was a major engineering feat and a drain to the national treasury. Beijing's city walls withstood the test of time from then on until they were completely torn down five hundred years later in the name of modernization.

At the middle of the newly completed capital, a 9-kilometer (5.6 miles) wall demarcated the Imperial City, the domain of the emperor, which occupied 20 percent of the entire walled city at the time (the Inner City). The Imperial City housed royal gardens, shrines, temples, and court services as well as the offices of key bureaucracies. City streets were designed to divert traffic from the Imperial City. At the center of the Imperial City, and indeed at the very center of Ming Beijing, there was the rectangular-shaped Forbidden City, the emperor's outer court–inner court compound. It was protected by a wall that was 10 meters (33 feet) tall and 3.4 kilometers (2.1 miles) long and a moat that was 52 meters (170 feet) wide.

Visitors to Beijing today are inevitably drawn to the sprawling and majestic Forbidden City, where they enjoy a visual feast of Chinese history and culture. The impressive royal complex is the best-preserved imperial

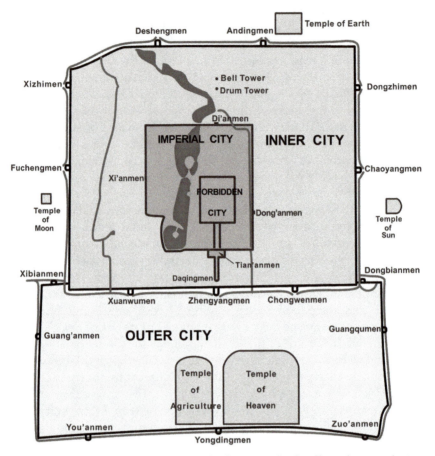

Imperial Beijing's fortification consisted of a network of walls and moats during much of the Ming and Qing Dynasties (1368–1911). Construction of the Forbidden City, the Imperial City, and the Inner City dates back to the early 1400s, and the Outer City was added in the mid-1500s. The walls and gates were demolished in the 1950s and 1960s. (Courtesy of Kallgan)

complex in China and one of the largest of its kind in the world. The Forbidden City was home to the emperors of the last two imperial dynasties in China, the Ming (1368–1644) and the Qing (1644–1911), and its design epitomized the absolute power bestowed upon the sovereign from heaven. The Forbidden City, and indeed all of Beijing during the Ming and Qing Dynasties, was a project intended to be a return to "purer" Chinese traditions, as defined by Confucian doctrines and Daoist metaphysics.

The Mongols had splintered into a number of tribes by the end of the fourteenth century but continued to pose a threat to China proper. The

The Forbidden City in Beijing, China is the largest palace complex in the world. It covers 183 acres and comprises 9,999 buildings. The Forbidden City was commissioned in 1406 by Ming emperor Yongle and served as the Ming imperial palace. (Chen Lirong/Dreamstime.com)

Mongols carried out frequent invasions and demanded favorable trade terms along the frontier and exorbitant rewards from the traditional tribute system. Invasions, pillaging, and all-out wars became a major theme of the Mongol-Ming relationship through much of the Ming Dynasty, although there were also prolonged periods of peace.

The most dramatic and traumatic of the Ming-Mongol conflicts was the Tumu Crisis. In summer 1449, Oirat Mongols led by Esen Tayisi (1407–1455) advanced on Datong in today's Shanxi Province. An ill-planned counterattack led by Emperor Zhengtong turned into a disaster. The five hundred thousand–strong Ming army was annihilated, and Emperor Zhengtong was captured by the Mongols at the post station Tumu, just outside the Juyong Pass of the inner Great Wall. The Mongols then laid siege on Beijing. The emperor's younger brother was installed as the new emperor, who rejected the Mongols' demands for border trade as well as offers for ransom. Fierce battles took place near the city gates on the west side, and the defenders were able to repel the Mongols with both resolve and the capital's outstanding defense infrastructure. The Mongols retreated to the steppes in November. The captured emperor was returned the next year and was put under house arrest by the reigning emperor. The encore of the Tumu Crisis was a bloody court coup d'état seven years later and the restoration of the former POW emperor.

It became imperative to further improve Beijing's defenses after a Tatar Mongol incursion led by Altan Khan of the Tümed in 1550. The Ming court decided to construct an outer wall around the existing city. The proposal was first presented in 1476 to build a new 35-kilometers-long (21 miles) outer wall encircling the existing city, which would cost 600,000 Chinese tael of silver (1 tael is about 1.3 ounces). The plan was put aside due to concerns of cost overruns. In 1553, construction finally started on the south side, but it was abruptly halted within a month because of funding shortages and complicated groundwater conditions on the southwest side. Only the southern outer wall was completed, with a total of roughly 14 kilometers (8.7 miles).

The new wall provided protection to a densely settled area as well as the Temple of Heaven and the Temple of Mountains and Rivers (later renamed the Temple of Agriculture), which came to be known as the "Outer City" or the "South City." At the same time, the original walled city became the "Inner City." The Outer City had seven gates, and its middle south gate, Yongdingmen Gate, became the new southern terminus of Ming Beijing's central axis. The Outer City gave Ming Beijing a distinct 凸 shape and four distinct walled sections: the Forbidden City, the Imperial City, the Inner City, and the Outer City.

In terms of civil management, Ming Beijing was divided into five large districts using the names of the five elements in Daoist metaphysics with different colors. The northern section of the city was the "water" district, the southern section was the "fire" district, the eastern section was "wood," the western was "metal," and the central section was "earth." Each district had a number of city blocks, or fang, a residential community where most residents shared a similar socioeconomic profile. Each fang was divided into a number of pai, and each pai was divided into a number of pu, which would be the equivalent of a neighborhood that included eight or nine hutong. The government would select local residents to be in charge of rudimentary management duties, such as safety patrol, fire prevention, and information reporting. This model of localized urban governance is still being used today.

While not as open to cultural diversity as Yuan Beijing, Ming Beijing welcomed the arrival of Christian missionaries. Christians (Nestorians) had reached Changan, the imperial capital of the Tang Dynasty, in the seventh century, and Christianity had a strong presence in China during the Yuan Dynasty. It was during the late Ming Dynasty, however, that Christian missionaries left remarkable imprints in Beijing's cultural landscape. Matteo Ricci (1552–1610), an Italian Jesuit who arrived in Beijing in 1598, gained trust as well as resources from the Ming court for his proselytizing and earthly activities. He built the Cathedral of the Immaculate Conception in 1605, the oldest Christian church in Beijing. Also known as the Southern Church locally, it burned down during the 1900 Boxer Rebellion but was rebuilt in 1904. Matteo Ricci died in Beijing in 1610 and was granted special permission to be buried in the city. His gravesite eventually grew into a cemetery for Catholic missionaries, which is located on a small college campus.

The Ming Dynasty collapsed in 1644. In the late Ming period, inefficiency, corruption, and a failed taxation system nearly incapacitated the Ming court in its response to major natural disasters, which were in part caused by a climate cooling period. Massive revolts spread in China proper, and the Manchus, a hunting and farming group under Aisin Gioro Nurhaci (1558–1626), emerged from the northeast forests, later known as Manchuria, or the Manchu Homeland. They waged war against the Mongol tribes, subjugating them and then forming alliances with them, an exploit that the Ming Dynasty had failed to achieve. The alliance with the Mongols was a most crucial strategic victory for the Manchus, without which they could have fallen into the same geopolitical trap that the Jurchens, their distant kin, did centuries earlier. In the early seventeenth century, the Manchus began to breach the Great Wall and reached Beijing and its environs numerous times. In 1629, for example, they laid siege to Beijing for months. Both domestic instability and foreign threats, especially the Wanli Korean Campaign (1592–1598), known as the Bunroku Geichono Campaign in Japan and the Imjin War in Korea, exhausted the Ming treasury and shook its confidence in confronting domestic unrest and foreign threats.

Qing Dynasty Period (1644–1911)

Amid nationwide revolt, in 1644, the largest rebel forces led by Li Zicheng marched on Beijing. Emperor Chongzhen failed to summon reinforcements to Beijing's rescue. Refusing to flee Beijing, he hung himself on Longevity (Coal) Hill. Beijing fell to the rebels, and Li's army then advanced toward Shanhaiguan (Mountain and Sea Pass), the vital fortification on the flat pass between the northeast plains, where the Manchus had risen to be the dominant power, and the vast North China Plain to the south. As fate would have it, the commanding general at Shanhaiguan defected to the Manchus, and they joined forces to route Li's army. Li evacuated Beijing, which his forces had held for only forty-one days, but not before crowning himself as emperor of the Shun Dynasty in the Forbidden City and then setting ablaze the royal palaces and several gates. Fortunately, the fires did limited damage. On June 6, 1644, the Manchus entered Beijing, and on July 8, they declared Beijing the capital of the Qing Dynasty (1644–1911). On November 8, Emperor Shunzhi was enthroned in the Forbidden City after paying homage to heaven at the Temple of Heaven.

The Manchus chose Beijing as their capital, first of all, because of the same geopolitical imperatives that dictated capital selection by successive dynasties (Jin, Yuan, and Ming): the site's commanding location at the interface of vastly different environmental and cultural realms. Second, Beijing had already retained superior resources and infrastructure that would support the needs of an imperial capital, such as its location at the northern terminus of the Grand Canal. Third, Beijing was the largest city closest to Manchuria, the Manchus' homeland, providing easy retreat to the northeast if necessary.

The Qing rulers swiftly made the Forbidden City their own home without any major alterations to the layout and design of the Ming palaces except for rebuilding some of the damaged buildings and renaming others. The Manchus appeared to recognize the Ming Forbidden City as the supreme form of imperial palaces and, as a matter of fact, had built a smaller replica of it in Mukden (today's Shenyang), the Qing's first capital. The Manchus had adopted much of Chinese cultural tradition and the political system over several generations of interactions with Chinese society, including being appointed to official positions by the Ming court. It was a clever public relations maneuver to win Chinese hearts and minds, as the Manchus claimed to be the legitimate heir of the Ming Dynasty, hence possessing the mandate to rule China. The Manchus also knew that it would have been prohibitively costly to demolish the old palaces and build new ones at a time when war was raging in much of China. As a result, the Forbidden City we can visit today, in its unsurpassed conformity to Chinese tradition and culture, is two and a half centuries older than it could have been.

Despite overwhelming success in their military campaigns, the Manchus felt extremely insecure because of their small numbers and rudimentary economy. Upon taking over Beijing, the Qing court issued an edict ordering all residents to move out of the Inner City so that soldiers of the Eight Banners, the elite core of the Manchu fighting force, could settle around the Forbidden City. Bannermen and their families were allocated free housing in the Inner City as a form of reward, along with large-scale land seizures in Beijing and its environs. In total, there were eight Manchu banners, eight Mongol banners, and eight Han banners, each banner with roughly 7,500 fighters. The yellow and yellow-bordered banners were deployed in the north section of the Inner City, the white and white-bordered in the east, the red and red-bordered in the west, and the blue and blue-bordered in the south. The Manchu banners were positioned closest to the Forbidden City, and the Han banners were stationed on the outskirts of the city. As an additional security measure, wooden fences were built at all entryways of streets and lanes. The royal degree resulted in strict ethnic segregation, which prompted Westerners to refer to the Inner City as the "Tartar city" and the Outer City the "Chinese city."

The royal decree, as the law, also prohibited most commercial activities and all entertainment in the Inner City because of the court's concern about the corrupting effect of such activities to its bannermen. The segregation law had a far-reaching cultural and economic impact on Beijing. Residents and businesses forced out of the Inner City, as well as newcomers to the capital, congregated in the Outer City, which, as a result, was transformed into the capital's hustling and bustling mecca of commercial, social, and cultural activities. Specialized clusters of commercial and entertainment activities sprung up throughout the Outer City, including Liulichang (Glass Mill), the famed district for craftwork, artistry, and antiques; Tianqiao (Heavenly Bridge), the low-brow folk culture center; Niujie (Oxen Street), the Chinese Muslim community; and Dashilan (Big Fence), the popular commercial district just to the south of the Imperial City. The Outer City also became home to numerous trade guilds and hometown associations, many of which originally provided lodging and food for their members but later became upscale hotels and famous restaurants open to the general public. In contrast, the Inner City was void of commercial activities and popular entertainment.

Another unintended consequence of the segregation law was the deterioration of the Inner City's housing stock. As peace and stability settled in, bannermen and their descendants became indulgent in an exorbitant but unsustainable lifestyle. As their financial conditions worsened, many bannermen found themselves in a bind: they could no longer afford to maintain their houses, and they could not sell these court properties. In desperation, some bannermen tore down their houses so that they could sell the scraps. The Qing court had to reiterate the original edicts in 1734, 1743, and 1754 in an attempt to stop such actions. It was not until after the early 1800s that, as enforcement of the segregation law became lax, Han officials and wealthy merchants began to buy houses from the bannermen, and their new investments led to a gradual ethnic desegregation and improvement of the Inner City's housing stock.

Although much of the imperial Ming Beijing was preserved, the Qing court did contribute many new additions in the Inner City. Unlike the Ming, Qing nobilities were not granted vassal states. Instead, they were permitted to build their estates in the Inner City according to strict imperial standards of size and configuration. At the peak of their dynastic wealth and prosperity, Qing emperors lavished in building new royal gardens and transitory palaces outside the walled city. Qing rulers, especially the longest-reigning emperor, Qianlong (r. 1735–1796), appeared to be smitten with delicate gardens in the Yangzi River Delta and built replicas of some of them in Beijing's royal gardens.

The most spectacular among these royal gardens was Yuanmingyuan (Gardens of Perfect Brightness), known in the West as the Old Summer Palace. Built in 1707 and located to the northwest of the walled capital city, it was originally the mansion of Prince Yong, and when Prince Yong became Emperor Yongzheng (r. 1722–1735), extensive expansions of the mansion began and continued for decades. At its peak, Yuanmingyuan had three distinct but integrated gardens, Yuanming (Perfect Brightness), Changchun (Eternal Spring), and Qichun (Elegant Spring), occupying a total of 3.5 square kilometers (1.35 square miles) of land and water. It was about five times the size of the Forbidden City and almost eight times the size of Vatican City.

Until 1860, Qing emperors often lived and ran the court year-round in Yuanmingyuan. New additions, including some designed and built by Europeans, made Yuanmingyuan an expo of traditional Chinese and European gardens and architecture and a supreme royal fantasyland, as the French literary luminary Victor Hugo described it:

> Imagine some inexpressible construction, something like a lunar building, and you will have the Summer Palace. Build a dream with marble, jade, bronze and porcelain, frame it with cedar wood, cover it with precious stones, drape it with silk, make it here a sanctuary, there a harem, elsewhere a citadel, put gods there, and monsters, varnish it, enamel it, gild it, paint it, have architects who are poets build the thousand and one dreams of the thousand and one nights, add gardens, basins, gushing water and foam, swans, ibis, peacocks, suppose in a word a sort of dazzling cavern of human fantasy with the face of a temple and palace, such was this building. The slow work of generations had been necessary to create it. This edifice, as enormous as a city, had been built by the centuries, for whom? For the peoples. For the work of time belongs to man. Artists, poets and philosophers knew the Summer Palace; Voltaire talks of it. People spoke of the Parthenon in Greece, the pyramids in Egypt, the Coliseum in Rome, Notre-Dame in Paris, the Summer Palace in the Orient. If people did not see it they imagined it. It was a kind of tremendous unknown masterpiece, glimpsed from the distance in a kind of twilight, like a silhouette of the civilization of Asia on the horizon of the civilization of Europe.[3]

Hugo's acclamation of Yuanmingyuan came as he angrily denounced its destruction by the Franco-British forces during the Second Opium War in 1860. By the end of the eighteenth century, the Qing Dynasty appeared to be at the zenith of power and prosperity, which was reflected in the court's apathetic reception of the Macartney Embassy (1793). In reality, however, by this time, China had lagged behind Europe, which was in the midst of the industrial revolution; the Qing Dynasty had passed its prime. It was, as

Lord Macartney observed, poor and backward, lacking motivations and efficiency. Macartney did not achieve the primary objectives of his mission, to open more trade with China, but the British would later return with a product with which China would become insatiable: opium from British India. And it was the modern guns from HMS sloops, frigates, and ships that blew open the gates of China a half century later.

The Qing Dynasty was at its most vulnerable state in the mid-nineteenth century. Having barely recovered from the First Opium War (1839–1842), which ended in China's defeat and cession of the island of Hong Kong to Britain among the restitutions. The Qing Dynasty was faced with an existential threat from the Taiping Rebellion (1850–1864) as well as the Nian Rebellion (1851–1868). Both the Taiping and Nian armies reached the suburbs of Beijing but failed to advance farther. Prior to this time, the only major uprising against Qing rule was that of the White Lotus Sect from the late eighteenth century to the early nineteenth century, with the climax of a siege on the Forbidden City by a couple hundred followers of the cult. The British and the French exploited the Qing's vulnerable position and tried to extract further trade and economic concessions. In 1860, the Anglo-French forces, some twenty thousand strong, landed in Port Dagu near today's Tianjin and launched an assault on Beijing.

On September 20, the Anglo-French forces were confronted by a large but ill-equipped Qing army at a bridge over Tonghui Canal. The Baliqiao (Palikao) Bridge, so named because it is 8 li (1 li = 0.5 kilometer or 0.3 miles) from the town of Tongzhou, was the last stand for the defenders of Beijing. The Battle of Palikao ended with resounding defeat of the Qing army. The best Mongol cavalry under the fabled Mongol prince Sengge Rinchen (1811–1865) was annihilated by the Anglo-French forces equipped with modern canons and rifles. The Qing court fled before the allied forces reached Beijing. Amid widespread looting, news broke that some of the Western hostages had been killed. On October 18, the order came to burn Yuanmingyuan as revenge. The fire raged on for three days, demolishing the sprawling gardens, killing over three hundred eunuchs and maids in hiding, and decimating countless treasures housed there.

The specifics of the plundered treasures have remained a contested subject to this day. Among the war spoils, there was a Pekinese puppy that was later presented to Queen Victoria and properly renamed "Looty." The resultant Peking Convention ratified the Treaties of Tianjin and ceded the southern Kowloon Peninsula, opposite of the island of Hong Kong, to Britain. Scholars divide the Qing Dynasty into two phases separated by the First Opium War. The first phase encompasses the early and middle Qing Dynasty, when there was a demonstrated continuity between Yuan Beijing (Dadu), Ming Beijing, and Qing Beijing in terms of the capital's management and governance. The second phase, or late Qing, is marked by the

involuntary opening of China to Western influence and eventual dominance, pushing China into a semicolonial, semifeudal society. The Second
Opium War, however, may be a more precise chronological demarcation
for Qing Beijing's evolution; it forced open the capital city to Western
influence and began its transition to modernity.

After the Second Opium War, Western powers acquired a large tract of
land on the southeast side of the Imperial City. For the first time in Chinese history, foreign diplomats obtained a physical presence in the imperial capital. The Legation Quarter encompassed a rectangular area between
the southern wall of the Imperial City and the Inner City, about 700 meters
(2,300 feet) from north to south and 1,300 meters (4,300 feet) from east to
west. The Legation Quarter became a foreign enclave of diplomatic missions, residential areas of expatriates, and the home to hospitals, schools,
banks, clubs, parks, and churches. The European landscape was a window
to Western civilization that reshaped the socioeconomic geography and
engendered urban changes in Beijing. One of the landmarks in the Legation Quarter was the Grand Hotel des Wagons-Lits (1901), which was one
of the few places for Beijing's high society and Western expatriates to
lodge, dine, and mingle in the first half of the twentieth century.

Beijing in the last decades of the nineteenth century was the stage of a
fierce struggle between reformers and conservatives. After the devastating
defeat in the so-called First Sino-Japanese War in 1895, the reformers, supported by Emperor Guangxu, initiated a series of reform policies through
the emperor's edicts. The reform was crushed by a coupe d'état backed by
Empress Dowager Cixi (1835–1908) after merely 104 days. The emperor
was placed under house arrest in yiheyuan, known in the West as the new
Summer Palace, until his death ten years later. Six leaders of the reform
were executed, and others went into exile.

As Western powers continued to pressure for further economic, political, and cultural concessions, extreme nationalism began to rise among
both conservative elites and the masses. Xenophobia turned into violence
against foreigners and Chinese Christians, incited in part by the court's
acquiescence, and culminated in the Boxer Rebellion, an uprising led by a
secret society, Yihequan (Righteous and Harmonious Fists), which aimed
to drive all foreigners out of China. In 1900, thousands of Boxers entered
Beijing and, with collusion from some Qing troops, laid siege to the Legation Quarter for fifty-five days (June 20–August 14).

An international force of some nineteen thousand troops was assembled from eight countries. The largest contributions were from Japan and
Russia, but many were also from Britain, Germany, the United States,
France, Austria-Hungary, and Italy. The international force reached Beijing on August 14, 1900, and engaged Qing forces at the eastern city gates.
The Qing forces included troops that had been trained by Europeans and
equipped with modern weapons, the Manchu bannermen, and Muslim

Northeastern corner tower of Beijing, China. This 1860 photo by Felice Beato is the earliest known photographic image of Beijing's wall fortifications, which the Franco-British forces encountered during the second Opium War. (Wellcome Collection)

troops from Gansu led by Dong Fuxiang (the Gansu Braves). After defeating the Qing troops, the allied forces rushed into the city and relieved the Legation Quarter. This event marked the first and only time in history that the walls of Beijing were directly breached.

In the early hours of August 15, the Qing court escaped from Beijing. As the court fled to Xian, the allied forces occupied Beijing and started days of officially sanctioned looting, rape, and summary execution, as witnessed by both the Chinese and Western reporters. Fierce fighting left serious damage to the city, especially to some of the city gates. The most important Inner City gate, Zhengyangmen (Qianmen), literally the "front door" to the Inner City, the Imperial City, and the Forbidden City, became the focal point of attack. British troops shelled it from the Temple of Heaven, roughly two miles away, destroying its archery tower. Later, during the occupation, Indian soldiers in the British troops damaged the gate itself by igniting an accidental fire while cooking inside the gate.

After extensive negotiations, the Peking Protocol, also known as the Boxer Protocol, was signed on September 7, 1901, ending the hostilities and providing reparations amounting to 450 million taels of fine silver (1 tael = 1.3 ounces), which was equal to USD 333 million in 1901 (roughly USD 10 billion in 2019) over a course of thirty-nine years, mainly to the eight countries that had contributed to the Legation relief forces. The Peking Protocol allowed foreign troops to be stationed in Beijing and at key points between Beijing and the sea. It also included conditions that expanded the physical and legal perimeters of the Legation Quarter, such as status of extraterritoriality and a residential ban of Chinese nationals. There were eleven embassies and eight military barracks in total, a number of international banks, two clubs, and several churches in the Legation

Quarter; three countries, Germany, France, and Japan, opened their own hospitals. The streets received European names. In other words, the Legation Quarter became a de facto international concession similar to concessions in Shanghai after the First Opium War.

The Grand Hotel des Wagons-Lits was the prime social venue and upscale hotel for the Legation Quarter; it also became a shelter for Chinese dissidents, political exiles, and those who wanted to escape persecution or even execution, though high-profile assassinations did take place on a number of occasions. The internationals obviously enjoyed their lives in the Legation Quarter, so much so that some diplomats refused to relocate after the government of the Republic of China (ROC) under Kuomintang (KMT, the Chinese Nationalist Party) moved its capital to Nanjing in 1928. It was also in the Legation Quarter that, in early 1937, a nineteen-year-old woman, Pamela Werner, the stepdaughter of former British diplomat E. T. C. Werner, was found murdered in a most brutal and bizarre manner. The case was never solved and has been the inspiration for several books, including Paul French's *Midnight in Peking* (2012), which has vivid details of Beijing's cityscape in the 1930s, especially the exclusive and depraved social circle of the expatriates in and around the Legation Quarter.

Christian communities in Beijing also grew rapidly after the Boxer Rebellion. These communities often formed around churches and their schools or hospitals. The largest among them was established by the American Methodist church near the Legation Quarter, which, in addition to the church, included the Peking Methodist Hospital (originally for male patients only), a hospital for women and children, and several schools that gained prestige in time. These church-centered areas became prominent in Beijing for both their religious and charitable services and distinct architectural landscape.

During the final years of the Qing Dynasty, Beijing was an ancient capital city that suffered from irreversible decline. China had been reduced to the "sick man of East Asia," and its capital was the showcase of its ills. Historical photographs show the decay of Beijing: large sections of the city wall were in a deteriorated state after four hundred years of weathering, weeds were overgrown on the grounds of the Forbidden City, and paint was peeling off the palace walls. The urban infrastructure, once on the leading edge of the world, had fallen into disrepair or become badly outdated. Open sewers were running along unpaved streets. Residents of the Legation Quarter complained about the noxious smell from the creek (Jade River) running through the international enclave. The lack of collective waste management turned many areas in the city into garbage dumps and open-air restrooms, which were not only a public nuisance but also a serious health hazard. After the Boxer Rebellion, the allied forces issued a ban on public excretion and enforced it with harsh punishment, which caused great consternation among the masses. Some, including the Americans, built public restrooms in their occupied zones, but others, like the Germans, failed to do so.

Beijing also faced a worsening living environment in the late Qing Dynasty. Sand and dust storms had been exacerbated since the Ming Dynasty by both long-range climate change and desertification on the steppes due to overcultivation and overgrazing. Unpaved streets in Beijing were often dusty until rains turned them into muddy traps. The heavy dependence on coal for fuel contributed to the poor air quality. Worse still, the poor in the city could only afford to use the hazardous honeycomb briquet, a cylinder-shaped cake of coal and wood dust mix, for cooking and heating. As a result, Beijing's winter was choked with stifling smoke from a hundred thousand household stoves.

At the same time, Beijing was being nudged into modernization as Western technology, management, and popular culture were introduced for consumption by the court and the elites as well as Western expatriates. In 1888, Empress Dowager Cixi received the first direct-current electric light in her residence. In 1890, a generator was installed that provided electricity to the Summer Palace. In 1899, the Legation Quarter installed its own electricity service. In 1905, the first Chinese power company in Beijing was founded and powered over eight thousand lights in government and public places.

It was the transportation infrastructure in Beijing, however, that underwent the most dramatic transformation. In 1864, a British merchant built a 600-meter (2,000 feet) rail track outside the south wall of the Inner City as a business stunt, which the court found disturbing and ordered dismantled soon thereafter. A municipal trolley service started in 1899, which operated a 7.5-kilometer (4.6 miles) tram service between the main railroad station in Majiapu, a town to the south of Beijing, and the Yongdingmen Gate. The track and trams were destroyed during the Boxer Rebellion, and municipal trolley service in Beijing would not resume until the early 1920s.

Between 1900 and 1901, the British troops tore a gap in the southern wall of the Outer City to extend railroad tracks from the south to the Inner City, a project the Qing court had previously rejected. The railway extension ended at the eastern entrance of the Legation Quarter, where Beijing's main railroad station was later erected. The first Chinese-designed railroad was completed in 1909, connecting Beijing to Zhangjiakou, an important city on the Mongolian Steppes (and the cohosting city with Beijing for the 2022 Winter Olympics). Japanese rickshaws and European horse-drawn wagons replaced traditional wheelbarrows and oxen carts as passenger transportation. Motor vehicles first came to Beijing in 1902 as a tribute to Empress Dowager Cixi, a four-cylinder car most likely made by the American company Duryea Motor Wagon.

The Imperial Examination System, the pipeline for supplying literati to the imperial bureaucracy since the seventh century, was officially abolished in 1905 and replaced by a Western-style curriculum and degree system. In 1898, the forerunner of Peking University, dubbed the "Harvard of China," was founded, and more Western-style education institutions followed. In 1902, the predecessor of Beijing Normal University was founded and went on to become the flagship campus for the huge national system of normal schools. Tsinghua University, known as the "MIT of China," was founded in 1911. Beijing, as the imperial capital and China's cultural center, had the largest concentration of modern schools and colleges as well as faculty and students in higher education.

Despite the seemingly insurmountable hardship that China faced during the last decades of the Qing Dynasty, some saw a new dawn for the ancient civilization in its capital city. William Edgar Geil (1865–1925), a prominent American traveler, author, and lecturer, expressed his appreciation for the capital city's cultural heritage and confidence in its rebirth through modernization in his *Eighteen Capitals of China* (1911):

> We spent one midsummer day riding round on the wall, Erving Leroy Johnson being my brilliant guide, donkeys being our bearers. Eight hours did the trip take to cover the fourteen miles around the Manchu or Tartar city. But out of the very centre is to be subtracted the Imperial city, within its own fortifications, covered with bright tiles of the Imperial yellow, so that the available area is not much over ten square miles. This is gridironed by regular, broad streets, newly lined with electric standards, metalled down the centre, sprinkled, and policed; no other city in China is so homelike to an American in this respect. But walls! and within the walls a forest! Where can this be matched?
>
> Could one live on the walls, to enjoy the breeze, to picnic in the shade of a fort, to survey the scenery of the great North Plain, Peking might be attractive. Curious sights met us, old and new jostling one another.
>
> Here is the old Examination Hall being demolished. The classical education is gone, never to return. The "modern side" has displaced it, and on this site will arise the Imperial Parliament intended to crown the eighteen Provincial Parliaments.
>
> . . .
>
> Contrast the forts, foreign forts, on the wall, the hostages given to the foreigners who not only claim to dwell in the Manchu city, but oblige part of the wall to be prohibited to Chinese lest the foreign settlement be overlooked! Imagine a section of Washington taken possession of by Moroccans and Tripolitans, with Turks and Arabs and Persians settling alongside. Oriental soldiers garrisoning it, free-born Americans bidden keep away lest the Eastern susceptibilities be hurt! Would America tolerate that long, after her new army was in working order?
>
> . . .

Near-by rumbles a railway right into the Chinese city and alongside the Front Gate. Five lines converge here now, and others will; then easily the forces of the Empire can be mobilised. There rises a mast, from which the radio-telegrams flash away to the coast.

The new age has dawned. Smoke-stacks in the city, in the Tartar city! Electric lights! But where are the temples! There are now as many churches in Peking as important temples! Peking is already a city of churches! The temples are going, going, gone! Here is a school; here the Education Office rises; here is the novel College of Interpreters, and there the College of Finance![4]

The deaths of both Emperor Guangxu and Empress Dowager Cixi in 1908 ushered in the curtain call for the Qing Dynasty. As armed uprisings led by Chinese Nationalists took place throughout China, Beijing became the epicenter of political assassination and espionage. On March 31, 1910, Wang Jingwei, a high-profile Nationalist, attempted to assassinate the regent prince and father of the boy emperor, Emperor Xuantong (Puyi), by planting a bomb under a bridge on the daily route to court by the prince. The plot was foiled, and Wang was arrested. An uprising finally succeeded in Nanchang, Jiangxi Province, on October 10, 1911. Dubbed the "Xinhai Revolution," after the name of the Luna year, it set nationwide upswell to topple the Qing rule. On January 1, 1912, the provisional government of the Republic of China (ROC) was founded in Nanjing with Sun Zhongshan (known in the West as Sun Yat-sen, 1866–1925) as its provisional president. In January 1912, the revolutionaries carried out two assassinations; the one on Yuan Shikai (1859–1916), the most powerful Qing military commander, failed, but the other succeeded in killing Liangbi, the leader of the hard-liners in the court. With his own political ambitions, Yuan Shikai started secret negotiations with the Nationalists and pressured the Qing court to abdicate.

On February 12, Empress Dowager Longyu signed the abdication agreement on behalf of Emperor Xuantong, the five-year-old Puyi (the "Last Emperor"), effectively ending both the Qing Dynasty and the two thousand-year-old Chinese feudal system. On February 15, Yuan Shikai was installed in Beijing as the provisional president of the ROC after Sun Zhongshan resigned based on a previous agreement stuck between the Nationalists and Yuan.

THE REPUBLICAN ERA (1912–1949)

The Republican era engendered rapid, almost unhinged, modernization in Beijing. This era, though brief in time, can be divided into four distinct periods: the ROC capital period (1912–1928), the special municipality

period (1928–1937), the Japanese occupation period (1937–1945), and the
Civil War period (1946–1949).

The ROC Capital Period (1912–1928)

The ROC government during this period is also referred to as the Beiyang government, a label derived from the name of a Western-style army
established during the late Qing Dynasty that became the military foundation for Yuan Shikai's ascendance to and hold on power. This period started
with a fierce national debate over the selection of the ROC capital. In early
1912, the Nationalists pressured Yuan Shikai to move the government to
Nanjing, as the various factions had agreed to do. Yuan refused to depart
Beijing, his power base, for Nanjing, which was considered the power base
of the Nationalists. Allegedly, Yuan instigated a mutiny by his own troops,
which broke out on March 3, 2012, and used it as excuse to keeping the
central government in Beijing. National public opinion, meanwhile, was
decidedly tilted toward keeping Beijing as the capital for the sake of
national unity and security. The ROC Senate also overwhelmingly voted
for Beijing to be retained as the capital. As a result, Beijing became the
official ROC capital, commencing a period when the northern political
factions dominated China's central government while the Nationalists agitated in the south. On August 25, 1912, the Nationalists formally founded
the Nationalist Party of China (Kuomintang, or KMT) at the grand theater
of the Hunan-Hubei Guild in the Outer City of Beijing.

The debate and political maneuvers continued over whether Beijing or
Nanjing should be the national capital, echoing opposing perspectives in
the early Ming Dynasty. While China's geographical core of population
and economy had long shifted to the south, especially the Yangzi River valley and delta, where Nanjing was located, China's front line of national
security had to be held in the northeastern frontier, where Beijing was
located. The last three unified dynasties, the Yuan, the Ming, and the Qing,
had chosen Beijing as their capital mainly because of this geopolitical
imperative. The capital debate focused on whether the geopolitical imperative was still paramount in modern times, especially when the nomadic
threat had passed. For many Nationalists, Beijing was rather a symbol of
ethnic oppression in the hands of the Manchus and national humiliation
in the hands of the Westerners, who continued to enjoy super-national
treatment. Nonetheless, for the first sixteen years of the ROC (1912–1928),
Beijing remained the national capital.

Beijing experienced civic upheaval and political intrigue as the national
political center. The fledgling parliament was repeatedly disbanded and
ceased to function completely after 1923. Yuan Shikai was sworn in as the

ROC president in 1913 and was immediately confronted with a major crisis. In 1914, Japan pressured China to sign a treaty similar to the one it forced upon Korea in 1910, which effectively allowed Japan to annex Korea. After World War I broke out later that year, Japanese and British troops took over the German Protectorate in Jiaozhou Bay and Qingdao (the hometown of Tsingtao Beer, a German-style pilsner) in the Shandong Peninsula. When the ROC government requested the return of these territories, Japan instead imposed the so-called twenty-one demands as it tried to further colonize China. The ROC government rejected these demands, but it signed several other unequal treaties with Japan in May 1915, which triggered massive protests throughout China. In Beijing, two hundred thousand protestors jammed Central Park (the former Altar of Earth and Harvest in the Imperial City), demanding retraction of the treaties and calling for a boycott of Japanese products. These protests were precursors of Beijing's role as the national center of political activism.

Political paralysis cast doubt over the effectiveness of the ROC government among some Chinese and rekindled their interests in reviving the monarchy. There are still debates as to how specific events unfolded, but President Yuan Shikai appeared receptive to the idea and started canvasing support. On November 20, 1915, a rubber-stamping parliament voted unanimously to approve the founding of the "Empire of China" with Yuan as its first emperor (Emperor Hongxian, which literally means "constitutional abundance"). The accession rites were planned for 1916, but opposition to monarchical resurrection quickly turned into widespread armed resistance, called the National Protection War, by the end of 1915. Caught by surprise, Yuan was forced to halt imperial restoration on March 22, 1916, and resumed the ROC presidency. Amid the turmoil, Yuan fell ill and died on June 6, 1916.

After Yuan's death, his power base splintered, and the ROC government in Beijing struggled to govern the entire country, which was descending into sectionalism and warlordism. Beijing's status as a national capital began to weaken as the KMT gained strength. Nevertheless, Beijing remained the center stage of political activism and cultural revolution during the 1910s and 1920s.

In May 1917, President Li Yuanhong and Premier Duan Qirui had a falling out over whether China should enter World War I, with the latter demanding China's immediate declaration of war against the Central Powers. Li subsequently dismissed Duan but encountered opposition from military governors. He then requested mediation by Zhang Xun, a warlord and a monarchist. Zhang entered Beijing on June 14 with five thousand of his troops, who retained their Qing-style queues as a sign of allegiance with the Qing. On July 1, supported by Qing loyalists, Zhang carried out a coup d'état and ceremoniously restored Puyi, the abdicated Qing emperor Xuantong, in the Forbidden City. Denouncement was swift from national politicians, famous intellectuals, and military governors and generals as well as the entire country. Duan Qirui, who was himself a powerful war-lord, counterattacked and recaptured Beijing on July 14, twelve days after the so-called Manchu Restoration. Zhang sought asylum in the Dutch Legation. After a brief encounter with Republican forces in the Temple of Heaven, Zhang's army scattered in defeat, but not before cutting off their queues, adding to the victors' booty.

China was sidelined as a member of the victors during the Versailles Peace Conference after World War I. It did not even receive support to compel Japan to return the former German Protectorate to Chinese sover-eignty. On May 4, 1919, thousands of college students and their supporters protested in Tiananmen Square against the mistreatment of China by its Western allies. Known as the May Fourth Movement, the protests sparked nationwide demonstrations and marked a major awakening of Chinese nationalism. The two most inspiring concepts emerging from the May Fourth Movement were *science* and *democracy*, an indication that the new generation of the Chinese intelligentsia embraced Western-style cultural enlightenment and political mobilization. It was a departure from China's traditional social structure and cultural norms and, hence, encountered criticism from the likes of Sun Zhongshan.

Many political and social leaders emerged from this movement. The Chinese Communist Party (CCP) was founded two years later, and its offi-cial historical account would have the May Fourth Movement as a key incubator of the Chinese Communist movement. Throughout the late 1910s and 1920s, Beijing's college campuses were hotbeds for introducing and spreading new knowledge and ideas from the West.

During this period, Beijing was not only invigorated by the dynamics of the political and social movement but also at the forefront of urban mod-ernization. As the national capital, Beijing's revitalization plans and proj-ects had direct policy guidance and financial support from the ROC government, which reflected the deeply embedded conviction that the capital be "the model for all places" and the central government must be directly involvement in achieving this goal.

Beijing was spared major damage due to the bloodless revolution that overthrew the Qing Dynasty. The preservation of Beijing's imperial capital layout, however, was a mixed blessing to modern urban development. The immense and impassible Imperial City occupied the center of the Inner City and accounted for nearly 20 percent of its total area, presenting an obstacle to through traffic and overall flow in the city. Early in the Republi-can era, Zhu Qiqian (1871–1964), a visionary manager and minister of internal affairs in the ROC government, launched numerous transportation and construction projects with strong support from President Yuan Shikai. Legend has it that, in confronting opposition to redevelopment projects, President Yuan presented Zhu Qiqian with a silver pickax. On June 16, 1915, Zhu used it to ceremoniously knock off the first brick from the barbican of Zhengyangmen Gate, breaking ground for the reconstruction project that opened up east–west traffic along the southern wall of the Inner City. It is interesting to note that the German supervising architect for the project, Curt Rothkegel, was responsible for the European-style motifs and stairways on the renovated archery tower, which can still be seen today.

Other infrastructure projects were less theatrical but more important for Beijing's modernization. First, two more new east–west thoroughfares were opened. The first one went along the southern wall of the Imperial City and became the predecessor of modern Changan Avenue. The other thoroughfare extended between the Forbidden City and Jingshan (Prospect Hill). Second, in 1923, the northern, eastern, and western walls of the Imperial City were torn down, and openings were made on the southern wall to provide passage of two new north–south thoroughfares in the Inner City. Third, in 1919, a railroad track was laid between the Inner City wall and its moat on the north and east sides of the city and was connected with the existing interregional railroads on the south and west sides to form a ring railroad around the entire Inner City. Fourth, barbicans at four additional city gates were demolished, and a new opening were made near the southeastern corner tower to allow through traffic.

This period also saw a continuation of the building boom in Beijing that had started in the last years of the Qing Dynasty, driven by both a desire to emulate the West and the needs of the capital. New government offices, college campuses, and commercial complexes sprung up throughout the city. Many new buildings were in Western or mixed architectural styles, and collectively they began to transform Beijing's landscape. The Legation Quarter and its adjacent areas, where many Western religious and benevolent organizations had built up, provided the most convenient showcase to this building boom.

Modern commercial and entertainment districts also emerged, including Wangfujing (Wells of Princely Mansions), a new upscale shopping and entertainment district to the immediate north of the Legation Quarter. Beijing's planners and developers also attempted to copy the success of Shanghai's Great World, a famous indoor complex of amusement arcades and other forms of entertainment, with a planned development of a new open-air mall in the hustling and bustling Outer City.

Unlike modern Western cities, traditional Chinese cities lacked large public green space. This was particularly true to Chinese imperial capitals, where the emperors and the aristocrats enjoyed their private gardens that were completely closed off to the general public. The Republican era ushered in a period of rapid public space expansion by converting former imperial resorts and gardens into public parks. The Altar of Earth and Harvest became Central Park (later renamed Zhongshan Park) in 1914, the first public park in Beijing. Other renowned imperial complexes, such as Prospect Hill, Beihai (Northern Sea), Yiheyuan (the Summer Palace), and Tiantan (the Temple of Heaven), would subsequently open to the public. The passageway to the Imperial City was expanded into a public square. Known as Tiananmen Square, it would become the most prominent public space in China.

There was a reshuffling in Beijing's socioeconomic profile. When the Qing Dynasty collapsed, there was an exodus from Beijing as many nobility and officials took refuge in nearby Tianjin. As the last vestiges of Beijing's ethnic residential segregation quickly faded away during the Republican era, many bannermen, having lost their privileges, including a regular stipend, fell into poverty and had to sell their residences in the Inner City and other belongings. The Inner City remained affluent and supported upscale businesses and cultural venues. The Outer City, in contrast, had a predominantly low-income population and was a major destination for many rural poor from nearby provinces fleeing the countryside to escape poverty, famine, and wars.

In the 1920s, KMT and its allies, including the Communists, began to challenge the government in Beijing. At the same time, the Beiyang (northern) warlords continued to wage war against each other. In 1920, warlords of the Zhili (today's Hebei Province) Clique took control of the central government after they and the Fengtian (today's Liaoning Province) Clique defeated Duan Qirui's Anhui Clique. In 1924, a general from the Zhili Clique, Feng Yuxiang, carried out a coup d'état in Beijing and toppled the central government. Feng, who was known for his populist propensity, ordered the expulsion of the Qing royal family from the inner court of the Forbidden City, where it had resided under the 1912 abdication agreement. On November 5, Feng sent troops to expel the former emperor Puyi and his family. Allegedly, Feng set up artillery on top of Prospect Hill to intimidate those who refused to depart. With the Manchu royal family gone, the Forbidden City became home to the Palace Museum, which was officially founded on October 10, 1925. It would later become China's premier collection, research, and exhibition repository for classic artifacts.

Feng then invited Sun Zhongshan to Beijing for unification talks. Sun fell ill soon after he arrived in Beijing and died of liver cancer on March 12, 1925. Wars among the Beiyang warlords continued. In March 1926, foreign powers issued ultimatums to Feng's troops, pressuring them to withdraw from Dagu batteries in Tianjin. When the news broke, college students in Beijing organized protests against what they deemed as foreign impingement on China's sovereignty. When protestors tried to breach the Chancellery, guards opened fire on them, killing many, including several leaders from the Beijing Women's Normal University. The incident, known as the March 18 Massacre, was widely condemned and further weakened the standing of Beijing's ROC government.

In 1926, KMT launched the Northern Expedition and eventually gained the upper hand against Beiyang warlords. On June 4, 1928, Zhang Zuolin, of the Fengtian Clique, was assassinated by the Japanese as he was retreating to his home base in the Northeast (Manchuria). On June 8, KMT forces peacefully took over Beijing, ending the reign of Beiyang warlords over the ROC government. At the end of 1928, Zhang Xueliang, now the leader of the Fengtian Clique, declared allegiance to the KMT-dominated ROC government. China became nominally unified.

After unification, the debate over a national capital resumed. KMT, led by Sun Zhongshan, had aspired to build a postfeudal modern China freed from alien Manchu rules and Western domination, both of which were most ostensibly manifested in Beijing. This nationalistic mind-set was on full display when Sun Zhongshan and the ROC provisional government in Nanjing offered ritualistic sacrifice to Zhu Yuanzhang, the founding emperor of Ming Dynasty, three days after the Qing court's abdication. The historical parallel was uncanny: Nanjing was where the Ming Dynasty was founded (by Han Chinese), and a successful Northern Expedition was launched to expel the alien (Mongol) rule in Beijing (Dadu). KMT seemed to have duplicated the exact success of the Ming Dynasty nearly six centuries before. On April 15, 1927, KMT reaffirmed Nanjing as the official capital of the ROC, where it began to set up the government bureaucracy. As the Northern Expedition triumphed on the battlefield, KMT encountered little resistance to ratify Nanjing's capital status. Some northern media and academic community voiced strong disagreement, but to no avail. On June 21, 1928, the ROC government renamed Beijing "Beiping," just as Zhu Yuanzhang did in 1368, and Beijing ceased to be the ROC's national capital.

The Special Municipality Period (1928–1937)

Beijing was devastated by the loss of capital status because it did not have the location and hinterland advantages to attract modern industries, trade, and commerce. As the national capital, Beijing was home to the largest securities market, many high-level financial activities, and upscale service industries. In the early 1920s, roughly half of the major banks in China had their headquarters in Beijing, apparently in an effort to have better access to their major client, the ROC government. Beijing's share of banking headquarters fell drastically to just 2.8 percent by the end of 1928, and all of them had left by 1935. In 1933, the entire business volume of Beijing's securities market was barely equal to one day's volume in Shanghai's securities exchange. Shanghai took the lion's share of financial services from Beijing, though nearby Tianjin had experienced growth in this sector at Beijing's expense even when Beijing was the capital.

Beijing's robust redevelopment in the previous decades slowed to a halt due to the loss of support from both the central government and the private sector. The Xinhua Avenue Reconstruction Project, for example, was an ambitious plan to open a north–south thoroughfare along the west side of the Imperial City. The southern section of the thoroughfare would connect the planned Xiangchang District, Beijing's version of Shanghai's Great World, with the Inner City. The plan included detailed steps to attract businesses to the new commercial, entertainment, and office structures along the new thoroughfare. It was met with opposition from the nearby long-established Dashilan business community. As a result, the plan was delayed for more than a decade. With strong support from the central government, it finally started in 1926. A new opening on the Inner City wall, named Peace Gate, was to create a passage for traffic between the Inner City and the Outer City. The entire project collapsed two years later, however, after the central government left Beijing.

Beijing turned to its historical and cultural assets to generate economic vitality. As a result, historical preservation became a booming business as the city endeavored to promote international tourism. Photographs from this period, especially those by Hedda Hammer Morrison (1908–1991), a German photographer who worked in Beijing between 1933 and 1946, show ample evidence that Beijing's historical landmarks had been refurnished. The city became the major antique trade center in China, attracting merchants and tourists alike from China and abroad. It also boasted the largest flea market in China. At the same time, Beijing retained its reputation as the high-culture capital of China. With the largest concentration of colleges and universities in the country, the city was a magnet for intellectuals. Scholars and academics exited Beijing in droves after 1928, but many returned in the 1930s for the laid-back lifestyle, historical nostalgia, and robust intellectual community.

Beijing was on the front line during the Sino-Japanese conflicts in the 1930s. The Japanese took control of Northeast China (Dongbei, or Manchuria) by instigating the September 18 Incident in 1931 and subsequently installed the puppet state of Manchukuo (1932–1945) with Puyi as its "emperor." Tensions mounted in Beijing as the Japanese began to advance southward. At the end of 1931, expecting an imminent Japanese takeover, the Palace Museum began to prepare for evacuation of the high-value artifacts in its collection. After the Japanese launched multipronged offenses along the Great Wall in 1933, the Palace Museum decided to transport the selected artifacts, already packed in crates, to the south. The original plan was to temporarily store the treasures in French and British concessions in Shanghai, but the ensuing all-out war with Japan and the Chinese Civil War in the late 1940s forced the convoy to embark on an epic journey of moving the nearly twenty thousand crates of historical treasures through southern China, with only limited losses and minor damage. Between 1948 and 1949, the ROC government shipped three thousand crates of selected relics to Taiwan, which today constitute the core content for Taipei's National Palace Museum.

By the mid-1930s, Japanese forces in northern China began to encircle Beijing and Tianjin. The ROC government had no legal recourse for stopping the Japanese deployment as the Peking (Boxer) Protocol of 1901 permitted countries with legation in Beijing to station troops and conduct military exercises near Beijing, despite the fact that the Japanese military contingents near Beijing exceeded the limits set by the protocol. Once again, Beijing became the flash point where foreign invaders and Chinese defenders were on a collision course that would change the historical trajectory of Beijing and China.

The Japanese Occupation Period (1937–1945)

On the night of July 7, 1937, Japanese and Chinese troops came to a standoff outside the town of Wanping near Lugou Bridge (Marco Polo Bridge) after the Chinese refused a Japanese request to search for a Japanese soldier who went MIA during a military exercise. Over the next several hours, both sides began to send in reinforcements. The first shots were fired in the morning of July 8, and a full-scale armed conflict followed. Known as the July 7 Incident or Luguo Bridge Incident, the clash marked the beginning of what the Chinese refer to as the Eight-Year Anti-Japanese War, which is known in the West as the Second Sino-Japanese War. The Japanese took over Beijing after a fierce fight in the suburbs and installed a puppet Provisional Government of the Republic of China (1937–1940), which changed the city's official name to "Beijing." The Japanese went on to occupy the city for eight years (1937–1945).

The period of Japanese occupation was characterized by brutal oppression and planned development in Beijing. During the first few years of occupation, the Japanese updated Beijing's infrastructure and services and continued with historical preservation. Major construction projects concentrated on areas of Japanese settlements in the western suburbs. After the attack on Pearl Harbor, these projects were stopped as Japan began to extract resources from occupied territories for its war efforts. Among the resources that the Japanese were eyeing were the trees in Beijing. The city had long fostered an urban forest, in part because of the abundant groundwater and in part as a coping strategy against sand and dust storms. The earliest photographic images of Beijing by Felice Beato (1832–1909), a British photographer embedded with the Anglo-French forces during the Second Opium War, recorded an urban landscape covered by a thick tree canopy.[5] Other visitors to Beijing in the late Qing and early Republican era also marveled about "a forest" in the walled city. The Japanese logged so many of the trees in Beijing during this period that they nearly denuded the city.

The Civil War Period (1946–1949)

After World War II, the victorious ROC government changed the city's name back to its prewar name, Beiping. Debate over the choice of a national capital briefly rekindled, but the KMT-dominated ROC government could not have considered the matter because the Civil War (1945–1949) soon broke out between the forces of the ROC government and the Communists. Meanwhile, Beijing's population grew rapidly, reaching 1.5 million in 1948 despite a serious population undercount outside the walled city. The rapid population growth also drastically changed Beijing's demographic profile. First, the migrant population accounted for two-thirds of the entire city population. Second, there was a severe imbalance in gender and age distribution, with young males counting nearly two-thirds of the migrant population. Third, socioeconomic polarization worsened with a significant increase of low-income and uneducated migrants. The poor migrants disproportionally concentrated on the outskirts of the city, while the well-to-do occupied the Inner City and some upscale areas of the Outer City.

From late 1948 to early 1949, a half million Communist troops trapped a quarter million government troops inside Beijing. A battery was set up on Jingshan (the Prospect Hill) with 122 howitzers facing all four directions; hundreds of canons on the Communist side were deployed on the outskirts of Beijing. Both sides, however, were keenly aware that an all-out clash would destroy the largest and best-preserved historical capital. After several rounds of intense negotiations, the two sides reached a peace accord that handed control of Beijing to the Communists, henceforth sparing Beijing from destruction. On January 31, 1949, the Communist forces officially took over Beijing (Peiping).

Beijing was in a state of transition and uncertainty during the Republican era. For the first sixteen years, as the national capital, Beijing appeared poised to become the showcase for a postimperial new China with bold and large-scale redevelopment schemes. All the efforts were cut short, however, by the city's loss of capital status, Japanese occupation, and the Civil War. On October 1, 1949, Beijing turned a new page in its long and tumultuous history when Mao Zedong (1893–1976), the leader of the

Chinese Communist Party (CCP), declared the founding of the People's Republic of China (PRC). After a twenty-one-year interval, the city, now called Beijing, once again became the capital of a nearly unified China.

SUMMARY

The history of Beijing was intrinsically linked to the long-range environmental changes of East Asia. The evolution of Chinese civilization after the late eighth century was driven by the interactions among three distinct but interwoven cultural realms: sedentary agriculture, nomadic pastoralism, and a mixed forest-based, hunting-farming economy. They profoundly influenced each other through wars, intermarriage, and trade and commerce. Located at the crossroads of the three realms, Beijing became the most logical, if not the only, capital choice for a unified empire to command all three realms.

Visitors to Beijing today are likely to tour the most famous landmarks that Beijing has to offer, such as the Forbidden City, the Temple of Heaven, and the Summer Palace. They should recognize that the historical landscape in front of them was a product of the Ming and Qing Dynasties, the last two in a long procession of imperial dynasties in Chinese history. They may detect rigidity and conformity beneath the facade of the imperial grandeur, which is a far cry from the bigger, innovative, more daring, and more exciting atmosphere that filled Changan, of the Tang Dynasty, or Yuan Beijing (Dadu). As a matter of fact, the historical landscape of Beijing represents the desperate attempt by the ruling class to preserve the status quo as China was facing a crisis of deteriorating traditional economy and culture.

The visitors may be eager to try out some famous foods that Beijing is known for, such as Peking roast duck, instant-boiled mutton, and variety snacks. They should be reminded that the Beijing cuisine, if there is such a thing, is but an example of Beijing Culture, an amalgamation of material and nonmaterial traits from the (Han) Chinese of different regions, the Mongols, the Manchus, the Muslims, and many others. Beijing as the capital has indeed been a cultural melting pot.

If the visitors are more adventurous, they can go to visit the ruins of Yuanmingyuan, now a popular park, or the former Legation Quarter, now a historical district. They may be informed of the humiliations that the foreign powers inflicted on China and the Chinese in recent history. These sites may also be enduring reminders of how China first resisted and then eagerly partook in the tides of modernization. For China, the course leading to opening up started in Beijing, the imperial capital. It took decades for Beijing and China to embark on the ship of globalization; once the ship sailed, however, there was no point of return for either.

LIFE IN THE CITY **REVISITING MY CHILDHOOD HOME**

Beijing, the stomping ground of my youthful years. As a little girl, Beijing was a city of red walls and green tiled roofs, perhaps because our siheyuan was in the shadows of the Bell and Drum Towers. Our siheyuan had three sets of houses and two enclosed courtyards, and my family occupied the third set of houses with a courtyard. The front gate was wide and guarded by two stone lions. There were even two horse-mounting masonry blocks next to the lions.

There was a veranda that led from the front gate into my home. Its posts and eaves were covered with beautiful paintings. The main house had a wide porch and four red columns that made the house look grand to me. As a child, I used to think that our house was not much less than where the royal wives lived in the Forbidden City!

The courtyard was truly a garden, with carefully laid out and manicured trees and hedges, such as lilac, starfruit, pomegranate, and grape vines, as well as many annual flowers. There was a large rose bed, which was my grandfather's favorite, and a huge stoneware bowl for gold fish. I remember doing my homework on the porch and being enchanted by the many shades in the light and the drifting scent from the flowers.

Oh, these wonderful times of my childhood! The turmoil of the Cultural Revolution was raging outside, but my home was the harbor of safety and comfort for us. I am still visiting my mother in Beijing every year, not at the siheyuan where I grew up but in a twelve-story condo on the North Second Ring Road, where my family has lived since the 1980s. Traveling from the airport to my mom's, I sometimes feel baffled about whether I am arriving in Beijing or Chicago: I see in both cities a dazzling cityscape of skyscrapers, neon lights, fancy cars, and fast-food joints. Where are my red walls and green tiled roofs?

A couple of years ago, I made an effort to go to see our old home. To my surprise, the front gate and the horse-mounting blocks were still there! Inside, though, I saw little matching my memories. The walls and doors between the courtyards were gone, and so were the trees and flower gardens; the courtyards were crowded with makeshift shacks that also took over the veranda. I could barely squeeze through between the shacks to reach our former home, which was by now in a dilapidated state. Fortunately, I found a couple of intact wooden window frames that had survived the "building boom." On them, I saw a few chiseled flowers that were almost the same as I remembered. Staring at them in faded colors, I felt reassured that I did once live in this siheyuan, and in a Beijing of red walls and green tiled roofs.

—Di

NOTES

1. Marco Polo, "Concerning the City of Cambaluc," in *The Travels of Marco Polo*, trans. Henry Yule, the complete Yule-Cordier ed. (Mineola, NY: Dover Publications Inc., 1993), Chapter XI in Book Second, https://ebooks.adelaide.edu .au/p/polo/marco/travels/complete.html#book2.11.

2. Marco Polo, "Concerning the City of Cambaluc, and Its Great Traffic and Population," in *The Travels of Marco Polo*, trans. Henry Yule, the complete Yule-Cordier ed. (Mineola, NY: Dover Publications Inc., 1993), Chapter XXII in Book Second, https://ebooks.adelaide.edu.au/p/polo/marco/travels/complete.html #book2.22.

3. Victor Hugo, "The Sack of the Summer Palace," *UNESCO Courier*, November 1985, 15. http://unesdoc.unesco.org/images/0006/000669/066943eo .pdf.

4. William Edgar Geil, *Eighteen Capitals of China* (Philadelphia: J. B. Lippincott Company, 1911), 415–417, https://archive.org/details/eighteencapitals 00geiliala/page/n10.

5. Felice Beato, "View of the Imperial Winter Palace, Pekin, Showing the Artificial Hill, October 29, 1860," National Gallery of Art, accessed May 31, 2019, https://www.nga.gov/collection/art-object-page.163376.html.

4

Politics

The politics of Beijing must be understood in the context of its political status: it is the national capital of a unitary political state, the People's Republic of China (PRC). Beijing is one of the four province-level centrally administered municipalities, and its governance, especially major decisions and policies regarding development, has been directly influenced and in some cases decided by the central government. It may not be far-fetched to regard the Beijing Municipal Government as the caretaker of Beijing, the home of the central government. The politics and its outcome in Beijing's governance and development, therefore, reflect the interactions of national rather than local forces. As a result, Beijing's political history is particularly volatile, amplifying the great symbolism and distinct landscape that the city embodies.

CURRENT MANAGEMENT SYSTEM

China's administrative hierarchy consists of four tiers of division under the central government. The provincial tier includes twenty-two provinces, if Taiwan is excluded; five autonomous regions; four centrally administered municipalities (Beijing, Shanghai, Tianjin, and Chongqing); and two special administrative regions (SARs, Hong Kong and Macao). The second tier covers prefecture-level administrative units, including prefecture-level municipalities and urban districts in centrally administered municipalities such as Beijing. The third tier consists of over twenty-eight hundred counties and equivalent administrative units, such as urban districts in prefecture-level municipalities. The fourth tier is township (township, nationality township, and town). Its urban counterpart is the so-called subdistrict, which is an urban residential area that comprises a number of adjacent city blocks managed by the representative office of an urban district or the municipal government. All first-level administrative units, except for the two SARs, have the same management infrastructure, although the five autonomous regions are also governed by the Law of the People's Republic of China on Regional National Autonomy.

Structure of Government

The PRC government is composed of the legislative branch (the National People's Congress), the judicial branch (the Supreme People's Court and the Supreme People's Procuratorate), the legislative advisory body (the People's Political Consultative Conference), the executive branch (the State Council), and the PRC presidency. The military forces represent a separate political entity controlled by the Central Committee of the Chinese Communist Party (CCP). With the exclusion of the presidency and the military contingent, all levels of administrative divisions, including Beijing, have the same government infrastructure. Most departments of the Beijing Municipal People's Government (the executive branch of the Beijing Municipal Government) are subordinate counterparts to the ministerial agencies of the central government.

Although there are specific constitutional mandates for each branch of the government, the PRC Constitution stipulates that the ultimate political power is vested in the Communist Party over all matters of governance. Therefore, China's political system operates in a power structure in which the CCP has the final say over administrative and personnel decisions in ensuring that the CCP's policies and strategies are implemented correctly and in a timely manner. Consequently, the CCP's top official, the secretary, outranks the highest-ranking administrator of an administrative division, though the two positions could be held by one person concurrently. It must be noted that most bureaucrats and public servants in China are also members of the CCP, which explains the lack of conflicts of interests between the parallel apparatuses of the CCP and the government.

With two exceptions during the early reform years (late 1970s–early 1980s), all of Beijing's CCP secretaries have been members of the CCP's politburo, the highest policy-making body and the nexus of China's political power. In addition, Beijing's CCP secretary has the mandate to hold the position as the first political commissar of the Beijing Garrison Command, which is the military security apparatus for the capital. This arrangement is typical of China's political power relationship in which the CCP exerts absolute control over the military forces and their operations. It is important, therefore, to include Beijing's CCP secretaries along with the city's mayors during the PRC era (Table 4.1).

Table 4.1   Top Executives of Beijing, 1900–Present

Name	Term
Magistrates, Shuntian Fu, Qing Dynasty (1900–1912)	
He, Naiying	?–May 1900
Wang, Peiyou	May–August 1900
Chen, Kuilong	June–July 1900 (Acting)
	August 1900–April 1901
Zhang, Renfu	April–July 1901
Chen, Bi	July 1901–September 1903
	February–September 1906 (Acting)
Shen, Yuqing	September 9, 1903–March 1905
Li, Xijie	March 1905–February 1906
Yuan, Shuxun	February 1906–February 1908
Sun, Baoqi	September 1906–April 1907 (Acting)
Ling, Fupeng	February 1908–February 2010
Wang, Naizheng	February–June 1910
Ding, Naiyang	June 1910–February 1912
Magistrates, Shuntian Fu Prefecture (1912–1914), Republic of China	
Ding, Naiyang	February 1912–December 24, 1912
Zhang, Guangjian	December 24, 1912–September 19, 2013
Wang, Zhixin	October 16, 1913–March 23, 1914
Shen, Jinjian	March 23, 1914–October 2, 1914
Magistrates, Capital District (1914–1928), Republic of China	
Shen, Jinjian	October 3, 1914–September 26, 1915
Wang, Da	September 26, 1915–August 3, 1920
Wang, Hu	August 3–September 18, 1920
Sun, Zhenjia	September 18, 1920–May 19, 1922
Liu, Menggeng	May 19, 1922–November 5, 1924
Wang, Zhixiang	November 5–December 31, 1924

(continued)

Table 4.1   (continued)

Name	Term
Xue, Dubi	December 31, 1924–October 20, 1925
Liu, Ji	October 20, 1925–May 5, 1926
Li, Yuan	May 12, 1926–September 24, 1927
Zhang, Jixin	September 24, 1927–June 4, 1928
Li, Shengpei (Acting Magistrate)	June 4, 1928–June 25, 1928
Mayors, Beiping Special Municipality (1928–1931), Republic of China	
He, Chengjun (Acting Mayor)	June 25, 1928–July 13, 1928
He, Qigong	July 13, 1928–June 12, 1929
Zhang, Yinwu	June 12, 1929–February 27, 1931
Wang, Tao (Acting Mayor)	October 1930–March 1931
Zhou, Dawen	February 27, 1931–April 26, 1931
Mayors, Beiping Municipality (1931–1937), Republic of China	
Zhou, Dawen	April 27, 1931–June 16, 1933
Hu, Ruoyu (Acting Mayor)	April 1931–June 1931
Yuan, Liang	June 16, 1933–November 1, 1935
Song, Zheyuan	November 1, 1935–November 8, 1935
Qin, Dechun	November 8, 1935–July 28, 1937
Zhang, Zizhong	July 28, 1937–August 8, 1937
Mayors, Beijing under Japanese Occupation (1937–1945)	
Jiang, Chaozong (Appointed by the Japanese)	August 6, 1937–January 7, 1938
Yu, Jinhe	January 7, 1938–February 9, 1943
Su, Tiren (Acting Mayor)	1941–February 9, 1943
Liu, Yushu	February 9, 1943–February 20, 1945
Xu, Xiuzhi	February 20, 1945–August 16, 1945
Mayors, Beiping Municipality (1945–1949), Republic of China	
Xiong, Bin	August 16, 1945–July 15, 1946
He, Siyuan	July 15, 1946–July 1948
Liu, Yaozhang	July 1948–February 4, 1949
Mayors, Beiping and Beijing (September 27, 1949–Present), People's Republic of China	
Ye, Jianying	December 8, 1948–September 8, 1949
Nie, Rongzhen	September 8, 1949–February 26, 1951

(*continued*)

Table 4.1   (continued)

Name	Term
Peng, Zhen	February 26, 1951–May 1966
Wu, De	May 1966–April 20, 1967
Xie, Fuzhi	April 20, 1967–March 26, 1972
Wu, De	May 1972–October 9, 1978
Lin, Hujia	October 9, 1978–January 25, 1981
Jiao, Ruoyu	January 25, 1981–March 24, 1983
Chen, Xitong	March 24, 1983–February 1993
Li, Qiyan	February 1993–October 1996
Jia, Qinglin	October 1996–February 1999
Liu, Qi	February 1999–January 2003
Meng, Xuenong	January 2003–April 20, 2003
Wang, Qishan	April 20, 2003–November 30, 2007
Guo, Jinlong	November 30, 2007–July 25, 2012
Wang, Anshun	July 25, 2012–October 31, 2016
Cai, Qi	October 31, 2016–May 27, 2017
Chen, Jining	May 27, 2017–Present

Secretaries, Beijing Municipal Committee of the CCP, 1948–Present

Name	Term
Peng, Zhen	December 1948–May 1966
Li, Xuefeng	May 1966–April 1967
Xie, Fuzhi	March 1971–March 1972
Wu, De	October 1972–October 1978
Lin, Hujia	October 1978–January 1981
Duan, Junyi	January 1981–May 1984
Li, Ximing	August 1984–December 1992
Chen, Xitong	December 1992–May 1995
Wei, Jianxing	May 1995–August 1997
Jia, Qinglin	August 1997–May 2002
Liu, Qi	May 2002–June 2012
Guo, Jinlong	June 2012–May 2017
Cai, Qi	May 2017–Present

Source: Magistrates of Shuntian Fu, Qing Dynasty. https://zh.wikipedia.org/wiki/Category:清朝順天府府尹; Mayors of Beijing. https://zh.wikipedia.org/wiki/北京市市长列表; The CCP Secretaries and Mayors of Beijing. http://xinwenlianbo.tv/xinwen/40853.html.

Historical Evolution of Capital Governance

The Qin Dynasty (221–206 BCE) established China's first nationwide administrative system that consisted of prefecture and county. This system remained largely intact through the imperial times, and, despite modifications, it retained the county as the basic administrative division. Cities were under the governance of counties and did not constitute an independent tier of the administrative hierarchy. Deeply entrenched agrarianism might have been responsible for the city's lack of power and influence despite its being the seat of government and the center of regional economic and cultural activities. Cities lacked their own independent governments, and so their civilian affairs were under the jurisdiction of the county where they were located. The lack of power might have spilled over to a lack of identity for some cities; some did not even have distinct names. For example, during much of the Tang Dynasty (618–907), Beijing was referred to as Youzhou cheng, or the city of Youzhou Prefecture, instead of Jicheng, its traditional and common name, in official chronicles or elsewhere.

The imperial capital was by rule the largest city in size. It was first and foremost the home of the monarch, where the vast royal complexes were exclusive domains directly controlled and managed by the court. The remainder of the capital city was usually divided between two counties that belonged to Jingshi, the capital region, which consisted of a number of counties and large rural areas around the capital. During the Ming and Qing Dynasties, Beijing was under Shuntian Fu (Shuntian Prefecture), and its magistrate was also the "mayor" of Beijing, who only had nominal power and no control over city security and policing nor affairs of the banners during the Qing Dynasty.

Because of its size, Beijing's civilian affairs were governed by two counties, Wanping and Daxing, and their jurisdictions were roughly divided by the central axis. In turn, Wanping and Daxing were two of the counties under the jurisdiction of Shuntian Fu. This explains why Beijing had no "municipal" government nor "mayors" between 1900 and 1928 (Table 4.1). Furthermore, there was a large turnover of the magistrate for the capital region and scanty records of what these magistrates actually accomplished in Beijing. As a result, major development projects in Beijing during the early Republican era (1910s) were directly sponsored and administered by the central government of the Republic of China (ROC), as shown by the leadership of Zhu Qiqian in a series of redevelopment projects in the 1910s.

In 1920, Guangzhou became the first city in China to become an independent administrative entity directly under the provincial government. Other cities followed its lead. After the KMT-led ROC government moved the national capital to Nanjing in 1928, Beijing, the walled city and its immediate suburbs, became the Beiping Special Municipality, and the Capital Region was abolished. This was the first time in history that Beijing was an independent administrative entity.

In the aftermath of the Boxer Rebellion (1900), the allied forces established a public safety apparatus in their respective occupation zones, which became the forerunner of police districts in Beijing. The districts were first drawn based on the domains of the banners' geographical locations, and they underwent frequent changes during the late Qing Dynasty. In the Republican era, the districts evolved to include other civic functions, such as residential registration management, public health services, and business permitting procedures; they did not, however, become formal administrative divisions.

In 1925, the Inner City was divided into six districts, and the Outer City was divided into five districts. In addition, there were four suburban districts encompassing much of the Chaoyang, Fengtai, and Haidian Districts in today's inner suburbs, or the expanded urban function zone. The establishment of the suburban districts provided an important security buffer and economic hinterland for Beijing, which was a model that successive municipal governments would emulate. By the end of the Chinese Civil War (1946–1949), Beijing consisted of thirty-two numerically named districts.

Current Management System

During the PRC era, Beijing became not only the capital but also, with Shanghai and Tianjin, one of the three centrally administered municipalities (1954). The city formally constituted a municipality-district administrative hierarchy, and consolidation in 1952 formed thirteen new and larger districts, each with a unique name instead of a number. In the same year, Beijing expanded its administrative area by 1,961 square kilometers (750 square miles) and its population by 130,000. In 1956, the PRC State Council approved another expansion that increased Beijing's administrative area by over 600 square miles and its population by nearly 300,000.

The most significant and drastic expansion came in 1958, when China commenced an ambitious national development campaign. Dubbed the "Great Leap Forward" (1958–1962), the campaign aimed to leapfrog China from an agrarian economy to an industrial economy in a short period of time through mass labor employment and national mobilization. Driven by the zealous campaign, Beijing began to undergo rapid growth in population and economy, which could no longer be accommodated by the existing space and resources within Beijing proper. To remedy the problem, the central government implemented large-scale annexation for Beijing. In March, five neighboring counties and one municipality, all major agriculture producers, came under Beijing's jurisdiction. In October, Beijing annexed four more counties to the north, which gave the city direct control over water resources, as each of the four counties had a sizable reservoir. In total, the annexation in 1958 added 12,000 square kilometers (4,600 square miles) of land and more than two million people to Beijing. This set up the administrative perimeters for Beijing that have been maintained to the present day.

There were further mergers of urban districts. In 1960, Beijing's thirteen districts and four counties were reorganized into eight urban districts and nine rural counties. Influenced by Soviet-style urban planning, the PRC government promoted industrial growth to make Beijing more economically independent. Three districts were added to Beijing as a result: a coal mining area to the west of Beijing was incorporated into the Mentougou District in 1958; the Shijingshan area regained its district status in 1967 because of the expansion of an iron and steel complex; and the Yanshan District (1980–1986) was formed to accommodate a large petrochemical complex being built in the area.

Counties and urban districts under a municipality are administratively equivalent in China; the major difference is that the former is mainly rural and agrarian and the latter is predominantly urban in land use and economy. An urban district must meet official quantitative criteria: 70 percent of its employment must be in nonagricultural sectors, and 75 percent of its gross domestic product (GDP) must be from secondary (mainly manufacturing activities) and tertiary (services) sectors. As urbanization accelerated in the reform era, the nine counties in Beijing transitioned from rural to urban in terms of land use and economic structure. Consequently, from 1986 to 2010, these nine counties were restructured into districts, though only the six at the urban core are classified as "urbanized." As of 2019, Beijing is composed of sixteen districts.

Below the district level, there are 140 municipal subdistricts, 142 urban townships, and 35 village townships. It should be noted that subdistrict offices are branch offices of respective districts and do not legally constitute an independent level of administrative division. There are also over 2,500 neighborhood committees and nearly 4,000 village committees, which are similar to homeowners' associations in the United States in activities and functions but are under direct guidance of their subdistrict offices. This administrative hierarchy has proven effective in ensuring the execution of government policies and decisions.

POLITICS AND MODERN DEVELOPMENT

Beijing's development during the PRC era has been driven by two sets of forces. First, the politics of Beijing, unlike other Chinese cities, has been a direct reflection of the politics of the PRC as the bearer of the national political landscape. As in the cases with China's central government in general, the PRC government has played the deciding role in major developments of the capital. With unwavering efforts, the central government has intended to make the capital the model of all places, with no resources spared and no oversight omitted on any long-term plans or major projects. The characteristics of Beijing's development, therefore, are what the PRC government has envisioned for how China must look. Second, ideological persuasions and changes have left enduring and contrasting imprints on Beijing's urban development. Although Soviet-style Socialist urban design dominated Beijing's development between the 1950s and the 1970s, China's economic reform and globalization have introduced the ethos of neoliberalism to Beijing's rapid transformation.

Geostrategic Continuity in Capital Selection

It is important to outline the PRC government's reasons for selecting Beijing (Beiping) as its capital, because the decision has had profound repercussions for Beijing's development. As the Chinese Communists were gaining the upper hand in the Civil War (1946–1949), they began to survey candidate cities for their new capital. There might have been debates over whether Beijing (Beiping), Nanjing, or Xian should be the capital of the new Communist-led state, but historical accounts show that there was a broad consensus among the CCP leaders and their political allies that Beijing be the capital.

The decision over the new capital was based on strategic considerations. First, by selecting Beijing as the capital, the Chinese Communists recognized the historical concerns over control of Northeast China (Manchuria), which had become the leading heavy industrial region of China during Japanese occupation (1931–1945), and Inner Mongolia (the southern part of the Mongolian Plateau). After World War II, these two regions were under Chinese control, but they remained vulnerable to foreign encroachment and invasions. Selecting Beijing as the new capital was a strategic posture that the PRC wanted to show to the major powers, the United States and the Soviet Union, its determination to protect its sovereignty and territorial integrity.

Second, northern China had suffered from environmental degradation caused by long-term climate change and continuous unsustainable human activities, which had resulted in depopulation and lack of modern development. Northern China had, in a sense, regressed to becoming a Chinese frontier and was much less developed than southern China, especially the Yangzi River Delta region where Shanghai and Nanjing are located. A national capital located in the north would help mobilize national resources for economic development and environmental conservation. Beijing was best suited for such a strategic function with its advantageous accessibility to both the coastal regions and the hinterland in contrast to Xian and other northern cities, which were isolated in the interior where the economy and environment had declined.

Third, Beijing's selection was in part dictated by the geopolitical configuration in East Asia in the late 1940s. Beijing's strategic depth overlapped with the Soviet Union's sphere of influence in the north through Mongolia and Northeast China, providing a paramount security guaranty for the fledgling Communist state. After the fallout between the PRC and the Soviet Union in the 1960s, however, Beijing came under threat of Soviet invasion. In the late 1960s, the PRC government had to evacuate government agencies and senior officials while mobilizing the local population to construct fallout shelters and rehearse air raid drills.

Fourth, Beijing provided the CCP with a largely intact city that had been unified China's imperial capital for most of the previous six centuries. Its layout, urban architecture, and land use patterns presented both challenges and opportunities to government agencies, urban planners and architects, and advocates as Western modernization, Socialist urban policies, and efforts of cultural conservation converged on the city. The fundamental transformation that Beijing has since undergone must be understood in the context of these political dynamics.

Rapid Urban Development in the 1950s

Once Beijing became the PRC capital, the central government had to cope with the disadvantages that Beijing presents as the capital. Soviet urban planning principles, in part through direct involvement by Soviet experts in Beijing's urban planning, greatly influenced Beijing's development due to ideological and geopolitical motives during this period.[1] The development plan needed to accommodate the capital's key functions based on available economic resources, the image projection of the state, and the handling of historical heritage. A convergence of revolutionary ideology and practical considerations left profound imprints on Beijing's changes during this decade. First, the PRC government decided to build a complete and independent economic foundation for Beijing, a departure from the traditional dependency on the south. Second, the PRC government attempted to strike a balance among diverging needs and interests in building a modern infrastructure for the swelling central bureaucracy.

A major construction boom ensued to accommodate the influx of several hundred thousand employees and their families. Soviet-style superblocks were constructed in designated locations with a network of government office compounds, affiliated housing, and auxiliary services, and services expanded rapidly in the sectors of education, health care, retail, utilities, and transit systems. New sports complexes, hospitals, and college campuses sprung up throughout the city, some showing apparent Soviet influence while others were a combination of Soviet, European, and Chinese architectural traditions.

Large tracts of land in the suburbs were put aside for designated government agencies and installations, which resulted in specialized land use zones on the periphery of the city. For example, the western suburbs became the largest cluster of military headquarters, and the northwestern suburbs were designated as the district for scientific research and higher education. Today, this district, dubbed "China's Silicon Valley," has the highest density of colleges and universities in China and is home to most of the research institutes of the Chinese Academy of Sciences located in Beijing. Industrial zones were set in the west, south, and east suburbs, where kindred manufacturing facilities were clustered in the same industrial parks. Most government ministries were located in the central northern sections of the city. Part of Zhongnanhai (central and southern lakes), the former imperial gardens where national and local governments had been housed during the Republican era, became the home of the State Council, the PRC's executive branch. The rest of the sprawling gardens housed the residences of many top PRC leaders.

TIANANMEN SQUARE

DID YOU KNOW?

Tiananmen Square took political center stage during the May Fourth Movement in 1919, when college students mounted the first political protest in modern times. Revamped and expanded during the PRC era, Tiananmen Square has been transformed into the largest city square in the world and China's political center both functionally and symbolically. It is surrounded by the PRC's vital offices. It is also where the PRC government stages military parades, pays homage to the national heroes, and conducts welcome ceremonies for foreign dignitaries. During celebrations of important occasions, such as the National Day (October 1), up to a million people fill the square, and there are spectacular fireworks at night as the curtain call. Tiananmen Square is also the stage for political activism and protest, where the June Fourth prodemocracy movement commenced and was eventually suppressed in 1989.

Tiananmen (the Gate of Heavenly Peace), overlooking Tiananmen Square on the south and leading to the Forbidden City to the north, serves as the symbolic power center of the People's Republic of China. It is the platform from where national leaders inspect military parades and mass celebrations. (Kenishirotie/Dreamstime.com)

The 1950s saw a drastic transformation in Beijing's land use and landscape beyond the utilitarian construction and development projects. The PRC government aimed at creating a symbolic landscape in the capital that could showcase the progress in a modern Socialist China under the leadership of the CCP. An ambitious plan was drafted to achieve this goal that included monumental public buildings strategically purposed and located in the city and reconfiguration of the landscape and land use in the city center in commemoration of the tenth anniversary of the PRC in 1959. Tiananmen Square, which had been enlarged in 1954, was greatly expanded in 1958; remaining structures of the Imperial City in the square were demolished to increase the total area of Tiananmen Square to 44 hectares, nine times larger than the Red Square in Moscow. Legend has it that when the chief architect of the Tiananmen Square expansion suggested a narrower square than the central government had instructed, he was told that the proposed size of the new square must not be altered because it was set by none other than Mao Zedong himself. As intended by the PRC government, Tiananmen Square has been the symbolic, geographical, and functional center of China's politics. In 1976, Mao's Mausoleum was built where the Gate of China once stood on the square.

Changan Avenue, the street running east to west between the Gate of Tiananmen and Tiananmen Square, was widened substantially, making it one of the widest avenues in the world and the de facto east–west axis. Unlike the traditional central axis, which runs north–south through the middle of the walled city of Beijing and functioned as a symmetrical guideline, the new Changan Avenue opened to through traffic and linked the eastern and western halves of the city.

Another transformative event for Beijing during the 1950s was the conceptualization and construction of ten landmark public buildings, dubbed the "Ten Great Buildings for the Tenth Anniversary of the Founding of the PRC." Completed by the deadline of October 1, 1959, the National Day of the People's Republic of China (PRC), these ten public buildings were intended to show the CCP's vision for China as a modern and progressive country that was still steeped in Chinese tradition. These buildings included (1) the Great Hall of the People, (2) the Museum of the Chinese Revolution and the National Museum of Chinese History (they were merged in 2003 and renamed the National Museum of China), (3) the Military Museum of the Chinese People's Revolution, (4) the Cultural Palace of Nationalities, (5) the Minzu (Nationality) Hotel, (6) the Beijing Railway Station, (7) the Diaoyutai (Fishing Terrace) State Guesthouse, (8) the Workers Stadium, (9) the National Agriculture Exhibition Hall, and (10) the Overseas Chinese Hotel. The architectural styles for these buildings were eclectic, a rare display showing inspirations from international modernism to Soviet-influenced Socialist realism, and from Western classicism to traditional Chinese architecture.

The construction projects consumed national resources and involved around-the-clock operations by over twelve thousand architects, engineers, and construction workers from all over the country. All the buildings were completed in good quality within ten months. The construction projects displaced twenty-one hundred households, and the provision of new housing for them was a major budget buster at the time. There would not be another comparable construction feat in China until the country's economic reform more than two decades later. In the end, the Ten Great Buildings may be considered a great success for their intended purposes. They remain the most remarkable landmarks for Beijing despite the construction craze over the last several decades that has produced new landmark behemoths. The buildings completely reconfigured Beijing's landscape and geographical orientation. The Great Hall of the People and the National Museum of China anchor Tiananmen Square on the west and east side, and six of the ten buildings are located on Changan Avenue, solidifying the boulevard's status as the major east–west thoroughfare of the capital and earning it the reputation as the "First Avenue of Sacred China."

The Clash of Visions: Historical Preservation
versus Modern Development

As Beijing underwent drastic changes in the 1950s, contentious debates broke out between some academics and government policy makers over what to do with Beijing's immense historical layout and structures. Uncannily reminiscent of Moscow's layout, Soviet experts suggested housing the central government in the garden section of the former Imperial City, from which new urban development would radiate outward. Their suggestion was also based on the reality that China was poor and underdeveloped and lacking the resources for building a new urban center in a short time. In addition, there was a precedent of converting the Imperial City into modern government facilities since the early ROC government operated in the Imperial City. Some Chinese experts, represented by architect Liang Sicheng and his wife, Lin Huiyin (an aunt of Maya Lin of the Vietnam War Memorial fame), proposed building a new capital administrative center in the western suburbs so that the entire old city could be preserved. The PRC government adopted the Soviets' more realistic plan. Notwithstanding some demolitions and reconstructions, much of the imperial complex was kept intact, and a traditional façade was added to new constructions to keep a consistent appearance.

Major clashes broke out over the fate of city wall among those involved in Beijing's development plans. The wall, along with its towers and barbicans, was an outstanding example of ancient Chinese urban fortification, but it had become an obsolete defense system in modern times, providing little advantage to the defenders during the Second Opium War (1860) and the Boxer Rebellion (1900). Liang Sicheng and colleagues argued, nonetheless, that the wall was an integral part of the irreplaceable imperial capital and therefore must be preserved with the rest of the city.

There were two practical problems with the proposal to preserve the city wall. First, the wall, along with the gate towers and barbicans, had become severely deteriorated by the early 1950s. Some gate towers had been destroyed during the siege of 1900, and others were in disrepair. Complete renovation was cost prohibitive at the time, and the status quo was not acceptable in light of the new outlook that the PRC government was trying to create for Beijing. Second, the city wall was a barrier to modern transportation infrastructure and, hence, to long-term planned urban development. After the Boxer Rebellion, British troops demolished a southern section of the Outer City wall to extend the railroad track to the Legation Quarter. In the 1910s, the government bored several more openings in the city wall for the circle line railroad. During the Japanese occupation (1937–1945), new openings were made in the city wall for through traffic. The Outer City wall, which was constructed in a haste and of inferior quality, was quickly demolished during the early 1950s. The gate towers of the Outer City were subsequently removed in later years.

Liang Sicheng and his colleagues implored the government to give a reprieve to the Inner City wall and most of its gate towers. Their efforts came to a crushing end when the central government intervened and ordered the complete demolition of the wall and most of the gate towers. By the late 1950s, the wall demolition was largely complete. Only a couple of small sections of the wall survived. By 1969, most of the remaining Inner City wall was cleared to make space for subway construction. Today, the circular No. 2 line of Beijing's subway system approximates the foundation of the Inner City wall.

Debates have continued to this day over whether the demolition of the city wall resulted in an irreversible loss of a priceless historical heritage. While many mourn the loss of the city walls, these debates often neglect the political, economic, and ideological realities of the time. Indeed, there were pragmatic concerns and urgent needs for removing the city wall, such as the lack of financial resources to preserve and refurbish the city wall and the urgency for modernizing Beijing's infrastructure so that it could function as the country's capital. The ideological motivation, however, might have been more important for the top decision makers in reaching the decision to demolish the city wall.

Since the late Qing Dynasty, an increasing number of Chinese politicians and intellectuals began to view traditional Chinese culture as being backward, unenlightened, and even obsolete. The prejudice extended to their perception of traditional urban design and historical cities, and Beijing became a symbol of feudalism and, in the case of the Manchu Qing Dynasty, alien domination as well as the humiliation that China had suffered at the hands of foreign powers. It was one of the most cited reasons that the KMT-led ROC government moved the national capital from Beijing to Nanjing in 1928, and it played an important role in how the PRC officials were suspicious, if not outright hostile, toward Beijing's city wall and some of the imperial complexes.

The CCP had a unique take on the traditional and the foreign, as Mao Zedong famously said, "Use the past to serve the present, the foreign to serve China." Using the past meant not only making use of the imperial compounds for government and public use but also removing the elements that hindered using "the foreign" to serve Beijing's modernization and industrialization. In the 1950s, the PRC government avidly prescribed to Soviet urban policy and was eager to transform Beijing from a city of economic dependency and consumption to one of economic independence and production. Legend has it that Mao stated that he would like to see a "forest" of smokestacks from the Tiananmen Gate, where the PRC leaders inspected parades on May Day (International Labor Day) and National

Day. It is ironic that by the 1950s Beijing had lost much of its real (urban) forest. Beijing's layout as the imperial capital was an impediment to building a modern infrastructure and, therefore, had to go.

American urban planner Edmund Bacon, when visiting the city in 1934, described Beijing as "possibly the greatest single work of man on the face of the earth."[2] Bacon was most impressed by the human-environmental harmony that exuded from Beijing's urban design, and his praise might have reflected the ethos of neo-urbanism that he saw in Beijing. It may be strange to observers today that many Chinese did not share Bacon's enthusiasm about Beijing. In contrast, the Chinese intelligentsia, with notable exceptions such as Liang Sicheng and Lin Huiyin, had become obsessed with Enlightenment and were determined to emulate its success in China. Some Beijing residents may play revisionists today regarding the loss of the city wall and other cultural heritage, but many were actually happy when the city wall was demolished because it meant improved traffic flow for their convenience.

The Chinese perspective on preservation has evolved since then, and the government today has found new value in historical relics. A park near the Beijing Railway Station has a nearly one-mile-long section of the old city wall, the longest of its kind, which was only saved because the station builders had inadvertently shielded it from demolition with their camps. It has been restored as the centerpiece of the Beijing Ming City Wall Ruins Park. Visitors are charged a small fee to ascend the wall and enjoy a panoramic view of the imposing high-rise apartments and hotels nearby. They should be reminded that historical preservation was not part of the Chinese tradition and would not have been high on the list of priorities for the PRC government that was struggling economically in the 1950s.

URBAN DEVELOPMENT IN THE SHADOW OF THE CENTRAL GOVERNMENT

As the capital, Beijing is the center of political intrigue, the home of the central bureaucracy, and the place of choice for demonstrating political dissent. The central government has been directly involved in making Beijing the national showcase, and its unequivocal involvement has at times resulted in tension, and even clashes, with the municipal government. The central authority reigns supreme, however, in all important policies and plans concerning the capital's long-term and major development. On the one hand, Beijing can expect almost unlimited national support for its plans sanctioned by the central government. On the other hand, the municipal government is limited in its own initiatives and has to contend with the central government's bureaucracy, which is often beyond its reproach.

Beijing as the Center Stage of Political Intrigue, Liaison, and Dissent

The central government influences Beijing's politics and development strategies, first of all, through personnel appointment. Beijing's top political figures, the CCP secretary and the mayor, must closely align themselves with the PRC top leadership or risk their political careers. Changes in the PRC top leadership can cause political instability in the municipal government, and the ripple effect would adversely affect Beijing's governance and development. For example, Peng Zhen, Beijing's long-term CCP secretary (1948–1966) and mayor (1951–1966), and a politburo member of the CCP, was accused of being a member of a political faction challenging Mao's paramount leadership and became one of the first to be purged during the Cultural Revolution (1966–1976), a decade of political chaos and national instability. With his downfall, the bureaucracy that had governed Beijing for nearly twenty years collapsed, leaving the city in near anarchy during the early period of the Cultural Revolution.

Wu De, another CCP secretary and mayor of Beijing (1972–1978), rose to power during the Cultural Revolution and gained the trust of Mao and his loyalists. During the spring of 1976, Beijing witnessed unprecedented political unrest. With the pretense of commemorating Zhou Enlai (1898–1976), the long-term premier of the PRC who passed away in January 1976, political rumors began to swirl in the capital that the radical left in the politburo plotted to undermine the political heritage of Zhou and other moderate leaders. Large crowds gathered in Tiananmen Square. Provocative speeches were given, protest leaflets were handed out, and heaps of wreaths were piled up at the Monument to the People's Heroes. The protesters' goal was to stop the imminent purge of Deng Xiaoping, the heir apparent to Zhou, who had irked Mao and his key allies in the politburo with his reform-minded policies. Wu took a hard-line stand against the protesters by declaring a curfew in Tiananmen Square. He then mobilized a militia that mainly consisted of factory workers to clear the square with force and prosecuted many protesters. In the fall of 1976, Mao passed away, and his allies in the politburo, including his widow and the rest of the so-called Gang of Four, were purged through a bloodless coup d'état. Wu's loyalty to the now deposed faction in the CCP leadership doomed his political fortune, and he was removed from his Beijing posts soon thereafter.

A more drastic clash unfolded in the mid-1990s between leaders of the central government and the Beijing Municipal Government. Chen Xitong (1930–2013) was a reform maverick who rose from the ranks of Beijing's political establishment. As the mayor (1983–1993) and CCP secretary (1992–1995) of Beijing, Chen implemented a number of groundbreaking reform measures that included trimming bureaucratic red tape and endorsing limited private enterprise. Beijing's Pearl Market, today a retail-wholesale market specializing in pearl jewelry, was one of the few "free farmers markets" in Beijing in the early reform era where free enterprises first thrived. Chen was instrumental in refurbishing it into an enclosed privately owned multiple-use market, which bore his calligraphic inscription, "Hongqiao Shichang" (Red Bridge Market), as the signage until his downfall. Chen was also an avid promoter of Western urban planning and was responsible for the expansion of green spaces and plans for sustainable public infrastructure. His fondness of a peculiar architecture addition, the Ming-Qing–style pavilion on top of modernist high-rises, has left enduring marks on some of Beijing's landmark buildings from the early reform era, the most notable of which is the imposing towers of the Beijing West Railway Station.

As a politburo member and state councillor (equivalent to a vice premier), Chen was close to the PRC's power center. He allegedly became overconfident and challenged the CCP's new leadership headed by Jiang Zemin and others from Shanghai in the aftermath of the Tiananmen Square Incident in 1989. He was removed from his position and put on trial in the mid-1990s with trumped-up charges. One of his alleged crimes was official corruption in a gigantic real estate development of the Oriental Plaza. This project involved financial interests from Hong Kong, including an investment of USD 2 billion from Li Ka-shing, the Hong Kong billionaire and real estate tycoon. The Oriental Plaza is on East Changan Avenue and adjacent to Beijing Hotel, where the famous "Tank Man" shot was taken during the Tiananmen Square Incident. The Oriental Plaza occupies 100,000 square meters (25 acres) of prime real estate with a total built area of 800,000 square meters (8.6 million square feet), despite a scaleback directly ordered by the PRC government after Chen's downfall. It completely recreated the cityscape along East Changan Avenue. Chen became the first politburo member to be tried and convicted of graft and corruption in the PRC's history.

Tiananmen Square is the symbolic pivot of China's political power and, consequently, the converging spot for display and challenge of this power. On the one hand, the PRC government has organized many political rallies and parades. At the beginning of the Cultural Revolution in 1966, for example, Mao and his supporters held eight rallies of the Red Guards, totaling about eleven million people, as a declaration of mass mobilization against political rivals. On the other hand, the PRC government managed to prevent unsanctioned political activities in Tiananmen Square until 1976. In spring 1989, a crackdown on mass demonstrations on the square solidified its status as the physical center stage of China's political movements. Since then, Tiananmen Square continues to serve as the venue for promoting national identity and pride, with daily flag ceremonies and periodic parades, while also attracting the determined few who show dissent and rebellion.

It is hard to miss the overwhelming presence of the central government, despite the lack of systematic and quantitative data. The enormous bureaucracy of the central government is the leading employer as well as the major purchaser and consumer of goods and services in Beijing's economy. There are several components in the PRC's central government, including the CCP apparatus, the State Council (the executive branch), the legislative and judicial organs, and the military services, each with its own complex structure and budget. The State Council, for example, has twenty-six cabinet-level ministries and agencies. In addition, there are nearly thirty subministry-level agencies directly under the State Council. Each of these agencies employs thousands of people and has substantial annual appropriation. The Ministry of Treasury alone had a public budget of CNY 750 million in 2017, the equivalent of USD 108 million, for employee compensations and office expenditures. Most of the employees and their families live in Beijing, and much of the budgeted expenditure goes into the local economy. Central government agencies usually have the ability to directly acquire and manage their local resources, such as offices space, housing provision, and auxiliary services. The Beijing Municipal Government has limited control over these operations, even if they disrupt the city's general plans or undermine local regulations.

A unique characteristic of Beijing's political landscape is the large number of liaison offices. The liaison office is, by function, the capital branch office of provincial and local governments as well as large state-owned enterprises. It dates back in Chinese history as the instrument for local authorities to lobby the overpowering central government through a variety of activities. This is a unique phenomenon and a real factor in Beijing's development. Modern liaison offices are equipped with facilities and operations for intelligence gathering, entertainment and socialization, and accommodations for local officials. Collectively, these liaison offices present a formidable economic presence in Beijing not only for their employment and purchasing roles but also for their share in the capital's hospitality industry. Beijing's food connoisseurs have concluded that most of the authentic and upscale regional cuisines could be found in the in-house restaurants of these liaison offices, which nowadays often dwell in their own high-rise and multiple-use guest houses.

While playing a vital role in advocating local interests, the liaison offices have also been accused of being facilitators of political corruption by their design and actions. There was a proliferation of liaison offices in the reform era, and even some six hundred counties set up their own liaison offices. In 2010, there were more than six thousand liaison offices in Beijing! The central government has tried to overhaul government liaison offices in Beijing by requiring more strict accounting and reporting and by ordering delisting of most of the county-level offices. Liaison offices are, however, alive and well because they are a product of the political ecology of China's political system.

Impact of Beijing's Capital Functions

China's economic reform ushered in rapid urbanization driven by industrial expansion and explosive rural-to-urban migration. Beijing and other Chinese megacities have been confronted with a wide range of problems, such as overcrowding, housing shortages, traffic congestion, and environmental pollution, which could worsen the quality of life and threaten sustainable development. Dubbed "megacity ills," these problems in Beijing are further exacerbated because of the city's unique political and historical conditions in comparison to other major cities in China. Beijing's historical urban core became coveted by unscrupulous real estate industries that have conducted large-scale and wholesale demolition of traditional residential neighborhoods. Despite being in deteriorated conditions due to decades of neglect, many of these neighborhoods had maintained the traditional configuration of *siheyuan* (the traditional courtyard dwelling) and *hutong* (traditional alleyways), which were of great cultural and even commercial value. The central government was so alarmed by the decimation of Beijing's old city that it issued a directive to stop any further demolition projects in 2017. Instead, the PRC government has been promoting decentralization as the resolution to Beijing's housing and overcrowding problems.

As early as 1991, the Beijing Municipal Government drafted a twenty-year plan (1991–2010) in which it attempted to address the worsening megacity ills by decentralizing the population and businesses in the urban core to planned suburban satellite centers. This was the sixth master plan that Beijing had drafted (previous plans being in 1950, 1957, 1958, 1973, and 1983). For the first time, the plan emphasized historical preservation with a focus on retaining the integrity of the central axis and maintaining the hutong network. However, the plan underestimated the pace and scale of Beijing's growth and quickly became outdated. After winning the bid for hosting the 2008 Summer Olympics, Beijing commenced new planning efforts, and in 2005, the State Council approved Beijing's new fifteen-year plan (2004–2020), which broke with the tradition of a single center model and proposed a development plan that included two axes, two belts, and multiple centers.

These long-term plans, despite their actionable undertakings, merely played catch-up with not only Beijing's unprecedented urban growth but also the changing vision of the PRC's top leadership for the capital's future development. As early as 2002, there were discussions that the Beijing Municipal Government might need to relocate to the suburbs, and a large tract of land was reserved in Tongzhou District for this purpose. The relocation plan stayed on paper, however, until 2014, when Xi Jinping, the newly appointed PRC president, dictated a plan in which Beijing would be transformed into a most livable city exclusively operating as the center of four functions: the national political center, the cultural center, the center of international exchange, and the center of technological innovations. Once again, the Beijing Municipal Government had to revise its master plan and development strategies accordingly and face the real, albeit undesirable, possibility of relocating to the suburbs. A new development proposal in 2012 set the goal of adopting Tongzhou as the "capital subcenter" or "the subcenter." Beijing's top officials were dragging their feet, however, in putting the relocation process in motion. The Beijing Municipal Government had been situated in the historical Legation Quarter, which is centrally located within a stone's throw of the Forbidden City. Top Beijing officials were reluctant to abandon such a convenient and prestigious location for the wilderness of the suburbs.

In May 2016, the central government increased its pressure on the Beijing Municipal Government by naming Tongzhou the subcenter of Beijing in a major strategy paper that pinpointed Tongzhou and Xiongan New Areas as the two key growth poles for integrated regional growth of northern China. Rumors had it that President Xi, frustrated by passive resistance to his directive from top officials in Beijing, threatened that if the Beijing Municipal Government opposed to or even delayed the relocation plan, the central government would move instead! The mayor of Beijing was forced to resign in October 2016, and his counterpart in Tianjin was purged in September of the same year on corruption charges. The new mayor of Beijing, also an ally of President Xi's, saw the writing on the wall and immediately set the relocation process in motion.

By the end of 2017, the judicial and legislative branches, along with the Beijing Political Consultative Conference, had moved to Tongzhou. The executive branch of the municipal government, a much larger bureaucracy, moved to the subcenter in January 2019. It was projected that the relocation of the Beijing Municipal Government would channel roughly four hundred thousand people to the eastern suburbs, where much of Beijing's suburbanization had been taking place since 2005. The central government hopes that Beijing and Tianjin will continue to expand toward each other geographically and soon merge to form an integrated and powerful metropolitan region that could economically rival those on the Yangzi and Pearl Deltas.

The birth of Beijing's subcenter is illustrative of the political relationship between the central government and the Beijing Municipal Government. In Chinese tradition, the national capital must always be controlled by the central government, which is in turn obligated to make the city into the best showcase of the country. The municipal government has limited authority in regard to long-term development that involves Beijing's capital image and functions. The PRC government envisions regional integration in North China as a long-term national development and security strategy in which Beijing must play a leading role. The Beijing Municipal Government is obliged to carry out the task assigned by the central government.

The latest twenty-year plan (2016–2035) points to a departure from Beijing's imperial capital design by facilitating emerging "edge cities" on the periphery of Beijing proper. The PRC government has directed Beijing to decentralize businesses and institutions that are not integral to the four capital functions (political, cultural, international exchange, and technological innovations), whether they are state-owned enterprises, such as the Capital Iron and Steel Corporation (Shougang Group), or private enterprises, big and small. Even the Beijing Municipal Government must move out of the urban core of Beijing. The Xiongan New Area, a rapidly developing region in Hebei Province, will be the receiving destination for those decentralized from Beijing. Among the first to depart Beijing are traditional manufacturing industries and wholesale businesses.

The relocation of the Beijing Municipal Government to the subcenter as well as the ongoing decentralization in Beijing are mainly driven by initiatives of the central government, which intends to make Beijing more specialized in its capital functions. Beijing is first and foremost the national capital and a city that has a unique heritage as the national capital. The Beijing Municipal Government and its top officials must keep in mind that their initiatives and ambitions for Beijing are only valid and feasible if they fit in the strategic framework and long-term visions of the central government, and their primary duty is to execute these visions within the strategic framework. The central government has clearly defined its vision for Beijing as one that would slim it down to overcome its megacity ills so that it can function effectively as the national capital. Realizing this vision may push Beijing into uncertainty and exact tremendous human costs, but it may also provide unprecedented opportunities for Beijing to preserve its historical heritage while building a city for the future.

MEMORIES OF 1966

I was born and raised in Beijing but have been living in New York City for nearly thirty years. I try to visit Beijing as often as possible, perhaps as a feeble attempt to hold on to a past that has already faded away. The memories of my youth, however, have become sharper in my mind, and one particular experience stands out most vividly: it was the summer of 1966, when my life changed suddenly and forever.

On June 1, 1966, we took the last exam for intermediate school of Number Four Middle School (including both intermediate and high school divisions). It was an exceptionally hot and humid day with thunderstorms brewing in the horizon. Loudspeakers in the schoolyard were blaring the editorial from *People's Daily*, calling on "sweeping away cow demons and snake spirits," which, I knew, meant some in the government were in trouble. It was the eve of the Cultural Revolution, and the political atmosphere must have been just like the weather of that day. I could care less. I was looking forward to having a carefree summer and then, in the fall, attending the high school division of Number Four Middle School!

My school was founded in 1907 and became one of the top middle schools in Beijing. It was one of the few schools attended by children of the top PRC leaders, some of whom were my classmates. Lately, they had been flashing Chairman Mao's *Quotations*, or "the little red book," dressing in their parents' military uniforms and wearing red arm bands, the emblem of the Red Guards. They were ready to revolt against the status quo that their parents had fought for.

Two days later, my school was closed and sealed off. I was heartbroken as Beijing, and indeed the entirety of China, fell into chaos. After two years of aimless wandering, we were dispatched to the countryside. I was sent to a remote and poverty-ridden region on the northern Loess Plateau several months after my seventeenth birthday. Little did I know that I would not see Beijing again until five years later, and another five years would pass until I had the chance to attend school again.

—*Chie Soong*

NOTES

1. Victor F. S. Sit, "Soviet Influence on Urban Planning in Beijing, 1949–1991," *The Town Planning Review* 67, no. 4 (1996): 457–484, http://www.jstor.org/stable /40113418.

2. Edmund N. Bacon, *Design of Cities*, rev. ed. (London: Penguin Books, 1980), 244.

5

Economy

Beijing has a large, diverse, and robust economy. In 2018, its total gross regional product (GRP), that is, the total annual market value generated by an economy in an administrative subdivision, was more than CNY 3 trillion (USD 440 billion) based on the average exchange rate in 2018 (1 USD = 6.62 CNY). It ranks twelfth among the thirty-one province-level administrative divisions (not including Hong Kong and Macao, the two special administrative regions (SARs)). Between 2011 and 2016 (the PRC's twelfth five-year plan), Beijing was the largest province-level contributor to the national treasury. Beijing has continued its growth momentum despite some ominous predictions of economic downturns. A.T. Kearney, an American global management consulting firm, ranked Beijing ninth of the 130 major cities in its 2019 Global Cities Index, noting its remarkable progress in human capital, information exchange, cultural experience, and politics as well as its steady growth in business activities.[1]

Beijing has gained great wealth in the era of China's economic reform. Its GRP increased by more than 400 times from 1978 to 2017, and its per capita GRP increased by more than 160 times. The city's per capita GRP in 2018 was CNY 140,221 (USD 21,188), the highest among the province-level administrative divisions, and moved up to about USD 40,000 when it is converted to purchasing power parity (PPP), that is, what the per capita GRP could actually buy. Although it was still significantly less than that of the United States (USD 62,996, or USD 62,606 PPP) in 2018, Beijing qualified as what the World Bank considers a "high-income economy." The

---

BEIJING'S WEALTH

Beijing competes with Shanghai for the accolade of being the wealthiest city in China. Beijing's USD 21,188 in per capita gross domestic product led all other province-level divisions in 2018, edging out Shanghai's USD 20,421. Beijing maintained the lead during the first half of 2019, and its total wealth of USD 2.1 trillion in 2019 made it the richest city in China and the fifth richest in the world, according to New World Wealth. In 2018, 110,000 households in Mainland China had net assets exceeding CNY 100 million (USD 14.5 million), according to a report by CCB Trust Co., Ltd., and the Hurun Research Institute, of which 19,900, or about 18 percent, resided in Beijing, exceeding those in Shanghai (16,700), Hong Kong (12,600), Shenzhen (5,759), and Guangzhou (4,450).

---

overall private wealth in Beijing places it as the wealthiest city in China and among the wealthiest cities in the world, according to a report by New World Wealth, a market research firm.[2] A 2019 report by CCB Trust Co., Ltd., and the Hurun Research Institute reveals that, in 2018, 19,900 of the wealthiest 110,000 households (with net wealth exceeding CNY 100 million or USD 14.5 million) in China, about 18 percent, were from Beijing. This is no small feat considering how much ground Beijing has covered in the last four decades in terms of economic growth and wealth building.

Beijing's economy underwent a remarkable structural transformation over the last two decades. Beijing covers a complete economic spectrum with formidable business activities, such as commercial gardening and traditional manufacturing. There is an emerging landscape in the new economy, however, with the growing central business district (CBD) hosting international and domestic corporate headquarters and research and development (R & D) parks reminiscent of Silicon Valley. Shopping malls, the symbol of fervent consumerism until a decade or so ago, are now much quieter as residents are increasingly doing retail shopping and booking services online with their mobile phones. The rise of e-commerce has also given rise to an infrastructure of express delivery and an army of couriers. In the age of smart city building, Beijing is one of seventeen Chinese cities that are building the 5G overlay network and has started providing limited 5G service since the end of September 2019. Beijing is also one of eight cities that will receive 5G services from all three of the largest telecommunications companies in China: China Mobile, China Unicom, and China Telecom (the other seven cities are Shanghai, Shenzhen, Chongqing, Nanjing, Chengdu, Hangzhou, and Fuzhou).

A snapshot of Beijing's Central Business District (CBD). CBDs in major Chinese cities often feature bold modern and postmodern skyscrapers as a statement of phenomenal growth and global economic ambitions. (Xiao Xiao/Dreamstime .com)

Although China as a country is still an emerging economy driven by industrial growth, Beijing has transitioned to a postindustrial economy. In 2018, Beijing's tertiary sector, which includes services, distribution, and R & D activities, accounted for 81 percent of its total GRP. Within the tertiary sector, finance services (16.8%), information technology (12.7%), and scientific research (10.6%) were responsible for 40.1 percent of Beijing's total GRP; wholesale and retail (8.4%), distribution (4.4%), real estate (5.8%), and leasing and business services (6.7%) contributed another 25.3% of the GRP. In contrast, manufacturing, the core of the secondary sector and the Socialist-era urban economy (1949–early 1980s) accounted for only 14.7 percent of the GRP. It is interesting to note that, in 2017, the sectoral structure of Beijing's GRP was similar to that of the GDP of the United States: they both had less than 1 percent from the primary sector and fewer than 20 percent from the secondary sector but about 80 percent from the service sector(s).

For much of history, Beijing was a frontier city on the periphery of China's economic core regions. It began to develop a consumption-based economy as the imperial capital. Economic production in Beijing and its environs was inadequate, and the rulers had to muster nationwide resources to sustain the capital's functions. Beijing began to develop a modern economy during the PRC era when, under Soviet influence, it actively pursued industrial development. Since the late 1970s, Beijing's economy has undergone changes driven by market reform and globalization, but the new economy only started to emerge after active intervention by the central government. Beijing's comparative economic advantages lie mainly in its status as the national political center and the leading academic hub, which attracts high-level economic operations, such as corporate headquarters (quinary activities), financial services, and research and development (R & D). This economic model, which is termed the *capital economy* in this book, is the outcome of Beijing's unique historical heritage and political power rather than its endowment of production factors.

A CONTEMPORARY HISTORY OF BEIJING'S ECONOMY

Irrigation, sericulture (the agro-industry of silk production), and fruit farming prospered as early as the seventh century BCE in Beijing and its environs. Iron farming tools became widely used as well as oxen and other draft animals. During the Warring States period (475–221 BCE), as the capital of the vassal state of Yan, the city of Ji became a major transportation hub in northern China and experienced growth in trade and commerce as well as robust handcraft. The machete-shaped bronze coins minted by Yan have been excavated as far away as Korea and Japan, showing its early trading outreach in East Asia.

Between the Qin and Tang Dynasties (221 BCE–907 CE), the economy of Beijing and its environs underwent three phases. First, there was overall stability and prosperity during the Qin and Han Dynasties (206 BCE–220 CE). New crops, including rice, were introduced, and new farming technologies were developed. Taxes remained low, and invasions by nomadic groups were relatively few and far between. In contrast, during the Southern and Northern Dynasties (220–589 CE), wars and invasions wreaked havoc on traditional sedentary agriculture, and large influxes of refugees resulted in an integration of various food systems and irrigation development. During the third phase, the Sui Dynasty and first half of the Tang Dynasty (581–mid-eighth century), the exchange among various economic systems created lasting prosperity that saw significant growth in agriculture, metallurgy, textile, and handcraft as well as a wide range of trade and commerce activities.

Overall, however, the economy in Beijing and its environs was not as advanced and prosperous as that farther south along the Yellow River valley, as reflected in the transitional and frontier characteristics of Beijing's economy. Starting in the eleventh century, long-term, large-scale environmental changes pushed the geopolitical interface among sedentary agricultural, nomadic, and hunting-fishing societies eastward. It was at this historical moment and geographical crossroad that Beijing saw its status being elevated to an imperial capital. The capital economy began to take shape thereafter.

The Imperial Capital Economy

Beijing's economy began to experience a transformation after it came under the control of the nomadic Khitans in the tenth century. Subsistence farming and animal herding coexisted in Beijing and its environs. As the imperial capital of the Jurchen Jin Dynasty (1153–1215) and the Mongol Yuan Dynasty (1271–1368), Beijing underwent substantial growth that fostered a unique economic system that focused on economic activities that essentially served the court, the aristocratic class, and the bureaucracy by mobilizing national resources. This economic system, which could be described as the *capital economy*, continued to mature through the Ming and Qing Dynasties (1402–1911) and was characterized by two unique traits.

First, the court and the nobility directly controlled much of the land and other natural resources in Beijing and its environs. The court's land was usually operated by military garrisons and ethnic civilian settlements, which is evidenced by the historical names of rural settlements in and around Beijing today. Royal Buddhist monasteries also possessed large tracts of land. Agriculture in was highly specialized to serve the court and the elites. Horticulture, fruit orchards, and aquaculture, for example, became highly developed in Beijing and its environs during Ming and Qing Dynasties. This special service provision still exists today, as high-ranking government officials and military services in Beijing receive high-quality, special supplies from government-controlled farms and ranches in the suburbs.

Second, the luxurious products of Beijing's handcraft industries were in high demand from the court and the elites, such as specialty textiles, high-quality ceramics, fine jewelry, artworks, and crafts. By far, Beijing had the largest number of craftsmen and artisans in the country who specialized in cloisonné enamel, jade, lacquerware, oblation articles, metal casting, and glazed building materials. Many of these businesses exclusively served the court, and so their products and services were not available to the common folks. By the late 1700s, clusters of craft makers in Beijing began to bear the names of the specialties. One of the most popular hutong tour routes goes through Luoguxiang (Gong and Drum Alley). The most popular antique district, Liulichang (Glass Factory), was the site where glazed building materials were manufactured exclusively for the court and high nobles.

The imperial capital economy can be characterized as parasitic in nature because it was centered on serving the court, the elites, and the central bureaucracy while depriving the common folks of the basic resources and opportunities. For example, there were a large number of upscale restaurants and shops that thrived in the capital because of the volume of official business and the rich and famous clientele. The imperial capital economy consumed enormous economic resources, both local and national, and created specialized and monopolized businesses that were often owned by the court. The dominance of the imperial capital economy in turn suppressed the development of private enterprises of, by, and for the commoners.

The Capital Economy in Transition (1860–1949)

Coastal China, especially treaty ports such as Shanghai and Tianjin, opened up to global trade and commerce under treaties with European colonial powers after the Opium War (1839–1842). The treaty ports became both gateway cities and international investment destinations. In contrast, Beijing remained insulated and held on to its unique capital economy. This insulation from new economic tides was not to last, however, as the Second Opium War (1860) resulted in new treaties that allowed foreign legations in Beijing and exposed the elites in the capital, from the royal family down, to the "forbidden fruits" of Enlightenment. Imports of Western manufactured goods increased dramatically due to demand from the elites and the growing expatriate community in Beijing. Foreign businesses also began to purchase local agricultural products in large volumes for both export and local clientele, which led to embryonic agricultural specialization in crops such as tobacco and cotton, oil crops, and commercial gardening in Beijing and its environs.

Traditional handcraft industries, especially the specialized royal workshops, experienced the most drastic decline for failing to compete with European imports because of their inability to expand their own markets and reach economies of scale, that is, obtaining optimal size based on available technology and management. Ordinance (weapon making and supply), special textile, and printing businesses were particularly hard hit. At the same time, direct foreign investments arrived and focused on coal mining, power generation, textiles, machinery, chemicals, and public works, such as public transit and railroads. Foreign commercial interests competed against each other and carved out monopolies in specific economic sectors. For example, Britain gained control over coal mining in Beijing and its environs, and the French had an advantage in manufacturing transportation equipment. The Japanese cast a wide net in their investment, and the United States had a solid presence in the import-export business. Foreign economic interests also formed various joint ventures with their Chinese counterparts.

The most remarkable event during this period was Beijing's emergence as a modern financial center in China. A key characteristic of the capital economy has always been its gravitational pull of high-level financial services. The first financial institutions were banks from Western industrial economies, and HSBC (Hong Kong and Shanghai Bank Corporation, the seventh-largest bank in terms of assets in the world today) was the first to open a branch in Beijing in 1886. These banks provided banking services to businesses and individuals, but they derived the bulk of their business from financial services to the Chinese government, including making loans, minting currencies, and overseeing China's customs service. The first Chinese government bank was established in 1905 and became the predecessor of the present-day Bank of China. Most Chinese banks were located to the west of the Legation Quarter, along the same street that went through the Legation Quarter and was properly named Legation Street. It became the financial district of Beijing in the late Qing and early Republican periods. It must be pointed out that being located in the capital was crucial to these banks; they needed to stay informed of government decisions to quickly adjust their operations and depended on relationships and networks to obtain highly lucrative government contracts.

During the last years of the Qing Dynasty and the first two decades of the Republic of China (ROC, 1912–early 1930s), Western-style commercial services grew substantially in Beijing as diplomatic and expatriate communities grew and the capital's elites adopted modern consumption preferences. Retail shops and professional services sprung up along Wangfujing Boulevard. This commercial strip, marked on Western maps as Morrison Street between 1915 and 1948, after President Yuan Shikai's Australian confidant and adviser George Ernest Morrison (1862–1920), was at a most convenient location for its clientele: it was on the east side of the Imperial City and to the immediate north of the Legation Quarter. It became Beijing's premium shopping district, with a large cluster of various businesses. One of the princely mansions (Mansion of Prince Yu) near the street was purchased by the Rockefeller Foundation in 1916 and later became the campus of the Peking Union Medical College (PUMC) in 1919, where its hospital was opened in 1921. Both the college and the hospital are top-ranked institutions in China today.

In an ironic historical twist, Beijing became the booming center of China's antique trade in the early ROC era. After the Qing Dynasty came to an abrupt end in 1911, the large banner population in Beijing lost their political and financial privileges, including generous guaranteed stipends.

Without work skills or habits, many Qing patricians had to pawn or sell their assets, ranging from jewelry and artworks to land and dwellings. The reversal of fortune subsequently made Beijing an antique and arts trade mecca, and the reputed antique community has continued to this day. The fabled Liulichang (Glass Factory) became the center for antiques shops and high-quality artwork reproduction.

Beijing's capital economy was dealt a fatal blow when the KMT-dominated ROC government moved the capital to Nanjing in 1928, and it had collapsed by the early 1930s as major banks and government-oriented consumer services followed the central government and left town. Beijing fell into a deep economic recession, and growth became stagnant despite efforts to promote tourism and the hospitality industry and a brief economic boost during the Japanese occupation (1937–1945). Beijing was stuck in parasitic consumption, with a weak industrial base and an outdated service sector. Without being the national capital, Beijing appeared to be regressing to a medium-sized regional city and as a transportation and defense hub in northern China. Fortunately for the city, this period only lasted two decades (1928–1949).

Beijing's Socialist Capital Economy (1949–1978)

Beijing's political and economic fortunes changed after a twenty-year interval (1928–1949). In the 1950s and 1960s, Beijing experienced a revival of the capital economy, albeit in the confines of a fledgling Socialist economy, as hundreds of thousands employees of the central government and their families flooded the city. The capital underwent a construction boom of housing, offices, and infrastructure, and the PRC government adopted Soviet style superblocks as the development blueprint to jump-start government operations and speed up urban modernization. Most of the new development projects were designed to be the live-work space of a *Danwei* (a place of employment), either a large manufacturing facility or a ministry-level government agency. These superblocks were often physically enclosed and provided essential services, such as health clinics, retail shops, and recreational facilities, exclusively for the employees and their families. Superblock construction dominated Beijing's development and resulted in a new pattern of service activities. On the one hand, there was a lack of growth in citywide services and infrastructure; on the other hand, repetitive service provisions created a landscape adorned by smokestacks for the boiler rooms of the new superblocks.

The central government was the impetus behind the rapid expansion of Beijing's capital economy during this period. In 1956, as the story goes, the Indian ambassador to China, Ratan Kumar Nehru, complained to the

Chinese government after he failed to get his suit properly fitted in Beijing. After the incident, the central government moved reputable merchants from other large cities to Beijing as a quick fix for the capital's inadequate service sector. Shanghai and Tianjin contributed the largest number of these businesses, including tailors and clothiers, photographic studios, upscale restaurants, specialty laundry and dyeing shops, and hairdressers.

The PRC government made a major push for Beijing's industrialization based on national security concerns and ideological principles. The PRC's first five-year plan (1953–1958) called on Beijing to transform its economy from one of parasitic consumption to one of proactive production. The emphasis was on promoting heavy industries, industries mainly serving other industries rather than consumers, because they are considered the foundation for an industrial economy. During the ensuing decade, Beijing underwent rapid industrial growth with over eight hundred new or expanded factories. Employment in the secondary sector, which includes material processing and some segments of construction and transportation, increased from four hundred thousand in 1949 to over three million in 1978. During the 1960s and 1970s, a large petrochemical facility was assembled, and the local iron and steel plant underwent a major expansion.

Beijing's traditional service-based economy was transformed to an industry-based economy during the first three decades of the PRC (1949–1978), centered on textile and apparels, chemicals (especially petrochemicals), metallurgy, and machinery. In 1949, about 37 percent of Beijing's GRP came from the secondary sector (mainly manufacturing industries); by 1978, the figure had increased to 71 percent, with heavy industries alone accounting for 65 percent of Beijing's total GRP. Heavy industrial development, however, accounted for much of the government investment at the expense of the consumer goods industry and the service sector. In 1978, only a little more than 20 percent of Beijing's GRP came from the tertiary (service) sector. This Soviet style industrial economy resulted in a series of problems for Beijing's environmental quality, infrastructure, and consumer services.

In the early 1980s, at the advent of China's economic reform, the PRC government began to encourage a shift of Beijing's economic focus from heavy industries to technology and services as the PRC government rediscovered and reaffirmed the importance of the capital economy. It takes time and effort for economic transformation, however. By the early 1990s, Beijing still had 120 of the 130 industries identified in the national classification. Industrial use accounted for 19 percent of Beijing's total land, and commercial use added another 4 percent, far exceeding the 5–12 percent range of industrial and commercial land use in cities such as London, New York, Tokyo, and Paris.

BEIJING'S CAPITAL ECONOMY TODAY: TRENDS AND CHALLENGES

Beijing's economy has undergone substantial structural changes since China's economic reform commenced in the late 1970s, especially in the last two decades (Table 5.1). At the advent of economic reform, Beijing's primary sector accounted for 5.1 percent of the city's total GRP, and secondary activities, especially manufacturing, were the core of the economy, contributing a whopping 71 percent of the total GRP. The tertiary sector, which includes service and high-tech industries and is comparable to what the United States covers under tertiary and quaternary sectors, amassed less than a quarter of the city's total GRP.

The Transition (Back) to the Capital Economy

In 1994, Beijing's tertiary sector surpassed the secondary sector in its respective contributions to Beijing's total GRP for the first time. In 1997, the Beijing Congress of the Chinese Communist Party (CCP) conceptualized "the capital economy strategy" that would strengthen the economic sectors that would support the functions and tasks of the national capital. Since then, Beijing has accelerated its economic transition from manufacturing industries to service industries. In 2005, the State Council approved Beijing's "Urban Master Plan for Beijing, 2004–2020," which reaffirmed Beijing's primary functions as the national capital and cultural center of

Table 5.1   Economic Indicators, Beijing, Selected Years

Year	GRP (CNY 100 million)	Primary Sector (%)	Secondary Sector (%)	Tertiary Sector (%)	GDP per Capita (CNY)	GDP per Capita (USD)
1978	108.8	5.1	71.0	23.9	1,257	797
1987	326.8	7.4	55.8	36.8	3,150	846
1997	2096.8	3.7	37.4	59.0	16,778	2,024
2007	10,071.9	1.0	25.2	73.9	61,470	8,084
2017	28,000.4	0.4	19.0	80.6	129,000	19,892

Sources: Beijing Statistical Yearbook, 2017. Table 2-1, Gross Domestic Product (1978–2016). http://tjj.beijing.gov.cn/nj/main/2017-tjnj/zk/indexee.htm.
"Statistical Bulletin of Beijing National Economy and Social Development, 2017" (in Chinese). http://www.bjstats.gov.cn/zxfb/201802/t20180225_393332.html.

China with the goals of becoming a highly livable urban area and a world city. By 2006, the tertiary sector was contributing 70 percent of Beijing's total GRP, marking the city's ascension to a postindustrial economy and a capital economy. In 2017, the tertiary sector's share rose to 80 percent of Beijing's GRP, higher than that of any other provincial division of Mainland China.

Beijing needs a large service sector because of the rapid increase of the capital's population, its growing affluence, and the expansion of the central government. National capitals in general are attractive to high-level corporate operations because they benefit from having timely access to the executive, judicial, and legislative branches of the national government. Even capitals in a federal political system, such as Washington, DC, have seen phenomenal growth. Beijing, the national center of a unitary state, is bound to be a national and international magnet for service industries, especially those in financial services and banking, which is reminiscent of how Beijing became a leading banking center in China in the late Qing and the early ROC periods.

Transition to the capital economy has manifested in other aspects. First, it has led to fundamental changes in employment structure with rapid growth in the tertiary sector and steady decrease of primary and secondary sectors, as shown by their respective GRP contributions (Table 5.2). The most remarkable change, however, was the faster employment growth of white-collar STEM-based occupations, such as research and development, financial services, and information technology services, which posted annual increases between 2015 and 2017 (Table 5.3), indicating Beijing's transformation into the leading national center of the new economy.

Table 5.2   End of Calendar Year Employment by Sector, Selected Years

Year	Total Employment (10,000)	Sector Share (%)		
		Primary	Secondary	Tertiary
1978	444.1	28.3	40.1	31.6
1987	580.2	15.9	45.5	38.6
1997	655.8	10.8	39.2	50.0
2007	942.7	6.5	24.2	69.3
2017	1,246.8	3.9	15.5	80.6

Source: Beijing Statistical Yearbook, 2017. Table 3-14, Employed Persons in Three Industries and Their Composition (1978–2016). http://tjj.beijing.gov.cn/nj/main /2017-tjnj/zk/indexee.htm.

Table 5.3   Year-End Employment by Business Classification, 2016 and 2017

Business Type	2017 Total	2016 as % of 2015	2017 as % of 2016
Agriculture and Food	32,611	94.4	90.8
Mining and Quarrying	41,053	85.7	90.9
Manufacturing	803,278	94.2	94.9
Public Utilities	88,465	110.7	99.6
Construction	437,825	102.7	102.0
Wholesale and Retail	711,066	99.1	101.6
Transport, Storage and Post	560,823	96.6	99.0
Lodging and Catering Services	242,753	96.5	98.8
Information Technology and Services	761,923	102.6	112.0
Financial Intermediation	405,438	103.3	104.9
Real Estate	413,787	104.7	100.8
Leasing and Business Services	851,978	99.9	110.8
Research and Development	668,723	117.0	104.8
Environmental Services	101,950	100.6	104.0
Residential Services	80,460	96.3	100.4
Education	462,178	102.0	105.3
Health Care and Social Services	276,571	104.7	102.8
Culture, Sports and Entertainment	179,873	102.2	102.5
Government and Public Services	442,924	100.8	102.4
Total	**7,563,679**	**101.2**	**103.1**

Source: Beijing Statistical Yearbook, 2017. Table 3-19, Year-End Number of Fully Employed Staff and Workers in Urban Entities. http://tjj.beijing.gov.cn/nj/main /2017-tjnj/zk/indexee.htm.

Leading High-Tech Center

Beijing is a top destination and incubator of high-tech industries. On November 1, 2018, the Springer Nature Group published "The Nature Index 2018 Science Cities Supplement" in the famed science journal *Nature*, which included the first Nature Index's global science city ranking. The United States and China dominated the top-ranked cities, and Beijing ranked first based on the city affiliations of authors who published in eighty-two high-quality natural science journals.[3] This rating could be better appreciated considering Beijing's unmatched resources for research and

CENTER OF SCIENTIFIC RESEARCH AND HIGHER EDUCATION

Beijing is a leading center of China's new economy because of its unmatched resources in higher education and research in China. The city is the largest center of higher education in the country with more than ninety officially recognized and accredited universities and colleges and more than eight hundred thousand enrolled students. Beijing is home to 16 of China's top-ranked 100 universities, 8 of the 39 universities officially designated as China's "first-class universities in the world," and 26 of the 116 universities receiving special funding from the central government. Among the most prestigious and best known are Peking University, Tsinghua University, Peking Union Medical College, People's University, and Beijing Normal University. Beijing also has the largest concentration of scientists in China, with the headquarters of the Chinese Academy of Sciences and about half of its research institutes.

higher education. It is home to over ninety institutions of higher learning with over a half million undergraduate and graduate students, in addition to their large faculties. Beijing is also the headquarters for the Chinese Academy of Science (Academia Sinica), one of the top scientific research institutions in the world, and nearly half of its 114 research institutes, 68,000 research scientists, and 770 academy fellows. It should not come as a surprise that Beijing tops China, and even the world, as a scientific research center with these unrivaled human and hardware resources and its immeasurable economic potential, especially when China starts to secure an enforceable intellectual property regime. Beijing's unrivaled human resources give the city a superior production factor that can support cutting-edge economic activities, such as financial and informational services and R & D activities for new technologies and their applications. Beijing's R & D activities are strong in number, topping all Chinese province-level divisions in patent ownership: in 2018, Beijing recorded 111.2 patents per 10,000 population, more than doubling the runner-up, Shanghai (47.5), and four times as high as Jiangsu, the third-place holder (26.5).

Beijing leads the country in R & D funding in the form of both government grants and private venture capital. In 2017, for example, Beijing ranked twelfth among the provincial administrative units in total GRP but fifth in R & D funding. It has the largest concentration of private equity and venture capital in China, providing an environment similar to that of Silicon Valley for R & D funding sources. Startups by both Chinese and internationals have been major drivers in the growth of Beijing's economy. Venture capital firms, such as Sequoia Capital and tech giants, such as

Tencent and Microsoft, have tapped into Beijing's rich high-tech resources to foster technology incubators and accelerators. In 2018, Beijing led China in both the number and total valuation of China-based unicorns, or privately held startups with over USD 1 billion valuation. It was home to 74, or 46 percent, of the 161 Chinese unicorns that had a total valuation of USD 298 billion. Both were the highest in China.[4] Since 2012, Beijing has garnered USD 75 billion for startups, ranking second in the world after Silicon Valley, which raised nearly twice as much during the same period. Beijing added 16 new unicorns in 2018, and 5 of the 10 largest Chinese unicorns are located in the city. Such rapid growth even caused some observers to call Beijing the next world leader in startups.[5]

"Headquarter Economy"

An important component of the capital economy is the so-called quinary (executive decision-making) activity that is concentrated in corporate headquarters. The economic impact of the "headquarters economy" transcends substantial local employment and income as well as its multiplier effect, that is, the disproportional expansion of auxiliary goods and services generated by the quinary, that is, executive corporate, activities. For example, Beijing has the largest number of convention hotels among Chinese cities. Business headquarters accounted for less than 6 percent of the total number of businesses in Beijing, but they contributed 70 percent, 60 percent, and 90 percent, respectively, for total accumulated assets, operating revenues, and profits of all businesses that had an annual revenue exceeding CNY 20 million.[6]

In 2018, Beijing was home to over 4,000 business headquarters, including 100 of China's top 500 companies based on their stock market values, the most among all Chinese cities. Fifty-three of the 111 Chinese companies in the 2019 Fortune Global 500 largest corporations were headquartered in Beijing, making it the city with the largest number of Fortune Global 500 headquarters in the world six years in a row. Among them, 18 of the top 25 largest Chinese corporations are headquartered in Beijing. Many of these corporations were state-owned banking institutions and enterprises in energy and telecommunications, such as Sinopec Group (#2, natural gas and petroleum), China National Petroleum (#3), State Grid (#5, power generation), China State Construction Engineering (#21), Industrial & Commercial Bank of China (#26), China Construction Bank (#31), Agricultural Bank of China (#36), Bank of China (#44), China Life Insurance (#51, the second-largest insurance company in China), China Railway Engineering (#55), and China Mobile Communications (#56). There were also about 900 international businesses that had their China or Asia-Pacific headquarters in Beijing.

While more corporations are eyeing Beijing, the municipal government is actively courting their headquarters, too. The Chinese tech giant Tencent officially opened its second headquarters in Beijing in late 2018. Alibaba, the leader of China's e-commerce headquartered in Hangzhou, Zhejiang Province, broke ground for its second headquarters in Beijing in the spring of 2019. It is almost a certainty that Beijing will continue to strengthen its status as the headquarters capital of China and will enjoy the benefits of its headquarters economy in the years to come.

International Trade

Beijing is a major player in China's international trade. Beijing's total import-export value in 2018 reached CNY 2.718 trillion (USD 393 billion), an increase of 23.5 percent over that of 2017. Import value was CNY 2.23 trillion (USD 322 billion), an increase of 24.1 percent over 2017. Export value was CNY 488 billion (USD 71 billion), an increase of 15.5 percent over 2017. The growth ratios were higher than the national average. Beijing's major trade partners were, in terms of monetary value, the European Union (13.5%), the United States (9.9%), and the Association of Southeast Asian Nations (8.4%). Beijing's trade with the European Union and the United States grew 12.9 percent and 12.4 percent, respectively, between 2016 and 2017, and grew a whopping 35 percent with the Association of Southeast Asian Nations. Japan and Korea were also major trade partners.

With about 1.5 percent of the national population, Beijing's export value counted for 2.5 percent of China's total export value in 2017. In 2017, Beijing's major export commodities included refined petroleum products (43.3%), steel products (7.7%), phones (6.9%), integrated circuit boards (5.6%), clothing and clothing accessories (5.5%), and automobile parts (4.2%). Boats and ships, automobiles, textile yarn, and fabrics were also significant. The top five exporting destinations were the United States, Hong Kong, Japan, Singapore, and South Korea. This pattern is similar to China's export sales in 2018, with the United States, Hong Kong, Japan, South Korea, and Vietnam rounding out the top five. The European Union accounted for 16.4 percent of China's export sales. The data shows that Beijing's traditional industries, established during the pre-reform decades, have remained competitive internationally, though they have declined in relative importance in Beijing's economy.

It is Beijing's role in China's imports, however, that truly impresses. Beijing accounted for 14.4 percent of China's total import value in 2017. This is due to the effect of the capital economy, which presents strong demand on a wide range of goods and services for government functions. In 2017, the two imports with the highest value were crude oil (56.5%) and automobiles (13.2%). Adding the value of imported auto parts (2.4%), over 70 percent of

Beijing's import values are from petroleum and automobiles, fueled by the needs of the enormous PRC bureaucracy along with that of business and private consumers for modern mobility. Other important imports included iron ore, grains, automated measuring and analyzing equipment, medicine, and refined petroleum products. Countries that led in exports to Beijing in 2017, by value, were the United States (10.3%), Germany (8.2%), Switzerland (6.6%), Australia, (5.1%) and Japan (5.0%). These were the leading countries that export automobiles and auto parts to China, especially Beijing's huge luxury car market, a major component of Beijing's capital economy. Switzerland was a major source of precision equipment, including the famed Swiss watches coveted by the affluent Chinese. It is also interesting to note the next five largest exporters to Beijing in 2017, again by value, were Saudi Arabia, Angola, Russia, South Korea, and Oman. Obviously, four out of the five were major exporters of crude oil, with South Korea a leading exporter of automobiles, mobile phones, and home electronics.

The capital economy clearly translates into Beijing's international trade pattern, in which imports exceed exports by a large margin. As the current PRC policy is designed to transition Beijing's economy to one centered on R & D, cultural products, and government-centered services, Beijing may find itself increasingly becoming a consumption-driven economy.

Beijing's Economic Geography

The current distribution of Beijing's economic activities shows the effects of the environment and historical development. In recent years, urban sprawl has squeezed agricultural operations in Beijing and its environs. Even commercial horticulture has come under pressure from development and has been forced farther and farther to the western and northwestern hilly areas. In recent years, Beijing's needs for horticultural products have been increasingly fulfilled by large specialized commercial horticulture operators from nearby provinces, especially those in Shandong, thanks to greatly improved regional transportation infrastructure.

Borrowing from the Soviet model, Beijing established many of its manufacturing facilities in industrial superblocks on the urban fringe during the pre-reform decades. By the late 1950s, Beijing had established specialized industrial clusters on the outskirts of the urban area: a textile cluster in the east, electronics in the northeast, machinery and chemicals in the southeast, and iron and steel in the west. These industrial clusters are mostly in today's fast-growing suburbs (the expanded urban function zone and the new urban development zone) and have been under great pressure from, ironically, both urban sprawl and environmental conservation. Many have departed Beijing proper and relocated in neighboring Hebei Province.

A prime example of manufacturing decentralization is the Capital Iron and Steel Corporation (Shougang Group). It started steel production in 1958 and remained as the largest state-owned enterprise in Beijing and was the onetime leading steel producer in China in 1994. Environmental constraints, however, limited its expansion in the reform era. In addition, its role as the largest polluter in Beijing came under fierce scrutiny. It started a multiphased relocation to Tangshan, Hebei Province, in 2005 and ceased smelting operations Beijing in 2011. Today, the enormous former plant site is being converted to a multiuse park for museums, expo centers, high-end enterprises, and offices. It is also home to the Beijing Organizing Committee for the 2022 Olympic and Paralympic Winter Games.

In contrast, modern industrial parks are established in the urban periphery to host new industries with high added value, such as pharmaceuticals, electric motor vehicles, robotics, electronics, and telecommunications devices. In addition, the Beijing Municipal Government has planned three "science cities" to accommodate the needs of R & D firms and high-tech industries, which tend to cluster to be close to funding sources, major research universities, and horizontal and vertical integrations. One is in the heart of the higher education district (Zhongguancun) in Haidian District, known as "China's Silicon Valley," which is also home to many research institutes of the Chinese Academy of Sciences. Many corporations also locate their headquarters and research centers there, including the Founder Group, Lenovo, Baidu, and many international tech giants, such as Google, Oracle, and Intel.

Poverty and Inequality: Economic Disparity in a Booming City

As a shining example of China's economic ascendance, Beijing can testify to its economic achievement with displays of postmodern corporate skyscrapers, sleek high-tech parks, and upscale shopping centers. According to the market research group New World Wealth, Beijing led all Mainland Chinese cities in the number of millionaires and billionaires in 2018, which also places it within the top ten cities in the world.[7]

In the shadows of such unprecedented prosperity and wealth, however, there are economic hardships and glaring poverty in Beijing. Rapid economic development has created a nouveau riche community and a swelling middle class, but there is also a large socioeconomic underclass. As a matter of fact, economic disparity is large and increasing. In 2018, the average wage for Beijing's urban residents was CNY 94,000, but there were great gaps among the wage earners. According to government classifications, nonprivate employers, which include government agencies, state-owned enterprises, and publicly traded companies, paid an average annual salary of CNY 145,000 (USD 21,000). Employees of international businesses had the highest average annual salary of CNY 188,538 (USD 28,000). In contrast, employees of private businesses, many of which were small and privately held, were paid an average annual salary of only CNY 76,908 (USD 11,000). The monthly minimum wage in Beijing was a paltry CNY 2,120 (CNY 25,440, or USD 3,700, annually), which was about 27 percent of Beijing's average wage and only 17.5 percent of the nonprivate sector's average wage. The average annual minimum unemployment benefit was CNY 18,600 (USD 2,700), and the average annual pension was CNY 48,000 (USD 7,000), 33 percent of the average wage.

Beijing presents a landscape of economic contrasts. On the one hand, visitors are dazzled by mushrooming upscale condo high-rises, five-star hotels, and suburban gated communities; on the other hand, they may come across pockets of dilapidated inner-city neighborhoods and large tracts of slum-like communities on the urban fringe. Official statistics, such as the *Beijing Statistical Yearbook*, from which this chapter draws most of the quantitative data, do not detail information that has to do with poverty. However, there are numerous investigative reports and academic research on poverty in Beijing. According to these sources, there are three overlapping types of poverty, similar to other large Chinese cities, as shown in wage and benefits statistics: poverty of disenfranchisement, poverty of aging, and poverty of alienation.

China's economic reform has created both winners and losers. The blue-collar working class was disproportionally marginalized by the introduction of the market economy, which forced state-owned factories to downsize and lay off a large number of workers. The workers who lacked transferable skills lost the safety net of compulsory employment during the Socialist period. When outright layoffs were prohibited in the early stage of reform by the PRC government, factories used various schemes to realize de facto layoffs. Indefinite furlough was a widespread method. According to a 1997 study, half of the 6,500 enterprises surveyed stated that they had to furlough about 10 percent of their workforce. Buyout was another method to induce workers to terminate their employment with a generous severance package. Many factories also persuaded workers to file for voluntary early retirement, through which the workers became the responsibility of the state pension system before the standard retirement age. Middle-aged (forty to fifty years old) male workers represented the largest share of workers who became separated from employment. These forms of de facto unemployment may have been seriously underrecorded because they did not meet the official unemployment definition, which in part explains the low ratio of unemployment in official statistics. Between 1979 and 2016, Beijing's registered unemployed urban residents consistently accounted for fewer than 2 percent, or one hundred thousand, of working-age residents, with the highest ratio, 2.11 percent, in 2005.

The PRC government provides subsistence allowance or minimum living security to people whose income is below the official poverty line. The poverty line is determined by local governments annually and is different for urban and rural residents in the same municipality. Families and individuals with income below the poverty line receive monthly cash payments from the local governments. In 2016, Beijing's poverty line for urban residents was CNY 1,210 per person per month, and each individual below this income level received an allowance of CNY 800. In 2017, the poverty line was CNY 1,410 per person per month, and the allowance was increased to CNY 900 per person per month. For 2018, the poverty line jumped to CNY 2,000 per person per month, and the allowance was increased to CNY 1,000 per person per month. In recent years, the number of welfare recipients has decreased, reflecting both strict government regulations on eligibility and overall success in poverty relief among Beijing's permanent residents (Table 5.4).

The Economy of an Aging Population

China is undergoing rapid population aging, with nearly 18 percent of its population being above sixty years of age, exceeding the 10 percent threshold for an aging population set by the World Health Organization (WHO), due to a continued increase in longevity and a decrease in fertility. Beijing's population aging is accelerating; in 2018, 17 percent of the permanent population, or a quarter of its registered household population, was over sixty years of age. Poverty among the elderly population has become an open secret. Many elderly people depend on a fixed pension that cannot keep up with inflation and rapidly increasing living costs in one of the most expensive urban areas in China.

Despite pension adjustments and asset value improvements, the rapidly aging population in Beijing has resulted in an increasing number of poor elderly people. Recent research has shown that elderly people under the poverty line increased by twenty-five thousand in Beijing between 2000 and 2015. The same research also found that elderly women were more vulnerable than their male counterparts to falling into poverty because of the gender gap in education, career options, and consequent earnings and asset accumulation. Many elderly people try to conceal their financial hardship due to the social stigma associated with poverty. Some may have assumed that the elderly would receive financial and other assistance from their children, but the repercussions of the one-child policy and fading traditional values have weakened traditional support for the elderly from

Table 5.4 Persons Receiving Subsistence Allowance, Beijing, 1996–2016 (10,000 persons)

Year	Persons Receiving Subsistence Allowance in Urban Areas	Persons Receiving Subsistence Allowance in Rural Areas
1996	0.9	
1997	0.9	
1998	2.8	
1999	4.3	1.2
2000	6.7	1.6
2001	7.8	1.8
2002	12.0	5.4
2003	16.1	6.7
2004	16.1	7.5
2005	15.5	7.8
2006	15.2	7.1
2007	14.8	7.8
2008	14.5	7.9
2009	14.7	8.0
2010	13.7	7.7
2011	11.7	7.0
2012	11.0	6.3
2013	10.4	6.0
2014	8.9	5.1
2015	8.5	4.9
2016	8.2	4.7

Source: Beijing Statistical Yearbook, 2017. Table 22-2, Social Security Participation in Beijing (1995–2016). http://www.bjstats.gov.cn/nj/main /2017-tjnj/zk/indexee.htm.

family and kinship networks. The alarming prospect of the aging population and elderly poverty has prompted the Beijing Municipal Government to waive all medical costs for people older than ninety years of age.

Poverty is widespread among the millions of migrant workers and their families in Beijing. They suffer from not only limited education and a lack of transferable skills but also neglect and discrimination from the municipal government and the hosting society in general. Migrant workers fulfill low-skill, low-paying jobs that the urbanites do not want to take, such as retail service, construction, delivery, and homemaking, all of which are traditionally low paying. They are highly motivated in working hard on their jobs in contrast to the low-income local residents. Their role in Beijing, and in other major cities in China, is comparable to that of undocumented immigrant workers in the United States. Beijing and other major cities suffer from a near shutdown of services for two weeks around the time of Chinese New Year, when most migrant workers return home for this most important traditional Chinese holiday. Despite their irreplaceable role in the local economy, migrant workers and their families are not eligible for support and benefits from the municipal government, such as pension, health insurance, housing subsidies, and K–12 public education.

There has been a geographical decentralization of Beijing's poverty. First, rampant urban renewal in the old city has displaced a large number of low-income residents in Beijing and pushed them to the suburbs. Second, and more importantly, the migrant population has congregated in the urban fringe, where there is abundant supply of low-quality but less-expensive housing in the villages. As a result, a ring of low-income migrant communities has emerged in the periphery of the urban core of Beijing, roughly between the Fourth and Fifth Ring Roads, which is out of most of the commercial sprawl zone but still within commuting distance of the urban core, or the six urban districts.

The Capital Poverty Belt

In contrast to the capital's economic boom, there is a contiguous zone of stagnant development and poverty encircling Beijing in the north, west, and south now known as the "Capital Poverty Belt." Dubbed as the "Beijing-Tianjin Poverty Belt" in a report by the Asian Development Bank (ADB) in 2005, this region had 2.7 million people in 32 counties and 3,798 villages under the national poverty line. The three neighboring cities to Beijing, Chengde, Zhangjiakou, and Baoding, have 25 poverty counties and 1.5 million people in poverty. Official figures from the end of 2009 showed that in these counties, the net average income of a farmer was only one-third of his or her counterpart in Beijing, per capita GRP was one-quarter, and per capita local revenue was only one-tenth of those in Beijing. Some observers described the shocking contrast of economic landscapes between Beijing and the Capital Poverty Belt as "traveling from a European city to an African village in an hour." This dichotomy of economic geography was also in sharp contrast to the Yangzi Delta and Pearl Delta, where the leading cities, Shanghai and Guangzhou, appeared to have had the most positive economic effects on their respective regions.

A number of factors may have contributed to this stunning economic disparity. First, the Capital Poverty Belt in general and the poor counties in particular are less accessible to more developed coastal regions and, hence, do not have locational advantages to attract either international or domestic investment. Second, the poverty counties suffer from a lack of natural resources and long-term environmental degradation. Third, inefficiency and mismanagement of local governments are also responsible for the underdevelopment. Fourth, the development in this region is severely restricted by the PRC government as a means to reduce environmental pollution in Beijing. Areas located in the upwind direction of Beijing are required to carry out conservation projects, but they receive far less in subsidies than their counterparts in Beijing proper, which are used to offset the lost revenue from restrictions on development. For example, communities in Beijing once received ten times as much in subsidies as their neighbors in Hebei Province for similar conservation projects.

Causes of the Poverty Belt are multifold, but the main one may be their unfortunate geography for being in the shadow of the national capital. As a result of historical and environmental causes, northern China has long been at a disadvantage to compete with the Yangzi Delta and the Pearl Delta for economic development. Beijing's prosperity has mainly been driven by its political power, which does not extend beyond the capital's administrative boundaries. As a result, economic disparity between Beijing and its surrounding areas has been worsened.

Between 2004 and 2010, the central government and local governments began joint efforts to remedy the problem. A series of policy and funding initiatives have since taken place to even the playing field for Hebei Province. The Xiongan New Area may be the most ambitious and impactful strategy that has been aimed at generating economic diffusion from Beijing to the southern flank of the Capital Poverty Belt. The upcoming 2022 Winter Olympics will have many outdoor venues in Zhangjiakou, to the northwest of Beijing, which has already brought a construction boom and significant business investment to several poor counties there. Communities in the mountainous western and northern flanks of the Capital Poverty Belt are designated for developing ecotourism and are receiving more adequate compensatory subsidies for conservation and infrastructure projects. The jury is still out as to how effectively government policies and local initiatives would slow down or even reverse the increasing gap between Beijing and the Capital Poverty Zone. The long-term solution, however, depends on the success of integrated development among Beijing, Tianjin, and Hebei (Jing-Jin-Ji), the same metropolitan development model that has achieved great success in the Yangzi Delta and Pearl Delta.

In summary, the economy of Beijing must be examined in the context of the capital economy in a large and growing unitary state. The central government can draw investment, resources, and operations to the capital city with its political power and disperse those that are deemed not suitable for the capital. Beijing is promoting sustainable development by upgrading the service sector, supporting R & D activities, planning suburban satellite communities, and participating in Jing-Jin-Ji economic integration. The central government has also dictated the decentralization of traditional industries, which is restructuring Beijing's economy and demographics.

At the same time, the benefits of locating and operating in the capital are immense for executive corporate decision making, hence the large concentration of corporate headquarters in Beijing. In addition, the massive central government bureaucracy presents the most desirable clientele for high-level financial services. Beijing has become a mecca of R & D activities in the new economy as the national center of higher education and scientific research, and the city is a magnet for government funding and venture capital as a result.

One of the most daunting challenges for Beijing's sustainable economic development is improvement of its environmental quality. Environmental deterioration has not only blemished Beijing's global image but also hindered sustainable and high-quality economic growth that the city so desires. Tackling environmental challenges has become the priority for both the central government and the Beijing Municipal Government. The outcome of their endeavors will determine the future of the capital city.

MOVING TO BEIJING

I came to Beijing six years ago after college. Beijing had been the paradise in my dreams because it has so many top-notch universities and research institutions. I was impressed right away that the older Beijingers I came across were all very proper and willing to assist hapless newcomers like me.

I got a job working in the booming real estate industry, but at the bottom of the corporate hierarchy, the workload was brutal and the pay was meager. I didn't care because I knew the job was transitional, since my goal was to go to graduate school and pursue research in the field of my interest. I spent all the nonwork time preparing and succeeded in getting into an ideal graduate program. Three years later, I got my master's degree. Then, the real challenge came: I could either get a high-paying job in a private business without Beijing household registration (legal residency status) or secure a position at a government research institute, which does not pay much but would give me Beijing household registration.

I was tempted to go with the high pay in the private sector, since I always feel a moral obligation to help out my parents financially. As poor farmers, they had made great sacrifices supporting my education. My parents, on the other hand, insisted that I obtain legal residency status in Beijing. It was always their dream to see me settle in Beijing, which to them is the best place in China. So here I am, a leading researcher of two major projects at a government institute, and a legal resident of Beijing!

Looking back, I have no doubt that coming to Beijing was the best decision I ever made, despite all the hardship in the first couple of years. Beijing is indeed the best place for young, ambitious college graduates, to whom it offers the most and best opportunities for career success. In addition to my satisfactory career, I want to explore and enjoy the rich and diverse culture and history of Beijing. Beijing is my home now, especially this is where I met my love, with whom I am hoping to buy a condo of our own. By then, my parents will be able to come and visit!

—Junwen Wang

NOTES

1. "A Question of Talent: How Human Capital Will Determine the Next Global Leaders: 2019 Global Cities Report," A.T. Kearney, accessed September 22, 2019, https://www.atkearney.com/global-cities/2019.

2. "Global Wealth Migration Review 2019," AfrAsia, accessed September 1, 2019, https://www.afrasiabank.com/en/about/newsroom/global-wealth-migration-review-2019. The data in this report reflects the total amount of private wealth held by all the individuals living in each of the cities on the list. The ranking is not based on gross domestic product (GDP) but on the values of all assets, such as property; cash; equities and business interests, excluding liabilities; and government funds.

3. "Nature Index Launches First Global Science City Ranking: Beijing Number One," Springer Nature Group, November 1, 2018, https://group.springernature.com/gp/group/media/press-releases/nature-index-launches-first-global-science-city-ranking/16242958.

4. WalktheChat, "Study of 151 Chinese Unicorns Shows Beijing #1 City for Startups," Technode, May 2, 2018, https://technode.com/2018/05/02/beijing-best-place-for-unicorns.

5. Chris O'Brien, "Beijing on Track to Eclipse Silicon Valley as World's Top Startup Hub," Venturebeat, July 3, 2018, https://venturebeat.com/2018/07/03/beijing-on-track-to-eclipse-silicon-valley-as-worlds-top-startup-hub.

6. "Beijing Holds World's Most Headquarters of Fortune 500 Firms," eBeijing, June 6, 2018, http://www.ebeijing.gov.cn/BeijingInformation/BeijingNewsUpdate/t1526446.htm.

7. "The AfrAsia Bank Global Wealth Migration Review 2019," New World Wealth, April 2019, https://e.issuu.com/embed.html?u=newworldwealth&d=gwmr_2019.

6

Environment and Sustainability

The mention of Beijing usually conjures up an image of mildew-colored air blanketing the entire city and mask-wearing residents hurrying through city streets. Smog, a term coined in Britain in the early twentieth century to describe an air filled with smoke and fog, has come to accompany Chinese cities a century later. The frequency and severity of Beijing's smog has reached such cataclysmic levels in recent years that it has become synonymous with the down side of China's meteorite rise as an economic powerhouse. The Camp Fire in California was raging as this chapter was being drafted in November 2018. A persistent southward wind brought heavy smoke from the fire zone to the San Francisco Bay Area, resulting in unhealthy air and the cancellation of schools and most outdoor activities. As the air quality index (AQI) exceeded 150, the threshold for unhealthy air, local weathercasters bemoaned that the air was as bad as that of Beijing.

Was this sentiment based on reality? Instead of the AQI used by the United States, the level of PM2.5 (particulate matter with a diameter of less than 2.5 micrometers) may be a more comparable indicator of air quality among different counties. The World Health Organization (WHO) recommends that the PM2.5 level be at or lower than 10 micrograms per cubic meter ($\mu g/m^3$). In 2018, Beijing's PM2.5 annual mean was 50.9, much higher than Paris (15.6), Rome (15.0), Tokyo (13.1), London (12.0), and New York (7.0), the other world cities in this series. It was also worse than that of other Chinese megacities: Shanghai (45.0), Guangzhou (36.0), and Shenzhen (27.0). Only nearby Tianjin (51.0) was at the same unhealthy level.

It must be pointed out that air pollution is but one aspect of a wide range of environmental challenges that Beijing faces. Others include water scarcity and pollution, the solid waste crisis, noise and light pollution, deficient green space and traffic congestion. Improvement of environmental quality has become the life-and-death issue for Beijing to achieve sustainable development and its goal of being "the model for all places."

The Economist Intelligence Unit (EIU) publishes the Global Livability Index, which uses five categories to measure the quality of life in major cities of the world. Beijing was ranked 75th among the 140 cities rated in 2018. Only a much smaller Mainland Chinese city, Suzhou, ranked one place higher than Beijing.[1] The EIU livability ranking shows that Beijing benefits from its social and cultural assets, such as low crime, political stability, education and medical care access, and high-quality provision of goods and services, which catapulted the city into the ranks of most livable cities. On the other hand, Beijing's ranking was adversely affected by its subpar environmental conditions, such as poor air and water quality, outdated energy provision, inadequate public transit management, and a lack of green space. Analyses behind the ranking confirm the perceptions of local residents and visitors alike: Beijing has much to improve in its physical environment and infrastructure. Assessments of environmental and management factors could provide better insights into assessing Beijing's challenges and strategies for sustainable development.

ENVIRONMENTAL DEGRADATION AND RESOURCE DEPLETION

Air Quality

Visitors are often shocked by the poor air quality that frequently reaches an unbearable level in Beijing. It has become a devastating blemish on the public image of the city domestically and internationally. However, poor air quality is not a new problem for Beijing. In 1997, Tom Foley, a former speaker of the U.S. House of Representatives (1989–1995), declined the nomination to be the ambassador to China by President Bill Clinton because of his concerns about Beijing's poor air quality that might exacerbate his wife's respiratory problems.

As a matter of fact, Beijing's reputation of having bad air dates back to historical times. As the climate in northern China turned colder and drier, sand and dust storms increased in frequency and intensity. In addition to climate change, the deterioration of air quality was exacerbated by large-scale deforestation, the increased use of coal, unpaved earthen streets, and rampant sand mining for construction in the Beijing environs. Sand and dust storms began to appear regularly in official chronicles during the Yuan Dynasty and increased during the Ming Dynasty (Table 6.1). In late winter and spring, Beijing was often shrouded for days by fine dust from the Eurasian interior, which obscured visibility to less than a mile.

Reforestation was the main coping strategy to combat sand and dust storms. Over time, Beijing became an urban forest and impressed foreign visitors, such as American traveler and lecturer W. E. Geil (1911).[2] The regional ecological conditions continued to deteriorate, however, and air quality was worsened by the widespread use of honeycomb briquet, a coal and sawdust mix for cooking and heating, by Beijing residents.

Beijing was put on fast track for development during the PRC era, and the air quality worsened as a result of rapid population growth, industrial development, and the construction boom. The worst air was in winter and early spring, when the hundreds of boilers for the government superblocks and hundreds of thousands household stoves ramped up for heating. Beijing's air quality became a public concern in the era of reform. As living standards improved, the PRC government began to pay more attention to its public image. Sand and dust storms got the most attention for their

Table 6.1   Time Period Distribution of Sand and Dust Storms in Ming Beijing, 1425–1644

Time Period	Number of Sandstorms
1425–1444	1
1445–1464	6
1465–1484	9
1485–1504	11
1505–1524	17
1525–1544	6
1545–1564	23
1565–1584	15
1585–1604	8
1605–1624	18
1625–1644	19

Source: Gao Shouxian, "Mingdai Beijing shachen tianqi jiqi chengyin" ["Dust Weather and Its Contributing Factors in Beijing of Ming Dynasty"], *Beijing jiaoyuxueyuan xuebao* 17, no. 3 (2003): 33–38. https://www.ixueshu.com /document/376cc8c1b0f62d9d.html#pdfpreview.

Tourists at the National Stadium, dubbed "the Bird's Nest," wear masks to fend off heavy air pollution. Beijing's air pollution has reached extremely harmful levels in the last two decades, and the city has launched major efforts to improve air quality. (Xi Zhang/Dreamstime.com)

dramatic impact on daily life. There was a spike in respiratory problems, women covered their faces with colorful scarfs to repel sandy dust, and a layer of fine dust was left on everything in the aftermath.

Since the late 1990s, the central government has launched a series of policy initiatives and invested heavily in massive rangeland reclamation and reforestation projects in and around Beijing proper. Two decades later, conservation efforts may have paid off, as the frequency and intensity of the sand and dust storms appear to have subsided in Beijing and northern China. However, new environmental challenges have emerged.

Smog has been bad in Beijing, and it caught much greater attention as Beijing gained international exposure and the emerging middle-class majority demanded a better, more livable environment. Horror stories and negative reporting about the bad air spread around the world,[3] hurting not just the image but also the business that Beijing and China so wanted to sustain its economic growth.

Beijing intensified its efforts in improving its environment after it failed to win the bid for hosting the 2000 Summer Olympics. Systematic monitoring of air quality began in the early 1980s with a focus on total suspended particles (TSP). The first annual environmental report was issued in 1994. Between 1998 and 2011, the monitoring focused on bigger pollution particulates, PM10 (particulate matter with a diameter of less than 10 micrometers). In 2011, the U.S. Embassy in Beijing set up its own devices on the embassy grounds to measure the city's air pollution levels and then broadcast the results over social media, focusing on the PM2.5 level, which has a more direct impact on visibility and smog intensity.

The PRC government was agitated and embarrassed at first but could not stop the broadcast. Western media and some Chinese nongovernmental organizations (NGOs) accused the government of concealing or doctoring air quality data. This controversy turned out to be a wake-up call for the PRC government and the Chinese citizens. Beijing residents did not need quantitative data to know the air quality was bad, but with that information, they began to demand greater government transparency and more effective actions for environmental improvement. Beijing's annual environmental report began to include PM2.5 data in 2012, which has become a key indicator for the government to measure air quality and devise coping strategies. Overall, China's environmental management has become more transparent and receptive to public feedback since 2011.

After winning the bid to host the 2008 Summer Olympics, the Beijing Municipal Government implemented a series of drastic measures to improve the overall environment in preparation for the Olympic Games. These measures included moving heavy-polluting factories to the suburbs or out of Beijing proper, restructuring Beijing's energy structure by reducing the use of coal, and raising automobile emission standards. The government used its authoritarian power to manufacture a period of "Olympics Blue Sky," but after the Olympic Games ended, the incentives for sustaining or increasing "blue sky" days also disappeared.

The Beijing Municipal Government was increasingly held responsible by both the central government and the general public for improving the air quality in Beijing. Billions of dollars have been invested to help switch from coal to natural gas as the main energy source (Table 6.2). By early 2017, the last coal-burning power plant in Beijing ceased operation. Restructuring energy consumption has nearly doubled the average heating costs, but the government has absorbed most of the extra cost through subsidies. Between 2000 and 2015, Beijing's natural gas usage increased tenfold, which might have contributed to reducing PM2.5 by 36 microns per cubic meter during this period alone.

Has Beijing's air quality improved over the last several years? Opinions differ among both the public and the experts, and public perception may not entirely concur with scientific research. In 2005, for example, a survey conducted by Peking University showed that of the one thousand Beijing households randomly sampled, 70 percent stated that air quality had improved; only 13 percent felt that it had worsened. In contrast, a 2015 national survey showed that 50 percent of the two thousand plus Beijing

Table 6.2   Percentage Composition of Primary Energy Consumption, Beijing 2010–2017

Year	Coal	Petroleum	Natural Gas	Nuclear and Renewable Electricity	Net Transferred Electricity	Other Energy
2010	29.59	30.94	14.58	0.45	24.35	0.09
2011	26.66	32.92	14.02	0.45	25.62	0.33
2012	25.22	31.61	17.11	0.42	25.38	0.26
2013	23.31	32.19	18.20	0.35	24.99	0.96
2014	20.37	32.56	21.09	0.41	24.03	1.54
2015	13.68	33.54	28.97	0.40	21.55	1.86
2016	9.81	32.93	31.68	0.66	23.20	1.72
2017	5.65	33.80	31.80	0.64	25.99	2.13

Source: Beijing Statistical Yearbook, 2018. Table 7-2, Primary Energy Consumption and Its Composition (2010–2017). http://tjj.beijing.gov.cn/nj/main/2018-tjnj/zk/indexeh.htm.

households surveyed said that air quality had worsened; only 21 percent believed that it had improved. There may be several reasons for the lack of cohesion in the public perception of Beijing's air quality.

First, research shows that Beijing's air quality has improved (Table 6.3). The most improvement is seen in the decreased TSP levels since 2000, when the PRC government took radical measures to mitigate the sources of sand and dust storms in and around Beijing proper. For example, the Beijing Municipal Government invested USD 3.53 billion in 2017 alone in projects for environmental improvement. The reduction of coal use has significantly reduced sulfur dioxide (SO_2) in the atmosphere, which is a major cause of acid rain. Even PM2.5 levels have had a slight decrease of about 2–3 microns per cubic meter per year.

Beijing residents and visitors alike have already noticed better air quality.[4] The most obvious is the reduction of TSP, which some claim is directly related to life expectancy. Beijing's TSP level reduced by 150 microns per cubic meter between 2000 and 2016, and life expectancy during this period increased by 4.6 years to 82 years. As Beijing continues to implement drastic measures to curb pollutant emission, such as the promotion of electric cars, stricter regulations on construction, and decentralization of traditional industries, the residents can expect further air quality improvement.

Second, air quality in Beijing is still poor compared to world cities in developed countries and to its Chinese peers, such as Shanghai and

Table 6.3   Beijing Air Quality Indicators by Month, December 2013–
November 2018

Year and Month	AQI[1]	Range	PM2.5[1,2]	PM10[2]	SO_2[2]	CO[2]	NO_2[2]	O_3[3]
2013-12	100	23~291	73	97	37	1.73	56	38
2014-01	125	26~402	94	123	51	1.948	65	37
2014-02	184	33~428	148	155	56	2.171	69	42
2014-03	130	35~319	94	138	34	1.39	62	83
2014-04	127	65~279	89	145	16	0.927	57	129
2014-05	107	46~205	61	118	15	0.839	47	149
2014-06	116	50~179	54	74	6	0.79	39	168
2014-07	140	39~252	89	100	6	0.939	39	170
2014-08	120	46~200	62	88	5	0.839	43	172
2014-09	99	43~200	65	88	6	0.983	49	106
2014-10	154	28~381	118	148	9	1.339	70	54
2014-11	117	29~342	86	127	16	1.567	65	37
2014-12	86	21~267	58	95	28	1.552	53	42
2015-01	126	28~378	97	120	34	1.91	66	39
2015-02	127	36~334	93	114	26	1.457	51	60
2015-03	127	40~281	86	146	20	1.194	53	87
2015-04	107	38~212	71	118	9	0.76	43	124
2015-05	105	42~203	55	97	8	0.745	37	153
2015-06	111	35~231	60	70	6	1.303	35	156
2015-07	122	41~200	61	74	4	0.823	35	177
2015-08	104	37~202	45	66	3	0.79	31	159
2015-09	83	34~201	50	59	5	0.837	43	109
2015-10	106	27~344	74	86	6	0.955	55	74
2015-11	153	37~450	119	85	12	1.983	62	25
2015-12	187	23~485	152	172	20	2.865	76	26
2016-01	97	32~316	68	88	20	1.584	53	42
2016-02	71	34~238	44	59	15	0.903	35	68
2016-03	132	37~365	93	136	18	1.229	57	79
2016-04	106	43~209	69	118	10	0.803	44	116
2016-05	111	49~234	54	90	8	0.665	38	160
2016-06	126	50~189	59	70	5	0.767	35	183
2016-07	118	40~177	69	74	3	0.916	33	159

(continued)

Table 6.3   (continued)

Year and Month	AQI[1]	Range	PM2.5[1,2]	PM10[2]	SO_2[2]	CO[2]	NO_2[2]	O_3[3]
2016-08	94	34~179	47	60	3	0.832	35	135
2016-09	86	0~211	55	73	3	0.76	43	104
2016-10	116	29~292	85	101	4	1.155	56	47
2016-11	133	28~315	100	134	11	1.797	68	28
2016-12	168	54~431	133	159	17	2.51	80	28
2017-01	146	34~470	116	131	18	2.203	65	41
2017-02	100	36~305	71	84	18	1.318	53	65
2017-03	94	40~273	63	84	11	0.913	50	86
2017-04	87	38~174	53	104	7	0.693	48	101
2017-05	134	53~500	48	104	7	0.674	37	161
2017-06	125	50~200	42	75	6	0.783	38	184
2017-07	118	38~208	52	71	3	0.894	34	174
2017-08	85	34~162	38	56	3	0.803	35	131
2017-09	98	36~189	58	100	4	0.913	49	123
2017-10	84	25~221	57	63	3	0.923	46	47
2017-11	75	30~201	46	73	5	0.903	49	44
2017-12	81	23~254	44	68	8	1.09	49	25
2018-01	66	29~175	34	64	8	0.832	42	52
2018-02	81	35~219	50	72	10	0.861	34	76
2018-03	119	0~294	85	108	10	1.084	58	88
2018-04	105	39~273	64	116	7	0.743	41	125
2018-05	100	0~185	48	93	5	0.7	40	146
2018-06	123	48~203	48	74	4	0.803	35	183
2018-07	100	31~173	50	53	3	0.926	26	147
2018-08	93	39~172	35	51	3	0.861	28	145
2018-09	59	26~130	28	45	3	0.603	34	92
2018-10	74	25~202	41	62	4	0.71	45	70
2018-11	103	39~270	70	75	5	1.011	58	40

Source: China Air Quality Monitoring and Analyses Online Forum. https://www.aqistudy.cn/historydata/monthdata.php?city=北京.

Notes:
[1] Monthly AQI and PM2.5 were calculated by averaging the hourly data from the Environmental Protection Administration.
[2] $\mu g/m^3$.
[3] mg/m^3.

Shenzhen. The public perception of a lack of air quality improvement, misconstrued or not, is in part due to the psychological effects of frequent smog attacks. It is more difficult to tackle pollution caused by PM2.5 and PM10 than that caused by TSP because scientists are still trying to figure out the sources and mechanisms that cause frequent and severe smog in Beijing and other northern Chinese cities.

In 2012, the PRC government issued the Airborne Pollution Prevention and Control Action Plan (2013–17), which would invest CNY 1,700 billion (USD 277 billion) and specifically target PM2.5 particulates in the Beijing, Tianjin, and Hebei areas. It required that Beijing lower its annual average PM2.5 level to below 60 micrograms per cubic meter by the end of 2017, which Beijing achieved with an annual mean PM2.5 level of 58 micrograms per cubic meter in 2017 and 51 micrograms per cubic meter in 2018. However, the progress fell far short of WHO's standard for clean air, which is an annual mean of 10 micrograms per cubic meter. Notwithstanding an improvement in overall air quality, smog attacks still take place, and heavy air pollution is obvious and persistent, reminding the government and residents alike that there is still a long way to go in achieving sustainable good air quality. In late November 2018, as this chapter was first being drafted, there were two red alerts issued in Beijing as official warnings of heavy smog and extremely unhealthy air.

The latest scientific research may shed new light on Beijing's smog.[5] Beijing's sheltered topographic setting, similar to that of Los Angeles, traps pollutants and enhances smog when the atmosphere is calm and the humidity is high. On November 13 and 14, 2018, a heavy fog blanketed the entire Beijing metropolitan area just as the central heating systems started operation for the winter season as mandated by the government. Beijing's AQI jumped to well over 200. Government mitigation has so far focused on curbing SO_2 emission, but the real culprit for the smog may be the hydroxymethane sulfonate that was generated by a chemical reaction between formaldehyde and SO_2 from coal-burning and oil refineries. The findings, if verified, would allow the government to zero in on the sources of formaldehyde and make further progress in improving air quality.

In early 2019, a major two-year research project sponsored by the PRC government concluded that Beijing's air pollution was caused by three major factors: the local accumulation of pollutants, the external transport of pollutants, and secondary chemical reactions in the atmosphere. With these findings, governmental agencies began to crack down on violators of air quality regulations, including shutting down their operations and pursuing legal actions. Large heavy industrial sites, such as metallurgical and petrochemical plants, are still the main culprits of smog generation, but they are unlikely to be shut down due to potentially devastating economic impact. The ban on coal as fuel has already caused an uproar among residents and businesses in Beijing. The clampdown on big polluters has encountered even greater resistance outside Beijing proper, where provincial and local governments are in desperate need of economic growth. How to strike a balance between long-term environmental protection and economic development remains a tough challenge facing Beijing in particular and China in general.

Water Scarcity and Management

Air pollution is but one of the environmental challenges that Beijing faces. A 2013 Blue Book report by the Chinese Academy of Sciences and Renmin University of China (People's University of China) stated that water resource scarcity was the most daunting resource challenge for the entire metropolitan area of Beijing, Tianjin, and northern Hebei Province. Historically, Beijing had ample water resources from both rivers and artesian aquifers. Until the late Qing Dynasty, marshland, bogs, and lakes were widespread in Beijing and its environs, many of which become centerpieces of royal gardens and aristocratic estates. By the late 1970s, however, Beijing's explosive growth began to exceed the sustainable level of water use and caused a series of problems.

Beijing's water shortage was exacerbated when it experienced a dry period between 2000 and 2010 with an average annual precipitation of only 440 millimeters (17.3 inches), less than the 18.5 inches of annual precipitation in Sacramento, California. Beijing's replenishable annual water resources have been between 2.3 billion and 2.7 billion cubic meters (81–95 billion cubic feet), which translates into an annual per capita water supply of 119 cubic meters (4,200 cubic feet) for its 21 million permanent residents plus another 2.5 million of mobile population (non-household registered residents). In contrast, Beijing's annual water consumption has been about 3.5 billion cubic meters (123.6 billion cubic feet), which translates into an annual per capita water consumption of 345 cubic meters (12,000 cubic feet). As a result, Beijing has an annual water shortage of 0.8–1.2 billion cubic meters. Demand has long exceeded local supply by an increasing margin, forcing Beijing to extract its own groundwater above the replenishable level and to divert water resources from Hebei Province, where water scarcity was already a serious threat to economic and societal development. In 2012, for example, Beijing received 200–300 million cubic meters of water from Hebei Province.

As surface water sources became completely tapped, Beijing began to rely on its groundwater resources. By 2008, 65 percent of Beijing's water supply came from groundwater, exceeding the replenishment level and resulting in both deteriorating water quality and severe ground subsidence. Beijing's groundwater hardness, measured by the amount of dissolved calcium and magnesium carbonates, increased from 230 milligrams per liter in the 1980s to 400 milligrams per liter in 2012. It is difficult to get a lot of bubbles from soaps and shampoos when using water this hard! The depth to the groundwater table dropped from 12 meters (39 feet) in 1999 to about 24 meters (58 feet) in 2010 in the Beijing Plain. Research shows a subsidence zone of 2,650 square kilometers (1,023 square miles) that is spreading in the north and east of Beijing proper and threatening to trigger a series of natural hazards.

In anticipation of Beijing's rising water demand, the central and local governments have been carrying out extensive public works on water infrastructure since the 1950s, including constructing several major reservoirs in the northern and western mountains. The two largest reservoirs were the Miyun and the Guanting; each could retain almost one year's water supply for Beijing. A new problem with water resources emerged in the early 2000s, as all five drainage systems in Beijing proper had become polluted. The Guanting Reservoir was so polluted that it could no longer supply safe water for Beijing by 1997 due to severe pollution in the upper streams of the Yongding River, the main feeder of the reservoir. Today, water from the Guanting Reservoir can only be used for general industrial and recreational uses. In addition, Beijing's treatment facilities could no longer handle the large and ever-increasing volume of wastewater, which at its peak exceeded treatment capacity by at least 12–15 percent.

Diversion is a common engineering strategy in redistributing water resources. The regional water imbalance has long presented a major challenge to China's development. As early as 1952, the PRC government conceptualized a grand scheme of diverting water from the humid south to the north. After decades of feasibility studies, the PRC government launched the epic South-North Water Diversion project in the early 2000s, and the diverted water officially reached Beijing in 2014. Since then, the diversion project has been bringing about 1 billion cubic meters of water to Beijing per year. Two-thirds of the diverted water is used to supplement Beijing's various water needs, one-quarter is channeled into major reservoirs, and about one-tenth is used to replenish the groundwater. Beijing's per capita water resource increased from 119 to 137 cubic meters in 2017 (Table 6.4). Water quality has also slightly improved, mainly from the infusion of diverted water.

Of course, the water diversion project has incurred enormous socioeconomic, political, and environmental problems. In addressing environmental and economic justice issues, Beijing has taken a reciprocal approach

Table 6.4 Water Resources (2001–2016) (100 million cubic meters)

Item	2001	2003	2005	2007	2009	2011	2013	2015	2017
Total Volume of Local Water Resource	19.2	18.4	23.2	23.8	21.8	26.8	24.8	26.8	29.8
Surface Water Resource	7.8	6.1	7.6	7.6	6.8	9.2	9.4	9.3	12.0
Underground Water Resource	15.7	14.8	15.6	16.2	15.1	17.6	15.4	17.4	17.7
Per Capita Water Resource (cubic meters)	139.7	127.8	153.1	145.3	120.3	134.7	118.6	123.8	137.1
Total Volume of Water Supplied by Source in the Year	38.9	35.8	34.5	34.8	35.5	36.0	36.4	38.2	39.5
Surface Water	11.7	8.3	6.4	5.0	3.8	4.8	3.9	2.2	3.6
Underground Water	27.2	25.4	23.1	21.6	19.7	18.8	17.9	16.7	16.6
Water Transit South–North					2.6	2.6	3.5	7.6	8.8
Recycled Water		2.1	2.6	5.0	6.5	7.0	8.0	9.5	10.5
Total Volume of Water Consumed by Purpose in the Year	38.9	35.8	34.5	34.8	35.5	36.0	36.4	38.2	39.5
Water Used by Agriculture	17.4	13.8	13.2	12.4	12.0	10.9	9.1	6.5	5.1
Water Used by Industry	9.2	8.4	6.8	5.8	5.2	5.0	5.1	3.9	3.5
Domestic Water Use	12.0	13.0	13.4	13.9	14.7	15.6	16.2	17.5	18.3
Water for the Environment	0.3	0.6	1.1	2.7	3.6	4.5	5.9	10.4	12.6
Water Consumption per CNY 10,000 GDP (cubic meters)	104.91	71.50	49.50	35.34	29.92	22.13	18.37	16.60	14.10

Source: Beijing Statistical Yearbook, 2018. Table 7-17, Statistics for Water Resources (2001–2017). http://tj.beijing.gov.cn/nj/main/2018-tjnj/zk/indexeh.htm.

Notes:
[1] Water consumption per CNY 10,000 GDP is based on current prices.
[2] Per capita water resource are calculated based on average permanent population.
[3] GDP data used since 2016 include R & D expenditure in water consumption and decrease rates per CNY 10,000 GDP; the historical data were not revised based on the new calculation coverage of GDP.
[4] Source: Except for per capita figures and water consumption per CNY 10,000 GDP, other figures are from the Beijing Water Authority.

by providing funds for economic restructuring and poverty relief in areas that supply the water diversion, reaching CNY 2.5 billion (USD 370 million) between 2014 and 2019. These funds are used for over seven hundred projects that have supported water quality control, poverty relief, and alternative agriculture. In addition, the Beijing Municipal Government has helped channel nearly CNY 100 billion (USD 14.5 billion) in investments from businesses in Beijing to the source areas that have lost part of their local water resources and had to conduct large-scale relocation and, therefore, suffered great economic losses.

In the long run, Beijing must establish a sustainable system of water utilization. An increase in natural precipitation would certainly help. Beijing's annual precipitation has rebounded in recent years with an average annual precipitation of 606 millimeters (23.8 inches) between 2011 and 2017. However, climate change, especially short-term fluctuations, may not be a reliable source for water resource improvement. Seawater desalinization has sometimes been discussed, but there is no feasible plan due to energy consumption, production cost, and a wide range of environmental problems associated with seawater desalinization. It may still become an alternative to south–north water diversion in the future with new technological development.

Sustainable water strategies are available, especially water recycling, to remedy the water shortage. In 2010, Beijing treated and recycled 680 million cubic meters of wastewater. By 2017, this figure exceeded 1 billion cubic meters, more than a quarter of the total water supplied to the city. Recycled water is mainly used for replenishing public water bodies, industrial cooling, some agricultural operations, and green space maintenance (Table 6.4). Conservation has become a key component of the sustainable water strategy, and Beijing leads the country in water utilization efficiency in all major categories, including agricultural, industrial, and domestic uses. Beijing has also implemented numerous policies to protect major water sources by reclaiming agricultural land, deactivating factories, and banning polluting businesses, such as poultry farms.

Beijing has succeeded in reducing water usage by the two biggest water users: agriculture and industries. It has had success in managing gray water, the wastewater generated in households and office buildings without fecal contamination, for a variety of uses. New drilling for groundwater was banned in the early 2000s. More than 50,000 acres of wet rice in southeastern Beijing were converted to dryland crops. Some of the largest industrial water users, such as steel and coking plants, have been relocated to Hebei Province. Beijing's efforts to decentralize economic activities and population, if successful, may also help alleviate water shortages. Policies and laws are needed to implement effective water-pricing regimes and to promote the adoption of water-saving technologies for domestic use.

Solid Waste Management

All cities are confronted by solid waste management. Beijing's domestic waste growth poses a major challenge to its environmental sustainability. In modern times, Beijing's unsorted garbage was hauled out to rural land-fills. As early as the 1950s, Beijing experimented with sorting garbage through increased composting and recycling, which was aimed at reducing landfill use. Before economic reform, Beijing's domestic waste generation was small due to its meager per capita consumption, and 40 percent of it was compostable materials.

In recent years, industrial waste has decreased because Beijing is phasing out most mining and traditional manufacturing activities. At the same time. its domestic waste has skyrocketed. In 2017, Beijing generated nine million tons of domestic waste, the highest among Chinese cities with Shanghai a close second. Traditional landfills are no longer a feasible waste management strategy because of land scarcity and the environmental harms associated with them. In the meantime, Beijing's traditional recycling business, which attracted a large number of migrant workers, has withered over the years due to the lack of profitability. Despite progress in adopting the latest technology and strong government support, Beijing still faces the threat of being overwhelmed by its solid waste. Beijing's thirty-two waste treatment facilities could handle twenty-four thousand tons of domestic waste daily, but it has been projected that Beijing will generate twenty-eight thousand tons of domestic waste daily by 2020.

Waste management has become a big and lucrative business in China, with a significant portion of the revenue from government subsidies. To better monitor and regulate waste management, especially in light of the increasing involvement of the private sector, the Beijing Municipal Government issued the "Regulation of Beijing Domestic Waste" in 2011, which provided guidelines and legal support for environmentally friendly waste management. However, government monitoring and regulatory actions over both government and private operators remain inconsistent and inadequate, which results in lax law enforcement, operational mishaps, and incident cover-ups.

Beijing has been advocating transitioning from landfills to incineration and biochemical treatment in managing domestic waste. Today, garbage is first sorted and then disposed by incineration (40.3%), biochemical treatment (22.2%), or landfill (37.5%). It is notable, however, that landfill's share increased by 7 percent between 2015 and 2017, and biochemical treatment decreased by 7 percent. Some proposals suggest that waste treatment should become more dependent on incinerators, treating up to 70 percent of domestic waste and phasing out raw garbage in landfills by the end of 2020. The largest waste incinerators in Beijing, the Lujiashan

Waste Incinerator, came online in 2010. It can treat up to three thousand tons of domestic waste daily and generate enough electricity to support two hundred thousand households or supply heating for one million square meters, an area roughly equal to the immense floor space of Beijing Capital International Airport (986,000 square meters).

Waste treatment facilities inevitably expose nearby communities to deteriorating environmental conditions, especially when the operators shortchange required hazard mitigation. Waste treatment facilities directly affect the residents whose homes are within a short distance from landfills and incinerators. The harmful environmental impact due to physical proximity hits rural residents particularly hard. Land and water contaminations have caused frequent crop failures and skyrocketing health problems related to environmental degradation. Worse still, many rural villagers are too often voiceless because of their lack of effective organization and sufficient resources to fight against unscrupulous private businesses and inefficient, and often corrupt, local government bureaucracy.

There are signs that Chinese citizens are increasingly taking environmental concerns into their own hands. Communities near major waste treatment facilities have launched grassroots efforts to demand transparency, participation, and mitigation in major waste treatment projects. In 2017, for example, a plan was made public for Phase II of the Lujiashan Waste Incinerator, which would double its capacity and make it the largest in the world, surpassing the one in Shenzhen with a five thousand tons per day capacity. Although the developer and government agencies promised that the expansion would meet the European Union standard for 1,4-dioxin emission, residents and homeowners from nearby gated communities organized to sign petitions to stop the project from going forward before further environmental impact studies. Their protests, extensively covered by the media, appear to have halted the progress of both the Lujiashan II project and another ambitious project, a CNY 1.9 billion (USD 230 million) 7,500 tons per day waste treatment facility in Beijing.

The latest development in China's waste management is a strategic shift to reducing the volume of waste at the source through mandatory household garbage sorting. Chinese cities such as Beijing have promoted garbage-sorting programs, but the lack of incentives, facilities, and enforcement have undermined the effectiveness of these programs. On July 1, 2019, Shanghai issued strict waste-sorting guidelines with a strong regulatory enforcement regime, including punishing fines. The new sorting guidelines divide household waste into four categories—recyclable, wet (compostable), hazardous, and dry (common)—and the entire waste management system is being updated to make the new process sustainable.

Beijing is facing similar challenges as Shanghai with its waste management. There is an acute concern over costs: the traditional landfill-incineration treatment cost Beijing CNY 2,253 (USD 346) per ton of waste in 2015, far exceeding the government's targeted cost of CNY 40–300 (USD 6–46) per ton. Research found that waste sorting would have reduced the cost by up to 64 percent for Beijing in 2015. In spring 2019, the Beijing Municipal Government launched pilot programs to test the effectiveness of waste sorting and, based on the outcome of the pilot programs, proposed seven measures to promote waste sorting as a regulation and a civic duty. Recognizing the lack of a market-driven value chain for waste management and the lag in public participation, the authorities pushed for more enforceable steps of waste sorting, including banning the use of disposable utensils and containers for government agencies and mandatory waste sorting by education, health care, and hospitality entities.

Beijing may be slightly behind Shanghai in the implementation of waste sorting, but, as pointed out by some studies, its waste-sorting proposals are more realistic and easier to sustain in the long run. On November 27, 2019, the standing committee of Beijing People's Congress approved the amended 2011 Regulation of Beijing Domestic Waste, which requires compulsory domestic waste sorting starting on May 1, 2020. Violations will result in warnings and then fines. Beijing is on the right track for sustainable waste management because both the residents and the government realize that they must succeed in their efforts or be buried by their own waste.

Noise and Light Pollution

There are less publicized environmental problems that, if not addressed adequately and timely, have equally dire consequences as air, water, and garbage pollution. Noise pollution has been identified by many urban residents as being the second-worst environmental hazard after smog. It is also a major culprit for a wide range of health and social problems. In 2001, the average street and traffic noise level in Beijing's urban core was 67.9 decibels. By 2010, it had increased to 69.6 decibels, approaching the 70-decibel level (comparable to the noise of a vacuum) that would be directly harmful to health, and many locations near suburban transit hubs have long exceeded the 70-decibel threshold. The average city noise also increased by half a decibel to 54.1. A 2017 study on hearing loss, with two hundred thousand participants, found a 64 percent correlation between hearing loss and noise pollution. Based on its somewhat controversial methodology, the study listed the cities with the least and most noise pollution, and Beijing was ranked sixth for the most noise.[6]

Beijing's noise pollution was worsened by interminable large-scale constructions and the explosive growth of private automobiles. However, a worse offender was the rapidly expanding public transit systems because of the lack of noise mitigation in transportation planning. This is ironic because public transit is billed as the alternative to private automobiles for improving environmental quality. A study from 2009 showed that Beijing's buses accounted for 5–10 percent of the traffic flow but generated 40–52 percent of the traffic noise. One bus could generate a noise level equal to that of twenty-one sedan vehicles. Fixed-route mass transit, such as the light rail, is also a major source of harmful noise levels. Records show that 40 percent of citizen complaints about noise pollution was related to traffic. Some estimates put over one million Beijing residents at risk of transit-related noise pollution. Construction sites also generate tremendous around-the-clock noise as well as dust and solid waste pollution.

China's first noise control law was passed in 1996, and Beijing's first noise regulations were issued in 2007, which have been updated since then to employ a multiprong approach—regulatory, engineering, and planning measures—to mitigate noise pollution. There have also been efforts to introduce information technology that would allow the public to obtain information, voice opinions, and take action. Older buses have been phased out in the six districts of the urban core, and noise insulation barriers have been universally installed along freeways and rail transit corridors. Construction is no longer allowed at night. Progress appears to have been made: government data shows that Beijing's average noise level in the first ten months of 2018 was below 54 decibels in urban, suburban, and rural areas, which is already slightly lower than the government's target of below 55 decibels by the year 2020.

Light pollution is another major environmental problem, as Beijing, like its peers in China and other emerging economies, is lit up at night by fancy neon signs, office towers, and motor vehicle headlights. The public's initial fascination with night lights, which they originally associated with modernization and progress, quickly faded and was replaced by irritation, resentment, and even protests. In 2014, Beijing issued regulations for light control, restricting the use of searchlights, high-powered floodlights, landscape lighting, and commercial neon lights. The government opened tip lines for residents to file complaints. These measures seem to have stemmed further proliferation of light pollution in the city.

Lifestyle and pop culture can be the culprits of noise and light pollution, too. One peculiar pop culture item has become a new source of noise pollution in recent years. Improvised mass dancing for both fitness and entertainment, called *guangchangwu* (public square dancing), has come in vogue throughout China. Participants, who are mostly retirees, usually start to congregate in public spaces, such as parks and communal squares, at sundown and begin to dance away to deafening music. The noise that the activity generates is so annoying, especially to those who live nearby and are ready to retire for the day, that it has caused friction in the community.[7] The problem became so serious that the Beijing Municipal

Government revised its "Regulations of Beijing Municipality on Mass Body-Building" in 2017 in an effort to reduce the contention caused by the unruly masses in public spaces.[8]

BUILDING A MORE LIVABLE CITY

World cities like Beijing are the driving engines of the new economy centered on advanced technological innovations. Environmental amenities, that is, the attributes that make daily routines easier and personal health better, are imperative for a city to attract capital and retain labor in the new economy amid fierce global competition. A story recently circulating on the Internet was about a young AI (artificial intelligence) engineer relocating from Beijing to Hangzhou because he had finally given up on Beijing because of its high housing cost, traffic congestion, and the stifling air, all of which had made his life miserable. At the same time, he lamented the loss of career opportunities and top-notch infrastructure in Beijing, as it is also the dominant center for his field with the best funding and human resources in China. His experience is not unique. As Beijing's deteriorating quality of life starts to drive away the R & D workforce, there will be an adverse impact on the growth of high-tech firms and investment capital.

The concept of a *livable city*, which has been embraced by the United Nations Environment Programme, may provide a more effective framework for rating the development sustainability of cities because it focuses on the aspects of a city's environment that directly influence the quality of life of its residents, such as the condition of the natural environment and service infrastructure. The 2018 annual ranking of most livable cities by the Economist Intelligence Unit (EIU) placed Beijing among the most livable cities in the world with improvements in infrastructure and public service.[9] Consistent with this rating, Beijing was ranked as the leader based on the PRC government's green development index in 2018.[10] Beijing has made strides in improving its overall livability. Much remains to be done with monumental challenges, but the momentum seems to be set for building and maintaining a healthy environment and efficient infrastructure compatible to this world city.

Green Space

Beijing was a city of trees. During the imperial times, there was little communal green space; however, the royalty and the elites enjoyed their lush private gardens. During the ROC era, Beijing's citizenry gained access to numerous parks converted from imperial estates, such as the Temple of Heaven and the Summer Palace. During the 1950s and early 1960s, Soviet influence led to citywide greening efforts, but progress was halted by the ensuing political chaos during the Cultural Revolution (1966–1976). During early reform, rampant urbanization, both in situ expansion and urban sprawl, swallowed up much of Beijing's public green space. Using the impetus of its successful bid for the 2008 Summer Olympics, Beijing has been carrying out massive projects to increase urban green space (Table 6.5).

Table 6.5   Green Space Statistics, Selected Years

Year	Parkland Greenery (hectare)	Per Capita Parkland Greenery (m²/person)	Total Green Land Coverage (%)
1978	2693	5.07	22.30
1981	2751	5.14	20.10
1984	2878	5.14	20.10
1987	3570	5.07	22.90
1990	7110	6.14	28.00
1993	4452	7.76	31.33
1996	5147	7.54	33.24
1999	6457	9.10	36.30
2002	7907	10.66	40.57
2005	11365	12.00	42.00
2008	12316	13.60	43.50
2011	19728	15.30	45.60
2014	28798	15.90	47.40
2017	31019	16.20	48.42

Source: Beijing Statistical Yearbook, 2017. Table 5-25, Statistics for Landscaping and Forests (1978–2016). http://tjj.beijing.gov.cn/nj/main/2017-tjnj/zk/indexeh.htm. 2017 Beijing Urban Greening Resources, Beijing Landscaping and Greening Bureau. http://www.bjyl.gov.cn/zwgk/tjxx/201804/P020180425535648094242.pdf.

Notes:
[1] Parkland Greenery means the green land open to the public, with the main function of recreation, together with ecological, landscaping, and disaster preventing functions, and with more than 65% green coverage, provided with multiple arbors, shrubs, and ground-cover plants, along with certain facilities and artistic layouts. They include parks, community parks, street-side green land, and other green land in gardens.
[2] Per Capita Parkland Greenery is calculated on the basis of nonagricultural household registered population.
[3] Total Green Land Coverage means the ratio between the green land area and the total area of a region in the reporting period. The formula is: Green Land Coverage = Area of Green Land in a Region/Total Area of the Region × 100%.

By official statistics, Beijing stands out as a leading city in terms of public green space. In 2017, Beijing's per capita public green space reached 16.2 square meters (175 square feet). Although far behind such cities as Vienna, Berlin, and London, Beijing's per capita green space is slightly ahead of New York City, Rome, Paris, and Tokyo. It has also made great strides in the last forty years in greening the city through reforestation and other endeavors of increasing vegetation coverage (Table 6.5): Beijing now boasts a 43 percent coverage of green space for the entire city. Those who have visited peer world cities, however, may have quite a different impression and point out that Beijing feels amiss of ample and accessible public green spaces. The geography of Beijing's green space may be the cause for the disparity between statistics and perceptions.

First, the geography of Chinese urban administrative configuration may exaggerate the extent of green space. A large Chinese city usually consists of an urban area, its suburbs, and surrounding rural areas that have large tracts of "production green space," that is, land used for horticulture, and "protective green space," which includes woodlands maintained as windbreaks. Although both types of green space are abundant in Beijing proper, their distribution is quite uneven among the four development zones of Beijing (Table 6.6) and is in a reversed pattern compared to population distribution. In 2017, the core capital function zone, which includes areas within the historical walled city, had 9.5 percent of the city's population but merely 2.6 percent of the city's green space and 3.6 percent of the city's parkland green space. Both its per capita green space (10.8 square meters) and parkland green space (5.7 square meters) were the lowest among the city's four zones. The expanded urban function zone, which includes both the rapidly growing suburbs and the largely rural exurbs, matched its share of the city's population with that of the city's green space and parkland green space. As expected, the new urban development and ecological conservation development zone have far higher per capita green space than the urban core and the city's average.

Second, base numbers for calculation can make a difference. "Permanent resident population" was the population base for calculating per capita green space, but there were several million transient laborers and their families, classified as "nonpermanent resident population," who were not included in the equation but shared the green space with permanent residents. As a result, Beijing's per capita green space may be significantly overestimated in statistics. Residents and visitors alike, however, would feel the squeeze by the inadequate provision of public green space.

Third, Beijing's green space, especially in the urban core, is in two contrasting configurations. One type of green space, large parks, dominates the statistics of parkland green space. These large landmarks include Olympic Park (1,200 hectares), Yuanmingyuan Park (the Old Summer

Table 6.6   Green Space Resources by Urban Function Zones* of Beijing, 2017

Indicator	Capital Core	Contiguous	New Development	Ecological Conservation
% of City Total Population[†]	9.5%	46.1%	35.1%	9.2%
Population Density, % of City Average[†]	1,747.0%	611.9%	87.6%	16.8%
Green Space, % Share of City Total	2.6%	44.7%	42.4%	10.2%
Per Capita Green Space (m²/person)	10.8	43.5	52.6	46.2
Parkland Green Space, % Share of City Total	3.6%	43.7%	38.1%	14.6%
Per Capita Parkland Green Space (m²/person)	5.7	14.8	19.1	25.9
Green Space, % of Total Land	23.7%	48.1%	47.8%	52.2%
% of Residents within 500 Meters of Parkland Green Space	92.7%	89.2%	68.9%	90.1%
Trees, % Share of City Total	3.3%	44.7%	42.1%	9.9%

Source: 2017 Beijing Urban Green Space Resources, Beijing Landscaping and Greening Bureau. http://www.bjyl.gov.cn/zwgk/tjxx/201804 /P020180425535648094242.pdf.

[*] The sixteen districts in Beijing are grouped into four zones: (1) Core capital function zone: Dongcheng and Xicheng; (2) Expanded urban function zone: Chaoyang, Fengtai, Shijingshan, and Haidian; (3) New urban development zone: Fangshan, Tongzhou, Shunyi, Changping, and Daxing; and (4) Ecological conservation development zone: Mentougou, Huairou, Pinggu, Miyun, and Yanqing.
[†] *Source:* Beijing Statistical Yearbook, 2018. Table 3-3, Total Number and Density of Permanent Population (By District) (2017). http:/tjj.beijing.gov.cn/nj/main/2018-tjnj /zk/indexeh.htm.

Notes:
a. Parkland Green Space is the green space that is open to the public and has more than 65% green coverage, such as municipal parks, community parks, street-side green land, and other green land in gardens.
b. Per Capita Park Green Space is calculated on the basis of nonagricultural household population.

Palace, 350 hectares), the Summer Palace (290 hectares), Chaoyang Park (289 hectares), the Temple of Heaven (273 hectares), and Beihai Park (71 hectares). Each of these landmarks provides a large parkland green space, but there are very few smaller, communal green spaces between them. With fewer parks overall, Beijing's park density (number of parks per ten thousand square kilometers) was 545 in 2016, lower than that of other first tier Chinese megacities: Shenzhen (3,110), Shanghai (1,033), and Guangzhou (862). In addition, most parks in Beijing are historical or cultural landmarks where large numbers of tourists impede the activities of local residents. In contrast, other Chinese megacities and many of the world cities may have smaller but more communal parks that are convenient and integral to the daily lives of local residents.

The second type of green space in Beijing, the communal park, is often too scarce to allow easy accessibility, and the parks are too small to accommodate neighborhood needs. Research shows that urban green space smaller than three hectares (7.4 acres) usually does not provide adequate benefits for cooling and improving air quality in the surrounding area. Most of the communal green space in Beijing's residential areas looks like a planning afterthought, just small patches of green that provide little space for communal gatherings and relaxation, and is too small to help mitigate the effects of the urban heat island. Competing uses often cause conflicts among residents because of their limited space and close proximity to living quarters, as shown in the case of public square dancing.

In addition to distribution and configuration, there are ecological issues in maintaining and expanding green space. Traditionally, locally acclimated trees, such as the Chinese scholar tree (*Sophora japonica*), composed most of Beijing's green space. In recent years, large-scale grassy lawns were created as a way to quickly expand green space—a rush job for subordinate bureaucrats to meet their greening targets as mandated by the municipal government. In comparison to most trees, lawns are costly to maintain, water consuming, and much less effective in ameliorating urban heat island or absorbing greenhouse gases. Ironically, lawns in Chinese cities are not accessible to the general public! As a result, the proliferation of lawns in Beijing boosted government statistics but did little to improve community access to green space. Beijing has come to recognize and confront some of the challenges and problems in greening the city. Official plans call for increasing Beijing's forest coverage to 45 percent of the city's total land area and 32 percent of the urbanized area of the Beijing Plain by 2022, when per capita green space should reach 16.6 square meters. The plans also set the goal of distributing new green space more evenly so that up to 87 percent of the population will live within 500 meters (1,640 feet) of green space in a public park. Projects are underway to improve the ecological conditions in the existing green space by limiting new grassy lawns and fostering multilayered tree and grass canopies. Perhaps one day Beijing will regain its reputation as the city of forests, as it is tasked to lead China in building a new "ecologically based civilization."

Public Transit Infrastructure and Traffic Management

Locals and visitors are more likely now than ever to find themselves stuck in Beijing's traffic. An inquiry of Beijing's traffic conditions would solicit unanimous complaints and even condemnation. Traffic congestion was cited as the number one social issue to 82.8 percent of residents surveyed according to the "Beijing Development Report on Social Governance, 2018–2019," published by the Beijing Academy of Social Sciences in June 2019. The 2018 TomTom Traffic Index ranked Beijing 30th among the world's most congested cities among the 403 cities from 56 countries surveyed and 16th among the megacities (having a population larger than eight million). It is noteworthy that Beijing's 2018 ranking was actually an improvement from what it had been two years earlier, when it was ranked 10th worst in traffic congestion among the surveyed cities and 6th among the megacities. In 2018, Beijing's congestion index was slightly better than Guangzhou (13th) and Tokyo (15th) but worse than London, Paris, New York City, Shenzhen, and Shanghai.[11]

On average, a person in Beijing spent forty-seven more minutes a day to get where he or she needed to go than if there had not been traffic congestion. The hundred thousand stop-and-go cars in the streets have become a major source of greenhouse gas emissions that, among other damages, contribute to Beijing's horrendous smog as the city's crackdown on stationary polluters, such as manufacturing facilities, has gained progress.

Four decades ago, China was truly a kingdom of bicycles, reaching 670 million in the early 1990s. Most people in Beijing, like elsewhere in China, exercised their mobility by walking, taking public transit, or riding bicycles. Most city streets became dead quiet at dusk. Today, there are a half billion bicycles in China, a sharp decline from a quarter century ago; in contrast, private car ownership has skyrocketed, cramming highways and city streets in a nightmarish manner. There are over six million registered automobiles in Beijing now. How did Beijing, notorious for its gridlock traffic, get here in merely four decades?

To a certain extent, Beijing's traffic debacle has to do with its inherited urban design. As the imperial capital, Beijing was built in three rectangular zones centered on the royal palaces: the Forbidden City, the Imperial City, and the city itself (which came to be known as the Inner City after the southern walled addition was added in mid-1550s). Walls were used

Heavy traffic on North Fourth Ring Road of Beijing. Symptomatic of megacities in emerging economies, Beijing's traffic problems are the results of its historical layout, rapid expansion, and inadequate planning. Worsening traffic has resulted in most pressing environmental and socioeconomic challenges to the city. (Xi Zhang/Dreamstime.com)

for socioeconomic and, during the Qing Dynasty, ethnic segregations as well as for defense. Such a morphology became a physical hindrance for modern urban traffic that both the early ROC government and the PRC government tried to overcome but failed, in part because the central government occupied the center of the city. Furthermore, the PRC government put even greater symbolic emphasis on the center of Beijing, including expanding Tiananmen Square and building political landmarks around the square, making it the converging point for traffic. Records show that the core capital function zone, which accounts for 0.6 percent of the total municipal area, had 30 percent of the city's total traffic in the early 2000s.

It is wrong, however, to blame the historical urban design for today's traffic woes. Until recent years, Beijing's traffic was busy but by no means horrendous. The ultimate culprit, undoubtedly, is the car: the number of cars, the number of private cars, and the way the cars are used. Beijing has the largest number of cars and the largest number of private cars among all Chinese province-level divisions. The large number of private cars shows both overwhelming private wealth and the government's failure to control the number of private cars. In addition, the central government is responsible for its physical occupation of the city center and the enormous fleet of official vehicles.

Until the late 1980s, Beijing was a city on bicycles. Public transportation was limited, and there were very few taxis and even fewer private cars. There were more than seven million bike riders, and the number of bikes outnumbered motor vehicles by a ten to one margin. Bicycles, almost all nonsport models with only one gear, were not built for speed but for durability.

Economic reform ushered in a period of rapid development and growth of wealth, which made private automobiles desirable and more affordable. In 1994, the PRC government opened up the private car market and encouraged citizens to purchase and own cars. Beijing's privately owned automobiles skyrocketed from about 7,000 in 1987 to a whopping 4.67 million in 2017. The percentage of privately owned cars jumped from a mere 3.6 percent to consistently over 80 percent since 2009 (Table 6.7). In addition, there are thousands more motor vehicles registered in other provinces but used regularly in Beijing. In contrast, Beijing residents who use bicycles as their transportation mode drastically declined, from 60 percent in 1995 to barely 20 percent in 2010.[12]

Driving has become the preferred way of travel in Chinese cities. Beijing's private car use exceeds that of its peer cities. For example, a report stated that Beijing's private car use was 1.5 times that of London and

Table 6.7   Automobiles Statistics, Selected Years[1] (1,000)

Year	Total	Registered for Civilian Use[2]	Privately Owned	% Privately Owned
1987		193	7	3.6%
1992		341	49	14.4%
1997		784	298	38.0%
2002	1,899	1,339	811	60.6%
2007	3,128	2,778	2,121	76.3%
2012	5,200	4,957	4,075	82.2%
2017	5,909	5,638	4,672	82.9%

Source: Beijing Statistical Yearbook, 2017. Table 15-1, Transport, Post and Telecommunication (1978–2016). http://www.bjstats.gov.cn/nj/main/2017-tjnj/zk/indexeh.htm.

Notes:
[1] The first year with statistics for privately owned cars.
[2] Vehicles registered for civilian use (nongovernmental).

2.3 times that of Tokyo. Nearly half of the car trips were for a destination within 5 kilometers (3.1 miles). This stunning car dependency is in part due to the lifestyle change; it may be an overcompensation for the many who lived through an era of spartan lifestyle. Another reason for the car dependency may be due to the separation of residential and service functions in new urban development. Massive high-rise residential communities often lack adequate basic services such as retail, health, and public transit facilities. Some residents complained that it was not worth their while to walk fifteen to twenty minutes to the nearest subway station or grocery store, so they ended up driving to get to where they needed to be.

Parking has become an insurmountable challenge in Chinese cities, which were ill prepared to accommodate the explosive growth of private automobiles with both road networks and parking facilities. In Beijing's core capital function zone alone, it is estimated that there is a shortfall of 150,000 parking spaces. Streets are overspilling with both legally and illegally parked cars, which choke off the already crowded streets and slow traffic even further. Beijing authorities have identified poor management for roadside parking as one of the exacerbating factors of traffic congestion, but sustainable solutions are yet to be found.

In the meantime, Beijing has made substantial progress in developing public transportation. The city has twenty-two subway lines with a combined length of 602 kilometers (374 miles). An additional 397 kilometers (245 miles) of subway lines are planned to be added by 2021. But there are issues with the long-term planning of public transportation. Some experts have pointed out that the rapidly growing subway system in Beijing has the same checkerboard pattern, basically as a complement rather than an alternative to the already congested surface public transportation. Also, demand caused by the skyrocketing population growth has outpaced public transit growth, bringing the transit system to the brink of failure. On a regular weekday, Beijing's subway system handles about ten million riders, and conditions during rush hours are every bit as challenging as those in Tokyo, which is known for its encumbering jam-packed cars during rush hours.

Beijing's traffic problems also have to do with the reckless and illegal behaviors of some cyclists and pedestrians on the one hand and motorists on the other. They violate traffic rules and encroach on each other's lanes, causing frequent slowdowns and accidents. Traffic can be improved in this regard with better design and management as well as more effective law enforcement. More importantly, public awareness and increased civility can greatly help alleviate traffic congestions.

Beijing is making continued efforts to improve traffic conditions, which is crucial to boosting environmental quality and achieving sustainable

YIKATONG

Visitors should take advantage of the so-called Yikatong (One-Card Pass, or the Beijing Municipal Administration & Communication Card), which is a smart card for public transit that receives a 50 percent discount for normal bus fares in Beijing's urban districts. It can also be used as a debit card for a wide range and increasing number of goods and services, such as KFC and Walmart. Yikatong can be purchased and refilled at most ticket counters at Beijing subway stations and some bus stations. It can also be refunded at many designated locations, including the Beijing Capital International Airport (Terminals 2 and 3). Yikatong does not have photo ID capability and can be transferred. Read the instructions and explanations for more details (https://www.bmac.com.cn).

growth. A successful measure, called the odd-even license plate policy, was implemented during the 2008 Beijing Summer Olympics. Since then, new traffic control measures have included road space rationing regulations such as the end-number license plate policy; a strict lottery system for new motor vehicle registration; the yellow-labeled car policy that keeps cars that fail national emission tests out of the Fifth Ring Road; and encouragement to purchase clean energy vehicles through rebates and the expansion of electric charging stations. There is also increasing public support for congestion fee regulations. Nonetheless, the key to reducing traffic congestion is to discourage private car use, especially for short travel distances and stop-and-go driving. It would be a more achievable goal with better access to services and innovative public transportation alternatives.

A stunning recent development was the surge and fade of bikeshare in China. There were 2.2 million bikeshare bicycles in Beijing in 2016, and an average of four million passenger trips were made each day in Beijing using Mobike alone, about 50 percent of which were to or from subway stations. The fervor of bikeshare as a business venture has subsided due to the traffic chaos and economic losses that unregulated and unaccountable bikeshare services created. Some small bikeshare companies have failed, and the major players, such as Ofo and Mobike, are under financial pressure. What happened to China's bikeshare experiment, however, may have revived the interest in bicycle use in major cities such as Beijing. There is a push to reclaim and renovate bicycle lanes and pedestrian walkways, which had been encroached on by motor vehicles as side streets and parking spaces. There are currently over 1,014 kilometers (630 miles) of bicycle lanes and pedestrian sidewalks in Beijing, and the municipal government has set the target of increasing them to 3,200 kilometers (1,988 miles) by 2020.

Other Environmental Challenges

For many years, travelers and locals alike encountered an acute problem in China: public restrooms were primitive, few and far between, and invariably filled with flies and stench. Until the Ming Dynasty (1368–1644), Beijing was ahead of its time in human waste management, and travelers from Renaissance Europe had high praise for Beijing's sewer system. By late 1800s, the premodern sanitary system had become outdated and deteriorated, coinciding with China's overall decline. The Legation Quarter was often overwhelmed by the pervasive odor from open sewers, spoiling the otherwise good life of the expatriates. In the 1950s, Beijing replaced thousands of open-air restrooms with enclosed brick outhouses and converted many to flushable squatting toilets in the 1970s. However, public restrooms in Beijing, and indeed throughout China, have remained substandard and a public health nightmare.

As China began to undergo economic growth and achieve higher living standards during the reform era, public restrooms in good quantity and quality became an emergent matter for not only public service but also public health. Beijing began to build sanitary modern restrooms for the 1990 Beijing Asian Games, though these upscale restrooms were few and far between, and users often had to pay a fee. Beijing became highly motivated to modernize its public restrooms after winning the bid to host the 2008 Summer Olympics, but the real game changer came in 2015, when the PRC's National Tourism Administration launched a three-year campaign to build or modernize 25,000 public restrooms across China with USD 2 billion in funding. It also implemented an evaluation method that culminates in a rating system dubbed the "toilet index." Also, smartphone apps have been developed to help people locate the nearest public restrooms.

Beijing took the lead in this nationwide "revolution." It tops Chinese cities with about fourteen thousand upgraded public restrooms and has the second-highest ratio for public restrooms over residential population. In 2016, the municipal government announced plans to build state-of-the-art public toilets. These public restrooms feature Wi-Fi, ATMs, and even charging ports for electronics as well as new ventilation and heating and air-conditioning. Public restrooms in bars and restaurants around the city also began to provide transgender restrooms that are labeled "all gender toilet" in English. In the remaining traditional neighborhoods, where there is no indoor plumbing, the modern public restrooms have become a source of neighborhood pride and a place for neighbors to meet and socialize. Residents have also complained and intervened when passersby fail to follow hygiene norms while using the neighborhood restrooms, a sign of fledgling civic pride and accountability.

CONCLUDING THOUGHTS

Beijing is tackling its wide range of environmental challenges head-on. A clean and healthy environment is a prerequisite for the city to support the capital's functions as the national political center, cultural center, center of international exchange, and center of technological innovation. Progress has been made in improving environmental quality. For example, in 2013, Beijing's annual mean PM2.5 concentration was 89.5 micrograms per cubic meter; it went down to 51.0 micrograms per cubic meter in 2018, a 75 percent decrease. The Beijing-Tianjin-Hebei region (Jing-Jin-Ji) also saw a 48 percent decrease of PM2.5 concentration during the same period of time. Beijing residents hail the progress because the air quality, though still not good, has indeed improved.

The alleviation of one environmental problem may sometimes exacerbate another environmental problem. Large-scale reforestation to the north and west of Beijing has reduced the impact of sand and dust storms, but the reduced wind frequency and velocity has also weakened nature's ability to disperse smog. There are also setbacks in improvement efforts. In 2017, there was great fanfare when the last coal-fired power plant in Beijing ceased operation. In the early winter of 2018, however, an unexpected natural gas supply shortfall, coupled with a strong cold wave, forced the Beijing Municipal Government to restart part of the coal-fired power plant to ensure adequate heating service. Some of Beijing's environmental challenges, such as air pollution and water scarcity, are due to both natural and human causes that Beijing can only deal with through regional coordination, which requires support from the central government and cooperation from other jurisdictions.

The jury is still out as to whether Beijing can sustain the environmental improvements it has achieved in recent years. Beijing has identified some of the root causes—natural, socioeconomic, cultural, and political—for its environmental woes. To move forward, Beijing would need intensified research, increasing public awareness, sound public policy, and adequate government funding. Beijing must succeed in its endeavors because failure is not an option for the capital and model for the rest of China.

BEIJING'S ORGANIZED CHAOS

I have been to Beijing numerous times in the last twenty years. There were so many changes in people, infrastructure, and living conditions. June 1997 was my first time ever to China. Compared to O'Hare, with which I was familiar, Beijing's airport terminal was very dated, small and dark. As we drove into the city, I was amazed by the organized chaos. Large numbers of bicyclists and pedestrians swarm the streets, competing with each other and with motor vehicles, most of which were Volkswagens and Japanese cars. Noisy tractors driven by villagers crawled along and blocked traffic at the intersections. There were some tall buildings, but a lot of old, one-story dwellings were still sprawling in many parts of the city, where folks had lived for generations.

One thing that struck me was that I felt intuitively safe in this chaotic city of millions. People appeared to be amicable and carefree, and they were everywhere, all the time. There were large groups of people playing mahjong, dancing, and singing in the neighborhoods and parks during the day and night. I also noticed some older folks wearing red arm bands standing at street corners and inspecting the surroundings. I was told they were community volunteers for public safety. I had never thought "neighborhood watch" could become so up close and personal, but it must be working well to deter crimes. It was annoying, though, to experience a lack of civility in crowded public places, where people would almost always push and shove their way through.

I went to Beijing in the fall of 2012 again. Fifteen years had passed since my first visit to the city, but it might as well have been a century! The new airport terminal (the third one since 1997) was very fancy and cavernous, but a bit too out of human scale. There were so many more cars, and so many luxury ones. There were still lots of bicyclists but not nearly as many as fifteen years ago. The new expressways were such a far cry from the narrow, jammed streets, and now there were another two business loops, which they called "ring roads," encircling the city. Skyscrapers were everywhere, many with exotic, postmodern designs. People I knew lived so much better! Better housing, good cars, quality food, fashionable clothing, and plenty of personal services.

All these changes, however, diminished my unnamed nostalgia: I missed "the old city" that was not as clean and tony, but was full of humanity. When the new bulldozed over the old, progress triumphed; lost were the cultural heritage and the sense of place, which could not be made up by the BMWs and high-rise condos.

—Elizabeth

NOTES

1. Economist Intelligence Unit, "The Global Liveability Index 2018: A Free Overview," *The Economist*, accessed September 2, 2019, https://pages.eiu.com/rs/753-RIQ-438/images/The_Global_Liveability_Index_2018.pdf.

2. William Edgar Geil, *Eighteen Capitals of China* (Philadelphia: J. B. Lippincott Company, 1911).

3. Jonathan Watts, "China: The Air Pollution Capital of the World," *The Lancet* 366, no. 9499 (November 19, 2005): 1761–1762, https://doi.org/10.1016/S0140-6736(05)67711-2.

4. Some of the media headlines include, "Air Quality Improvement Drive Paying off in the Capital," *China Daily*, March 21, 2018, https://www.telegraph.co.uk/china-watch/society/air-quality-improvement/; "'Airpocalypse' Over? Beijing

Breathes Easier as Clean Air Drive Pays Off, US Embassy Smog Readings Suggest," *South China Morning Post*, August 20, 2018, https://www.scmp.com/news/china /policies-politics/article/2160444/beijings-clean-air-drive-paying-swift-recovery; "Beijing Enjoys the Bluest Skies in a Decade," *Bloomberg News*, August 19, 2018, https://www.bloomberg.com/news/articles/2018-08-19/xi-s-clean-energy-drive -paints-bluest-sky-over-beijing-in-decade; and Michael Greenstone, "Four Years after Declaring War on Pollution, China Is Winning," *New York Times*, March 12, 2018, https://www.nytimes.com/2018/03/12/upshot/china-pollution-environment -longer-lives.html. The technical support document for the above article can be found here: https://epic.uchicago.edu/research/new-evidence-on-the-impact-of -sustained-exposure-to-air-pollution-on-life-expectancy-from-chinas-huai-river -policy/.

5. Harvard John A. Paulson School of Engineering and Applied Sciences, "A Clearer Path to Clean Air in China: Formaldehyde—Not Sulfur Dioxide—May Be the Key to China's Stubborn Problem of Wintertime Air Pollution," *Science Daily*, October 18, 2018, https://www.sciencedaily.com/releases/2018/10/181018124948 .htm.

6. Alex Gray, "These Are the Cities with the Worst Noise Pollution," World Economic Forum, March 27, 2017, https://www.weforum.org/agenda/2017/03 /these-are-the-cities-with-the-worst-noise-pollution.

7. Nick Kirkpatrick, "China's War on Square-Dancing Grannies," *Washington Post*, March 25, 2015, https://www.washingtonpost.com/news/morning-mix/wp /2015/03/25/chinas-war-on-square-dancing-grannies/?noredirect=on&utm _term=.600b425f3d74.

8. Serenitie Wang, "Beijing Gets Tough on Dancing Grannies," CNN, February 28, 2017, https://www.cnn.com/2017/02/28/asia/china-gets-tough-on-dancing -grannies/index.html.

9. "Beijing Joining the Ranks of the World's Most Liveable Cities," United Nations Environment Programme, July 12, 2018, https://www.unenvironment.org /news-and-stories/story/beijing-joining-ranks-worlds-most-liveable-cities.

10. "China Unveils Green Development Index Ranking," *China Daily*, December 26, 2017, https://www.chinadaily.com.cn/a/201712/26/WS5a41bd83a 31008cf16da3800.html.

11. "Traffic Index 2018," TomTom, accessed September 21, 2019, https://www .tomtom.com/en_gb/traffic-index/ranking/?population=MEGA. Rome was not included in the 2018 survey.

12. Jeffrey Hays, "Bicycles and Cycling in China," Facts and Details, last updated July 2011, http://factsanddetails.com/china/cat13/sub86/item1914.html.

7

Local Crime and Violence

Crimes and violence are entrenched in the city, the theater of humanity. As a megacity and the capital of the largest emerging economy, how does Beijing fare in comparison to its peers in China and the world in terms of public safety? Is it safe to walk alone on the streets at night in Beijing? Are locals and visitors alike vulnerable to theft and robbery? Are there frequent public disturbances? What is the situation of crimes and violence hidden from public view, such as criminal gangs and organized crime, domestic abuse, and sexual exploitation? What are the measures for crime prevention?

China's criminal law classifies crimes into ten categories or "chapters" (Table 7.1), and most common crimes fall under chapters 2, 4, 5, and 6. It is difficult to quantitatively compare the conditions of urban crimes among different countries because they vary widely in criminal codes, law enforcement, statistics collection, and data reporting. It is possible, however, to compare Beijing's public safety with cities of comparable size and importance using qualitative information from government data, media coverage, police reports, and academic research. Analyses based on such comparisons can reveal common and unique characteristics of Beijing's patterns and trends of crimes as well as their causes and prevention.

The Economist Intelligence Unit (EIU) evaluated the overall security of sixty cities in the world, including thirty-one megacities, in its "Safe Cities Index 2019."[1] EIU selected fifty-seven distinct factors in four categories for its research, and Beijing landed right in the middle of the ratings at

Table 7.1   The Criminal Code of PRC, Part II Special Provisions (2018)

Chapter I Crimes of Endangering National Security

Chapter II Crimes of Endangering Public Security

Chapter III Crimes of Undermining the Order of Socialist Market Economy

Chapter IV Crimes of Infringing upon the Rights of the Person and the Democratic Rights of Citizens

Chapter V The Crime of Encroaching on Property

Chapter VI Crimes of Disrupting the Order of Social Administration

Chapter VII Crimes of Endangering the Interests of National Defense

Chapter VIII Graft and Bribery

Chapter IX Crimes of Dereliction of Duty

Chapter X Crimes of Violation of Duty by Military Personnel

Source: "Criminal Law of the People's Republic of China." Permanent Mission of the People's Republic of China to the United Nations and Other International Organizations in Vienna. https://www.fmprc.gov.cn/ce/cgvienna/eng/dbtyw/jdwt/crimelaw/t209043.htm.

thirty-first place, behind the other five cities in the Contemporary World Cities series: Tokyo (first), London (fourteenth), New York (fifteenth), Paris (twenty-third), and Rome (thirtieth). It fared better among cities in developing countries versus those in developed and oil-rich countries, placing first and followed by Shanghai, Santiago, Buenos Aires, and Kuala Lumpur. It was a one-spot improvement for Beijing over 2017's EIU safe city report, in which it was ranked behind Kuala Lumpur.

In terms of the four categories, Beijing was mostly in the middle range, but it did better in terms of personal security, ranking twenty-fifth overall and second among cities in developing countries (Table 7.2) and ahead of Chicago, San Francisco, New York City, and Los Angeles. Some may take issue with the methodology and findings of this report, but neither appeared to be skewed in Beijing's favor. EIU's relatively high rating for Beijing's personal security, an indicator based on an evaluation of risks from crimes, violence, and other man-made threats, shows that it is a safe city for most individuals in terms of crimes and violence.

The Chinese central and local governments do not regularly publish statistics regarding crimes affecting personal safety, which makes quantitative assessment difficult. Media reports and academic publications on crimes and violence provide snapshots that help establish a qualitative sketch of Beijing's conditions for personal security. For example, in 2013, the Beijing Academy of Social Sciences published a report on Beijing's public safety in which Beijing was compared with London, New York, Tokyo,

Table 7.2   Beijing's Rank by Factor, Safe Cities Index 2019

Criteria	Beijing's Rank, All 60 Cities	Beijing's Rank, Cities from Developing Countries
Overall Rank	31	1
Digital Security	36	6^1
Health Security	33	2^2
Infrastructure Security	33	2^3
Personal Security	25	2^4

Source: "Safe Cities Index 2019: Urban Security and Resilience in an Interconnected World." Economist Intelligence Unit. https://safecities.economist.com/wp-content/uploads/2019/08/Aug-5-ENG-NEC-Safe-Cities-2019-270x210-19-screen.pdf.

Notes:
[1] Behind Buenos Aries, Santiago, Istanbul, Johannesburg, and Mexico City.
[2] Behind Buenos Aries.
[3] Behind Istanbul (31st).
[4] Behind Shanghai (23rd).

and Paris as well as Shanghai, Tianjin, and Chongqing (the other three centrally administered municipalities in China). It showed that, between 2009 and 2011, Beijing ranked first among the eight cities in regard to crime prevention. It also revealed that Beijing's crime rates were trending down, and the clearance rate of criminal cases was increasing.

For Americans traveling overseas, a useful source of information on personal security is a specific country's "Crime & Safety Report" by the Overseas Security Advisory Council (OSAC) under the Bureau of Diplomatic Security of the U.S. Department of State. In 2019, the OSAC considered Beijing as having "minimal risk from crime,"[2] the same assessment as Tokyo. In comparison, London, Paris, and Rome were considered as having "moderate" threat or risk from crime. The OSAC's conclusions and advisories are generally consistent with the observations and experiences of foreigners who have visited or lived in Beijing in recent years. The report pointed out that the United States and other foreign nationals were mostly subjected to petty crimes such as pickpocketing, credit card fraud, and financial scams. Violent crimes against foreigners were relatively rare and would most likely take place in bars and night clubs.

High crime rates and violence are common among the megacities in developing countries because of poor governance due to poverty and corruption. Crimes in Chinese cities, Beijing included, increased exponentially after reform started in the late 1970s, as government's ironfisted control

---

PUBLIC SAFETY CONDITIONS FOR U.S. VISITORS

The Overseas Security Advisory Council (OSAC) states that "there is minimal risk from crime in Beijing. China's capital has a population of more than 21.5 million people and is generally safe when compared to other global cities." Criminal activities that affect foreign visitors include property crimes, financial scams, prostitution, and illicit drugs. Slow police response (emergency number 110) may be partially compensated by the strong presence of public safety volunteers who sport distinct red armbands. Random violence does occur in Beijing but is uncommon. The general caution and common sense that a person exercises in Western cities should suffice in improving personal safety. OSAC recommends U.S. citizens register with the Smart Traveler Enrollment Program (https://step.state.gov/STEP).

---

from the previous decades began to loosen. This prompted Nicholas Kristof, then a *New York Times* correspondent in Beijing, to report in 1992 on the public outrage over the rising crime waves.[3] It is remarkable that Beijing has since become a much safer city for residents and visitors despite permeating inequality and injustice in economic, social, and environmental realms. There are similarities among Chinese cities regarding the types and intensity of crimes as well as prevention measures, although Beijing receives more resources and broader powers in crime prevention under the mandate to safeguard the capital's key functions.

Serious crimes and violence do exist in Beijing. There have been over one hundred thousand cases recorded annually in recent years involving social order and public safety, far exceeding the fewer than forty thousand cases recorded in Tokyo during the same period, despite increasing pressure on crimes by authorities. Crimes and violence affect communities quite differently based on their socioeconomic status, which also manifests in distinct spatial patterns.

CRIMINAL GANGS AND ORGANIZED CRIME

Criminal gangs and organized crime are cancerous segments of society. The distinction between the two may lie in their operational scope and organizational sophistication. Gangs are criminal groups that focus on gaining local control through violence, and they often thrive on racketeering and extortion in the community. In comparison, organized crime focuses on illegal operations that aim at achieving substantial financial gains and legitimizing their businesses. Some gangs evolve into organized criminal networks, and organized crime frequently resorts to violence to protect and expand its interests. Both represent challenges to the status quo by disenfranchised socioeconomic groups, which are often based on regional cliques, and as a result, they incur the wrath of the political-security apparatus of the society. In 2015 alone, Beijing authorities took down over four hundred crime organizations, most of which had committed crimes such as scalping and racketeering, but over thirty of them had engaged in sophisticated operations of financial fraud through invasion of privacy and telecommunications scams. At the same time, criminal gangs and organized crime are sometimes in collusion with the political establishment, gaining protection by doing the dirty bidding for corrupt members of the government and shady characters in the legitimate business community.

Chinese criminal gangs and organized crime have a long and complicated history. After 1949, the PRC government effectively weeded out traditional secret societies and underground criminal organizations, including the entrenched ones in Beijing. There continued to be violent street gangs that fed off their low-income neighborhoods, but they never amounted to more than small-time hooligans that the authorities cracked down on periodically. In the early years of economic reform, China's gang violence reached an alarming level largely due to economic hardship, spiking population mobility, and loosened government control. In Beijing, for example, over four hundred thousand local residents, about 8.6 percent of the city's urban population, were unemployed in the early 1980s. Many restless and disillusioned youth became involved in violence and crimes.

As crimes and gang violence swept through China, the PRC government launched the first major crackdown in the reform era in 1983, in which up to twenty-four thousand convicted criminals were sentenced to capital punishment and many more were sent to border regions such as Xinjiang to serve their sentences. The crackdown temporarily improved public safety, but violent crimes would spike again and again when new generations of marginalized youth came of age. The PRC government subsequently launched further crackdowns in 1996, 2001, and 2010 in an attempt to stamp out the resurgence of gang activity and violent crimes.

Criminal gangs in Beijing have undergone a transition in the last several decades. The overall trend appears to show a decline of "native" gangs. These gangs mainly consisted of those from the city's "household registered population," meaning the residents who have legal residential status and are entitled to a wide range of benefits in Beijing. The decrease may partly be due to the much improved socioeconomic conditions, which deemed it unnecessary and unwise to form criminal gangs. Another reason might be that massive and sustained urban renewal projects during the last several decades have effectively dismantled a large number of traditional neighborhoods in the city, which had, by default, destroyed the social fabric and cultural hotbed for the native gangs.

In the meantime, economic reform opened the floodgate for population mobility and brought millions of migrants from rural areas to the cities and from the interior to the coastal regions of China. The large disenfranchised migrant population became both a fertile recruiting ground and the most victimized target of gang activities. These gangs became dominant in common crimes such as racketeering and extortion, property theft, human trafficking, and prostitution. They sometimes specialized in criminal activities and employed violence to get their way. They often thrived on oppressing the migrant communities, who often lack resources and government support to protect themselves.

An infamous example of migrant gangs was the rise and fall of an ethnic Korean criminal group from Northeast China (Manchuria) in the 1990s. Headed by Li Zhengguang, the group built an extensive network that spanned from Northeast China to Beijing and carried out a violent takeover of dining and entertainment businesses in the fast-growing Chaoyang District of Beijing. Their rivals and victims were mostly also ethnic Koreans from Northeast China. Through extortion, kidnapping, torture, and assassination, the gang had taken over a significant portion of restaurants and night clubs in the district before it was crushed by the authorities. Key members of the group were convicted, and its leader, Li, was sentenced to capital punishment for his crimes.

Crime organizations in Beijing have become more sophisticated in disguising their activities and avoiding publicity. Criminal gangs usually stay underground and refrain from using violence in public to evade pressure from the particularly vigilant authorities of the capital. In some cases, they have also found protection from corrupt officials through bribery or blackmail. Some entertainment establishments were known to be hubs of drugs and prostitution, but they continued to operate because of the ostensible protection from high-ranking officials in the government. Frequently, low-ranking officials and public servants are caught being protectors or even members of organized crime. In 2006, during the first major trial of a large organized crime group, the Hu brothers, three policemen and an officer in urban management (*chengguan*) were convicted of being "the protective umbrella" of the criminal gang, which was a major reason for the criminals' ability to continue their crime spree for more than a decade. Worse still, in 2007, a town's deputy mayor in the Tongzhou District of Beijing was convicted of being the head of a criminal organization and was sentenced to twenty years in prison.

Criminal gangs have penetrated lucrative businesses through intimidation, bribery, and technological know-how. One of the illegal and lucrative businesses for the increasingly sophisticated underground is operating as fraudulent intermediaries for a wide range of services in Beijing, such as the real estate rental market, medical services, the hospitality industry, and popular entertainment. Criminals have also established a scheme to defraud auto insurance companies by acting directly or coercing others to stage fake automobile accidents.

Beijing attracts white-collar organized crimes as China's leading financial and high-tech hub and upscale consumer market. The illegal manufacture of patented and trademarked consumer products has become a stubborn and costly organized crime in Beijing. The counterfeiters cluster in the large and transient migrant communities in the rural-urban fringe, making it difficult for authorities to monitor and control such crimes. During 2017 and the first half of 2018, over 90 percent of the busted counterfeiting operations in Beijing were involved in manufacturing fake or substandard health supplements for the local market, where there is a large and growing affluent middle-class clientele. These counterfeit products, however, are of very low quality at their best and contain harmful, even poisonous, ingredients at their worst, hence posing a public health threat.

There are more tech-savvy counterfeiters who break trademark and patent laws to make high-value commodities. In 2009, a criminal group manufactured thousands of fake tickets for sporting and concert events to be held in the "Bird's Nest," the main event stadium for the 2008 Beijing Summer Olympics. In 2015, U.S. authorities intercepted shipments of fake iPhones from China, and Beijing authorities subsequently uncovered a counterfeit operation that had six assembly lines, over a million cellphones and parts, and a stash of nearly USD 20 million in cash. The ring leaders were a couple who ran a technology company and built a factory in the suburban Shunyi District with several hundred employees. Their factory assembled fake iPhones for the underground market in the United States from old or broken cellphone motherboards imported from overseas and cellphone shells and parts from Shenzhen.

Organized crime in China has become interregional and international in the age of the Internet, with human trafficking and sexual exploitation as the two most heinous examples. Beijing's sex outlets were closed down within months of the Communist takeover in 1949, while it took Shanghai two years to accomplish the same. Prostitution has roared back during the reform era and has gone international. Women have disproportionately become victims by being coerced or forced into prostitution. Prostitution permeates personal services and entertainment venues in Chinese cities, often under the disguise of massage parlors, public bathhouses, and night clubs. There are exclusive clubs in Beijing with purported backing from high-level officials that are staffed by "high-class" courtesans. Prostitution rings have also infiltrated the hospitality sector. Single male hotel guests can expect numerous soliciting calls every night offering "massages" and other services.

The sex trade is both the cause and result of exploitation, the public health crisis, and violence in Chinese cities. In May 1999, a man in Beijing murdered eight young women in their dormitory just because he suspected they were prostitutes. While Beijing shares similar challenges with other Chinese cities in terms of sex-related crimes, it stands out as a major destination for foreign prostitutes. Beijing authorities conduct frequent operations to suppress the proliferation of the sex trade in an effort to safeguard the capital's reputation and image. It has become increasingly difficult, however, for authorities to keep prostitution in check.

Drug-related crimes have also worsened in China during the reform era. The first spike of drug use and related crimes came in the late 1990s and early 2000s as wealth expanded and socioeconomic pressure mounted. Beijing is a major center for illicit drug use in China, where the large and diverse community of white-collar professionals and foreign nationals, especially those in the entertainment industry, creates a substantial market for illicit drugs. Celebrities are frequently caught using drugs and soliciting sex illegally; some have been criminally convicted and publicly disgraced. Registered drug users in Beijing have exceeded twenty-five thousand, with an annual increase of more than 10 percent in the past decade. Beijing's drug addicts are relatively young, averaging thirty-three years of age, and the alarming trend is the increase of underage (younger than seventeen) population involved in drug use and trafficking, accounting for 5–7 percent of drug-related criminal cases in recent years.

Organized criminal enterprises have been targeting Beijing for its lucrative drug market. As the traditional heroin source from the "Golden Triangle" (Thailand, Laos, and Myanmar) began to dry up, heroin from the "Golden Crescent" (Afghanistan, Iran, and Pakistan), especially Afghanistan and Pakistan, began to take over the Chinese market, and its transporters are often foreign nationals or members of certain ethnic minority groups from western China. There is evidence that cocaine cartels in South America have also begun targeting the Chinese market, with Beijing as the main hub via civil aviation.

The illegal online drug trade is quite rampant. In late spring 2018, Beijing authorities took down seven online trade and solicitation groups of illicit drugs, detaining more than fifty people, twelve of whom were later arraigned. In recent years, synthetic drugs such as methamphetamine have gained popularity in China, affecting more than 60 percent of registered drug users. There is also an impending opioid crisis in China, accounting for 38.1 percent of all registered drug users in 2016, and the use of amphetamine-type stimulants is also on the rise, according to the "2017 Annual Report on Drug Control in China" issued by China's Ministry of Public Security.[4]

Beijing faces a unique challenge in combating drug crimes. There is a special provision in China's penal code that places some suspects of drug crimes in "the special population": suspects who are underage, pregnant, AIDS/HIV positive, patients with acute diseases, ethnic minorities, and foreign nationals. Only about 1 percent of Beijing's drug crime suspects can be classified under the special population, but the prosecution of these suspects presents a challenge to Beijing authorities due to humanitarian, diplomatic, and ethnic concerns. Beijing's special population mainly consists of foreign nationals and China's Muslim minorities. Legal procedures for international suspects are often slow and costly because of cultural (linguistic) barriers and diplomatic sensitivities. Authorities have encountered different hurdles in pursuing drug networks of Muslim minorities due to the inability to infiltrate Muslim communities in Beijing and the need to strike a delicate balance between enforcing the law and appeasing the PRC's Muslim groups. As a result, these suspects often receive more lenient treatment. Even the convicted felons from the special population are often released on parole with little official supervision.

Organized crime has quickly acquired both sophisticated skills and substantial wealth and has increasingly encroached upon legitimate businesses. Research shows that China is in the fourth stage of organized crime syndicates, which are getting more and more involved in pyramid schemes, communications fraud, and Internet-based scams. Scams are rampant and multiplying, and Beijing is the most-coveted target for organized crime because it is the mecca of financial and technological resources with advanced service infrastructure and an agglomeration of white-collar professionals.

The most prevalent organized crime today is financial fraud and scams. In the summer of 2018, the Beijing news media reported on a number of cracked cases of white-collar organized crime. On May 31, police raided a financial consulting and investment company in a new office tower and detained dozens of people for illegal financial transactions. In early July, Beijing authorities broke up an online gambling operation with revenue of CNY 320 million (USD 47 million) and connections to international gambling networks, arresting more than forty people. In December 2018, Beijing police announced that they had exterminated three crime groups involved in telecom scams and fraudulent loans.

There have also been international swindling operations targeting Beijing residents. Many of these criminal operations are carried out from overseas call centers run by Taiwanese and Mainland Chinese and are located in Chinatowns in Southeast Asian countries, where the criminals find shelter in the Chinese ethnic enclaves and take advantage of the corruptible law enforcement. In some cases, overseas criminals disguise themselves as U.S. military veterans who have found fortunes in Afghanistan or Iraq and promise to share with those who loan them some money to complete the transactions. Even when the criminal cases are solved and suspects arrested, extradition is often tricky legally and diplomatically, and sometimes there is a tug of war between Taiwan and Mainland China over who should be eligible for custody of the suspects.

Chinese authorities appear to play "whack-a-mole" games with organized crime by carrying out periodic sweeps of certain types of criminal organizations.[5] There have been nationwide campaigns against organized crime every decade or so since economic reform started four decades ago. Recently, however, the PRC government became alarmed over the widespread collusion between some local governments and organized crime groups. In many cases, the crime bosses had usurped elected offices at the village and township levels, undermining the judicial and governing systems of the state. In January 2018, the PRC government launched a major campaign to combat crime syndicates by exposing and punishing corrupt officials who are either directly engaged in organized crimes or who provide a protective umbrella for local mafia.

The latest crackdown has cast a wide net against criminal gangs and organized crime, though in Beijing it focuses on white-collar crimes such as rent manipulation, foreign currency laundering, mobile payment fraud, illegal banking and financial transactions, pyramid schemes, and collusion between organized crime and corrupt government officials or agencies. The central government sends supervisory groups to province-level, in some cases even lower, administrative divisions to ensure thorough execution of the campaign. By mid-2019, Beijing authorities had cracked a number of organized crime networks and criminal gangs, detained over one thousand suspects, and convicted over three hundred of them in nearly one hundred court cases. The authorities also confiscated illegal assets worth over CNY 600 million (USD 100 million).

Although Beijing is a major battleground against organized crime and gang violence in China, most residents and visitors may not be able to detect the intense war on crime behind the scenes because even the criminal gangs try not to exert violence publicly to avoid government crackdowns. Peace in the streets cannot gloss over the reality that criminal organizations are well and alive in the shadows of Beijing's skyscrapers. Government crackdowns have managed to keep organized crime and gang violence at bay, but they have yet to weed them out entirely. They will persist as part of the dark underbelly of Beijing, as they do in other world cities, as long as there is deeply rooted inequality and poverty and a parasitic environment festered by political corruption.

COMMON CRIMES AND VIOLENCE

Anyone can be directly affected by common crimes that threaten personal safety and property. Police records show that property crimes are by far the most prevalent types of criminal activities in Beijing. In 2012, for example, property crimes counted for 88 percent of all crimes recorded in Beijing, including theft (59.4%), automobile theft (10.5%), and burglary (18.1%). In contrast, violent crimes, such as homicide (0.1%), rape (0.7%), robbery (3.5%), and assault (7.5%), are low because they are the focus of law enforcement. Beijing authorities claim that they have solved nearly all homicide cases, in comparison to the two-thirds clearance rate for all crimes.

In the early decades of the reform era, violent crimes were more prevalent, and the city suffered numerous armed bank robberies, serial murders, and attacks on military personnel. Violent crimes in Beijing are relatively rare today, but violent acts are not uncommon in public, though many are either not reported or do not escalate to the level of chargeable crimes. Random violence often arises from disputes over minor traffic accidents, the quality of goods or services, public nuisance, and disorderly conduct. Physical altercations against service providers, such as medical professionals and traffic controllers, are also common in major cities such as Beijing. News media frequently report on incidents in which hospital staff are attacked by unruly patients or their families or a policeman is dragged and injured by a driver who tries to evade a traffic violation citation. These types of violence could be better managed with more timely and forceful police response, enforcement of existing laws and regulations, and greater public awareness through legal and civility education. Overall, though, public violence has been declining, which makes Beijing feel safe for residents and visitors alike.

For various reasons, some disgruntled individuals choose to exert revenge on the entire society as their twisted way of expressing grievance. This type of violence is highly unpredictable and hard to prevent. It persists with widening socioeconomic disparity and worsening government corruption. Beijing is the ideal place for these angry, twisted individuals to maximize publicity by inflicting major property damage or committing mass murder in public, usually using explosives or knives due to China's strict gun control. On July 20, 2013, for example, a petitioner detonated an explosive device at the Beijing Capital International Airport when authorities tried to stop him from distributing leaflets, severely injuring his arms and wounding a policeman. He claimed to have been beaten and disabled by public safety personnel in Guangdong Province but had not been able to get a fair trial in the local judicial system. He was eventually sentenced to six years in prison but ended up serving his term on medical parole. On February 11, 2018, a thirty-five-year-old man from Henan Province launched a knife attack on shoppers in a popular mall in Xidan, not far from Tiananmen Square, killing one woman and wounding twelve other people. On December 20, 2018, one person set off firecrackers in Terminal 2 of the Beijing Capital International Airport. No injuries or property damage were reported, but the perpetrator achieved his intended purpose of gaining public attention through causing a disturbance of the peace. The worst random violence is committed against children. In January 2019, a maintenance worker at an elementary school attacked the students with a hammer, injuring twenty kids. The attacker, a migrant worker from the northeastern province of Heilongjiang, lost his mind when his work contract was not renewed by his employer and went on to commit the heinous crime.

On rare occasions, violence directed at foreigners, especially Westerners, does take place because attacks on Westerners in the national capital are bound to provide greater publicity and blemish the country's image. During the 2008 Beijing Olympics, an American was killed by a Chinese man at Beijing's Drum Tower. While security deemed it a random act of violence, the murderer did single out Westerners to attack.[6] In 2015, a Chinese woman was killed and her French husband severely injured outside a shopping mall in Sanlitun, a leisure and entertainment district in the Diplomatic Quarter known for its night life. It was rumored that the sword-waving offender from northeastern Jilin Province later claimed that he wanted to kill an American.

In recent years, domestic violence has gained increased attention from the government and public alike. Traditionally, domestic violence, especially spousal abuse, was considered a familial scandal that needed to be resolved within the husband's family. The PRC government took a more proactive role in preventing domestic violence by allowing the victim to seek protection from the legal system and through intervention by women's organizations (e.g., local branches of All-China Women's Federation) and community mediators. In the reform era, however, victims of spousal, child, and elderly abuse have become more vulnerable because social and community interventions have weakened. The lack of public outrage and legal recourse for spousal and child abuse may in part be due to entrenched cultural tradition, which considers such abuses necessary for family morals and pecking orders. Elderly abuse, on the other hand, is never considered acceptable and is dealt with by swift condemnation and legal punishment.

Domestic violence is best illustrated by a high-profile case involving a popular actress and her multimillionaire husband. Bai Jing, an up-and-coming actress, married one of her suitors, a wealthy businessman from Beijing named Zhou, in 2010. She later started an affair with their trainer, who in turn extorted money from her husband and tricked him into committing infidelity so that Bai could divorce him with cause. In 2012, realizing that he had lost his money and honor at the hands of his wife and her lover, the desperate husband stabbed Bai to death and then committed suicide. This case shows that domestic violence may have become heightened as the old values and institutions rapidly fade away without new ones to replace them during China's Gilded Age. With China's biggest concentration of money, power, vanity, and greed, Beijing may witness a disproportionately large volume of domestic violence. A survey conducted in 2013 showed that one out of four female respondents from Beijing claimed to have been a victim of domestic violence.

In 2013, Beijing's Chaoyang Intermediate Court issued its verdict to a divorce case that might have been the straw that broke the camel's back in regard to public ambivalence toward domestic violence, especially spousal abuse. In 2011, Kim Lee, a former teacher from the United States, sued her husband, Li Yang, for divorce and sole custody of their three children, accusing him of domestic violence with photographic evidence of bodily injuries. Li Yang had been a household name in China because of his unique English learning method, Crazy English, and its successful business spin-off. Now a multimillionaire, he tried but failed to discredit the abuse allegations in court and in public opinion. The judge granted the divorce on the grounds of domestic abuse, plus a three-month restraining order, to Ms. Lee. The court also ordered Mr. Li to pay Ms. Lee CNY 50,000 (about USD 8,000) for mental anguish, child support for their daughters until they turned eighteen, plus CNY 12 million (USD 1.9 million) general compensation. This high-profile divorce case thrust domestic violence, especially spousal abuse, into the public spotlight as a national education moment.[7] Many women were emboldened by this case to overcome shame and fear for their rights and dignity.

On March 1, 2016, the PRC enacted the Anti-Domestic Violence Law, which empowers the judicial system and victims with legal tools to combat domestic violence. In 2016 and 2017, for example, the Beijing branch of the All-China Women's Federation received more than eight hundred petitions involving domestic violence, almost all of which were filed by women. During the same period of time, 11 percent of plaintiffs in all divorce cases claimed spousal abuse, and the court issued 145 protective orders.

While the vast majority of court filings of domestic violence cases involved spousal abuse, the legal system has started to pay attention to other types of domestic violence, especially increasing elderly abuse. Social services and media, such as the women's service hotline, have also been strengthened to provide more effective support to victims of domestic violence. Interestingly, in late 2016, the same year the Anti-Domestic Violence Law was enacted, a man who claimed abuse from his wife was granted a protective order.

CRIMES AND MIGRANT COMMUNITIES

There is a clear correlation between crimes and poverty. Beijing's migrant communities are mainly composed of low-skilled migrant workers and their families from poor rural areas, and they are disproportionately both contributors and victims of crimes in Beijing. The migrant population is estimated to have accounted for 20–30 percent of Beijing's total population since the 1990s but is responsible for 50–80 percent of total criminal offenses, according to various sources.

China's economic reform brought unprecedented mobility to the rural population, and the cities became the frontier of hope for them. Once in the cities, however, the young and undereducated men from rural villages found themselves trapped at the bottom of the socioeconomic pyramid with little chance for upward mobility. They suffered from systemic discrimination, often failed to receive their meager pay on time or at all, and were deprived of basic rights and services, such as access to affordable health care and public education for their children. The despicable conditions for migrant workers have not significantly improved since the first-generation migrant workers arrived in the cities nearly four decades ago. Enduring poverty has aroused resentment among migrant workers, a minority of whom commit crimes in desperation or in contempt. Beijing residents are particularly vigilant before Chinese New Year, when there is usually a spike of theft and burglary cases. By tradition, most migrant workers go back to their villages for the Chinese New Year. They are under enormous social and financial pressure to show their success by providing gifts for their families and friends back home. When they have little to show for their efforts, some resort to committing property crimes to meet their obligations.

The majority of migrant workers are, of course, not hard-core criminals. Their crimes reflect the injustice inflicted upon them by the society. Research has shown that migrant workers usually commit petty property crimes in a random fashion, or crimes of opportunity, including stealing manhole covers or cutting power transmission wires for scrap metal. Research shows that they are responsible for the majority of petty property crimes, about 70 percent, in Beijing, and most of their victims, also about 70 percent, are their peers. Robbery and home invasion, on the other hand, sometimes result in serious injuries or even homicides.

In addition to financial despair, migrant workers endure separation from their familiar social networks in the villages and suffer from segregation and discrimination in the cities. To gain greater security and power, some migrant workers form gangs, which in some cases evolve into more sophisticated criminal organizations. These gangs and organized crime groups are usually based on hometown or regional origins, and the migrant communities are their first victims.

A truly alarming trend is the increase of crimes committed by the children of migrant workers, many of whom were born in the city but, as research shows, have limited access to Beijing's public services and have endured discrimination. Resentment, sometimes even hatred, drives them to commit crimes. They also lack adequate parental guidance either because of their parents' inability or the parents' work-required absence. Many become school dropouts and child laborers, which forces them to be street smart. Data from three Beijing districts between 2006 and 2008 shows that more than two-thirds of juvenile crime convictions involved migrants, and 15–25 percent of these migrants were city-born children of migrant workers. In addition to committing petty property crimes, the children of migrant workers are also more likely to fall victim to substance abuse, violence, and sex crimes. The future generations of China's migrant workers, estimated to be at least two to three hundred million, are in jeopardy without fundamental improvement in socioeconomic justice.

Personal and property crimes in Beijing show three types of concentrations. First, low-income migrant communities on the urban-rural fringe suffer from high crime rates, where crimes propagated by poverty come home to roost. A government report published in early 2019 shows that only about one-third of the residents in the urban-rural fringe rated their community's public safety as "good," a ratio significantly below that in the urban area and outer suburbs. The authorities and social organizations are unable and, in some cases, unwilling to commit adequate resources to the migrant communities because of their highly transient population and continuously changing geographical locations. In the 1990s, the outer boundary of Beijing's urban sprawl was roughly along the Third Ring Road. Two decades later, Beijing's urban area has expanded beyond the Fifth Ring Road, and this is where migrant communities now cluster.

The second high-crime concentration is in locations with heavy public traffic, such as transit hubs and shopping centers. Thefts are particularly prevalent during rush hours or peak shopping seasons, such as the eve of Chinese New Year. Authorities play a cat-and-mouse game with the thieves, who usually operate in gangs, on transit lines, and in shopping centers. As police and security resources stretch thin, the government urges citizens to use common sense and safeguard their valuables in crowded public places and to avoid the crowds if possible.

Major entertainment venues, such as night clubs, pop music concerts, and sporting events, also fester a high volume of criminal activities. Thieves and robbers take advantage of the judgment impaired folks, shady characters peddle drugs and the sex trade, and an unruly crowd can turn into a ravaging mob that causes personal and property damages. Overall, Beijing is safe for foreigners because the traditional courtesy toward foreigners remains intact, and crimes against foreigners tend to incur the harshest punishments. A major exception to the overall safe environment in Beijing would be the chaotic and crowded entertainment venues. Visitors should maintain common sense and caution, as they should anywhere in the world. Bad actions and stupid behavior increase one's vulnerability to crimes in Beijing and elsewhere.

CRIME PREVENTION

It may come as a surprise to foreign visitors that there is no heavy police presence in public in Beijing. It is rare to see armed police patrols on city streets, and calling 110, China's police emergency number (120 is for medical emergencies), may or may not get a police response as quickly as one would expect in the United States. The use of lethal force by the police is also limited in comparison to that in the United States. Chinese police do focus on solving felony cases, and their preferred approach to crimes is community-based prevention.

Traditionally, family and kinship networks took on the task of reining in members who were at risk of committing crimes. Community surveillance was the second line of defense against crimes, as reflected in the community-based *baojia* system, which assisted authorities in maintaining order and control and operated throughout the ROC era (1911–1949). During the PRC era, urban subdistricts are responsible for organizing neighborhood activists to assist civic control and law enforcement in their communities. The voluntary neighborhood mediation committees patrol the neighborhood, arbitrate domestic and community disputes, discourage disorderly conduct, and report any suspicious persons or activities. Neighborhood activists in the cities mainly consist of retirees and homemakers; they have always played a vital role in community surveillance. As early as 1953, there were over fifty thousand neighborhood activists when Beijing's population was only two million.

Grassroots crime prevention has proven effective in maintaining law and order at the community level. Neighborhood activists wearing red armbands congregate on street corners and pace neighborhood streets. They intervene with disorderly conducts and petty crimes and report to law enforcement about more serious matters of public safety. Their dedication and success in recent years have led Beijing authorities to establish formal procedures for recruiting and regulating neighborhood activists through registration and training at subdistrict offices. By mid-2017, it was reported that Beijing had a total of 850,000 neighborhood activists, called registered community volunteers, who had undergone basic training in providing basic services to the public and overseeing the safety of neighborhoods. Active volunteers received a monthly token stipend of CNY 300–500 (about USD 44–72) and may receive cash rewards for tips and information that lead to stopping unlawful activities or solving criminal cases. On June 26, 2018, Global Times, a media outlet with government

Two elderly women on duty as community volunteers for public safety in Beijing. There are several hundred thousand registered community volunteers in Beijing alone, who play a key role in crime prevention. (Tonyv3112/Dreamstime.com)

backing, revealed that Beijing residents had received CNY 2 million (USD 305,000) in rewards for tips on illicit drugs deals alone.

Located in the eastern part of Beijing proper, the Chaoyang District has the largest population among Beijing's sixteen districts. As one of the four districts in the expanded urban function zone, the district is demographically and socioeconomically diverse. It is home to over 170 embassies and other diplomatic missions, Beijing's primary downtown business district (CBD), three-quarters of the city's skyscrapers, and the largest concentration of entertainment venues and night life establishments, including the famous Sanlitun. It has the most Starbucks among Beijing's districts with ninety-one (the Haidian District has the second most Starbucks with thirty-one). Upscale real estate projects have made Chaoyang a favorite residential choice for the nouveau riche, celebrities, and many foreign nationals. It has the largest number of residential properties listed for sale with listing prices above CNY 10 million (USD 1.45 million). It also has the largest migrant population living in slums and, as a result, only ranks fifth among the city's districts in terms of disposable income. It is not surprising that, in 2017, it had the largest number of criminal cases (38,155) in comparison to the second-place district, Haidian, which had 22,340 cases the same year.

It should not come as a surprise that Chaoyang District also has the largest number of registered community volunteers in Beijing. The residents, most of whom are typical middle-class folks, have come to bear the brunt of the high crime rates and are eager to help improve public safety in their communities. The district had a total of 140,000 community volunteers in 2018, or 300 per square kilometer (777 per square mile). There are 2,700 volunteer-staffed observation locations within the district, usually at busy traffic intersections or crowded public sites, each marked by a distinct "public security umbrella" and staffed by volunteers throughout the day. On average, these volunteers can provide over twenty thousand tips to the authorities every month. These tips have helped intercept unlawful activities, and some have led to criminal convictions, including several high-profile cases of illicit drug use and sex solicitation by celebrities, such as the son of Jackie Chan, the Hong Kong film star. The authorities have affectionately referred to the community volunteers as *Chaoyang Qunzhong* (masses or residents of Chaoyang District) in their public safety announcements, a nickname that has stuck. After helping crack a drug case involving a famous actor in 2015, Chaoyang Qunzhong became a semiofficial code name for the network of community volunteers.

Community volunteers operate in all urban districts of Beijing, though the ones in Chaoyang District have garnered the greatest publicity. Volunteer networks in other districts have acquired nicknames such as *Xicheng Dama* (grandmas of Xicheng District), *Haidian Wangyou* (netizens of Haidian District), and *Fengtai Quandaodui* (counselors of Fengtai District). Occasionally, some expatriates also become volunteers, as the fascinating story of Terry Crossman tells. Crossman, a retired human resources consultant, had been living in Beijing for twenty-two years and found a home in one of the remaining siheyuan in Xicheng District. In early 2017, community volunteers in Xicheng District solicited his help in making a promotional video, and from then on, Crossman signed on to be a volunteer himself. He was often staffed at a post behind the Forbidden City. Wearing the red armband, Crossman gladly provided assistance to foreign tourists, which helped him immerse further into Beijing culture and gain notoriety in the process.[8]

With a focus on crime prevention, community volunteers are familiar with their own neighborhoods. They recognize strangers and newcomers and take note of any abnormal behavior or activities. Some volunteers have expanded their sentries by forging collaborative relationships with domestic workers and service personnel, who would alert them on matters that are out of the norm in the neighborhood. On the other end of the community safety apparatus, the authorities provide basic training and continued education to the volunteers on how to identify suspicious people and activities more accurately and intervene with emergencies within the legal boundaries. Public safety officials have monthly meetings with the volunteers to exchange information and ideas. The authorities may follow the tips from the volunteers and set up professional surveillance and information gathering to determine whether it is necessary to conduct further investigation or seek search warrants.

Westerners may find the actions by the likes of Chaoyang Qunzhong offensive to their privacy and may worry that communal vigilantism could usurp law enforcement authorities. To the Chinese, however, the traditional view places individual rights within a group's or community's well-being. The volunteers are enthusiastic and determined, the authorities are happy and supportive, and the general public is grateful to the Chaoyang Qunzhong because their presence makes the community safer. Beijing's community volunteer networks, for their enthusiasm and effectiveness, have earned the humorous accolade of being "the fifth-largest intelligence network in the world," after the CIA of the United States, the KGB of the former Soviet Union, the Mossad of Israel, and the MI6 of the United Kingdom. They are truly the eyes and ears for the public safety apparatus, and the PRC government considers this grassroots network a model of success for the rest of the country.

Witnessing the success and greater potential of the Chaoyang Qunzhong in recent years, Beijing's public safety authorities have also started reform that promotes more proactive community policing. Traditionally, subdistrict-level police stations were mainly charged with civic matters such as residential registration and domestic mediation. They were ineffective in crime prevention and were not equipped to deal with felonies. The latest reform significantly increased the staffing at the subdistrict stations, sometimes more than double the previous staffing level, and divided the staff into three divisions: 60 percent of the staff would carry out street and community patrols, 20 percent would handle case-specific investigations, and 20 percent would be command control at the station. The new organization would offer around-the-clock operations and adjust workloads for the staff. The preliminary assessment of the reform is encouraging because it has boosted police presence and crime deterrence at the community level.

The physical partition of urban communities has a long tradition in China's urban development. In modern times, gated communities were common in some Chinese cities, among which Beijing stood out with its large number of superblocks that housed government agencies and state enterprises during the Socialist era. One of the key features of these superblocks was exclusivity through controlled entry, which has morphed into a draconic measure for neighborhood security in Beijing in recent years. Called "closure of village" because of its closed-off management approach, the authorities impose stringent procedures to prevent crimes, including sealing off the entire community with fences and walls, controlling personnel movement through checkpoints, and installing closed-circuit television systems (CCTV). This measure was first adopted in the southern Daxing District, where cheap housing and easy access to the urban core had attracted a huge transient population, along with deterioration of community security and environmental quality. Dubbed the "Daxing Model" for its success in crime reduction, the measure has been implemented in some urban neighborhoods and many villages near the urban-rural fringe to stem the transient population, which has been responsible for a disproportionately high percentage of felonies and petty crimes. Critics decry discrimination, but most residents insist that this measure has indeed reduced crimes drastically. Beijing authorities have promoted the Daxing Model throughout Beijing, though they have become more muted in the last several years in part because of concerns over rights abuses.

The PRC government has also been active in adopting the latest technology to combat crimes, and Beijing is leading the way. CCTV is already a common tool in Chinese cities, and facial recognition technology is also being adopted. In 2014, Beijing's public security adopted a crime data analyses and trending forecast system that uses big data to analyze the temporal and spatial patterns of crimes and misdemeanors. Its findings have allowed the authorities to plan for their operations and effectively appropriate resources. When the system predicted high probability of car thefts at a specific location, for example, the police immediately increased patrols in the area and captured a car thief in the act. The government has also begun to use artificial intelligence (AI) software to mine data and build models in an effort to predict the time and place that crimes and public disturbances may take place. The adoption of these technologies for improving public safety has raised concerns and provoked opposition in the United States and other Western countries, but it is unlikely to slow down China's push for developing technological means in combating crimes. The public may benefit from a safer environment with new technologies and, therefore, overlook the intrusive nature of their adoption.

For foreign visitors and the local middle class, Beijing is a safe city; for low-income migrant workers and their families, the city can be a hostile and dangerous place. Beijing fares well as a megacity in an emerging economy based on available crime statistics. At the same time, the city faces paramount challenges in keeping crimes and violence under control. For foreign visitors and newcomers in Beijing, common sense is the best guide to safety. They need to be vigilant about property theft and financial scams. Most people are not directly impacted by white-collar crimes unless they are lured into traps due to greed or ignorance. Random crimes and violence do exist, but they are relatively few and far between. If a person can manage his or her safety in New York City, London, Rome, or Paris, he or she should be fine in Beijing.

NOTES

1. Economist Intelligence Unit, "Safe Cities Index 2019: Urban Security and Resilience in an Interconnected World," *The Economist*, accessed September 20, 2019, https://safecities.economist.com/wp-content/uploads/2019/08/Aug-5-ENG -NEC-Safe-Cities-2019-270x210-19-screen.pdf.

2. "China 2019 Crime & Safety Report: Beijing," OSAC, March 11, 2019, https://www.osac.gov/Content/Report/6e339bea-374b-4614-aab9-15f4aeb35923.

3. Nicholas D. Kristof, "Beijing Journal; Crime Is Up in China, and So Is the Public's Rage," *New York Times*, January 20, 1992, https://www.nytimes.com/1992 /01/20/world/beijing-journal-crime-is-up-in-china-and-so-is-the-public-s-rage .html.

4. Tianzhen Chen and Mina Zhao, "Meeting the Challenges of Opioid Dependence in China: Experience of Opioid Agonist Treatment," *Current Opinion in Psychiatry* 32, no. 4 (July 2019): 282–287, https://doi.org/10.1097/YCO .0000000000000509.

5. Choi Chi-yuk, "Detentions, Torture, Executions: How China Dealt with the Mafia in the Past," *South China Morning Post*, January 26, 2018, https://www .scmp.com/news/china/policies-politics/article/2130679/chinas-decades-long -battle-organised-crime.

6. "Relative of U.S. Coach Killed in Beijing Attack," NBC News, August 10, 2008, http://www.nbcnews.com/id/26104003/ns/beijing_olympics-beijing _olympics_news/t/relative-us-coach-killed-beijing-attack/#.XAzaNC-ZP1I.

7. "The Divorce of Li Yang," China Plus, February 23, 2014, http://english.cri .cn/7146/2014/02/23/2041s814323.htm.

8. Kyle Mullin, "Old China Hand: Terry Crossman, the American Who Joined the Ranks of Beijing's Volunteer Dama," The Beijinger, February 28, 2018, https:// www.thebeijinger.com/blog/2018/02/28/old-china-hand-terry-crossman -american-who-joined-ranks-beijings-volunteer-dama.

8

Security Issues

On September 11, 2001, nineteen hijackers took over four passenger airliners in the United States and weaponized them to attack symbolic Western political and economic institutions. Three of the planes reached their targets: two slammed into the Twin Towers of the World Trade Center in Lower Manhattan, New York City, and one hit the Pentagon in Washington, DC. The fourth plane crashed in a field in Pennsylvania after the passengers fought back against the hijackers. It was later speculated that the hijackers of the fourth plane intended to attack the U.S. Capitol or the White House. In the era of globalization, the world community has become vulnerable to the threat of terrorism, which is defined as the systematic and coercive use of terror for religious or political aims. The 9/11 terrorist attacks reminded us that leading cities are symbols of a country's identity, pride, and power that are cherished by its citizens and loathed by its enemies.

Few countries in the world today can have their past and present displayed alongside each other in their capitals; China is one of the few that can and does. The hallowed ground of Beijing's Imperial City, which incorporates the Forbidden City, Tiananmen Square, and the monumental modern state structures, is the symbolic and real center of China's power, hope, and pride. Any indignation to Beijing is regarded by the Chinese collectively as an ultimate threat to the PRC's legitimacy and a slight to the country's prestige. Security for Beijing has always been an overriding concern for the PRC government to which no resources are spared.

During the Socialist era (1949–1978), the only known incident in Beijing that would qualify as a foreign terrorist conspiracy was a case that involved a number of foreign nationals. In 1950, the PRC's newly formed security and intelligence apparatus cracked an alleged plot to assassinate the top leaders with an old mortar. The alleged ringleaders, Antonio Riva of Italy and Ruichi Yamaguchi of Japan, were sentenced to death and executed in 1951. The Catholic bishop for a parish near Beijing, Tarcisio Martina, was sentenced to life imprisonment but was expelled from China in 1954. The case also became the ostensible cause that ended the PRC's diplomatic contact with the Vatican.

The details of this case remain murky.[1] At the time, the PRC government alleged Colonel David Dean Barrett, the military attaché of the U.S. mission to the Republic of China (ROC), by then a government in exile in Taiwan, was the spymaster of the plot. This case would have qualified as state terrorism if it had been directed and supported by the U.S. government, as the PRC government then alleged. Evidence remains ambiguous, even after the PRC government declassified the case files in 2009. Some analyses show that the case might have been built on shaky ground. The plot's logistics appear unfeasible, and there is little convincing evidence that Barrett or any foreign government agents were involved.

Under extremely tight security, Beijing almost remained immune to any foreign terrorist threats during the Socialist era. The only danger of instability in the capital came during the tumultuous years of the Cultural Revolution (1966–1976), when China encountered what would qualify as domestic terrorism. As the capital, Beijing took the brunt of chaos as millions of marauding youths called "Red Guards," who were mostly high school and college students, descended on the city. The Red Guards held parades and rallies and went on a rampage against individuals and groups that they deemed as "bourgeois" or "counterrevolutionary." The PRC government was able to sideline the Red Guards quickly by purging their leaders and cutting off state support.

The ensuing power struggle among several factions in the PRC's top leadership eventually spilled over and led to an alleged coup d'état attempt by Marshal Lin Biao's loyalists in September 1971. Some alleged coup plotters commandeered a helicopter. After their escape attempt failed, they tried to crash the helicopter into Zhongnanhai, the former royal gardens of the Imperial City where the CCP's central committee and the State Council were located. The plotters chose the highly symbolic target to show ultimate defiance to their political enemies.

During the Socialist era, the PRC government was able to minimize public presence of the state security apparatus in the capital. The traditional approach to guard against political unrest and terrorist activities heavily depended on grassroots surveillance and intelligence gathering, which was effective in stopping any terrorist operations from moving forward. Furthermore, China was insulated from the outside world through much of the Cold War era, and tight control over every facet of society made it next to impossible for organized domestic or international terrorism to infiltrate the country. None of the rumored plots of sabotage or attacks on Beijing succeeded. Security through insulation, however, came to an end as China entered the era of reform and jumped on the bandwagon of globalization in the late 1970s. China would come to face the reality that it was no longer immune to terrorism, domestic or foreign, and Beijing was to become the major target.

TERRORIST THREATS

As China's economic reforms brought greater openness to its society, the Chinese government felt increasing pressure from a wide range of domestic and international security challenges. China has been confronted with consistent and serious terrorist threats in recent years. China ranked 36th among 163 countries in the 2018 Global Terrorism Index in terms of the potential impact of terrorism, and its rating (5.108) was worse than, for example, Israel (41st) and Iran (44th).[2] As the national political center, Beijing faces public safety threats on three fronts: violent acts by individuals or groups who aim to maximize the effects of terror by targeting the national capital; typical terrorist attacks, so far mainly from the Muslim Uyghur extremists who have become a part of the international jihadist movement; and organized or spontaneous mass unrest aimed at challenging the political status quo.

The first type of terrorist acts has more to do with the worsening socio-economic disparity during the reform era, when large segments of the population became disenfranchised, providing fertile soil for disillusionment, dissent, and unrest. During the early reform years, there were numerous incidents in which individuals detonated homemade bombs or committed arson in public places to exert revenge against the government and the society in general. These incidents could be considered either violent crimes or borderline domestic terrorism, but they did pose a sustained threat to Beijing's security.

Some ethnic minority groups in China have suffered from economic, cultural, and religious marginalization. In some cases, their struggle for equality or self-determination has been exploited by international terrorist organizations. The PRC government has become alarmed by signs of pan-Islamic tendencies in some Islamic minority groups in its western borderland regions. It is in the process of invalidating halal food standards in several provinces that have large Muslim populations, such as the Xinjiang

Uyghur Autonomous Region and the Ningxia Hui Autonomous Region. Authorities shut down an Islamic bookstore in Beijing's Haidian District and arrested its owner in October 2017, accusing him of terrorist activities. It is noteworthy that the news was first broken by an academic in Mainland China, who had sounded the alarm against the proliferation of Islamic activities in China. In reality, the main threat of terrorism that China faces is the regional unrest led by the Uyghurs that has proliferated into frequent and widespread violent terrorist acts.

The Uyghurs, a Turkic Muslim minority group that is concentrated in the Xinjiang Uyghur Autonomous Region, which the Uyghur nationalists prefer to call East Turkistan, in western China. Uyghur nationalism was inspired in part by the emergence of pan-Turkism in the late nineteenth century and prompted several failed insurgencies between the 1920s and 1940s, including a major uprising supported by the Soviet Union in the mid to late 1940s. The Uyghurs' aspiration for independence was dashed in 1949, when the Soviet Union and the Chinese Communists, triumphing in the Chinese Civil War, reached an agreement that reassured Chinese sovereignty over Xinjiang. The Uyghur separatist movement went into hiatus until the 1980s.

In recent decades, secessionist movements have been emboldened by the political devolution and pan-Islamism that swept through Central Asia after the collapse of the Soviet Union. Some extreme elements in the Uyghur separatist movement have coalesced with other Islamist groups, such as the Taliban, al-Qaeda, and the Islamic State of Iraq and Syria (ISIS). Some Uyghur militants have become organized and battle-hardened through participation in a series of clashes in the Middle East and Afghanistan, including the civil war in Syria. They have attempted to infiltrate Xinjiang to launch direct attacks on China. More importantly, a wide array of Uyghur secessionist and pan-Islamic propaganda through the Internet and other modern media channels have played a major role in radicalizing many marginalized Uyghurs, who have in turn swarmed to join the secessionist cause. The PRC government's assessment on violence committed by some Uyghurs has evolved from domestic ethnic conflicts to international terrorism.

Violence began to flare up in Xinjiang in the 1980s, as government pressure on the Uyghurs began to slack during the reform era. In 1990, a large riot took place in Baren Township, near Kashgar in western Xinjiang, where the Uyghurs had gathered to protest against the government. They ambushed and killed several Chinese Armed Police and seized their weapons. An armed uprising ensued. The uprising was quickly suppressed by the authorities, but it marked the beginning of an era of ethnic unrest and terrorist violence committed by Uyghur extremists against the Chinese state and Han Chinese. While most of violent acts have taken place in

Xinjiang, Uyghur separatists have tried to bring their fight to other parts of China, especially the major cities, to maximize the impact of their actions. Beijing is the number one choice of Uyghur extremists, though they have had a hard time reaching the city.

In March 1997, there were two bus bombings near Tiananmen Square within two days that killed five and injured many more. These bombings were blamed on Uyghur extremists who had been responsible for mass violence in Yining (Kulja) and three bus bombings in Urumqi, Xinjiang's capital, in February 1997. These attacks were highly symbolic because they were designated to take place during the annual sessions of the PRC's National People's Congress and the People's Consultative Conference in Beijing. The bombings caused widespread public panic and repercussions against the Uyghurs, who were frequently refused service by hotels and taxi drivers and were subjected to close scrutiny by the authorities. The Uyghur community in Beijing suffered disproportionately.

As China stepped onto the world stage as an emerging world power, it was ill prepared to cope with the new but quickly mounting threat of international terrorism. Its crackdowns on Uyghur separatism were crude and reactive and failed to garner international support until 2001, when China, Russia, and several other Central Asian countries formed the Shanghai Cooperation Organization (SCO). One of the primary missions of SCO is intermember coordination in countering terrorism. The September 11, 2001, terrorist attacks in the United States provided China with the opportunity to join international anti-terrorism efforts by framing Uyghur secessionism as part of international jihadist movement. The turning point of Uyghur terrorist activities in China and the PRC's anti-terrorist response, however, came during the countdown to the 2008 Beijing Summer Olympics.

THE 2008 BEIJING SUMMER OLYMPICS

The PRC's global fanfare for hosting the 2008 Summer Olympics in Beijing drew mixed reactions from the international community. As much as the PRC government wanted to make the Olympic Games the coming-of-age party for China's "peaceful emergence," there was a strong undercurrent that was determined to sabotage it. Foreseeing the challenges, the PRC government and Beijing authorities mobilized national resources to guarantee absolute security for the Olympic Games. In 2003, security officials from fifteen government agencies formed the Olympics Security Coordination Group. The group oversaw the formation and operational structure of the Olympics Security Command Center and Olympics Intelligence Center, both established in 2005. Each sports venue was equipped with an on-site security command; reinforcement staff with specialized equipment provided protection at the competition facilities, the Olympic Village, the travel routes for the athletes, and for the VIPs of the Olympic Games. The security network was extended to monitor every facet of Beijing, including the Internet, the workplace, and every neighborhood. Intensified profiling was conducted to identify any sign of potential threats.

In spring 2007, the PRC's Ministry of Public Security issued a classified directive to subordinate public safety agencies in China, calling for the identification of potential terrorists in eleven categories covering various individuals and organizations that were hostile to the PRC. The authorities believed that the terrorist threats came mainly from three sources: international terrorists who were targeting specific foreign individuals and entities; domestic terrorists, mainly the Uyghur extremists, who aimed to sabotage the Olympic Games; and criminal elements that intended to do harm to the Olympic Games to smear China's reputation and image.

As anticipated, Uyghur extremists plotted a series of violent acts that were designed to create an atmosphere of insecurity before the Olympic Games. Several succeeded in Xinjiang and other Chinese provinces, including a bus explosion in July 2008 in Kunming, Yunnan Province. In early August 2008, on the eve of the Olympic Games, two Uyghurs rammed a dump truck into a column of armed policemen during their morning workout routines in Kashgar, killing sixteen of them. In mid-August, a series of explosions and attacks on the police took place in the Kucha and Shule Counties of Xinjiang, resulting in casualties and major property damage. The primary target of the terrorists, however, was Beijing.

In spring 2008, the authorities announced that they had busted two Uyghur terrorist groups led by people who had been trained overseas. Official disclosure claimed that the first group was plotting to attack major hotels, government facilities, and military installations in Beijing and Shanghai with explosives and chemicals. The second group was preparing to kidnap foreign athletes and journalists and to carry out suicide bombings during the Olympic Games to maximize chaos and damage. Both groups appeared to follow instructions from the East Turkestan Islamic Movement (ETIM, later renamed the Turkistan Islamic Party). In March 2008, a passenger plane from Urumqi to Beijing made an emergency landing in Lanzhou in the western province of Gansu after a nineteen-year-old Uyghur woman was caught hiding in the restroom with three gasoline-filled Coca-Cola cans. Authorities arrested the woman and three other Uyghurs on the plane who had disguised themselves as Pakistani merchants.

There may have been other terrorist plots, but the PRC authorities did not make them public until much later to give the outside world reassurance that the situation was under control and terrorist operations were limited. In 2016, for example, the PRC government bestowed top honor upon a contingent of the Armed Police stationed in a county of Shandong Province. Official reports revealed that up to forty "terrorists" were hiding in the hills of southwestern Shandong Province, training and preparing to launch attacks in Beijing. On July 19, 2008, the Armed Police contingent ambushed the group as it was getting ready to depart for Beijing. "It was a clean sweep of the terrorists," stated the Central Political and Legal Affairs Commission through its official WeChat account.

During the 2008 Summer Games, the Chinese military deployed seventy-four aircraft, forty-eight helicopters, thirty-three boats and ships, and the most advanced surface-to-air missile systems, such as S-300 and HQ-7, in and around Beijing. The PRC government also built a "human shield" in Beijing to protect the Olympic Games, including one hundred thousand security forces, four hundred thousand neighborhood activists, and over one million volunteers. Three hundred thousand CCTV cameras were canvassing nearly every corner of the city. Beijing became a fortified and closed city before and during the Olympic Games.

The 2008 Beijing Summer Olympic Games proceeded smoothly, in part due to the overwhelming anti-terrorism measures that mobilized China's national resources. The most important heritage of the Olympic Games to Beijing, and to the PRC in general, was the anti-terrorism infrastructure that the city built for the Olympic Games, including systemic emergency response planning, interagency coordination, a traffic entry control system, a rapid response task force, and intelligence networks. One of the most effective anti-terror measures was also what had worked well for the PRC in all public safety matters; the authorities termed it "people's war," that is, the mobilization of extensive networks of community volunteers.

Anti-terrorism measures for the Olympic Games, however, may not be sustainable in the long run in terms of the consuming resource commitment. Indeed, although the 2008 Beijing Summer Olympic Games were a great success, terrorist threats have not dissipated since then. While most of terrorist violence has been in Xinjiang, other Chinese cities, especially Beijing, remain in the crosshairs of Uyghur extremists who have merged with and gained strength from international terrorist organizations.

CONTINUED TERRORIST THREATS

The conclusion of the 2008 Beijing Summer Olympics did not end terrorists' attempts to attack Beijing. On October 28, 2013, a Mercedes-Benz SUV sped through the pedestrian section of Changan Avenue on the northern edge of Tiananmen Square, mowing down tourists along the way. It finally made a fiery crash right in front of the Tiananmen Gate.

Smoke billowed into the air amid panic and chaos. Before the fire was extinguished and smoke dissipated, two pedestrians had died, including a Filipino tourist, and forty more were injured. All three occupants of the SUV died in the fire. They were Usmen Hasan, his wife, and his mother, all Uyghurs from Xinjiang.

Witness accounts described the car's occupants as having displayed a black flag from the car window before immolating themselves in the crash. Authorities later announced discovery of propaganda pamphlets from the Turkistan Islamic Party in the car and subsequent arrests of eight Uyghur accomplices. Uyghur exile groups and some Western observers, on the other hand, disputed the claim, and the U.S. government declined to call it a terrorist attack. On November 24, 2013, Abdullah Mansour, the leader of the Pakistan-based Turkistan Islamic Party (TIP), previously the East Turkestan Islamic Movement (ETIM), released a propaganda video praising the plotters and warned of future attacks. Two of the conspirators were eventually sentenced to death for their roles in the attack; the rest received various prison terms. Hasan's girlfriend, a Han Chinese, was also sentenced to two years in prison for "helping destroy criminal evidence."

This incident was by far the most shocking and successful terrorist attack in Beijing. It showed growing sophistication and determination by Uyghur secessionists. According to a study,[3] there were six stages of Uyghur terrorism in the 1990s. As time went on, the terrorist tactics became more sophisticated and brutal, evolving from creating an atmosphere of terror to targeted assassinations, and from attacks on government institutions to large-scale riots that besieged towns and cities. Into the twenty-first century, Uyghur terrorism appeared to be on the rise in both number and scale, as exemplified by the well-planned 2009 mass attack on Han Chinese in Xinjiang's capital, Urumqi, that resulted in about two hundred deaths, a monthlong paralysis of the city, and enormous property damage. These attacks had mostly been confined to Xinjiang, where Uyghur extremists had the communal, religious, and geographical advantages to execute their terror plots, though evidence shows they could conduct more coordinated and sophisticated operations outside Xinjiang, as shown by the 2013 attack in Tiananmen Square.

On March 1, 2014, five Uyghurs dressed in black suddenly attacked passengers with machetes in the waiting hall of the Kunming Railway Station in Yunnan Province. Before security rushed in and gunned down the attackers, thirty-one people had been killed, and many more were wounded. Four of the five attackers were shot dead, and the fifth attacker, a sixteen-year-old woman, was captured. She was later spared capital punishment because she was pregnant at the time of the attack. Three other Uyghurs belonging to this group had been detained before the attack and were sentenced to death in the subsequent trials.

During the reform era, Chinese citizens have gained unprecedented mobility and some freedom to make a living almost anywhere in the country. Many Uyghurs have moved to eastern cities in search of jobs, business opportunities, and a better life in general. In Beijing, a city of great cultural diversity, the Uyghurs congregated to form two communities dubbed "Xinjiang Villages," which thrived in the early years of reform with numerous popular eateries serving the renowned Uyghur cuisine. Unfortunately, many Uyghurs were not able to successfully compete because of social and cultural prejudice and their own inability to adapt. There were conflicts between the Uyghurs and other ethnic groups, often out of cultural misunderstandings. As ethnic tensions mounted, law-binding Uyghurs suffered from ethnic profiling by authorities and ordinary Beijing residents alike.

The 1997 Beijing bus bombing, which was blamed on Uyghur extremists, triggered a backlash against Uyghurs, though there was no solid evidence that the Uyghur community in Beijing had been aware of the attack in advance or condoned it afterward. Many Uyghurs began to encounter difficulties in finding housing and jobs as well as getting their children into public schools. Hotel management and taxi drivers often refused to serve them. The once thriving Uyghur community in Beijing has since declined, in part, as a result of prejudice and discrimination. Poverty often translates into desperation. Some Uyghurs resorted to petty crimes for a living, and a few became involved in using and trafficking illicit drugs. A few others may have become radicalized, believing the only way for them to get justice was to have their own independent country.

The causes of Uyghur-led terrorism are complex and rooted in contemporary Uyghur nationalism. The centripetal tendencies of the Uyghurs have been exacerbated by the growing socioeconomic gap between them and the Han Chinese during the reform era. At the end of the Cold War, the collapse of the Soviet Union created a power vacuum in Central Asia in which pan-Turkism and pan-Islamism quickly spread, providing ideological empowerment to Uyghur nationalism. Economic and cultural marginalization of the Uyghurs has resulted in resentment among the Uyghurs toward the Chinese state, which creates a fertile ground for radicalization.

Uyghur-led terrorist activities, in part rooted in the enduring Uyghur nationalism, will continue to be a clear and present danger to China, and Beijing is always the primary target for terrorist attacks. The PRC government has tried to tread a delicate line in its approach to Uyghur nationalism. On the one hand, eradicating Uyghur-led terrorism is imperative to the PRC's national strategies, especially the Belt and Road Initiative,[4] for which Xinjiang serves as the gateway. On the other hand, the PRC government attempts to reassure Islamic countries that its counterterrorist measures are against three forces—violent terrorism, ethnic separatism, and religious extremism—and not against Islam or China's Muslim community.

Since the mid-1990s, the PRC government has tried both hard-line crackdowns and conciliatory policies, only to see continued and worsening violence in Xinjiang and beyond. Since 2016, the new leadership in Xinjiang has implemented drastic measures that are aimed at striking the right carrot-and-stick balance. Large camps were quickly built to board a hundred thousand Uyghurs, ostensibly for job skills and Chinese-language training. The PRC government claims that these training camps are designed with the goal of helping the camp graduates to become competitive in the job market and the Uyghur-majority regions to achieve sustainable development. Uyghur activists, international organizations, and Western media have alleged that these are in fact concentration camps.

The true nature of these camps may be somewhere in the middle: they are facilities for the PRC to forcefully integrate Uyghurs into China's economy and society. Improved job prospects and better living standards would, the PRC government hopes, lead to secularization and an identity shift from being Uyghur to being Chinese Uyghur. It remains to be seen whether this ambitious and controversial project works out. In the meantime, official reports claim that there have not been any Uyghur-led violent terrorist attacks since the project was launched in 2016.

STRUCTURAL AND LEGAL SYSTEMS FOR COUNTERTERRORISM

The 2013 terror attack in Tiananmen Square galvanized the PRC government to establish more effective anti-terrorism infrastructures. The National People's Congress passed the Counter-Terrorism Law at the end of 2015, criminalizing what it defined as "the promotion of terrorism or extremism." The law is designed to be the legal deterrent to any organized and violent acts against the state and the general public. The new law defines terrorist activities as "use or advocacy of violence, destruction and intimidation to create social chaos, harm public safety, violation of personal property, or duress to state agencies and international organizations, in order to achieve certain political and ideological goals."[5] By the legal definition, terrorist crimes can be carried out by groups (defined as three or more members) or individuals, and they can be committed through international or domestic networks.

The new law provides the state with prosecutorial powers to prosecute parties that provide material support to terrorist activities and organizations. Critics argue that the new law allows prosecution of "advocacy," a vague term that can be extended to include "thoughts," which will lead to human rights abuses. The PRC government, on the other hand, insists that "advocacy," as the law defines it, includes any expressions that encourage violence and unrest against society. The authorities also point out that many Uyghurs became radicalized through underground religious gatherings or exposure to materials from overseas multimedia Internet and messaging sources advocating violent insurgencies.

In June 2018, the anti-terrorism law was revised and amended with more specific guidelines as to what constitutes a terrorist crime. One of the key clarifications was on how to persecute the use of online platforms to promote or incite terrorism or extremism, long considered by the authorities as a leading method of radicalizing certain religious groups. While the 2015 anti-terrorism law criminalized the promotion of terrorism or extremism in general, the new guidelines specify that terrorist acts do include authoring and disseminating materials in written, audio, or visual forms that promote activities against the Chinese government and the general public through violent means. The guidelines pinpoint specific activities that Uyghur extremists have effectively employed in their radicalization efforts, such as organized viewing of propaganda videos, group training in remote areas, and spontaneous jihadist attacks, such as the Kunming Railway Station massacre. Digital data can be used as evidence in court. People providing material support to terrorist activities, including finance, travel, and facilities, would be charged with the act of aiding terrorism.

The new guidelines also highlight the emphasis on prevention and rehabilitation through education and provision of economic opportunities. They provide the legal ground and methodological framework for the large compulsory camps that have been in operation in Xinjiang. Chinese authorities want to preempt mass radicalization through a three-pronged approach: political "detoxication" through exposure to government propaganda, cultural assimilation through Chinese-language education, and economic advancement through job-specific skills training. The PRC government hopes that the anti-terrorism law, with the new guidelines, will be effective new tools in combating the spread of ideology, social code, and propaganda that advocate violent acts against the Chinese state.

China has also increased its international cooperation in its anti-terrorism efforts with the United States and several neighboring countries through training, information exchange, and coordinated operations. The PRC is a founding member (June 2001) and a key member of the Shanghai Cooperation Organization (SCO) founded in 2001, which includes Russia, Kyrgyzstan, Kazakhstan, Uzbekistan, and Tajikistan as founding members. India and Pakistan joined in 2017. A major function of SCO is coordination among members in security and counterterrorism policies and operations.

The 2013 Tiananmen Square attack also motivated the PRC government to establish an integrative bureaucracy in combating terrorism. As early as 2001, the PRC government established an Anti-Terrorism Task Coordination Group headed by the minister of Public Security, which was renamed the Anti-Terrorism Tasks Leadership Group in 2013 with expanded power over a new vertically integrated national anti-terrorism network. This revamped and powerful state organ is jointly headed by top officials from the executive, judicial, military, and Armed Police branches of the PRC government; it issues operational directives and provides logistical support to its subordinate province-level anti-terrorism agencies. Its subordinate counterpart in Beijing is the Anti-Terrorism and Major Felony Emergency Command, which is headed by the secretary of the CCP's Beijing Political and Legal Commission and the city's police chief.

Beijing is at the forefront of the nationwide anti-terrorism campaign. In 2006, on the fifth anniversary of 9/11 terrorist attacks in the United States, the PRC government announced the designation of seven Anti-Terrorism Central Cities: Beijing, Shanghai, Tianjin, Chongqing, Guangzhou, Wuhan, and Shenyang. These cities began to receive more resources from the central government to establish high-tech systems and special security forces for monitoring and responding to terrorist activities. Extensive CCTV systems are already in full operation in Beijing and the other cities. New technologies, such as biometric facial recognition, are being introduced for collecting, analyzing, and disseminating personal data the authorities deem relevant to their tasks.

The wholesale introduction of such technologies has aroused concerns over privacy and civil rights. Authorities in some locales, for example, have use CCTV video captures to publicly shame jaywalkers and offenders of various misdemeanors, and the facial recognition system has been used against "deadbeats" in their job or loan applications. The government wants to employ the latest technologies to more effectively identify and monitor groups that are regarded as shelters and incubators of terrorist suspects. At the same time, new regulations have been passed over the use of new technologies, such as drones, as a preemptive measure against terrorist acts after the drone attack on top government officials in Venezuela on August 4, 2018.

Beijing authorities employ both hard power and soft power in managing public safety and countering potential terrorist threat. *Hard power* refers to the professional counterterrorist infrastructure. First, Beijing authorities have established close working relationships with their counterparts in other provinces that are at high risk of terrorism, such as Xinjiang and the Xinjiang Production and Construction Corps (XPCC), Gansu, Shaanxi, Ningxia, Qinghai, and Henan, most of which are northwestern provinces with large Muslim populations. The goal is to preempt terrorist attacks through intelligence sharing and coordinated operations. Second, Beijing continues to upgrade the anti-terrorist infrastructure built for the 2008 Summer Olympic Games and increasingly displays its anti-terrorism hardware to the public as a deterrent strategy.

In all, Beijing maintains three sets of defenses against terrorist attacks: entry control along the city border and at transit hubs, omnipresent deterrence and surveillance and rapid response for key public sites, and emergency response forces. There are a large number of highway checkpoints at the city perimeters as well as at railway stations and air hubs. The authorities now have the ability to shut down selected segments or entire systems of transit and public venues should an emergency arise. Rarely seen in public until recent years, SWAT teams and armored police vehicles are becoming a common sight in public venues. The authorities now even showcase the elite Snow Leopard Commando Unit (SLCU) under the Beijing command of the People's Armed Police. Fourteen public sites have been identified as high-risk locations, including the Beijing Railway Station and popular shopping districts in Wangfujing and Xidan, where armed security police patrol around the clock on motorcycles and in specially marked vehicles, sometimes equipped with K-9 units. There is a compulsory one-minute response time to any of these fourteen sites in the event of a terrorist attack.

On the other hand, *soft power* is built on the tried-and-true strategy of "people's war" and may prove to be more effective than the beefed-up hardware. The government conducts regular and high-profile anti-terrorist exercises both as a terror deterrent and as a public awareness campaign. Mobilization of local residents is the key to Beijing's soft power

---

PUBLIC AND EMERGENCY SERVICES

English-language service is only available to some emergency services in Beijing, though more are being made accessible in English. For police service call 110 (text: 12110); non-Chinese speakers can also call 384020101 (option 3) for English assistance from the Foreigners Section of the Beijing Public Security Bureau. For the medical ambulance hotline call 120 (nationwide) or 999 (for Beijing only); assistance in English is now available. Other useful phone or text numbers include directory inquiries, 114 (local directory service in English: 2689 0114); international assistance, 115; fire, 119; traffic accidents, 122; health hotline, 12320; tourist hotline, 6513 0828 (option 1 for English); and weather, 12121. In case of a terrorist attack, it would be suitable to employ training, common sense, and knowledge that one would use in Western cities.

against terrorism. The authorities have instituted regular public awareness programs, such as traveling exhibits and community drills in communities, schools and colleges, and large businesses, to increase public awareness. Community volunteer networks, highly effective in crime prevention, are the eyes and ears for the state security apparatus. Many community activists and service workers undergo basic training on how to spot and report suspicious persons and activities, and informants of valuable tips are financially rewarded.

As part of the People's War against Terrorism, Beijing authorities have also formalized reward procedures for informants of suspected terrorist activities based on the 2015 anti-terrorism law. Informants may receive large cash rewards between CNY 40,000 and 500,000 (USD 5,800–72,000) if their tips lead to stopping terrorist operations or solving major criminal cases. Within the first month of the passage of China's anti-terrorist law, the Beijing Municipal Government awarded CNY 60,000 (USD 9,000) to informants. In February 2016, a security guard saw a suspicious person trying to pry open a backdoor of a hotel. His tips to the police led to the arrest of the suspect, who had intended to blow up the hotel with explosives over disputes with the hotel management. The security guard received a CNY 50,000 (USD 7,230) reward from the Beijing Municipal Public Security Bureau.

As its global footprint grows, the PRC will be increasingly confronted by terrorist activities both inside China and overseas. The violent insurgency of ISIS has forced China to confront international terrorism, as there has been clear evidence that some Uyghur extremists have joined forces with ISIS and al-Qaeda. In a video released in March 2017, ISIS vowed to "shed blood like rivers" in attacks against Chinese targets.[6] In response, China tried to preempt the infiltration of overseas Uyghur militants through collaboration with Pakistan and Afghan authorities to intercept them. A fortified border outpost has been constructed on the eastern end of the Wakhan Corridor that leads into China's Xinjiang from Afghanistan, and there have been rumors that China may get collaboration and permission from the Afghan government to establish a military anti-terrorism base on the Afghan side of Wakhan Corridor in an attempt to stop Uyghur militants before they reach the Chinese borders.

There have been attacks against Chinese interests overseas, especially factories and construction sites. Originally concentrated in Central Asian countries, such attacks have spread to other parts of the world, such as the 2015 bombing of the Buddhist Erawan Shrine in Bangkok that targeted Chinese tourists. Islamic jihadists have also attacked the Chinese in Mali and other African countries. ISIS executed a Chinese national, Fan Jinghui, in 2015. On August 30, 2016, the Kyrgyzstan Chinese Embassy was struck by a Uyghur suicide bomber. In June 2017, a Chinese couple who worked as missionaries for a Korean Christian church was kidnapped and eventually killed by terrorists with alleged affiliations with ISIS in Pakistan.

Although the PRC must confront terrorist threats internationally, its priority still lies in containing and suppressing violent terrorist acts in Xinjiang, and safeguarding Beijing from terrorist attacks remains the utmost priority.

OTHER SECURITY CHALLENGES FACING BEIJING

Notwithstanding terrorist threats, there are other security challenges that confront Beijing. Large public unrest and mass incidents related to infrastructure failure are two top security issues. Felony crimes aimed at causing maximum damage or major disruption in Beijing can also have devastating impact on people's lives and property as well as China's reputation and Beijing's image as the national capital.

Large public unrest in Beijing is regarded as a major security threat to the PRC's efforts in maintaining societal stability. As the country's supreme political center, Beijing attracts the attention of admirers and dissidents alike. Tiananmen Square, the PRC's symbolic political center, is both the premier stage for the central government to embellish power and achievements with pomp and circumstance and the most prominent platform for protest and demonstration, which the authorities try their best to prevent from taking place. Tiananmen Square had its first non-government-sanctioned mass protest during the PRC era in April 1976, when large crowds gathered to denounce the radical faction in the CCP's top leadership. In the spring of 1979, at the dawn of the reform era, Tiananmen Square became China's forum where heated political debates and calls for democratic reform rang out before the authorities whisked the participants and their postings away to a relatively obscure site.[7]

The largest mass demonstration took place during the prodemocracy movement of 1989, when a hundred thousand college students, factory workers, government employees, and ordinary residents demanded the PRC government carry out democratic reform and anti-corruption actions. College students took over Tiananmen Square and occupied it for weeks; some went on hunger strike, and others erected a hastily created statue, dubbed the "Goddess of Democracy," that was ostensibly inspired by the Statue of Liberty in the New York Harbor. The occupation of Tiananmen Square paralyzed Beijing until June 4, 1989, when Chinese military was summoned to forcefully remove the demonstrators from Tiananmen Square.

China's unitary political tradition inspires today's dissenters and those who feel wronged by local governments to seek recourse and justice at the higher levels of the government; many eventually reach the central government in Beijing. The PRC government has even set up a ministerial agency, the State Bureau of Letters and Calls, to deal with complaints filed by letter petitions or personal appointments. The bureau processes complaints, reports findings, and oversees implementation of central government decisions. China is known for its large number of petitioners whose final destination is the national capital. They frequently crowd government offices, where they occasionally mount large demonstrations.

The central government does not want public disturbances caused by these petitioners, and it pressures the local authorities to resolve the issues. Too often, however, the local authorities try to forcefully intercept and repatriate petitioners to their respective jurisdictions. At the same time, some suspicious and angry petitioners are determined to make their grievances publicized. Tiananmen Square is usually their last resort to get themselves seen and heard. Clashes between the two sides have taken place there and caused public disturbances.

The authorities allocate immense resources to prevent mass unrest in the capital with a special focus on Tiananmen Square. Uniformed and undercover security personnel are scattered throughout the square, and police paddy wagons are on standby at strategic locations, ready to haul away protestors and other troublemakers at a moment's notice. The demonstrators occasionally succeed in their efforts, however, and no demonstrations have been more shocking than those staged by Falun Gong.[8]

Zhongnanhai, near Tiananmen Square, is the most highly guarded government zone and the PRC's political nerve center as the home to CCP's central committee and the PRC State Council. In April 1999, over ten thousand Falun Gong followers silently amassed outside Zhongnanhai in protest against the government crackdown on the cult. It stunned the PRC government that such mass mobilization could have been plotted by its leader, who had escaped to the United States, right under the watchful eyes of the capital's security apparatus. In the ensuing years, Falun Gong followers have launched protests in Tiananmen Square. Although much smaller than the ten thousand amassed in 1999, some groups of Falun Gong protesters have resorted to extreme measures of protest, including self-immolation in Tiananmen Square. On the eve of Chinese New Year in 2001, five Falun Gong followers traveled to Beijing and self-immolated in Tiananmen Square; one died on site, and her daughter died months later. Forty foreign Falun Gong followers unfurled the cult's banner and shouted slogans in Tiananmen Square in 2002.

An unpredictable threat to Beijing's security is violent acts committed by individuals who are bent to make a political statement by exerting maximum destruction and harm to the public. These violent acts, a form of domestic terrorism, are highly esoteric and difficult to detect early. The best prevention is for the authorities to depend on the intelligence networks and grassroots community volunteers for information and assessment of any suspicious activities. Despite the best efforts, however, some twisted individuals do succeed in carrying out their murderous plans, which have resulted in far-reaching repercussions, especially when the targets and victims are foreign nationals or international entities.

On September 24, 1994, Tian Jianming, an army lieutenant from the Beijing Garrison Command, the military security forces directly assigned to Beijing's security, suddenly opened fire on his commanding officers during the morning roll call with an unlawfully acquired automatic rifle. After killing four and wounding many, Tian hijacked an SUV and ordered the driver to go to Tiananmen Square. The driver intentionally wrecked the vehicle at the Jianguomen Gate overpass on the western edge of the diplomatic quarters. The ensuing gun battle between Tian, an army sharpshooter, and security forces resulted in at least fifteen more dead, including an Iranian diplomat and one of his four children in his car, and a number of security officers. Another sixty people were injured. Tian was eventually killed by an army sniper.[9]

In the aftermath of the worst mass shooting in Chinese history, a number of commanding officers of the Beijing Garrison Command were reprimanded and demoted; two years after the incident, the unit designation of Tian's regiment was revoked. This incident exposed a number of flaws in Beijing's security apparatus, including mismanagement in training and equipment of security forces, poor coordination among related emergency response agencies, and a lack of discipline and preparedness within the garrison itself. Prior to this incident, military personnel in the garrison were prohibited from possessing live ammunition. As a result of this incident, each garrison regiment is now required to have a standby armed squad for rapid response to emergencies.

On July 26, 2018, a man in his twenties detonated a homemade explosive near the U.S. Embassy. The perpetrator, who came from northeastern Jilin Province, suffered minor injuries and was arrested on site. There was no other injury or property damage. The government's official explanation was that the suspect had been mentally ill and unable to hold a job. It was called an isolated security incident. It must not be assumed as a coincidence, though, that the U.S. Embassy was where the perpetrator chose to detonate his improvised explosive device (IED).

Beijing, as the national capital, is in the crosshairs of terrorists and extremists. It is also the most heavily guarded city in China, with no state resources or efforts spared. Beijing has been building extensive tangible and intangible protections against terrorism and major violence. The only sustained known terrorist threat is from some of the Uyghur secessionists who have both domestic roots and international connections. China's capability to keep terrorist threats under control, especially in Beijing, depends in part on its authoritarian political system and in part on its heavy investment in building and maintaining both hard power and soft power against terrorism. As some experts have pointed out, the PRC has acquired tactical capabilities in protecting Beijing's security, but it remains to be seen whether it can formulate long-term policies and practices that will help eradicate the root causes of ethnically and religiously inspired terrorism. Meanwhile, Beijing is increasingly fortified and overall remains safe in comparison to its peer cities in the world.

REMEMBERING CHILDHOOD'S BEIJING

After graduating from college with a degree in recording engineering, I became a freelance musician, recording artist, and acoustic designer. I am on break now from designing a recording studio for Cui Jian, the most famous rock and roll musician of my parents' generation.

Beijing was a quiet city when I was a toddler. In the summer, crickets and street vendors seemed to echo each other, and the sound of whistles carried by pet doves left an enduring memory in me. I often played with other kids outside: soccer, marbles, and sports cards. It felt that there was little disparity among people, though some kids had a few more toys.

We moved to a new condo in the early 1990s. The West Third Ring Road was not completed yet, and the new home was surrounded by vegetable gardens and canals. Few families had cars, and my parents had one bicycle, which the three of us shared. Soon the city began to expand. The Fourth Ring Road was built, and streets became crowded with cars, lots of cars. I had to learn how to dodge cars when riding the bicycle to and from school. There were shacks selling pirated music CDs and DVDs in Zhongguancun, now known as the Silicon Valley of China, and how they were quickly replaced by malls selling computers and electronics. Now the malls are all closed with the rise of e-commerce.

The first decade of the twenty-first century was the most exciting time for my generation. Beijing began to show growing global flavors with the emerging central business district and places like Sanlitun. Opportunities abounded for the young and educated folks: starting ventures, making money, and enjoying the new cosmopolitan lifestyle. It was a good time to dream the China Dream or, more aptly, the Beijing Dream.

I will never forget two particular events during this decade. The first was Beijing winning the Olympics bid in 2001, and the second was the Chinese soccer team winning a spot in the 2002 World Cup. My friends and I went to join hundreds of thousands of revelers in the streets. Afterward, we sat on the steps of a church in Wangfujing, drinking Coca-Cola and talking about dreams. I told my friends that I dreamt of becoming rich, so I could buy one hundred

Cherys (a Chinese-made car) and give each of them one. We'd then cruise up and down Changan Avenue together all night long.

Entering the second decade of the century, however, many overlooked problems started to surface. More and more people began to feel alienated and disillusioned by insatiable material desires. Beijing began to feel like a strange place to me; it is losing its tradition, its humanity, and the soul of its people. I miss the time when I grew up: it was safe and peaceful. I know, however, that time is gone forever.

—*Xingyu Li*

NOTES

1. "Plot to Kill Mao—U. S. Accused," *The Sunday Herald*, August 19, 1951, p. 3, https://trove.nla.gov.au/newspaper/article/18496014. "CHINA: Old Hands, Beware!" *Time* 58, no. 9 (August 27, 1951), http://content.time.com/time/magazine/article /0,9171,815245,00.html.

2. Institute for Economics & Peace, "2018 Global Terrorism Index: Measuring the Impact of Terrorism," November 2018, http://www.visionofhumanity.org/app /uploads/2018/12/Global-Terrorism-Index-2018-1.pdf.

3. Justin V. Hastings, "Charting the Course of Uyghur Unrest," *China Quarterly* 208: 893–912.

4. "The Belt and Road Initiative," The State Council of the People's Republic of China, accessed August 2, 2019, http://english.gov.cn/beltAndRoad; "Belt and Road Initiative," The World Bank, March 29, 2018, https://www.worldbank.org/en /topic/regional-integration/brief/belt-and-road-initiative.

5. "Unofficial Translation of the Counter-Terrorism Law of the People's Republic of China," The US-China Business Council, accessed September 20, 2019, https://www.uschina.org/china-hub/unofficial-translation-counter-terrorism -law-peoples-republic-china.

6. Michael Martina and Ben Blanchard, "Uighur IS Fighters Vow Blood Will 'Flow in Rivers' in China," Reuters, March 1, 2017, https://www.reuters.com/article /us-mideast-crisis-iraq-china-idUSKBN16848H.

7. "Democracy Wall," BBC News, accessed September 21, 2019, http://news .bbc.co.uk/2/shared/spl/hi/in_depth/china_politics/key_people_events/html/7 .stm.

8. David Ownby, "Falun Gong," *Encyclopædia Britannica*, accessed September 19, 2019, https://www.britannica.com/topic/Falun-Gong.

9. "China Names Gunman in Shooting Spree," UPI, September 21, 1994, https://www.upi.com/Archives/1994/09/21/China-names-gunman-in-shooting -spree/2783780120000.

9

Natural Hazards and Emergency Management

Natural hazards are natural events that pose potential threats to humans and can turn into natural disasters without adequate mitigation, as was the case in 2005 when Hurricane Katrina hit New Orleans and caused devastating flooding. It should be pointed out that the concepts of natural hazards and natural disasters are anthropocentric, that is, they are considered potential or actual harms according to human values and interests. Nature and humans have intrinsically interactive relationships, and it is the impingement of human actions upon natural processes that can result in losses to human lives and property. Natural hazards are an integral part of our living environment to which we choose to adapt based on the assessment that the attainable benefits outweigh the potential harm from that environment and adequate, sustainable mitigation is possible for us to prevent the potential harm from becoming a disaster. Failed mitigation, on the other hand, may lead to tragic consequences.

Natural hazards can be classified into four general categories based on their mechanisms. First, geological hazards include earthquakes, volcanic eruptions, tsunamis, and mudslides. Second, meteorological hazards include cold waves, hurricanes (known as typhoons in Asia), and dust storms. Third, hydrological hazards include floods and droughts. Fourth, biological hazards include various types of diseases, including infectious diseases that can become pandemics and cause the deadliest disasters.

DID YOU KNOW?   EMERGENCY RESPONSE SYSTEM

Beijing has implemented an emergency response system that identifies twenty-seven types of hazards that can result in disasters, including air pollution, smog, sand and dust storms, rainstorms, hailstorms, flooding, cold wave, earthquake, influenza, food safety, explosive ordinance, and toxic chemical leakage. The system issues color-coded alerts, from blue for the lowest level (for some hazards) to yellow, orange, and red (the highest level), which forecast the probability, duration, and severity of the impending hazard. The alerts are correlated to potential human impact of the hazard and advise personal and community preparedness. They also trigger corresponding levels of emergency response measures. The alerts are relayed to the public through extensive information dissemination networks, including billboards, television, radio, cellphone services, the Internet, and social media.

Some scholars have identified a new category of hazards, which is termed *environmental hazards*. It covers environmental degradations caused by a combination of natural and human causes, such as air, water, and soil pollutions. Natural hazards and natural disasters may have causal relations among them; for example, earthquakes can cause tsunamis, such as the 2011 Japan earthquake and tsunami.

China is a country with complex geophysical and biological environments and has been prone to all natural disasters, except for volcanic eruption, since the eighteenth century based on available historical records. China is one of the countries most affected by natural disasters, where floods, drought, earthquakes, typhoons, and landslides have accounted for 80–90 percent of the losses resulting from natural disasters each year. Beijing is exposed to a multitude of natural hazards common in northern China, and its high concentration of human activities makes it particularly vulnerable to natural disasters. Major natural disasters can devastate the capital and paralyze the country's political and cultural systems. It is imperative that Beijing develop a resilient emergency response system as an integral part of its sustainable development strategy.

MAJOR NATURAL HAZARDS

Beijing is exposed to a number of natural hazards that pose varied threats to different physiographical and socioeconomic environments of the city. For example, the rural areas in Beijing proper are most affected by cold waves, frost, hailstorms, and pest outbreaks. Landslides usually occur in mountainous areas that are sparsely populated. Some meteorological hazards, such as snowstorms, heavy fog, lightning, and high winds, happen occasionally and, when they do, can cause injuries, property damage, and traffic paralysis. Several natural hazards, especially droughts, flooding, earthquakes, and sand and dust storms, have impacted Beijing in significant ways and sometimes turned into disasters. Biological hazards have become more dangerous to Beijing in recent decades as it emerges as a world city. Infectious diseases can turn into pandemics that wreak havoc on the city and beyond.

China is an earthquake-prone country, accounting for 33 percent of the continental earthquakes stronger than 6.0 on the Richter scale with only 7 percent of the world's land area. While western China has more frequent and bigger earthquakes, it is eastern China that would be most adversely impacted by earthquakes due to its high population density and intense human development. Situated in a complex tectonic zone, Beijing is dissected by many geological faults and particularly vulnerable to earthquake hazards. There have been a number of recorded big earthquakes centered on Beijing proper, starting in 294 CE. The strongest earthquake in Beijing took place in 1679, which is estimated to have reached the magnitude of 8.0, killing about one hundred thousand people and causing immeasurable property damage.

While the last strong earthquake centered on Beijing took place in 1730 (estimated at 6.5 Richter magnitude), earthquakes taking place in the North China earthquake area can also directly impact the city. The 1976 Great Tangshan Earthquake, which registered at magnitude 7.6, killed nearly a quarter million people. Meanwhile, Beijing, a little over one hundred miles southwest of Tangshan, was shaken by a 6.0 earthquake and suffered numerous injuries and widespread building damage, including cracks and foundation damage to some of the landmark buildings, such as the Great Hall of the People in Tiananmen Square.

Droughts in Beijing proper became more frequent and protracted as the climate in northern China became drier and cooler in recent centuries. Records show that Beijing had more than four hundred droughts between 1368 and 1949. Climatologists believe that northern China is undergoing a historical dry period, with annual precipitation reaching the lowest century mark in the 1980s. Drought has played a major role in Beijing's deteriorating water supply and quality, and rapid urban expansion and skyrocketing water usage in modern times have further exacerbated the problems with water resources.

Although it may not be the most sensational natural hazard for media coverage, flooding is the most frequent and costly natural disaster in many heavily populated and developed areas of the world. Historically, Beijing suffered from frequent and devastating flooding. The inability to mitigate river floods was the main reason that early settlers avoided building the

Beijing residents celebrate the first snow of winter 2011. Beijing's winter is usually very dry, and any sizable snowfalls can cause major traffic problems that may paralyze the city. (Li Dongliang/Dreamstime.com)

city on the banks of Yongding River, the largest river in Beijing and its environs. Historical records show that since the Yuan Dynasty (1271–1368), Beijing has suffered, on average, one major flood every two or three years. Summer flooding was often preceded by a spring drought, causing widespread crop and property damage.

In 1698, Beijing and its environs were hit by a major flood caused by the Yongding River, prompting the Qing court to launch an extensive mitigation project that included elaborate hydraulic and levee systems. The project largely alleviated the flooding hazard for Beijing, and an overjoyed Emperor Kangxi changed the river's name from Wuding ("indefinite") or Hun ("muddy") to Yongding ("ever-definite").

Historically, Beijing also suffered from the waterlogging hazard inside the walled city. The Yuan Dynasty built an extensive drainage system in Dadu, the new capital, which included interconnected flood channels and outlets on city walls. In 1801, days of torrential rain forced the water level in the moat around the Forbidden City to rise five to six feet. Terrified court officials called up boats to the Forbidden City in case the emperor and the royal family had to be evacuated. Urban flooding was particularly devastating for the southeastern portion of the city, where the poorest communities would get trapped in the waterlogged environment after summer rainstorms. Despite engineering projects aimed at relieving the waterlogging problem, rapid urban growth in recent decades has made Beijing more vulnerable to waterlogging and flash floods because of the change in surface conditions and the outdated drainage system.

Beijing's drainage system was once a showcase of China's leading-edge engineering feat. However, it had become dilapidated and antiquated by the late imperial era. Only a fraction of the nearly two hundred miles of drainage channels was still in service by the 1940s. While Beijing was no longer under direct and frequent threat from river flooding, waterlogging remained a major hazard in the urban area. In the early 1950s, the government carried out eight projects in Beijing to turn open drainage channels into underground ones to improve public sanitation. These drainage projects, dubbed the "Conscience of Beijing," would help the city avoid major urban flooding for decades to come. Massive underground sewers and culverts were built in the southeastern section of Beijing to alleviate the worst waterlogging problem in the vast slums along Longxu Gou ("Dragon Whisker Trench") and to improve the deplorable environmental conditions in the southeast part of the old walled city. The city's moats and lakes were completely dredged for better drainage. In the reform era, the city's rapid population growth and construction boom have worsened urban flooding due to increased surface runoff and lagging drainage modernization. Every major rainstorm in the summer has brought Beijing to the brink of disaster with major traffic stoppage, property damage, and even the loss of lives, as was the case on June 23, 2011.[1]

The most disastrous urban flooding in Beijing's history took place on July 21, 2012. A massive rainstorm wreaked havoc on Beijing, dumping an average of 170 millimeters (6.7 inches) of rain on the city, registering the highest daily rainfall total since the start of the city's systematic data recording of precipitation in 1951. The downpour caused unprecedented flooding that also triggered lightning and mudslides.[2] The disaster killed at least seventy-nine people by drowning, building collapse, and electrocution by downed powerlines. Over six hundred flights were canceled, ten thousand buildings collapsed (mostly in the rural areas), 1.6 million residents were adversely affected, and 60,000 of them had to be evacuated. The storm's direct economic impact was estimated at about CNY 116 billion (USD 19 billion). Fifty-nine other counties near Beijing also suffered major losses in the disaster. While this particular disaster was considered a 100-year event, Beijing's urban flooding caused by rainstorms and subsequent flooding has become a high-frequency disaster in the urban area. The Great Rainstorm of July 21 revealed a range of inadequacies in the city's emergency management and became a flashpoint for revamping the disaster response system.

Sand and dust storms are a type of meteorological hazard common in arid and semiarid regions, where strong winds lift large amounts of sand and dust from barren and dry surfaces into the atmosphere. Dust particles can be raised to the troposphere by turbulent mixing and convective updrafts. They can then be transported by winds for lengths of time, depending on their size and meteorological conditions, before being pulled back down to the surface again. Roughly 85 percent of sand and dust storms in northern China take place between January and April. The dusty, windy conditions become sand and dust storms when they reduce visibility to fewer than 1,000 meters (3,280 feet).

These storms may incur negative ramifications for public health, economic activities, and ecological conditions. First, airborne dust presents serious risks for human health. Dust particles larger than 10 micrometers (0.01 millimeters) are not breathable; thus, they can only damage external organs such as skin and cause eye irritation. Particles smaller than 10 micrometers, on the other hand, can result in respiratory disorders because they often get trapped in the nose, mouth, and upper respiratory tract. Finer particles may even penetrate the lower respiratory tract and enter the bloodstream, where they can affect all internal organs and be responsible for cardiovascular ailments. Second, dust reduces visibility and degrades the condition of transit routes, directly impacting travel and transportation. Dust deposits adversely affect the output of solar power plants and may also affect river and stream water quality. Third, surface dust deposits can be a mixed blessing. On the one hand, they are a source of micronutrients for both continental and maritime ecosystems, increasing environmental productivity. Sand and dust storms were a key force in the formation of the Loess Plateau and have been responsible for transporting large quantities of minerals to replenish soil fertility in eastern China. On the other hand, dust deposits can disrupt the photosynthesis process and damage plant tissues, thus posing a threat to agriculture.

The earliest record of sand and dust storms in Beijing and its environs was from 440 CE. During the Yuan Dynasty (1271–1368), Beijing began to have official and continuous records of the storms, which may be an indication of their increasing frequency and intensity as the result of long-range climatic and environmental changes. Yuan official records from 1323, 1328, 1329, 1330, 1338, and 1367 describe weather phenomena associated with sand and dust storms with such terms as *red sky*, *day turning into night*, and *raining dust*. During the Ming Dynasty (1368–1644), sand and dust storms in Beijing and its environs appeared to become even more frequent and intense, prompting bitter complaints by bureaucrats from the south, as shown in their personal letters and literary works. Sand and dust storms experienced a spike in the sixteenth and seventeenth centuries, coinciding with warming winters and decreasing annual precipitation.

In modern times, sand and dust storms often blanket much of northern China. Broad planetary and regional conditions may play a key role in the frequency and intensity, as global climate change has resulted in warmer and drier winters, hence exacerbating desertification and enhancing sand and dust storms. At the same time, human-induced environmental degradation, especially overgrazing and overcultivation, has degraded the vast interior rangeland, providing sand and dust storms more abundant material sources. Sand and dust storms began to increase in frequency during the second half of the twentieth century.

In recent years, the frequency of sand and dust storms in China has decreased, and Beijing has had no more than two such storms per year since 2010, though the only storm in 2015 was also the worst since 2002 (Table 9.1). Researchers attribute the decrease of sand and dust storms to both regional ecological restorations, especially conservation projects near Beijing, and global climate change in recent years. The key factor is a reduction of windy conditions in northern China in both frequency and intensity, which has lessened the lifting forces of sand and dust in the interior deserts. Sand and dust storms will continue to take place as a meteorological process, but effective mitigation, such as conservation and the reduction of local sand and dust sources, can help alleviate their negative effects on the human living environment.

Smog is a prime example of a disaster-prone event that is caused by a combination of natural and human activities. Recently, the PRC government decided to classify smog as a natural hazard. The academic basis for this is still up for debate, but environmental activists fear that the classification may reduce public attention and, hence, divert funding and other resources from combating human-induced environmental problems. It is interesting to note that lessened wind strength has exacerbated smog in northern China. Surrounded by mountains on three sides, the bay-like setting of Beijing's topography results in strong temperature inversion and frequent, heavy fogs in the winter and early spring. The foggy condition and drastic increase of pollutants result in catastrophic smog, and the decreasing intensity and frequency of strong winds in northern China diminish the environment's innate ability to disperse the smog.

As China's leading international hub in the era of globalization, Beijing has become more exposed to interregional and international influence. At the same time, a new challenge for this newfound openness is increased exposure to biological hazards because of the difficulties of monitoring population movement and maintaining an effective emergency response system. As a result, Beijing has become more vulnerable to infectious diseases and epidemics. China has paid a hefty price for the lack of modern

Table 9.1   Worst Sand and Dust Storms in Beijing since Year 2000

Date	Intensity and Damage
March 27, 2000	There was no warning. Wind speed reached more than 45 miles per hour; sand and dust blanketed the entire city. Two deaths were reported, caused by scaffolding collapse. There was other structural damages.
April 6, 2000	This was the fifth sand and dust storm in Beijing for the year. Visibility was less than 100 meters (328 feet).
March 15 and 20, 2002	The sand and dust storms lasted 49 and 51 hours, respectively. The second one was registered as the strongest on historical record, dumping 30,000 tons of sediment on Beijing (about 2 kilograms per resident).
April 7–12, 2006	Air pollution reached the highest level (V) in two of the five days.
April 16–18, 2006	There was an estimated 330,000 tons of dust sediments in Beijing.
April 24, 2006	This storm reached Level IV pollution.
March 20, 2010	This storm reached Level V pollution.
April 15, 2015	This was the strongest sand and dust storm since 2002, with the highest level of air pollution index (API) as PM10 exceeded 1,000 µg per cubic meter.
May 4, 2017	PM10 exceeded 1,000–2,000 in southern sections of the city.
March 26–29, 2018	Sand and dust storms and smog coexisted, which was rare. It achieved the highest level of API (VI). The PM10 level jumped from below 300 to 2,000 within two hours. The PM2.5 value in Beijing averaged 1,000–2,000; some locales exceeded 3,000.

Source: Various media reports and government news releases.

emergency management and has done a lot of catching up along the way. The 2003 SARS (severe acute respiratory syndrome) outbreak was both a wake-up call and a turning point in the modernization of China's biohazard mitigation and emergency response system to outbreaks of large-scale infectious diseases.

SARS is a contagious and deadly respiratory illness caused by a coronavirus that has been traced to cave bats in the Yunnan Province in southwest China. One hypothesis is that the virus was passed on in the wild to masked palm civets (*Paguma larvata*), which is a local delicacy in the Guangdong Province and Southeast Asia. The first outbreak of SARS took place in Shunde County, Guangdong Province, in late November 2002. Unfamiliar with the new disease, the local government did not take strong and quick measures to contain it, and the PRC government deemed it a local public health issue and did not notify the World Health Organization (WHO). In February 2003, an infected person from Guangdong brought SARS to Hong Kong, where the disease rapidly transmitted to other places, such as Taiwan and Vietnam, via visitors and travelers. Virus carriers soon brought the deadly disease to other parts of China. Eventually, twenty-six provinces in Mainland China had confirmed SARS cases, and Beijing, along with Guangdong and Hong Kong, suffered a heavy human toll and major disruptions to the city's operations (Table 9.2).

Beijing recorded the first SARS case on March 6, 2003. Both the PRC's Ministry of Health and the Beijing Municipal Government

Table 9.2   Summary of SARS Cases, November 1, 2002–July 31, 2003, Selected Countries and Chinese Provinces

Countries with 100+ SARS Cases*		Total Confirmed Cases	Accumulative Deaths	Cured/ Discharged
Mainland China	Beijing	2,434	147	332
	Guangdong	1,514	56	1,363
	Shanxi	445	20	218
	Inner Mongolia	289	25	41
	Hebei	210	10	57
	Tianjin	176	12	10
	Total	5,327	349	4,941
Hong Kong		1,755	299	1,433
Taiwan		346	37	*
Canada		251	43	194
Singapore		238	33	172

Source: For country data: "Summary of Probable SARS Cases with Onset of Illness from 1 November 2002 to 31 July 2003," World Health Organization (WHO). https://www.who.int/csr/sars/country/table2004_04_21/en.
For Chinese provincial data as of May 18, 2003: Shu Liu, "SARS Incident." October 29, 2014 (in Chinese). http://wap.pishu.cn/zggjaq/aqsj/139604.shtml.
* No adjusted data.

downplayed the severity of SARS in Beijing for fear of, allegedly, disrupting the power transition that was unfolding at the PRC's top leadership. The daunting reality came to light when a retired physician from the leading military hospital revealed more accurate and damning information about Beijing's SARS to an American journalist. Inadequate government action hindered an effective emergency response and wasted precious time for early containment. By late April 2003, when new leadership was installed in the Ministry of Health and Beijing Municipal Government, SARS had become an epidemic with scores of new cases diagnosed every day for two consecutive weeks. A series of emergency measures were hastily implemented, including mandatory quarantine and intensive care of all suspected SARS patients in designated hospitals, the citywide closure of schools and entertainment facilities, and cancellations of major public events. In panic, most migrant workers and many residents fled the city, leaving behind eerily empty streets and a capital that had come to a standstill.

Beijing was hit the hardest by SARS, with the largest number of cases and deaths in Mainland China, but it also received nearly unlimited support from the central government, which made a difference in containing the outbreak. May 29, 2003, was the first day that Beijing reported no new diagnosed cases of SARS. During the next month, the city gradually resumed normal activities. On June 24, 2003, the WHO formally withdrew its travel warning for Beijing and removed the city from the list of SARS-affected areas. The SARS pandemic was a heart-wrenching wake-up call for Beijing and China to build an effective biohazard emergency management system, as Beijing would inevitably be impacted by new epidemics in the coming years, such as H1N1 flu that hit the city in 2013.

Beijing is confronted with a wide range of natural hazards, such as flooding, sand and dust storms, earthquakes, and smog. It needs a mitigation system that adequately accommodates Beijing's size, growth, and functions and that has an integral emergency management component. It is imperative that such a system be in place and be upgraded to reduce disaster vulnerability and to respond to disasters when they happen. Failure to do so will result in adverse national and international repercussions, as the case of SARS demonstrated. In early November 2019, two patients from Inner Mongolia were transported to Beijing and were confirmed to have pneumonic plague on November 12. According to the emergency response protocols, everyone who had been in contact with the two patients were quarantined for observation; three lines of medical checkpoints were set up between Beijing and Inner Mongolia; experts from Beijing were dispatched to the hometown of the two patients in Inner Mongolia. No new cases were found in the ensuing days, and the quarantine related to these two cases was removed on November 21.

RAPIDLY EVOLVING EMERGENCY MANAGEMENT

Human societies must, first of all, mitigate natural hazards to prevent them from turning into disasters and, second, be able to respond effectively when disasters do strike. Conversely, an inadequate emergency management system would increase the potentially adverse effects of natural hazards. On December 7, 2001, for example, a snowfall of four to five inches sent the entire city of Beijing into near paralysis. The breakdown of emergency response, starting with inaccurate weather forecasts partly due to an antiquated computer system, caused citywide traffic jams that lasted for the entire day because of sluggish snow removal and a lack of emergency training.

In an increasingly globalized and integrated world, the lines are blurred between human and natural hazards as well as between domestic and international hazards and disasters. In response, there has been a convergence of strategies and institutional infrastructure for managing societal emergencies. An example of this trend is the establishment of the Department of Homeland Security (DHS) by the U.S. federal government. DHS encompasses federal agencies that had previously been charged with countering human threats (e.g., the Transportation Security Administration (TSA)) or with handling natural disasters (e.g., Federal Emergency Management Agency (FEMA)) or with both (e.g., the U. S. Coast Guard (USCG)). Under DHS, their traditional missions have become integrated, which has proven to be particularly efficient in emergency responses to natural disasters.

In the pre-reform era, the PRC's natural hazard mitigation emphasized traditional biological and engineer approaches, such as ecological improvement through afforestation, flood control levee and dam projects, and soil erosion reduction through hillside terracing. The crucial deficiency was the lack of standing emergency management, which would require substantial economic and technological resources that the PRC did not have. The PRC government instead encouraged self-reliance in rescue and recovery tasks by local communities during disasters. The absence of an integrated infrastructure for natural disaster response, however, exacerbated the toll of natural disasters.

During the early morning hours of July 28, 1976, a magnitude 7.6 earthquake took place with its epicenter in Tangshan, Hebei Province, 178 kilometers (110 miles) to the northeast of Beijing. The shake reached a magnitude of 6.0 in Beijing, causing widespread building damage and numerous personal injuries. In the aftermath of the earthquake, there was little government emergency response, such as material relief and public safety, for the local communities. It is said that even Mao Zedong, the PRC's paramount leader, was merely put up in a makeshift shelter near his residence in Zhongnanhai.

Beijing residents had to fend for themselves and depend on their relatives or neighbors for relief. Fearing collapse of their homes, they set up improvised tents using plastic sheets and wooden poles and camped out for months. In the meantime, there was a lack of official updates or clarification regarding seismic activity or disaster relief. As a result, rumors spread, and resentment mounted, causing great public anxiety. Remarkably, there was no spike in crime thanks to interventions by neighborhood activists and the vigilance of the public.

In the reform era, China adopted new hazard mitigation strategies to cope with emergencies caused by natural disasters. Emergency management remains highly centralized and top-down, with an emphasis on expanding coordination at different levels. The government's role is paramount in mobilizing and streamlining resources to support hazard mitigation and emergency management endeavors.

A good example of the top-down approach was the PRC's efforts in combating the disastrous sand and dust storms. Legend has it that the PRC government was alarmed and embarrassed by the onslaught of sand and dust storms in the early 2000s that seriously disrupted Beijing's daily operations and blemished the capital's international image. The PRC premier Zhu Rongji requested a number of presentations by renowned academic scholars on the causes and coping strategies of sand and dust storm. He was impressed by one particular presentation and decided on the spot to award CNY 30 million, a huge sum for research funding at the time, to the presenter to conduct feasibility studies of tactics and strategies in mitigating sand and dust storms.

Based on the research findings, the PRC government quickly moved to carry out massive projects near Beijing to eliminate sand and dust sources. A forest belt quickly emerged through expansive reforestation projects in the northern and western mountains of Beijing. An ecological recovery zone was established in the Otindag Sandland (20,000 square miles) in Inner Mongolia, the closest sandy desert to Beijing (about 110 miles), with a focus on grassland conservation. Significant progress was made in sand fixation on the Ordos Plateau, 480 miles to the west of Beijing and another major source of sand and dust storms. Today, immense woodlands have taken root in the hills and mountains near Beijing, completely transforming the barren landscape from several decades ago.

These new ecological projects are integral to the long-term afforestation project in the "three norths" (Northeast China, North China, and Northwest China). Together, they form a great green wall that has improved the local ecological environment and is bound to have positive effects on Beijing and northern China by helping to combat desertification and, therefore, diminish the major sources of sand and dust. The PRC also recognized the need for international cooperation, especially with Mongolia, perhaps one of the largest origins of sand and dust.

The PRC's top-down emergency management approach has achieved some success in alleviating the impact of sand and dust storms. This approach has some serious flaws, however. First, local governments lack autonomy and are afforded little flexibility for quick reaction during times of emergency. The PRC government's initial handling of the SARS pandemic shows how this top-down approach can go wrong. There was a communications breakdown, and the central government was not alerted in time. In the meantime, local governments, including the Beijing Municipal Government, waited for directives from the central government, showing little initiative in taking immediate actions to deal with the outbreak. It did not establish an emergency response command until weeks after the WHO had declared a SARS outbreak in the city and issued travel restriction advice. The lack of official assessment and response wasted precious time and caused widespread panic in Beijing and the rest of the country due to a lack of information and advice on coping strategies.

The PRC government has since abandoned its traditional reactive model for emergency management, which centered the emergency response on dealing with the aftermath of disasters or emergencies. The new system focuses on a proactive, mitigation-focused approach to deal with the most frequent and harmful natural hazards and other emergencies. For example, after the disaster caused by a moderate snowfall on December 7, 2001, the Beijing Municipal Government implemented a three-level emergency plan to mitigate snow hazards and prepare for disasters caused by snowstorms, which includes a snow day command center, an enhanced public weather alert system, a stockpile of deicing salt at strategic locations, a rapid-response team equipped with specialized vehicles, and mandatory street front snow removal by businesses and residents.

The new plan had its first test a year later when a round of heavy snow hit Beijing. The new emergency system kicked in. Traffic remained relatively smooth. Over one hundred thousand Beijing residents were mobilized to remove snow from the streets, and businesses that failed to remove snow from their street fronts were fined. There was no major incident during this snow event, and Beijing went on with its daily routines without a hitch.

Another example of a stopgap and piecemeal approach to natural hazard mitigation was the way that Beijing authorities dealt with the sudden spike of sand and dust storms in the early 2000s. In 2006, Beijing drafted the Contingency Plan for Sand and Dust Storms Hazards Emergencies, which outlined responsibility assignments for specific government agencies in managing emergencies if sand and dust storms rose to catastrophic levels. This plan, however, only targeted a particular natural hazard that posed the greatest threat to Beijing at the time. How would the city respond to other disasters, such as SARS, should disaster strike?

The PRC government has carried out broad improvement in emergency management. As a result, there has been positive development in China's emergency management in the aftermath of SARS. Official information dissemination has become more transparent; public officials are expected to be directly accountable for the outcomes of their decisions and actions in managing emergencies. There has been a flood of government-funded academic research on improving emergency management infrastructure. Legislations and regulations have been drafted and passed swiftly to support the establishment of sustainable and effective emergency management. Between 2003 and 2006, the PRC government invested CNY 25.7 billion (USD 3.3 billion) in prevention and control of infectious diseases that covered 95 percent of China's territories. For the first time in Chinese history, public health emergency management became part of regular government operations. The response and relief were overall quite efficient during the 2003–2004 bird flu outbreak,[3] the 2008 winter storm in central and southern China,[4] and the 2008 Wenchuan earthquake.[5] Sometimes, the system can overreact, however. When the WHO declared the 2009 flu pandemic, the PRC reacted with such heightened vigilance that it banned all passengers from Mexico, one of the worst-infected countries, from entering China, causing a diplomatic rebuff from Mexico.

The new emergency infrastructure focused on modernizing the "hardware" by adopting cutting-edge technical capacity and organizational structure that had proven to be effective in developed countries. In October 2003, the first emergency shelter in China opened in Beijing. It was located in the Yuan Dynasty City Wall Relics Park located between the northern Third and Fourth Ring Roads. The budget proposal for the shelter was expedited and approved in part because of the aftermath of the SARS pandemic and in part because of the decision to integrate the new shelter into the historic park, which had been slated to be part of the landscape project for the 2008 Summer Olympics. The shelter was designed to accommodate 250,000 people, with 1.5 square meters (16 square feet) per person, more than the 230,000 residents from the four subdistricts bordering the park. The shelter is equipped with emergency utilities, such as power generators, a water filtration and supply system, toilets, a broadcasting office, supply storage, and medical facilities. Plastic replicas of the park's manicured landscape are used to hide the shelter from visitors' view to preserve the park's aesthetics. The emergency shelter has since become the model for Chinese cities in densely populated areas.

The original conceptualization for the shelter was for the purpose of accommodating evacuees after a major earthquake. There are three types of earthquake shelters in Beijing with different accommodations based on projected duration of stay. Class I shelters have a complete range of facilities and can accommodate evacuees for more than thirty days. Class II shelters have most facilities and can accommodate evacuees for one to thirty days. Class III shelters have basic facilities and can accommodate evacuees for no more than ten days. As of 2018, there are eleven Class I shelters, thirty-seven Class II shelters, and forty-four Class III shelters in Beijing. Long-term plans call for Class I shelters within one-hour walking distance and Class III shelters within ten minutes of walking distance for all residents. The per capita shelter space is currently 0.76 square meters (8 square feet) for each permanent resident. The government's goal is to increase it to 1.09 square meters (11.7 square feet) per permanent resident by 2020 and to 2.1 square meters (22.6 square feet) by 2035. The distribution of shelters is uneven, however. Most shelters are located in the six urban districts, and the four rural districts in the ecological conservation development zone have no evacuation shelters.

Beijing was the first province-level administrative division that established a judicial framework for emergency management. In the aftermath of the SARS pandemic, Beijing drafted the General Contingency Plan for Public Emergencies in 2006 to serve the needs of the 2008 Summer Olympics. In 2007, the PRC's National People's Congress established the Emergency Response Law of the People's Republic of China to overhaul the existing emergency response infrastructure. In 2008, Beijing People's Congress passed a resolution to implement the national contingency law, laying out specific priorities and components of a new emergency management system with a "3+2" management structure: "3" stands for three operational levels of emergency response apparatus, that is, municipal-level agencies, thirteen event-specific command centers, and corresponding agencies at the district level, and "2" represents the two-tier information call centers, the 110 emergency and the 12345 nonemergency switchboards. The new approach emphasizes comprehensive and coordinated emergency management, government accountability, and public information transparency.

Despite progress since the 2008 Summer Olympics, Beijing continued to face serious challenges in dealing with major natural disasters, as evidenced by the 100-year rainstorm taking place on July 21, 2012, which is dubbed "the Great Rainstorm of July 21." This disaster exposed Beijing's hazard vulnerabilities and weaknesses in emergency response. Postdisaster assessment revealed several urgent problems in Beijing's emergency management infrastructure. First, the city's drainage system needed an overhaul. Many parts of the drainage system built in the early 1950s had deteriorated; the newer additions to the drainage system were mostly designed to prevent flooding generated by one- to three-year rainstorms in Beijing and its environs, which average 36–45 millimeters (1.4–1.8 inches) of rain per hour. In contrast, the drainage systems for Paris, Tokyo, and New York City were designed to accommodate five-year, ten-year, and fifteen-year rainstorms. Even the drainage system serving newer and vitally important development, such as the Olympic Park and Tiananmen Square, was only designed to accommodate up to a five-year rainstorm.

Second, the Great Rainstorm of July 21 exposed the failure of the Beijing Municipal Government to adequately invest in the costly, long-term, and largely invisible public infrastructure that is essential in keeping up with rapid urban expansion. Between 2000 and 2010, Beijing's built (urbanized) area more than doubled from 700 square kilometers (270 square miles) to 1,400 square kilometers (540 square miles). High-rise residential structures and business skyscrapers sprung up to crowd the skyline. The accompanying infrastructure, however, was often inadequately designed, hastily constructed, and poorly maintained due to both substandard construction and corner-cutting actions by some unscrupulous contractors. For example, an investigative report revealed that the underpasses of over ninety expressway interchanges in Beijing would become flood traps during rainstorms because of their flawed sunken design. Motorists often get stranded, and some have even drowned after their vehicles became inundated.[6] A temporary fix is to install large pumps at the underpasses. They would meet the emergent needs in case of underpass flooding, but the pumps take up a lot of space and blemish landscape aesthetics.

Beijing still has much to improve, notwithstanding its progress in acquiring the latest technology, hardware, and even personnel training in emergency management. Effective emergency management requires a systemic framework, similar to an engineered system, within which respective groups and agencies work in synergy to perform the system's designed functions.

Early during the 2012 rainstorm disaster, Beijing's emergency management suffered malfunction because of breakdowns in communication and coordination among key government agencies. Why were there no emergency personnel at freeway underpasses known for dangerous flooding to direct traffic and assist stranded motorists? Why had there not been any mitigation for manhole covers in the streets when it was known that most of them would be washed away by street flooding, posing a grave danger to pedestrians?[7] While the weather service had issued five warnings prior to the storm, it appeared to have underestimated the impending magnitude of the storm, first issuing a blue warning (weakest storm) in the morning, then updating it to yellow in the early afternoon, and then changing it to orange (second most severe level for storms) in late afternoon when the torrential rains were already wreaking havoc on the city.

Furthermore, the authorities failed to take precautions based on these warnings. As a result, over eighty thousand passengers did not receive flight cancellation information and became stuck at Beijing Capital International Airport, where there was no emergency evacuation plan, nor any accommodation, for them. A hundred thousand cars were stranded on the freeways and in city streets, and numerous stoppages happened in the subways. A lot of blame flew around in the aftermath of the disaster while the official media praised the top Beijing officials for being at the frontline of relief efforts during the storm.

The Great Rainstorm of July 21 was the most recent major disaster that tested Beijing's hazard mitigation and emergency management. In the aftermath of this disaster, the Beijing Municipal Government came to the conclusion that a comprehensive preventive system must replace the disaster-specific stopgap apparatus that had been proven not to work well, especially when Beijing's rapid growth poses greater and more complex challenges to hazard mitigation and emergency response. The exiting emergency management was overhauled to clear the way for a new systemic model of emergency management. The new system emphasizes integration of relevant government agencies, citywide risk assessment on potential human and natural disasters, an advanced warning system, infrastructure improvement, and enhanced public awareness.

BEIJING'S EMERGENCY MANAGEMENT AS A WORK IN PROGRESS

In recent years, China has made significant progress in developing a new system of emergency management that focuses on not only hazard mitigation and disaster relief but also, and more importantly, the transformation of traditional cities into resilient cities. While scientific studies on hazard mechanisms continue to be strong, research on the social aspects of natural hazards, such as risk analysis, socioeconomic vulnerability, and community resiliency, has become increasingly influential to policy making and long-term planning. The latest progress in Beijing's emergency management may be shown in three aspects.

First, there has been an institutional convergence of emergency management and natural hazard mitigation, which traditionally were parallel to each other. In April 2018, the PRC government inaugurated the Ministry of Emergency Management (MEM) as part of the overhaul of the existing emergency management apparatus. The new ministry consolidated resources and administrative powers for emergency management and disaster relief, which had been scattered in thirteen ministerial departments. It also absorbed the National Committee for Disaster Reduction (NCDR), which was first established in 1989 but never had administrative or regulatory authority. MEM appears to be modeled after the U.S. Department of Homeland Security (DHS), especially its Federal Emergency Management Agency (FEMA). It was given broad powers as the sole central government agency in charge of mitigating natural hazards and responding to consequent human crises.

Beijing established its subordinate counterpart to MEM, the Beijing Municipal Bureau for Emergency Response, in November 2018. It directly answers to the mayor of Beijing and has nineteen command posts, each specializing in a specific disaster or incident that had been managed under various government agencies. For example, the Earthquake Emergency Command Post had been under the Beijing Earthquake Agency, and the Counterterrorism and Criminal Case Emergency Command Post had been under the Beijing Bureau of Public Safety. While it may take some time for the previously fragmented operations to become fully integrated, the new emergency management structure is definitely a step in the right direction in developing a complete and responsive system of emergency management.

Second, Beijing is at the forefront of adding new hardware and adopting the latest technology to enhance emergency management capabilities. In its Emergency Plans for the Thirteenth Five-Year Plan, the Beijing Municipal Government set the goal of establishing the first aerial rescue and response system in the country, combining the use of helicopters, blimps, and drones with large funding and other resource support.

Beijing is in the process of expanding the size, number, and location of emergency shelters. Each of the sixteen districts is required to add a new Class I shelter per year. Beijing's medical emergency services comprises a three-tier hierarchy: the municipal emergency center, the district subcenters, and the first-aid stations. In summer 2018, the Beijing Municipal Government decided to set up 288 first-aid stations throughout Beijing, with Chaoyang, the most populous district, having the most with 55. This is aimed at shortening emergency response time, especially during times of major emergencies. The city has also set the goal of providing one mobile ambulance per ten thousand residents; the national average since 1994 has been one ambulance per fifty thousand people. A foreign language emergency service hotline is also being planned.

Beijing has plans to become a "sponge city" by enhancing its rainwater retention through sunken green space, impounding water reservoirs, and public spaces built with water-permeable materials. The concept of a sponge city describes a city that integrates urban water management into urban planning policies, including hazard mitigation and emergency management. For Beijing, building a sponge city is "a stone for several birds," as the initiative would empower the city to cope with a multitude of challenges related to water resources, urban flooding, and waterlogging. Extensive "sponge" surfaces can help Beijing increase storage and filtration of natural precipitation, reduce storm runoff as a mitigating tool for flooding hazards, control pollution, and improve groundwater quality. Water retained from the sponge surface qualifies as gray water—household and office wastewater without fecal contamination—and can be used for a variety of purposes, such as car washes and green space maintenance. The goal is to transform 20 percent of Beijing's built areas into sponge surfaces by 2020.

Beijing intends to adopt the latest technologies in boosting its emergency management by taking advantage of its position as a leading innovation hub in China. One innovative approach in emergency management is Beijing's move to tap into the rising "fusion media," that is, the seamless integration of all forms of media. Beijing is the first province-level administrative division that has set up one fusion media center in each of its sixteen districts by the summer of 2018. These centers immediately experienced a real-life test in July 2018 when a rainstorm hit Beijing. The municipal government's press office live cast rainstorm and flood information through the new media matrix and received more than twenty-three million viewings. The fusion media center in the rural and hilly Miyun District alone received over a million viewings.

As a crucial aspect of natural hazard mitigation, however, Beijing has been slow in dealing with the outdated infrastructure and inadequate public services that are critical in hazard mitigation and emergency response. Significant investment and bureaucratic streamlining are needed to revamp aged drainage systems to reduce waterlogging, to refurbish older buildings to improve earthquake safety, and to modernize outmoded components of public infrastructure, such as subway tracks and natural gas pipelines. Granted, infrastructure improvement projects are costly and time-consuming, which may not help appointed officials garner political credentials. However, it is analogous to planting disaster time bombs in the city to neglect or delay these projects. In late November 2019, the Beijing Municipal Government published a three-year plan for improving water environment, which includes replacing and repairing sewer and drainage systems. The plan aims to treat all wastewater in the six urban districts and the capital subcenter by 2022.

Third, the "software" of emergency management has improved in recent years in terms of government transparency and personnel training, public awareness, and grassroots participation in emergency preparedness. Government emergency personnel are required to have regular training and testing to guarantee their readiness. Many citizens have stepped up and risked their own lives to help others during emergencies and disasters; they fulfill a much-needed role in emergency management at the ground level.

They would be safer and more effective with basic training and timely support. There has been a concerted effort by the government to enlist the help of residents for emergency response, and, in the tradition of community activism, there is no shortage of volunteers. The government provides basic training to volunteers on evacuation procedures, first-aid application, neighborhood warning methods, and emergency monitoring and reporting.

Having learned the hard lesson from the SARS pandemic, Beijing authorities have become more transparent in their emergency management operations. In 2017, the Beijing Municipal Government made public the responsibilities in emergency management for respective government agencies so that residents could have better access to and oversight of the bureaucracy during time of emergencies. On June 1, 2018, the municipal government held a press conference informing the press about the rainy season forecast and predicted levels of flooding threat. During the 2018–2019 flu season, the Beijing government held press release sessions twice a week to update flu information and announce clinic locations and business hours for flu shots. There were over four hundred free flu vaccine stations for K–12 children and senior Beijing residents, plus over four hundred additional fee-based flu shot clinics.

The authorities frequently sponsor organized drills and education campaigns to promote public awareness and preparedness for natural disasters and other emergencies. The municipal and district governments have made it a routine to conduct emergency drills at workplaces and schools. Each year, May 12 is slated for mass drills, as it was the date when, in 2008, the devastating Wenchuan earthquake took place, marking the most catastrophic natural disaster in China in the twenty-first century.

An important development in China's emergency management is the unique and increasing role of grassroots participation and nongovernmental organizations (NGOs). Bursting onto the scene after the 2008 Wenchuan earthquake, social organizations have become actively engaged in disaster relief activities. In recent years, the Chinese government started procuring services from social organizations and engaging them in building disaster model communities, officially known as Comprehensive Disaster Reduction Demonstration Communities. There have been discussions on how to encourage further business participation in disaster relief and market-driven products and services, but skepticism and government entrenchment are barriers for businesses to play a more engaging role in emergency management.

The key to reducing disaster risk in cities is to build and sustain a mitigation-oriented system of emergency management. Such a system requires new conceptualization in urban policy and planning with legislative and financial support. Beijing leads China in legal and policy initiatives regarding hazard mitigation and emergency management. The municipal government updates its master plan for emergency management at the beginning of each five-year plan and revises respective laws and regulations accordingly. Beijing was the first province-level administrative division to adopt the resilient city model in its 2016–2035 Master Plan, which mandates the city to integrate sound emergency management into overall urban development through improvement of both the "hardware," such as infrastructure and equipment, and "software," such as public awareness and grassroots participation.

Since the 2003 SARS pandemic, Beijing has gone a long way in emergency management, from disaster-specific response to comprehensive hazard mitigation and disaster prevention. It has embarked on developing an integrated system composed of synergistic components in emergency management, and the signs of progress are surely encouraging.

NOTES

1. "Torrential Rains Hit Beijing, Disrupt Traffic," SINA English, June 23, 2011, http://english.sina.com/china/p/2011/0623/378825.html; "Downpour Paralyses Beijing Traffic," China.org.cn, June 24, 2011, http://www.china.org.cn/photos /2011-06/24/content_22847995.htm.

2. "Heavy Rains in Beijing," NASA Earth Observatory, July 21–22, 2012, https://earthobservatory.nasa.gov/images/78626/heavy-rains-in-beijing.

3. "Bird Flu—The Chronology of a Disease," United Nations World Food and Agriculture Organization (FAO), accessed September 10, 2019, http://www.fao .org/avianflu/en/chronology.html.

4. Kortney Smith, "2008 Chinese Winter Storms," Prezi, last updated May 9, 2011, https://prezi.com/9hardaylkkyc/2008-chinese-winter-storms. The snow storms that swept through eleven provinces in central and southern China killed 129 people and caused an estimated USD 23 billion of economic loss.

5. Kenneth Pletcher and John P. Rafferty, "Sichuan Earthquake of 2008," Encyclopædia Britannica, accessed September 22, 2019, https://www.britannica .com/event/Sichuan-earthquake-of-2008. Also known as the Sichuan earthquake of 2008, it was a magnitude 8.0 quake that killed ninety thousand people and destroyed 80 percent of the structures in the region.

6. Xu Chao, Huang Kaiqian, and Lilian Rogers, "Buried under Water," ChinaFile, July 26, 2012, http://www.chinafile.com/reporting-opinion/caixin -media/buried-under-water. During the July 21, 2012, rainstorm, a thirty-four-year-old magazine editor became trapped in his SUV at an underpass in the southern part of Beijing. It took more than four hours for rescuers to finally find him dead in his car, having apparently died of suffocation instead of drowning.

7. "China Rainfall: Beijing Resident Describes Deluge," BBC, July 22, 2012, https://www.bbc.com/news/world-asia-18943207.

10

Culture and Lifestyle

Beijing has fostered a culture centered on a lifestyle so unique and influential that it is worthy of a special designation: Beijing Culture. The city's political gravity has molded a landscape of rigidity and grandeur and codified social relations in an orderly and stratified fashion. Beijing citizens impress visitors with an aloof and paternalistic persona, as if they all have an inside track on the highest levels of political intrigue and cultural vogue. Native Beijingers appear to prefer leisurely activities over entrepreneurial pursuits, perhaps because of residual influence of the parasitic lifestyle of the Qing bannermen or the capital's ability to summon nationwide goods and services. Some describe their lifestyle as slow-paced and laid-back; others may consider it as being lazy and lacking initiative. To understand Beijing Culture, one must separate myth from reality and distinguish the past from the present. As the capital becomes a world city, Beijing appears to embrace national and global pop culture, at times awkwardly, while recreating its cultural legacy.

Beijing has been steeped in historical heritage as the national capital for much of the last seven and half centuries. It is the mecca of Chinese imperial architecture and the apex of traditional Chinese cityscape. It has seven historical and prehistorical landmarks designated as UNESCO World Heritage Sites,[1] the most among all cities in the world. Beijing is home to the Forbidden City, the Temple of Heaven, the Summer Palace, the Ming Tombs, and the Peking Man site. Beijing can also claim a section of the Great Wall and the Grand Canal, both of which played vital roles in the development of Beijing as the imperial capital. These landmarks still define the layout and place identity for Beijing and are the material sustenance of national pride and unity.

Beijing Culture is not limited to the tangible, of course. It has many intangible cultural traits that include the performing arts, such as the Peking opera; artworks such as cloisonné enamel and jade or ivory sculpture; and colorful folk handcrafts, such as clay figurines and dough figures. More importantly, the acclaimed Beijing Culture is rooted in a mind-set. An old-timer of Beijing would describe, in a distinct old Beijing accent, a patrician lifestyle centered on an aloof attitude and a laid-back daily routine as well as insistence on ritualistic formalities and high-brow sensitivity. The traditional tea houses might have been the best place to observe how the old-timers interacted, only the old-timers and traditional tea houses have both faded into history. And, lest we forget, there is the traditional Beijing food—Peking roast duck, anyone?

Beijing Culture has three distinct characteristics. First, Beijing Culture is the product of the capital's status and the political elites. The imperial capital's physical layout epitomized Chinese cosmic vision and supremacy of the ruler, which placed the royal compound at the center of the city straddling an imaginary central axis and dictated the location, size, and design of landmarks. The political elites have always insisted on showcasing Beijing as "the model for all places" by lavishing abundant resources and imposing ideological preferences to enhance China's national image and serve their own interests. The convergence of political, intellectual, and financial powers in the capital has long fostered an unparalleled and sophisticated fusion of arts and literature, cuisine and artifacts, and customs and rituals.

Second, Beijing Culture is the product of a cultural melting pot. Beijing has been at the crossroad of economic and cultural exchange among different societies of Eurasia. Nomadic and hunting-fishing cultures played a major role in Beijing's development: two of the last three unified dynasties in Chinese history were ruled by the Mongols from the steppes and the Jurchens (Manchus) from the northeastern forests and marshland. The city has been the national hub that witnesses the comings and goings of the capable, the ambitious, and the destitute from near and far, who have left their marks on Beijing Culture along the way. It is interesting to note that most of the cultural attributes that are associated with Beijing Culture, such as a the unique accent or classic dishes, are actually recent emulations, transplants, or fusions of various regional and ethnic cultures.

Third, Beijing Culture is never provincial and stagnant. Few in Beijing can claim to be "authentic" natives because the city's demographic profile has been undergoing constant flux—and so have the characteristics of Beijing Culture. For example, one of the most celebrated aspects of Beijing

Culture is the high-brow, ritual-driven, and slow-paced lifestyle of "old Beijingers." This lifestyle was indeed the way of life for bannermen during the Qing Dynasty, and it persisted briefly among the patrician community thereafter. It was never a lifestyle afforded to the masses, especially the urban poor, nor was it sustainable in postimperial times.

CAPITAL AND CULTURE

The Landscape of the Capital

Beijing is renowned for its landmarks; it is a living museum of historical and modern urban design and architectural renditions of epochal ethos. The most important landmark in Beijing is, however, the north–south central axis that has dictated the symmetrical layout of the city and the location of important buildings. Beijing's central axis dates back to the design of Yuan Beijing (Dadu), and it was during Ming Dynasty that Beijing was realigned and rebuilt based on the central axis, which still dominates the land use and landscape of Beijing's urban core today. The historical central axis was about 7.8 kilometers (4.85 miles) long. It started in the south at the Yongdingmen Gate, the middle gate of the historical Outer City; extended northward through Zhengyangmen Gate, the front gate (Qianmen) of the Inner City; and went through the Forbidden City, Jingshan (Prospect Hill), and the Bell and Drum Towers on the north end. More important structures aligned the central axis, including the Temple of Heaven (Tiantan), the Temple of Agriculture (Xiannongtan), the Imperial Ancestral Temple (Taimiao), the Altar of Earth and Harvest (Shejitan), the Middle and South Lakes (Zhongnanhai), and the North Lake (Beihai) as well as more shrines and temples, princely mansions, and government offices. The central axis is the epitome of how the Chinese metaphysical views and societal governance manifested in city planning; it is currently on China's Tentative List of UNESCO World Heritage.

The PRC government has inherited and reinforced the symbolic imperatives of the central axis with its own additions. The most high-profile monument in modern China, the Monument of People's Heroes, broke ground on the axis the day before the official founding of the People's Republic of China (October 1, 1949). In the 1950s, the PRC government expanded Tiananmen Square and built two of the ten monumental buildings during this decade on each side of the axis on Tiananmen Square: the Great Hall of the People (on the west side) and the National Museum of China (on the east side). In the 1970s, Tiananmen Square was further expanded, and the Mausoleum of Chairman Mao Zedong, the PRC's founding father, was erected on the site where the Gate of China (previously called the Gate of Ming and the Gate of Qing) once stood.

As China burst onto the world stage in the reform era, the PRC government and Beijing authorities decided to rebuild and extend the central axis as a visible showcase of China's achievements. Beijing restored the historical streetscape to the south of Zhengyangmen Gate in 2003; Yongdingmen Gate, at the historical southern end of the central axis, was rebuilt in 2005. The main site of the 1990 Asian Games was located on the northern extension of the central axis as well as the Olympic Park for the 2008 Beijing Summer Olympics. It must be noted that the two most visible structures in the Olympic Park were the squarish National Aquatics Center ("the Water Cube") and the circular National Stadium ("the Bird's Nest"). Straddling the northern extension of the central axis, they commemorate the ancient Chinese notion of heaven, which is spherical, and earth, which is squarish.

Beyond the central axis, Beijing also has many other historical landmarks. Among the most famous are the Summer Palace (Yiheyuan); Yuanmingyuan Park (ruins of "the old Summer Palace"); the Ming Tombs, one of which has been excavated; and the Great Wall constructed during Ming Dynasty. There are many architectural renditions that reflect period political and cultural characteristics. Places of worship featured prominently in imperial Beijing, the most famous include the Yonghe Lamasery, which was commissioned by the Qing rulers as a conciliatory effort toward their Mongol allies, who were Tibetan Buddhists. Islamic mosques, often built with a Chinese architectural façade, demonstrate the importance of the Chinese Muslim community in Beijing. Among Christian churches, the most famous has to be the Cathedral of the Immaculate Conception. Referred to by locals as Nantang (the South Church), it started as a small chapel by the famous Jesuit Matteo Ricci in 1605. The cathedral was razed to the ground during the Boxer Rebellion in 1900 but was rebuilt in 1904.

During late Qing Dynasty and early Republican era, many Western-style buildings sprung up in Beijing, an indication of the sea change in China's politics and culture. There is no significant landmark from this period, as China had fallen into crises and chaos. The 1950s saw Soviet influence in urban development with Chinese vernacular. The central government procured national resources to construct the Ten Great Buildings by 1959 to commemorate the PRC's tenth anniversary. Two of them, the Great Hall of the People and the National Museum of China, became anchor structures on Tiananmen Square.

In the reform era, Beijing has experienced an unprecedented building boom. Skyscrapers overcrowd the skyline. Most of the new landmarks are in eclectic postmodern styles and were almost all designed by Western architects, symbolizing China's embrace of Western concepts of urban design. Many are office towers and convention hotels, but the most notable are public structures. In addition to the National Aquatic Center and the

The Great Wall of China began when a series of smaller structures were linked during the Qin Dynasty in the late third century BCE, and it eventually extended over roughly 4,000 miles in northern China along the nomadic and sedentary agricultural divide. The wall that most tourists visit today was built during the Ming Dynasty (1368–1644) with the best preserved sections within Beijing Proper. (Corel)

National Stadium at the Olympic Park, the National Center for the Performing Arts, the CMG (China Media Group) Headquarters, the Galaxy Soho, and the tallest and newest of them all, the China Zun (its outline was inspired by the *zun*, a Bronze Age Chinese wine vessel) by TFP Farrells, are but some of Beijing's new landmarks that have been reshaping the city's skyline and landscape. Beijing's new landmarks and their resultant new landscape show an ongoing transformation of Beijing Culture, a process that started in the late Qing Dynasty but has sped up in the reform era.

The Capital and Mandarin: The National Tongue

What the capital has to offer is often eagerly emulated by the rest of the country, and the rulers in the capital can also impose what they are used to on the rest of the country. Take the case of Mandarin, for example. Spoken Chinese has undergone significant changes over time, and the dialect of a dynasty's core region, centered on the capital, usually prevailed to become the official tongue. As the official spoken Chinese, today's Mandarin has a relatively short history. The origin of Mandarin can be dated to the Yuan Dynasty (1271–1368). A seminal compilation by Zhou Deqing, *Zhongyuan Yinyun* (Rhymes of the Central Plain, 1324) illustrates that the northern Chinese used in Yuan variety plays (*Yuanzaju*) was very similar to today's Mandarin. During the early Ming Dynasty, when Nanjing was the imperial capital, the Nanjing dialect gained popularity and became the official dialect. Its pronunciation of *Beijing* was transcribed by French missionaries in the Yangzi Delta area as *Pékin*, which was later modified and adopted by the postal map romanization. The Beijing dialect emerged as a secondary official tongue after the Ming capital was moved to Beijing and remained so until the early part of the Qing Dynasty (1644–1911), when it became the official tongue with significant Manchu influence, thence known in Europe as "Mandarin." In 1728, Emperor Yongzheng (r. 1723–1735) decreed that the new Beijing dialect would be the national spoken Chinese for official affairs. By the late Qing Dynasty, the Beijing dialect had become the spoken Chinese of the bureaucrats and the literati, as the court tried to proclaim it the national *lingua franca* (the common tongue).

National debate over an official national dialect went on during the ROC era (1911–1949), but the Beijing dialect, or Mandarin, held a strong advantage over the alternatives because it had become the national lingua franca and Beijing had remained the national capital in the early ROC (1911–1928) era. In 1924, a consensus was reached that the national tongue would be based on the Beijing dialect. The ROC government actively promoted this new national tongue in the 1930s. At the 1955 National Language Reform Conference, experts voted fifty-two to fifty-one for the Beijing dialect to remain the basis of the national tongue, which was retitled *the Common Tongue* (Putonghua). In addition to this historical momentum, Beijing's political sway as the capital helped promote its dialect nationwide, making it a unifying cultural trait for China.

The Capital and Political Sensitivity

Beijing's capital status has also fostered an intriguing cultural characteristic, that is, a mentality of superiority and political sensitivity among "native" Beijingers. Beijing is where politicians, bureaucrats, and aristocrats have been engaged in ideological polemics and political intrigues. Beijing is the hustling, bustling hub that has attracted some of the most educated, ambitious, and capable folks who come to the national capital in search of upward mobility in the central bureaucratic hierarchy. In modern times, the large intellectual community is inherently robust; its engagement in political discourse has been infused by young college students from the many colleges and universities in town.

Notwithstanding the dynamics of political machinations, local residents also made an interest in politics a part of their pop culture. Merely residing in the capital, dubbed as living "at the emperor's feet," appeared to provide an ample credential for some native Beijingers to feel well equipped and more entitled to dissect national politics in both rumor mills and public forums as a great pastime. Observers and visitors took note that Beijingers were indeed keen on claiming to be well informed of national politics and were quite eager to discuss and participate in politics. Some found it amusing that almost every taxi driver would welcome a politically charged conversation. Too often, this political sensitivity caused trouble. In the play *Teahouse* by renowned native author Lao She (1899–1966), for example, the owner of the popular teahouse posted "No Politics!" on the wall as a reminder to his customers to refrain from debating politics.

THE MELTING POT THAT HAS BREWED BEIJING CULTURE

As the national capital, Beijing has been the hub for politics, trade and commerce, literature and arts, and diverse folk cultures. Beijing Culture is, therefore, the product of the interactions among regional cultures and even different civilizations. Its food scene may best illustrate the essence of Beijing Culture as a constantly evolving amalgamation.

A popular Chinese cuisine known around the world today is Peking roast duck. Indeed, Peking roast duck has earned Beijing, and even China, a special international reputation for its unique and delicate flavor and complex preparation procedures. Legend has it that the founding emperor of the Ming Dynasty, Zhu Yuanzhang, was very fond of duck, and so the court chefs perfected roasting duck in either an open or closed oven. His son, Emperor Yongle, brought the duck chefs with him when he moved the imperial capital from Nanjing to Beijing in the early 1400s. The first "Peking Duck" restaurant, Bianyifang, was opened in 1416 near Zhengyangmen Gate and is still in business today, representing the highest form of closed-oven roasting technique. For decades, the restaurant's sign had a small caption: "Jinling (Nanjing's historical name) Roast Duck."

The most remarkable part of Peking roast duck, however, was the contribution from the nomadic and hunting cultures of the north. During the Qing Dynasty, a special duck subspecies became exclusively used for Peking roast duck. The duck, allegedly known for its white feathers and superior flavor, was favored by the rulers of Liao, Jin, and Yuan in their ritualistic hunting expeditions. Some of these ducks were captured alive and raised in imperial hunting grounds. During the Qing Dynasty, a special feeding method was developed to fatten the duck to attain the ultimate tenderness in roasting. The "Beijing force-fed duck" eventually became the only authentic bird used for preparing Peking roast duck.

Another famous Beijing cuisine is a hot pot feast called Beijing instant-boiled mutton. The authentic version of instant-boiled mutton appears simple, but it is quite meticulous in preparation and selective in ingredients. The classic utensil is a pure copper pot, which is filled with broth (made with dry shrimp, chopped green onion, ginger, and mushrooms) and heated by charcoal. The best cuts of mutton are from the back neck, the fore shank, and the hind shank. They are sliced to roughly 13 centimeters (5 inches) long, 3.3 centimeters (1.3 inches) wide, and 0.9 millimeters (0.04 inches) thick pieces. The sauce is a concoction of sesame paste, Chinese leek flower, fermented bean curd, fermented shrimp sauce, chopped cilantro, and ginger. Hot chili oil can also be used as a side sauce. Diners use their own chopsticks to pick up the sliced mutton, rinse it for a few seconds in the boiling broth, and then dip the now cooked mutton in the sauce. Napa cabbage, mung bean vermicelli, and doufu (tofu) are used as sides; sesame biscuits or buckwheat noodles are served as the starch component of the meal. The meal concludes with sweet pickled garlic and some broth, now enriched by the meat. Green and jasmine tea are not served with the meal because the tannic acid in the tea hinders the digestion of mutton.

Hot pot has a long history, and legend has it that it was the Mongols who invented instant-boiled mutton. Specifically, Kublai Khan was served a meal quickly prepared in a copper pot before a major battle, which he won, and thereafter jubilantly bestowed the name "instant-boiled mutton" upon the meal. Its origin, however, may be dated to the Khitans, whose tenth-century murals show them eating mutton from a hot pot. Instant-boiled mutton was brought to Beijing after the Khitans established the Liao Dynasty (907–1125) and made Beijing its "Nanjing" (the southern capital, 938). Later on, the Mongols took a liking to it, but it was the hunter-fisher Manchus who invented its current elaborate version. It was the main course of the royal feast consisting of Manchu and Chinese delicacies. Beijing instant-boiled mutton became a full-meal dish after the mid Qing Dynasty and has maintained its popularity to this day. It is yet another reminder of Beijing Culture's nomadic and hunting-fishing heritage.

Beijing's traditional cuisine reflects three major streams of regional cultural influence. First, as exemplified by instant-boiled mutton, there is a strong cultural influence from the nomadic steppes and northeastern forests and marshland. In addition to instant-boiled mutton, Beijing has numerous time-honored restaurants renowned for their barbecued mutton and beef. As a matter of fact, the strong presence of mutton and beef in Beijing cuisine is an indication of the strong nomadic influence.

Second, Shandong cuisine, one of the top regional cuisines in China, had established itself as an influential school of cooking in Beijing partly due to the region's enduring affluence and elaborate food culture. Shandong's proximity to Beijing was also an important factor for its popularity in the capital, which gave it both a wealthy elite clientele and incentives for continued innovations. Most of the court chefs during the Ming and Qing Dynasties were from Shandong, and Shandong-style restaurants still have a prominent presence in Beijing.

Third, Chinese Muslims have played a key role in the development of Beijing cuisine. Chinese halal food is widespread and beloved in northern China, where the heavy-flavored fusion cuisine is embraced by nomads, hunters (the Manchus), and northern Chinese, who are fond of mutton and beef. The most famous halal restaurant, Hongbinlou, was founded in 1853 and became the top halal restaurant in Tianjin, but the central government relocated it to Beijing in 1955 to serve the capital's official needs and popular demand. The success of Chinese Muslims can also be attributed to their business acumen and high standards in food hygiene. The Chinese Muslims have taken over some of the famous Beijing dishes, such as instant-boiled mutton, and made them halal.

Parallel to the opulent fine dining tradition, Beijing is also known for its street food, which can be aptly called "Beijing tapas," small portions of great variety of delicacies that can be enjoyed as appetizers or snacks or as a full meal when adequate amount is consumed. Beijing tapas originated from two sources: the food of low-income communities and the snacks of the court and elite circles. The former uses low-cost ingredients such as cattle and sheep organs, fermented soy products, and starch and is often

---

RENOWNED DISHES

DID YOU KNOW?

All regional and international cuisines are well represented in Beijing, though the city has a definitive northern Chinese flavor in its food scene. Beijing's traditional fine dining was heavily influenced by Shandong and Jiangsu cuisines. The renowned culinary delight, Peking roast duck, for example, was made popular in Nanjing of Jiangsu and perfected by chefs from Shandong. Some of the famous dishes, such as instant-boiled mutton, reflect nomadic and hunting-fishing heritages of the ruling class of the Yuan and Qing Dynasties. Chinese Muslim food has a strong presence and is quite popular in Beijing. Traditional Beijing snacks, the rough equivalent of Spanish tapas, are varied and inexpensive. Beijing's unique breakfast foods, however, with their distinct tastes and texture, may be an acquired taste even for many Chinese.

deep-fried; to many, it is an acquired taste but strangely addictive. The latter is represented by delicate snacks that are made from coarse grain flours and often sweetened with a great variety of fillings.

Today, one can find any Chinese regional cuisine in Beijing, the best of which can often be found in the in-house restaurants of the provincial and regional liaison office complexes. The most authentic Beijing cuisine, however, remains the fusion dishes rooted in northern food traditions, especially those hailed from Shandong, nomadic and hunting cultures, and Chinese Muslims.

MYTH AND REALITY OF THE BEIJING LIFESTYLE

In 1986, a little-known film directed by Peter Wang won the Special Jury Recognition at the Sundance Film Festival. *A Great Wall* (also known as *The Great Wall Is a Great Wall*) is a feature film about a Chinese American man who takes his family to visit Beijing, his hometown that he left nearly forty years earlier. Coming from San Francisco, the family sees Beijing in its early reform years. While the Chinese youngsters marvel at American pop culture, Mr. Wang bemoans a culture that has been fading away. Mr. Wang's sister still lives in the traditional *siheyuan* (family courtyard house) in which he grew up, but the city walls and many traditional customs are gone. Fortunately, Mr. Wang realizes that the slow-paced, laid-back lifestyle has survived, and he leaves with a sense of rekindled cultural connection.

It was a film fitting for its time. In the mid-1980s, China began to get exposure to the West after decades of political, economic, and cultural insulation. As the national capital, Beijing was at the forefront of the profound changes that were about to take place. Today, Beijing is a megacity where most residents live in transient and isolated apartment high-rises and where the traditional nuclear family has largely been replaced by households of single persons and DINKs (cohabitating couples who have a double income but no kids). One wonders how Mr. Wang would feel today if he were to visit Beijing again. Would he be amused by the crowd of young high-tech workers who are almost the spitting image of their counterparts in Silicon Valley? Is his family's traditional siheyuan still standing? Could he enjoy sitting in a sleek café that is a global pop culture substitute of the old tea house where his grandfather spent countless hours? Mr. Wang's family was well-off before the Communist Revolution, which was hinted by his family's full-sized and well-preserved siheyuan. Would he have had the same nostalgia had his grandfather been a rickshaw puller or street vender?

The real life in historical Beijing was more complicated and dichotomic. While the elites enjoyed an opulent lifestyle and could afford to be laid-back, the majority of people in Beijing were the urban poor and mostly consisted of recent rural migrants who crammed in the slums that clustered in the Outer City. In the postimperial times, some former bannermen and new elites inherited the patrician attitude; they showed off their pet birds in special carriages, wandered in antique markets, and spent much of the daytime in tea houses bickering over politics. In contrast, the same urban poor, only more numerous by now, struggled to scrape by.

In his novel *Rickshaw Boy* (*Luotuo Xiangzi*, 1936–1937), which was adapted to a stage play (1957) and a feature film (1982), Lao She depicts a young, hardworking, and well-built rickshaw puller. He works as hard as he physically can but cannot escape exploitation and bullying and repeatedly fails to earn an honest living. For the novel's protagonist, a migrant worker from the countryside, and the urban poor in Beijing, the leisurely "Beijing lifestyle" is a far-fetched myth, a pie in the sky, as they face the harsh realities of primeval survival on a daily basis. Their "low-brow" lifestyle, while often misconstrued and rarely recorded by outsiders, is the underbelly of a real-life portrait of the historical and present Beijing.

It is true that those who could afford the Beijing lifestyle enjoyed it to the fullest in the neatly maintained neighborhoods fitted with hutong-siheyuan networks. It has been idealized in literature and popular culture, as exemplified by the writings of literary illuminati such as Lu Xun (1881–1936) and Yu Dafu (1896–1945). Yu, an avant-garde and influential writer with a best-selling book (1927), extolled Beijing as a cozy and nurturing place for intellectuals like himself, with its classy and grand environment and a slow-paced, leisurely lifestyle. The city remained an eternally enchanting capital covered by a vast tree canopy, supplied with all luxury necessities, and endowed by distinct seasons. The feature film *My Memories of Old Beijing* (*Chengnan Jiushi*, 1983) was adapted from the novel by Lin Haiyin (1960), who as a child lived in Beijing with her well-to-do family in the 1920s. Both the film and the novel provide nostalgic imagery of the Beijing for the socially and financially endowed. Today, commercial attempts abound in an endeavor to reproduce the Beijing lifestyle for postmodern consumption by the nouveau riche. In real life, however, the idyllic Beijing lifestyle of the past has been in decline for some time during the PRC era.

A new lifestyle emerged during the Socialist era (1949–late 1970s), when Beijing underwent large-scale construction that created many Soviet-style superblocks, which were large live-work-service compounds of government agencies, state enterprises, and colleges. These superblocks, walled in and gated, were where coworkers and their families were required to live together to receive subsidized housing and provisions. While the superblock was a regimental and refrained environment, the residents were entitled to certain privileges that other residents in Beijing did not have, such as better housing and a supply of daily necessities as well as access to their own recreational and entertainment facilities. Most residents were from outside Beijing, making the superblocks melting pots of regional cultures that fostered a new cultural identity that is literally referred to as "superblock culture" or "big courtyard culture" (*dayuan wenhua*). The superblocks in Beijing nurtured an entire generation that was born in Beijing but had little connection to the traditional Beijing culture; those of this generation were *from* Beijing but not *of* Beijing. Housing reforms in recent decades have to large extent diminished superblock culture in Beijing, as the superblock model has been abandoned and many existing ones have been privatized. Nonetheless, superblock culture diluted and diversified Beijing's cultural scene in the Socialist era and continues to represent a unique lifestyle.

During the PRC era, more and more hutong-siheyuan neighborhoods came under government control and were turned into de facto public housing. Many siheyuan became occupied by multiple, often low-income, families and came to be known as *dazayuan* (tenement-like, one-story housing compounds). Most suffered from deterioration due to decades of ill maintenance. In recent decades, large-scale urban renewal projects, driven by commercial real estate industries, have razed many hutong-siheyuan neighborhoods, completely and irreversibly destroying the residential fabric of the traditional way of life that had sustained for centuries.

It is easy to fall into nostalgia and become indignant in light of the demise of hutong-siheyuan residential neighborhoods. In reality, many siheyuan residents were eager to move into modern accommodations, where they would enjoy amenities such as indoor plumbing and natural gas stoves for the first time as well as more privacy, all of which were absent in the hutong-siheyuan living arrangement. In addition, most siheyuan were in dilapidated conditions that their owners, who did not get their private properties back from the government until recent years, could not afford to refurbish. It was not until later, after having lived in the isolated high-rise apartments, that many former hutong-siheyuan residents realized the social and cultural losses, but it was too late. The latest efforts to salvage hutong-siheyuan neighborhoods have mainly been driven by historical preservation sponsored by the municipal government, but the completed projects have mostly been used for guided tours and guest lodging.

The romanticized Beijing lifestyle is fading into history, as the people who sustained it are gone. The new residential pattern has contributed to the decline in interpersonal, familial, and community interactions, as multigenerational families are becoming an institution of the past. How does it feel to live in Beijing today? Is there an all-encompassing city ambience? How does living in Beijing compare to, say, living in Shanghai or Shenzhen? The answers to these inquiries depend on who is asked, as there are distinct lifestyles in Beijing that rarely intersect. However, several observations could be made in an attempt to sketch a picture of life in Beijing.

First, for the folks riding the waves of globalization, living and working in Beijing is just like living in any other world city, be it Shanghai or Paris, Shenzhen or Tokyo, Guangzhou or New York. Indeed, like their brethren elsewhere, the white-collar techies and businessmen are hustling and rustling to advance careers, make money, and get ahead every day, as evidenced by the morning crowd in suits, with Starbucks cups in hand and looks of indifference, hurrying into Beijing's numerous business centers. They cultivate and thrive in a cosmopolitan lifestyle that could fit any world city, and Beijing has plenty to accommodate their wallets, including fancy shopping malls, upscale restaurants, high-tech wellness clubs, and weekend suburban retreats. Meanwhile, they have not the faintest emotional ties to the traditional way of life in the hosting city. They may equate a slow-paced lifestyle to laziness and a lack of ambition. These people often continue to work into the night, while nearby night spots light up for the entire spectrum of clientele to frequent. Artsy salons and dive bars are also thriving as well as a lively pop music scene. Most white-collar workers should be able to find accommodation for their globalist lifestyle in Beijing and meet their kindred souls along the way.

Second, Beijing feels rigid and inconvenient for many common folks from other Chinese cities, especially those in the south. Many argue that life in Beijing is not as convenient as in Shanghai, nor as good as expected for the capital. Specific complaints include access to goods and services and a lack of traditional night life, especially in comparison to Shanghai and other southern cities. Beijing is 60 percent larger than Shanghai, but they have similar urban populations. At the same time, Shanghai has twice as many shopping centers and farmers markets as Beijing and 70 percent more convenience stores. In addition, convenience stores are more evenly distributed in Shanghai and usually open 24 hours a day. Beijing is also ridiculed for its lack of night markets. In contrast, many cities have night markets in every neighborhood that are open through the night with local foods and a variety of entertainment. Beijing turns its lights off while other cities turn the lights on after dark, as the joke goes.

Some have observed that Beijing residents appear to be indifferent toward convenience stores and night markets, and others have cited climate and city layout as reasons. Some say that Beijing's cold seasons are so long that most night markets could only operate for half a year. While this reasoning sounds plausible, it may not be valid, considering that other northern cities, such as Xian, have very vibrant night markets year-round. Beijing's layout, on the other hand, does perhaps present physical obstacles. Government superblocks have their own services and usually do not allow private businesses, which may explain the low number of convenience

A vendor at the night food market in Beijing sells fried silkworms, sea stars, scorpions, and seahorses. There are several popular night food markets in Beijing, where most vendors serve traditional street and snack foods instead of adventurous items. Night markets are less common in Beijing than in many other Chinese cities, especially those in the south. (Chrispyphoto/Dreamstime.com)

stores in the western and northern parts of Beijing, where most of the government superblocks are located. The surviving hutong-siheyuan neighborhoods have long had their own mom-and-pop stores and are otherwise too crowded for new, bigger convenience stores. Some have also speculated that Beijing's low population density compared to Shanghai may have made it more challenging for convenience stores, which depend on foot traffic for a chunk of their business. The wide streets, a renowned feature of the capital, are usually fenced in the middle to regulate traffic and deter jaywalkers and may have the inadvertent effect of deterring pedestrians from frequenting businesses on the other side of the street.

Another applaudable reason for the lack of community-based businesses such as convenient stores, however, may be the inefficiency of Beijing's municipal bureaucracy. Beijing's business licensing and regulation are more cumbersome than those of Shanghai, which shows Shanghai is ahead of Beijing in making its management system more incumbent for a world city. Many Chinese and foreigners alike have commented that it is just more convenient to get things done in Shanghai than in Beijing. The Beijing

Municipal Government has vowed to make swift improvements and set a goal of having three thousand convenience stores by the end of 2020. Public transit now has extended hours at night, and the bureaucratic process for the application and renewal of business licenses has been streamlined.

Many native Beijingers may still cling to its traditional lifestyle. Their laid-back attitude may result in a lack of motivation for starting small businesses. Unlike their counterparts in Shanghai, the Beijingers may prefer to sit and chat over a pot of tea instead of hustling for material gains with a cup of joe in hand. Visitors have found it attractive that native Beijingers appear to have plenty of patience to assist them and are willing to spend time to chat. Perhaps some native Beijingers have managed to hold on to the old motto, happiness lies in contentment, and just lay back and take it easy. By doing so, they may conserve a bit of the ambience that once permeated the fabled capital.

WATCHING BEIJING TRANSFORM

LIFE IN THE CITY

I was born and raised in Beijing, but I am not considered a native Beijinger, however, since my parents were from Suzhou. I grew up in a big ministerial compound that housed my parents' offices and apartment as well as the ministry's cinema, cafeteria, and clinics. Most of my friends were also children of my parents' colleagues, so we knew a lot about each other, no matter whether we liked it or not.

I experienced many important events in Beijing, such as the Three Years of Hardship (1959–1961) and the Cultural Revolution (1966–1976). After high school, I was dispatched to the countryside with many of my peers, where I spent three years working in the field with the villagers. Then, the reform era arrived, and I was one of the lucky ones to go to college, where I was trained as a teacher.

The transformation of Beijing in the last forty years has left me awestruck. When I was young, Beijing was dirty, with trash and spit everywhere. I remember feeling embarrassed to hear foreigners' negative comments. Beijing is a lot better now; people are more civil, and you rarely see people throwing trash or spitting in public. The city started mandating sorting household waste this year. It may take a few years for people to get use to the "inconvenience," but I am confident we will succeed in this endeavor.

What I hated during the reform era was rampant corruption. Beijing was crowded with upscale restaurants, hotels, and shops that were mainly frequented by those who were involved in the corruption. Many of these establishments have closed in the last several years, as the ironfisted anti-corruption campaign appears to have taken effect. Upscale restaurants have to reset their menus to attract regular folks like us.

Our pensions and savings allow us to enjoy a fulfilling retirement. We practice tai chi in the morning, and I take piano lessons in the afternoon. We regularly go to karaoke bars and often visit museums. We rented a village house in the mountains, which is our escape when the air quality in the city becomes intolerable. We grow vegetables there—definitely organic! We usually spend one day of the weekend taking care of my mother and mother-in-law, who are both in their nineties. We bought a small place in Suzhou and also have a condo in Hainan where we spend part of our winter, and we have traveled overseas, including the United States.

I am content with my life and confident things will get even better.

—Shaoyu Zhou

NOTE

1. "World Heritage List," UNESCO, accessed September 22, 2019, http://whc .unesco.org/en/list.

11

Beijing in Pop Culture

Beijing is a treasure trove for the production and consumption of Chinese popular culture. The perpetual capital city has been the backdrop of many major events with far-reaching ramifications throughout China. Beijing's landmarks, such as the Forbidden City and the Temple of Heaven, are ubiquitous cultural symbols for China that have been popularized in art, music, film, television, and other media. Beijing Culture, from eclectic food to bucolic neighborhoods, from ritualistic celebrations to folk performances, have been popularized and commercialized to provide sustenance for a rising society's longing for history and identity. As "the model of all places," Beijing is the reflection and indication of the past, present, and future of China.

Beijing enjoys the unmatched cultural heritage of a large, diverse, and vibrant community of daring and creative minds. It is home to the renowned international artist community 798 Art District,[1] which is housed in a converted industrial complex right off the expressway to Beijing Capital International Airport. It is the birthplace of Chinese rock and roll music, where in the mid-1980s the first Chinese rock band was founded by Cui Jian,[2] the "godfather of Chinese rock." Beijing also boasts one of the liveliest club scenes in China, where the district along Sanlitun Road[3] just inside the East Third Ring Road showcases the biggest and most robust cluster of bars and clubs and the in vogue styles and folks are on display. Indeed, as some have argued, Beijing may not be the only center for Chinese pop culture, but it is definitely the most diverse, original, and

The 798 Art District, also known as the Dashanzi Art District, is located in Chaoyang District in East Beijing. Located on the site of an old factory code-named 798 Factory, it has become a robust artist community and a new landmark of Beijing's urban culture. (Qin0377/Dreamstime.com)

productive one. It is also the largest urban market for pop culture products. Beijing enjoys unmatched support and advantage as the national capital from both the government and the private sector.

THE CAPITAL AND POP CULTURE

Beijing's cultural heritage and intellectual tradition have contributed to the design and promotion of pop culture enjoyed by the entire country. Unique genres in pop culture have been developed to tap into the city's heritage as the last imperial capital and as the modern political center. Beijing Culture is neither provincial nor stagnant. Although celebrated as "Beijing Culture," it is the product of cultural convergence that epitomizes and inspires national trends. In essence, Beijing Culture is the progenitor of Chinese pop culture shared and embraced by the entire Chinese nation.

Historical Heritage in Pop Culture

Beijing's historical heritage, both tangible and intangible, is a boundless source that has solicited meticulous documentation and inspired artistic creations. In postimperial times, however, Beijing's traditional culture experienced neglect and deterioration. It was foreigners who took methodical efforts to explore Beijing Culture and left us with invaluable period documentation. Swedish art historian Osvald Sirén (1879–1966) did extensive survey work of Beijing's walls and gates. His book *The Walls and Gates of Peking* (1924) may be the best source of qualitative and quantitative information on Beijing's walls and gates before they met their demise in the 1950s and 1960s. Hedda Hammer Morrison, a German photographer who spent thirteen years (1933–1946) in Beijing, was perhaps the best visual documentarian of Beijing's traditional culture of her time. A few Chinese intellectuals educated overseas also endeavored to save the layout and landmarks of the city. Liang Shicheng, a famous architect who received a master's degree from the University of Pennsylvania, was a vanguard in Beijing's historical preservation, though his efforts to save the city's walls and gates failed.

China's market reform and ensuing economic boom have provided economic incentives for historical preservation. Beijing's historical landmarks and cultural relics suddenly became trendy pop cultural icons from which lucrative business opportunities arise and national pride finds sustenance. The Forbidden City, in particular, has become the premium visual symbol used as the backdrop of imperial China that represents Chinese history and culture. In 1998, the opera *Turandot* by Giacomo Puccini was played at Taimiao (the Imperial Ancestral Temple) in the Forbidden City. Director Zhang Yimou, who later also directed the Opening Ceremony of the 2008 Beijing Summer Olympics, used the setting to create extravagant pomp and circumstance for the stage. It was the first major pop cultural event in the Forbidden City.

In early 2019, the Lantern Festival, which is the concluding part of the Chinese New Year celebration, was held in the Forbidden City. The Palace Museum, the museum sections of the Forbidden City, was decorated with traditional Chinese lanterns and door couplets. The last time that a royal celebration of the Lantern Festival was held in the Forbidden City was in 1725, during Emperor Yongzheng's reign. The celebration was then moved to Yuanmingyuan (the Old Summer Palace), where the festivities were captured in paintings by Giuseppe Castiglione (Lang Shining, 1688–1766), an Italian Jesuit brother and a missionary in China. The 2019 celebration was the first time that visitors were allowed into the Palace Museum at night since it was opened to the public in 1925. After nightfall, spectacular light shows entertained thousands of visitors who had snatched free tickets that were distributed online. There were also other performances and activities typical of the Lantern Festival celebration, except for the traditional fireworks.[4]

The gala was designed, in part, to entice the consumers with "creative cultural products" that the Palace Museum appropriates to generate

Located on Beijing's central axis, Taihedian (Hall of Supreme Harmony) is the largest hall in the Forbidden City. Destroyed by fire and rebuilt a number of times in its six hundred years of history, Taihedian was the symbol of imperial power, where coronations, royal weddings and celebrations, and, for a time, imperial exams were held. (Tonyv3112/Dreamstime.com)

revenue, as the central government covers only 54 percent of the museum's annual budget. Government regulations limit the number of visitors and the amount of the admission charge, so the museum has shifted its attention to creating new merchandise that is uniquely associated with the Forbidden City and cannot be mass-produced by others because of special techniques and trademark protection.

By the end of 2016, the Palace Museum had developed over nine thousand creative cultural products. Buyers can make new products on their own using the purchased merchandise; for example, batches of appliqué, when bought in their entirety, can be used to make one's own imperial robe. The museum has also tapped into the vast smartphone market by offering accessories with distinct Forbidden City themes, such as chargers and earbuds: the first batch of its smartphone accessories was sold out within hours. The museum has also established a strong presence on the Internet[5] and new media platforms, such as Weibo and WeChat, by developing its own apps that provide the official source of educational information and works as a subtle way of nudging people toward purchasing its exclusive merchandise. In 2017, the Palace Museum generated CNY 1.5 billion (USD 230 million) from selling its creative cultural products, which not only covered its share of the annual budget but also provided funding for thousands of free educational events in China and overseas. In return, the Palace Museum receives far-reaching positive exposure that serves both its primary mission and its needs for revenue growth.

The museum has also attempted joint ventures with outside businesses. The most publicized and controversial was a two hundred square foot Starbucks coffeehouse that opened in 2000 and immediately encountered protests from some Chinese who were either against its being a foreign business or commercialization of the hallowed ground in general. It was finally closed in 2007, ostensibly due to public backlash,[6] but a decision to shift to exclusive branding and merchandising might have been the more important reason. The latest scheme of cashing in on the imperial past was the opening of a hot pot restaurant at the northern wall of the Forbidden City. The average cost of CNY 200 per person (about USD 30, with no tip or sales tax) was considered by many as being overpriced, but what the diners got, in addition to the actual food, was a heavy dose of simulated imperial ambience: they were being accompanied by the images of royalty on napkins and utensils and a scroll menu in the imperial color scheme (apricot yellow). Not far from the restaurant, the Corner Tower Café opened at the end of 2018, selling coffee and tea beverages ranging from CNY 22 to 45 (USD 3.2 to 6.5) in cups adorned with imperial themes and traditional artworks.

The Beijing Municipal Government has also made concerted efforts to popularize and commercialize the city's cultural heritage. In its 2018 proposals for promoting creative cultural industry, the municipal government outlined major upcoming creative cultural projects, including establishing three cultural zones, constructing cultural parks that are based on the themes of imperial gardens in the western hills, and improving the environment of historical subdistricts, such as Dashilan Pedestrian Boulevard, bordering the south of Tiananmen Square; the Nanluoguxiang (South Gong and Drum Lane) Hutong Culture Strip; the Xianyukou (Fresh Fish Market Entrance) Delicacy Street; and the Shichahai (Three Rear Lakes) Historic Scenic Area. Beijing authorities intend to transform these historical areas into centers of creative cultural enterprise zones, which would generate broad public interests and pop culture consumption.

Historical Beijing has been popularized in artistic renditions, such as stage plays, feature films, television series, and literary works. Popular art forms, especially feature films and television series, have been the most favored venues of exploring the artistic as well as the commercial values of Beijing's traditional cultural milieu. These productions exploded as a young generation of uninhibited film directors, all graduates of the Beijing Film Academy in the 1980s, emerged as the first wave of postreform

Chinese filmmakers. These "fifth-generation directors," including Zhang Yimou and Chen Kaige, directed some of their classic films with historical Beijing as the backdrop, such as the highly acclaimed *Farewell My Concubine* (1993, directed by Chen Kaige) and *The Blue Kite* (1993, directed by Tian Zhuangzhuang).

Several feature film genres and television series have been developed based on Beijing's unique historical heritage. Beijing takes the lion's share of the milieu for historical dramas. One of the early Western feature films, *55 Days at Peking* (1963), dramatized the siege on the Legation Quarter during the Boxer Rebellion (1900). Famed Italian director Bernardo Bertolucci's *The Last Emperor* (1987), a feature film that won the Academy Award for Best Picture, in part portrayed the life of Puyi, the last emperor of the Qing Dynasty, in the Forbidden City during a time when China was undergoing transformations. A number of recent Chinese historical dramas, such as the *Opium War* (1997), the *Founding of a Republic* (2009), and *1911* (2011), have further reinforced Beijing's popular image as the leading center of important political and cultural events. In recent years, the Chinese became fond of television series embellishing historical characters, court intrigue, and aristocratic lifestyle, perhaps because of nostalgia for the rapidly fading traditional culture in general. These TV melodramas, true to the style of soap operas and deemed vulgar by many critics, thrive on the stereotypical imagery of imperial Beijing.

Nostalgia as Pop Culture

Beijing's cultural heritage has inspired its intelligentsia community, which in turn engendered a literary and artistic genre that stemmed from Beijing's history and culture. Beijing's literary society underwent a renaissance in the 1920s and 1930s. Literary works from this period reflected contrasting imageries and perceptions among foreign, provincial, and local Chinese writers. Foreigner authors, such as French ethnographer and poet Victor Segalen (1878–1919), often depicted Beijing as the distinct and exotic showcase of Chinese culture and history; provincial Chinese writers idealized Beijing as the urbane and enchanting capital city, as Yu Dafu (1896–1945) sentimentally prosed in "The Four Seasons of Beiping" (1936). Beijing's indigenous writers, on the other hand, often found decay and crises in the city, as depicted by Lao She. Intellectuals invariably embraced Beijing's discreet charm highlighted by its sophisticated lifestyle, patrician aloofness, and bucolic environment, which were reminders of the imperial past and an escape from the chaos that had swept through much of China. Such nostalgic notions reflected in their works have helped shape Beijing's persona for popular perceptions and consumption.

During the PRC era, feature films have helped popularize the old Beijing before the PRC era, when the city retained much of the traditional culture of the imperial capital. These film titles include *Teahouse* and *Rickshaw Boy* (1982, both adapted from works by Lao She), *My Memories of Old Beijing* (1983), *Farewell My Concubine* (1993), and *Forever Enthralled* (2008). Television series set in old Beijing have also thrived, including adaptations of classics by Lao She, such as *Four Generations under One Roof* (1985, 2007, based on his 1944 novel of the same title), *The Life of Mine* (2002, based on a 1937 novella), *Longxugou* (2009, based on a 1951 play), and *Teahouse* (2010); his *Rickshaw Boy* (1936) was adapted into stage play (1957), feature film (1982), dance drama (1987), Peking opera (1998), television series (1998), and animation film (2014). Other popular television series include *The Patrician* (1989, adapted from a 1982 novel, *Nuowu*, by Deng Youmei), *In the Shadows of the Imperial City* (1992), and *Last Princess* (2008). *The Grand Mansion Gate* (2001) was a national hit TV series about the members of a prominent merchant family and their experiences over several generations in Beijing. The stories of these film and television productions may cover the lives of aristocrats, celebrities, the middle class, or the urban poor, but they all depict nostalgic imagery of a past gone forever.

There are a number of works dealing with the Socialist era that carry the same sentiment, such as *The Blue Kite* (1993) and *In the Heat of the Sun* (1994), which is a coming-of-age story about a group of teenagers from a superblock community. Feature films such as *Shower* (1999) and *Mr. Six* (2015) and TV series like *The Bell and Drum Towers* (1986), on the other hand, portray how the last generation of old Beijingers struggles to balance the new and the traditional and would go down fighting for the old way of life.

Many film and television productions depict life during the reform era from the cross section of Beijing. These productions explore the uncertainty that comes with the changes and opportunities during the reform era. Some explore human relations in the era of rampant materialism, such as *Good Morning Beijing* (1990), *Keep Cool* (1997), *The Dream Factory* (1997), *Restless* (1998), *You and Me* (2005), and *Beijing Bicycle* (2001). Others show the clashes among locals and newcomers, the young and the old, and the wealthy and the poor as well as the overachieving and the downtrodden, such as *Together with You* (2002), *Summer Palace* (2006), and *Lost in Beijing* (2007). TV series include *I Love My Family* (1993, the first Mandarin sitcom), *The Pigeon Whistle* (2009), *Pinwheel* (2011), *The Story of Zhengyangmen* (2013), and *A Family Portrait* (2013). Beijing is arguably the most used urban setting for film and television productions because it is the capital, a megacity, and a place where the past, the present, and the future of China converge dramatically.

International collaborations have also produced a number of films depicting cultural clashes between the past and the present or between the West and China with Beijing as the backdrop, such as *The Great Wall Is a Great Wall* (1986), *Big Shot's Funeral* (2001), *The Karate Kid* (2010), *American Dreams in China* (2013), and *Beijing, New York* (2015). Beijing is always portrayed as an exotic and interesting place that most represents China and Chinese culture.

Politics as Pop Culture

Beijing's intelligentsia community has built a tradition of social activism and political engagement. After the May Fourth Movement (1919), the city became a hotbed of political activism and cultural revolution, which culminated in a productive literary community. A novel by Yang Mo (1914–1995), *The Song of Youth* (*Qingchun Zhige*, 1958),[7] tells the story of a young, educated woman's exploration of independence and ways to take part in China's salvation. An immensely popular novel in China for decades, it vividly portrays Beijing's social and cultural environment in 1920s and 1930s, in which young, idealistic intellectuals fought against "feudalistic" traditions and participated in political activism.

Reform opened a flood gate for political dissent and protest as well as exploration of the economic values of Beijing's political intrigue and activism. Writers, artists, and designers began to question and challenge the status quo, which manifests in pop culture products. A son of Yang Mo, the author of the aforementioned *The Song of Youth*, became one of the dissident authors rebelling against the political and cultural status quo, just like his mother did a half century earlier.[8] Ai Weiwei,[9] one of the best known Chinese contemporary artists in the West, more for his political activism than for his art, may attribute his notoriety, in part, to his home base in Beijing. Beijing's pop music scene, more subtle but no less vocal and influential than Ai's works, shows how the capital's political and cultural resources can enrich the creation and appropriation of China's pop culture.

Although Chinese popular music was very much part of the state propaganda in the Socialist era (1949–1978), China has experienced an unprecedented breakout of rebellious and provoking pop music since then. Guangzhou, due to its cultural and historical connections with Hong Kong, was the early center of pop music production and promotion in Mainland China, where the first Chinese pop music band, The Violet, was founded in 1977. In the 1980s, Guangzhou's pop music community thrived with many of China's leading pop musicians, recording studios, promoters, production companies, and marketing agencies. By the mid-1990s, however, Beijing had wrestled away Guangzhou's de facto status as the "pop music capital" of China. Guangzhou may have taken its status for granted. Beijing emerged as the new capital of pop music with unsurpassed artistic talents and financial backing and, more importantly, the tradition of political sensitivity and cultural rebellion that is the essence of modern pop music.

In the mid-1980s, Beijing and the rest of China were limited to songs and music sponsored and sanctioned by the government that were either recycled from the past or pop versions of Western classical music. A young trumpeter from the Beijing Symphony Orchestra, Cui Jian, began to feel restless and experimented with Western pop music genres. In 1986, Cui became an instant pop star with the first rock and roll song in Mainland China, "Nothing to My Name," which became the unofficial anthem during the 1989 Tiananmen Square demonstrations.[10] Cui's album, *Rock 'n' Roll on the New Long March* (1988–1989), aroused controversy and resulted in subsequent concert cancellations by the authorities, but he has not shied away from the spirit of political dissent and cultural rebellion, distinct characteristics of both Beijing Culture and rock and roll music. Deservingly called the "godfather of Chinese rock and roll music," Cui ushered in an era of pop culture by being the harbinger of indigenizing Western pop music forms in Beijing and for China.

Today, China's pop music scene is a benign version of its recent past.[11] Notwithstanding the watchful eyes of the government, the exit of financial investment from pop music may have been the major taming factor. Beijing nonetheless remains the undisputed capital of China's pop music. Eager to tap into the large and creative music community, over one thousand rock musicians from all over China live and work in Beijing, which has provided a vibrant underground rock music scene.[12]

Beijing also hosts the largest number of major music events among Chinese cities. In 2018 alone, there were quite a few multiday pop music festivals, including the Beijing Blues Festival, the Beijing Strawberry Festival, the Beijing Running Shark Pop Electronic Music Festival, the Beijing Yugong Yishan Festival, the Great Wall Festival, and the Beijing Rye Music Festival. In addition, there were concerts at smaller venues. Government-sponsored music venues include Beijing International Pop Music Week, the Sino-British Pop Music Festival, and the two-week-long Beijing Music Festival, which features a colorful spectrum of Chinese and international folk music, pop music, modern music and dance, and a classical music repertoire.

In recent years, the Chinese pop culture market has come to embrace other Western music genres, such as jazz, R & B, and especially hip-hop.

Electronic music and computer music are becoming more accepted and are regularly performed at festivals and concerts. It is noteworthy that music venues, big and small, increasingly feature Chinese musicians and their original works, which are more likely to be embraced by the Chinese populace beyond the avant-garde and urban youth communities. It may indicate the maturity of the Chinese pop culture industry.

CENTER OF CULTURAL CREATIVITY AND APPROPRIATION

Historically, Beijing as the capital was at once a melting pot of regional cultures and a cradle for cultural creativity. Forms of art and entertainment favored by the ruling class gained nationwide promotion. The history of Peking opera is a good example of how political power and cultural elitism could manipulate the conception and popularization of Chinese pop culture. Peking opera has a relatively short history, but it is the only traditional operatic style that enjoys national popularity today.

Historically, each region fostered its own operatic dramas, and it was not until the Ming Dynasty that *Kunqu*, original to Kunshan (between Suzhou and Shanghai), became the primary court opera. Kunqu is a highly sophisticated operatic style that is steeped in classic content and literary expressions. It was among the first nineteen Masterpieces of the Oral and Intangible Heritage of Humanity proclaimed by UNESCO in 2001.[13] Several of its most famous dramas, especially *The Peony Pavilion*, are still regularly performed today in China and abroad. Kunqu began to lose popularity by the mid Qing Dynasty, in part due to its high-brow style that most outside the literati community found difficult to appreciate, and its effeminate performing style may have caused ire in the male-dominated society. Kunqu's decline in popularity coincided with the rise of Peking opera.

CITY TREES AND FLOWERS

Beijing officially designated its city trees and flowers in 1987 based on votes from city residents. The votes between the top two trees and flowers were so close that the municipal government decided to have two in each category. The two city trees are the scholar tree (*Sophora japonica*) and the oriental cypress (*Platycladus orientalis*); the former is said to be a symbol of good fortune, joy, and well-being, and the latter symbolizes courage, strength, and longevity. The two city flowers are Chinese rose (*Rose chinensis*) and chrysanthemum (*Dendranthema morifolium*); the former is native to China, and the latter is extremely popular in Beijing with more than one thousand varieties.

Legend has it that the longest-reigning emperor of Qing Dynasty, Qian-long, when celebrating his eightieth birthday in 1790, summoned the Four Great Anhui Troupes to Beijing to perform their regional drama *Huiju* (the regional opera of Anhui Province). In the next several decades, the court favorite Huiju was infused by several other regional operatic styles, and a new and unique operatic style, Peking opera, was born. Peking opera became the only traditional opera form that gained national acceptance, largely due to its being favored by the court. Empress Dowager Cixi, the woman who ruled China from the 1870s until her death in 1908, was said to be extremely fond of Peking opera, which contributed to its great popularity in and beyond the capital. Peking opera was awarded "national treasure" status during the ROC era and was successfully promoted overseas as such. Its popularity continued during the PRC era. Revolution-themed new dramas were produced to promote Communist ideology in the 1960s and 1970s and performed throughout the country by local government-sponsored Peking opera troupes. Peking opera, which was recognized by UNESCO as an intangible heritage of humanity in 2010, is a prime example of how Beijing's capital status has played a vital role in the creation and proliferation of popular culture.

As China's center for international exchange, Beijing enjoys the priority for hosting national and international cultural events. When the Philadelphia Orchestra under Eugene Ormandy made its historical visit to China in 1973, it held four of its concerts in Beijing and two in Shanghai. The Berlin Philharmonic had its only concert on its 1979 China tour in a Beijing sports arena. In 1985, Wham!, the first Western pop band to visit China, performed two concerts, one in Beijing and the other in Guangzhou, the city at the forefront of China's market reform. Beijing is the official clearinghouse of international cultures and the most exposed and stimulated Chinese city for pop culture innovations.

Starting in Beijing, China has also embraced American fast-food culture. In November 1987, Kentucky Fried Chicken (KFC) opened its first restaurant on the southern edge of Tiananmen Square. It was the first American fast-food restaurant to open in China and gained instant popularity. For the first several years, the line at the original KFC was out of the door, and the wait was more than an hour. It became a must do for many Chinese visiting Beijing. From Beijing, American fast food, represented by the likes of McDonald's, Pizza Hut, and Burger King in addition to the KFC, quickly spread to the rest of China. Starbucks opened its first café in Beijing in 1999 and now has over four thousand outlets in more than 160 Chinese cities. Together with its Alibaba online virtual store, Starbucks has reached six hundred million Chinese.

What happens in Beijing's pop culture scene quickly transmits to and influences the rest of the country. It is from Beijing, for example, that newscasts by Chinese Central Television (CCTV) supersedes provincial and local TV programming at 7:00 p.m. every evening, providing the government-sanctioned news and information of the day that is viewed by hundreds of millions. A prime example of Beijing's central role in pop cultural production and promotion is the CCTV Spring Festival Gala. The variety show, televised live since 1983, provides instant and far-reaching publicity for its performers and programs. The live telecast of the gala is quite popular among the Chinese diaspora around the world and is available in Hong Kong, Macao, Taiwan, Japan, Malaysia, and the United States. The gala set a Guinness record in 2012 for viewership. It has since suffered from stagnant growth, however, because of its regimental format, worn-out content, and competition from new media platforms.

In response, CCTV has ventured into new content, formats, and media platforms to maintain and expand the gala's appeal. The producers of the gala infused more youth culture and international cultures into the show while maintaining the traditional popular programing. In 2016, TFBoys, an extremely popular Beijing-based Chinese boy band, was invited to appear at the gala and was invited back in 2017, 2018, and 2019. The band, with an estimated commercial value of a stunning CNY 300 billion (USD 43 billion), enhanced the gala's youth appeal. For 2019, Phoenix Legend performed at the gala. This Chinese popular music duo sold more than six million albums in China between 2005 and 2012, and ten songs from four of their albums have recorded one billion hits online. The band blends folk music with rap and hip-hop elements and has a wide appeal with fans across the demographic and socioeconomic spectra.

In March 2018, CCTV, China National Radio, and China Radio International merged to form a huge media conglomerate, China Media Group. For 2019, all its channels were used to promote the gala. Major Chinese online video services and new media platforms made live streaming available for the gala, including Tencent, iQIYI (under Baidu), Youku (under Alibaba) and Sina Weibo, as did Japanese video hosting service Niconico, which is known for its "bullet comment screen" technology. Since 2015, CCTV has also tried to live stream the gala on Twitter, YouTube, and Google+. For 2019, Baidu, one of the largest Internet and artificial intelligence (AI) companies in the world, obtained the sole authorization to be the gala's Internet interactive platform, while the popular video app Tik-Tok was the official social media for the event. Baidu conducted four rounds of digital "red envelope snatching" for the audience during the duration of the gala, who only needed to turn on Baidu's app to participate. With the highly developed mobile payment technology in China, red envelope snatching has become a most popular activity for special occasions, especially Chinese New Year, because of its incentives for monetary reward. Baidu's use of fusion media for designing the activity was a promotional success for both the gala and Baidu. In all, Baidu recorded more than twenty billion hits and subsequently distributed CNY 9 hundred million (USD 1.33 hundred million) digital cash rewards.

For the 2019 gala, according to China Global Television Network (CGTN), more than 621.4 million viewers in China and another 24.8 million overseas watched the show on television. In comparison, 527 million viewers watched the gala on new media platforms, such as apps, websites, video-streaming services, and social media.[14] Starting in 2016, producers of the gala, the ultimate symbol of pop culture procreation in China, also had three or four breakout venues in other locations. All eyes were on the capital, however, where Beijing as the symbolic national center and the gala as a feast of pop culture converged.

Beijing's strength in pop culture procreation is also partly due to its being a large market of cultural consumption with the highest cultural consumption index among all the province-level divisions of China. Beijing has the largest number of bookstores, 6,719 in 2017, or 3.1 bookstores for every ten thousand residents, compared to Chengdu, which was in second place with 3,463 bookstores, or 2.2 bookstores for every ten thousand residents. In early 2018, Beijing had 160 museums, far outnumbering any other city in China. Beijing is also home to the largest and best performing arts venues, including the National Centre for the Performing Arts near Tiananmen Square, the egg-shaped masterpiece by French architect Paul Andreu. There are also many modern movie theaters modeled after those in the West, where the old rule of no food and drinks had been abandoned and new concessions offer overpriced popcorn and soft drinks.

Beijing also has the most and some of the best arts academies. Beijing is home to ten of the top fifteen arts and performing academies or colleges in China, taking up the top seven spots. These institutions of higher learning continuously infuse fresh blood into the local creative arts community. In 2017, according to hihey.com, the largest Chinese art e-commerce company, Beijing had a community of 347,670 practicing artists, far more than the 160,820 artists in the second-place city, Jinan, in Shandong Province, or the 113,670 artists in Shanghai, the sixth-place city. No wonder a 2018 survey conducted by College Student Arts Expo, based in Guangzhou, showed that 34 percent of the responding young artists chose Beijing as their ideal base after college, in comparison to the 19 percent who chose second-place Shanghai. Respondents cited Beijing's abundant resources and strong artist community as well as infrastructure and a market for their works as the top reasons for their choice.

Beijing enjoys unsurpassed infrastructure for the creative cultural industry. In 2017, for example, 240 of the 585 Chinese publishers had their headquarters in Beijing, where many of the rest located their major printing and marketing operations. Beijing has more than twenty thousand design firms with more than one hundred thousand employees covering the entire spectrum of the industry. The design firms collectively generate about USD 20 billion in annual revenue and spawn ten times as much in related businesses. Beijing's computer software and media services, for example, account for one-quarter and one-third, respectively, of the total national revenues of creative cultural products.

Beijing has some of the largest creative parks, usually converted from old industrial facilities, for artist studios and R & D firms alike. The famed 798 Arts District and Songzhuang Artist Village[15] are the two best-known examples, but newcomers and startups regularly emerge, sometimes to the chagrin of the authorities.[16] The Beijing Municipal Government has been instrumental in the development of the CBD-Dingfuzhuang Corridor for International Media Enterprises, which extends from the central business district (CBD) to the Communication University of China in eastern Beijing along a section of the Grand Canal (Tonghui River). The target is to house twenty thousand media-related businesses in an area that is forty square kilometers (fifteen square miles) and to produce an annual revenue of CNY 100 billion (USD 15 billion).

The Beijing Municipal Government has provided regulatory and financial support in an effort to solidify the city's position as the leading center for China's creative economy and culture industry, a goal that fits into the four capital functions that the central government has set for the capital. In summer 2018, the Beijing Municipal Government issued "Proposals for Promoting Development for Innovative Enterprises of Cultural Creativity." Nine categories of business enterprises were identified in the proposals: (1) creative design (Beijing was designated as City of Design by UNESCO in 2012); (2) fusion media and new media platforms; (3) audio and visual production, including television, film, and new video sharing; (4) digital publishing and intelligent bookstores; (5) animation and gaming, especially esports; (6) performing arts and entertainment focusing on Beijing's traditional culture; (7) integration of intangible cultural heritage and modern commercial development; (8) streamlining the art market, including Internet sharing, trade, and funding infrastructure; and (9) think tanks in support of cultural creativity. The categories encompass all key areas for creative cultural industry.

Beijing's advantages in setting the trend for pop culture also have to do with the fact that the central government is directly involved in cultural production and appropriation. It may be a mixed blessing for Beijing, however, because the best academies and performing groups in the city are directly managed by the central government, and some of the pop culture productions are designed to serve the PRC's national and international interests. For example, the PRC government maintains an exclusive performing troupe, the China Oriental Performing Arts Group. It was established in 1962 through a merger between the Chinese Song and Dance

Troupe and the Oriental Song and Dance Troupe. Its mission was to function as a "cultural envoy" on the diplomatic front. The performing artists of the former specialized in music and dance of various ethnic groups in China and were tasked to convey China's diverse cultures to an overseas audience; those of the latter specialized in the music and dance of other countries and were tasked to bringing authentic but filtered foreign cultures to the Chinese.

The first Chinese-made film was shot in Beijing in 1905, but it quickly fell behind Shanghai, which became China's center for the motion picture industry. However, Beijing overtook Shanghai as the most important center of the Chinese film industry in the reform era, largely due to the capital's draw of resources and talent in the industry. Today, Beijing is home to the largest cluster of Chinese film-centered companies. Nine of the top ten most influential film companies in 2018 were headquartered in Beijing, including Huayi Brothers, Wanda, Bona, and the China Film Group Corporation. Two state-owned motion picture companies, the National Radio and Television Administration of China Film Group Corporation and the Huaxia Film Distribution Company, both located in Beijing, are the sole distributors of imported films in China, with the former controlling the review and decision procedures for film import and distribution.

THE MECCA FOR CREATIVE AND CULTURAL INDUSTRIES

The PRC government has been promoting supply-side growth of "creative and cultural industries" in China's ongoing efforts of restructuring and optimizing its economy. Creative and cultural industries form the foundation of the creative economy,[17] which specializes in developing and marketing intellectual rights that often overlap with pop culture production and consumption, such as broadcasting, television, animation, audio and video products, media, visual arts, performing arts, crafts and design, sculpture, environmental arts, software and computer services, fashion design, and commercial advertisements. Beijing has the best facilities and supply chain for cultural and creative industries in China and has strengthened its position as the dominant center in China for pop culture enterprises, which in turn has become one of the biggest segments in the city's economy. Beijing's long tradition as the cultural hub of China provides a fertile environment for an emerging creative economy driven by the mutually perpetuating dynamics between the community of pop culture talents and creators and funding and policy support from the Beijing Municipal Government as well as the private sector.

In 2016, Beijing's creative and cultural industries generated CNY 358 billion (USD 51.6 billion) of added value, which was about 14 percent of

Beijing's GRP, and contributed more than 10 percent of local taxes and 9 percent of the taxes Beijing paid to the national treasury. Between 2014 and 2016, Beijing's cultural and creative industries obtained over three thousand financing investments, about one-third of the national total. More than 70 percent of the financing investment came from private sources or from publicly traded corporate funding. In 2018, the total output value of Beijing's cultural and creative industries reached CNY 1070 billion (USD 156 billion). Beijing's comic and animation activities alone generated CNY 71 billion in 2018.

There are two interwoven dynamics for Beijing's leading role in shaping and consuming Chinese pop culture. First, as the national capital, Beijing benefits from its access to political power, financial resources, and social precedence in setting pop culture trends, standards, and appropriations. Second, Beijing benefits from its own tradition. It is the destination for the best and brightest Chinese who seek fame and power and to thrive on the famous and powerful. It is home of the largest cluster of institutions of higher learning, museums, and cultural venues and many of the most influential Chinese artists. Beijing also has the tradition of supporting cultural procreation.

Beijing has been ranked first eight out of nine times in the composite index of the Development Index of Provincial Cultural Industry, which has been published annually by the Institute of Creative Industries Technology at Renmin University of China since 2010. The composite index is based on categories of productivity, influence, and drivers. Beijing may not have ranked the highest in all categorical indices, but it has topped the influence and drivers indices in recent years, showing the combined effects of central and municipal government support, financial resources, a local testing market, and historical-cultural prestige. Beijing is indeed sitting at the apex of China's hierarchy of pop cultural origination and diffusion.

As "the model of all places" for the last seven and a half centuries, Beijing as the national capital has been endowed by a "halo effect;" pop cultural traits from Beijing are regarded to be in vogue by the rest of the country because the political and economic elites in the capital have endorsed them. In the ongoing rush to capitalize on the emerging creative cultural industry, Beijing will maintain its position as the leader in China with its unmatched support from the central government, progressive local policies, abundant capital investment, rigorous artist community, enormous market, and international exposure.

Beijing will host the sexcentenary celebration of the Forbidden City in 2020. What new pop cultural production will Beijing's creative and cultural industries present to the country and the world? How will Beijing be portrayed in the age of great change and uncertainty?

FOND MEMORIES OF THE 2008 OLYMPICS

Hi, I am Cary. I chose this English name because I was a fan of Cary Grant. After graduating from college with a degree in electronic science and technology, I got a job working for the China Cruise & Yacht Association. It was fun, but the pay was low. I also could not use my college training. I took some extension courses to get updated in coding and became a programmer with Mobile Ecosystem Group of Baidu, China's equivalent to Google.

Even to me, a local, Beijing's transformation has been no less than fantastic. Beijing has spread out so much! My grandparents worked and lived at a research institute in the northwest suburbs. When I was little, visiting them would take hours and several bus transfers. I always remember the smell of manure when riding the bus through the expanse of vegetable gardens. Now, over the concrete urban jungle called China's Silicon Valley, I can see the institute's rooftop from my office window and can only smell the exhaust from countless cars.

If anyone asks me about my most memorable time in Beijing, I'd have to say that it was during the 2008 Summer Olympics. I was a fifth grader in 2001 when Beijing won the bid to host the 2008 Summer Olympics. I remember the excitement around me and the ensuing boom of development. Within a month, my route to school was widened from a two-lane street to a six-lane boulevard; high-rises mushroomed throughout the city, and every public facility was either rebuilt or refurbished. Nothing came close to the day of the Opening Ceremony, though. My blood was boiling as the song "My Motherland" echoed throughout Beijing and the twenty-nine firework-simulated footprints marched across the capital's night sky. I still get teary-eyed even today when I recall the splendor and pride from that evening. Since then, the growth in Beijing's old city has slowed down while many other Chinese cities have caught up. But it was Beijing in the summer of 2008 that set the country in motion.

Today, I am leading a life of 996.icu: working 9:00 a.m. to 9:00 p.m., six days a week, and no relief until ending up in the intensive care unit. This is the lifestyle that we are expected to have in the extremely competitive world of high-tech economy. I am paid well, and I like my job; but this lifestyle is not sustainable in the long run! I heard that, in Beijing, only one out of every eight interviewees for high-tech jobs was a Beijinger, and most of my coworkers are from elsewhere. I may check out what my childhood friends are doing now. Perhaps 996.icu is the result of progress? I start to miss the laid-back and modest life that my grandparents enjoyed which we can no longer afford.

—Kexin Guo

NOTES

1. The 798 Art District's website is www.798district.com.

2. "Cui Jian," accessed September 22, 2019, http://www.cuijian.com/english /pages/main_interface.html.

3. "Sanlitun Bar Street," TripAdvisor, accessed September 22, 2019, https:// www.tripadvisor.com/Attraction_Review-g294212-d548083-Reviews-Sanlitun _Bar_Street-Beijing.html.

4. "China's Forbidden City Lights Up for Lunar New Year Show—In Pictures," *The Guardian*, February 9, 2019, https://www.theguardian.com/world/gallery/2019 /feb/20/chinas-forbidden-city-lights-up-for-lunar-new-year-show-in-pictures.

5. "The Palace Museum," accessed September 22, 2019, https://en.dpm.org.cn.

6. "Starbucks Closes Coffeehouse in Forbidden City," *NPR*, July 17, 2007, https://www.npr.org/templates/story/story.php?storyId=12026402.

7. Yang Mo, *The Song of Youth*, trans. Nan Ying, 3rd ed. (San Francisco, CA: China Books and Periodicals, 1978).

8. Binyan Liu, "Truth vs. 'False Realism': The Book That Stunned Beijing," *New York Times*, November 6, 1988, https://www.nytimes.com/1988/11/06/books/stark -truth-vs-false-realism-the-book-that-stunned-beijing.html.

9. "Ai Weiwei," accessed September 22, 2019, https://www.aiweiwei.com.

10. Hugh Grigg, "Nothing to My Name, by Cui Jian—A Decent Chinese Rock Song," East Asia Student, March 4, 2012, https://eastasiastudent.net/china/mandarin /cui-jian-nothing-to-my-name.

11. Henry Knight, "Inside Beijing's Underground Rock Scene," BBC, June 2, 2015, http://www.bbc.com/culture/story/20150602-how-to-be-a-rock-star-in-beijing.

12. William Hancock and Paula Jin, "Why You Need to Start Paying Attention to Beijing's Indie Rock Scene," Waytogo by Smile Magazine, January 19, 2018, https://waytogo.cebupacificair.com/beijing-indie-rock.

13. "Kun Qu Opera," UNESCO, accessed September 23, 2019, https://ich .unesco.org/en/RL/kun-qu-opera-00004.

14. Hong Yaobin, "China's Spring Festival Gala Sets Record with 1.17 Billion Viewers," CGTN, last updated February 7, 2019, https://news.cgtn.com/news/3d3 d414f334d544e32457a6333566d54/index.html.

15. Gavin Van Hinsbergh, "Songzhuang Art Village/Community," China Highlights, last updated March 12, 2019, https://www.chinahighlights.com/bei jing/attraction/song-zhuang-artist-village.htm.

16. Naomi Rea, "Beijing Police Evict Two Art Districts to Prepare for Demolition, Citing 'Unstable Factors' and Organized Crime," Artnet, July 12, 2019, https://news .artnet.com/art-world/art-district-beijing-eviction-demolition-1599433.

17. According to a 2013 report funded by the National Endowment for the Arts (NEA), the "American creative economy" includes these common categories: advertising; architectural and related; culture and heritage, including libraries; design; film, video, and sound; independent artists; Internet broadcasting and publishing; music production, distribution, and sales; performing arts and entertainment; printing and publishing; and television and radio. Christine

Harris, Margaret Collins, and Dennis Cheek, *America's Creative Economy: A Study of Recent Conceptions, Definitions, and Approaches to Measurement across the USA* (Oklahoma City, OK: National Creativity Network in collaboration with Creative Alliance Milwaukee, August 2013), https://www.arts.gov/sites/default/files/Research-Art-Works-Milwaukee.pdf.

12

The Future

The capital of China, as the old adage goes, must be "the model for all places." It is the moral obligation and governing priority for China's central authorities, who in turn dictate the process and amass national resources to reach this ambitious goal. This political dynamic is key to understanding the Beijing of the past, present, and future and for assessing the strategies for the city to confront the challenges and to achieve sustainable development. Beijing is destined to be China's showcase to the world and the paragon for the rest of the country to emulate and follow.

Beijing must strike a delicate balance between preserving the old, especially its unmatched historical heritage, and adapting to the new, mainly the technology- and innovation-driven economy, in its ongoing transformation. The central government has reconceived Beijing's essential functions as the national center of politics, culture, international exchanges, and technical innovation, which means Beijing must take on two interrelated challenges. First, it must greatly improve its environmental quality by addressing pressing issues such as air quality, water scarcity, and waste management. Second, it must tackle the antiquated economic structure and megacity ills such as congestion, overcrowding, and crime.

Beijing appears to be well positioned to succeed in its designated tasks. It is implementing a wide range of environmental and social policies to improve quality of life and build a sustainable future for the city's millions of residents and hundreds of thousands of visitors. It is leading China in key new economic sectors, such as R & D activities, high-end services, and creative cultural industries with government support, labor and institutional resources, and financial investment. Several aspects of Beijing's ongoing transformation may foretell where the city is heading to and what the city will be like a generation from now.

A STREAMLINED CAPITAL CITY

Beijing as the imperial capital was a city of consumption that depended on support from the productive south. The rulers in Beijing even built and maintained the Grand Canal, a great engineering feat. During the pre-reform decades (1950s–1970s), in the Socialist ethos of economic self-reliance, the PRC built a complete industrial base in Beijing ranging from textile to machinery, including some of the largest state-owned enterprises in China, such as the Capital Iron and Steel Corporation (Shougang Group) and the Beijing Yanshan Petrochemical Company Limited. Beijing's industrial growth, however, was state sponsored rather than driven by adequate production factors such as regional economy and historical inertia. As a result, Beijing's advances not only did not spur economic development in northern China but, worse still, siphoned resources and opportunities from its surrounding regions, resulting in their growth stagnation and environmental deterioration, which in turn directly and adversely affected Beijing's sustainable development.

In the reform era, the increasing economic disparity between Beijing and neighboring Hebei Province contributed to Beijing's skyrocketing population explosion, overcrowding in the urban areas, and a wide range of environmental problems. Millions of people have moved into Beijing's urban core, where its six urban districts account for 8 percent of Beijing's total area but 60 percent of the city's population. At the same time, the city's urban sprawl accelerated at an extremely fast pace. In 2000, Beijing's built area was about five hundred square kilometers; it has since tripled. The new skyline is dominated by imposing postmodern behemoths, often designed by Western architects, and the resultant landscape is devoid of historical continuity.

Beijing began to suffer from environmental degradation and worsening quality of life as motor vehicle expressways created a labyrinth clogged by millions of private vehicles. Infrastructure building, at the same time, has had to play catchup but may suffer from poor planning and design. Expansions of public transportation, for example, have followed the existing patterns of Beijing's transit system, in which subway, light rail, and bus routes converge on the urban core of the city, exacerbating overcrowding and worsening traffic congestion.

Community services have also lagged behind rapid urban development. One of the most pressing inadequacies is the network for senior services. China's baby boom generation in the largest cities has reached retirement age. With 25 percent of its native population older than sixty years of age by the end of 2018, Beijing suffers from inadequate senior services, especially in both availability and affordability of planned retirement and health care facilities.

The PRC government has diagnosed the root cause of Beijing's megacity ills as the city being overladen with functions and activities inconsistent with the capital's basic functions. In February 2014, Xi Jinping, the CCP secretary general and the PRC president, declared Beijing's role as "the center of four capital functions." Beijing should be the national center of political governance, cultural creativity, international exchange and technological innovations. Beijing's future development, therefore, will be guided by measures for highlighting these four capital functions and for dispersing the noncapital functions from the city's urban core.

Beijing must deal with its environmental and socioeconomic challenges in broad regional or even national frameworks, as the causes and impact of these challenges are not confined to Beijing alone. Furthermore, Beijing's realignment as the national center of the four capital functions is part of the PRC's grand strategy of revitalizing the sluggish development in northern China. The PRC government has unfolded the blueprint of interwoven national, regional, and Beijing-specific strategies that will fundamentally reshape Beijing for generations to come. This strategy focuses on regionally integrative development among Beijing ("Jing"), Tianjin ("Jin"), and Hebei Province ("Ji"), which, dubbed as "Jing-Jin-Ji," is a megaregion[1] and one of the nineteen supercity clusters in China. The central government has stepped in and initiated a number of major environmental, economic, and infrastructural projects that are designed to benefit from Jing-Jin-Ji's intraregional complementary relations. These projects will channel noncapital functions related to the traditional supply chain, such as manufacturing and wholesale, from Beijing's urban core to Hebei Province. The goal is to relieve Beijing's megacity ills and enhance its abilities to carry out the capital functions. Meanwhile, Hebei Province will receive much-needed growth through increased industrial investment and employment in the sectors, which include wholesale, traditional manufacturing, and some educational activities.

Beijing's latest Master Plan (2016–2035) was conceptualized to be in a "one core and two wings" pattern. Eastward development was to be led by a new suburban nucleus, the capital subcenter, and the southward development was to connect with a newly conceived development zone, the Xiongan New Area, in Hebei Province. Areas along the two axes were designated to be the new homes of relocated industries and services from Beijing's urban core. In mid-2017, the PRC government approved a master plan for the Jing-Jin-Ji megaregion that overlaps and expands Beijing's new Master Plan (Table 12.1). The Jing-Jin-Ji master plan proposes a development hierarchy of one core (Beijing), twin leading urban centers (Beijing and Tianjin), three axes, and four special districts. Together, the two master plans will dictate the spatial development of Beijing and the Jing-Jin-Ji megaregion in the years to come.

The Beijing Municipal Government has taken a number of steps to disperse economic sectors that are considered to be noncapital functions. Some enterprises may move to Hebei Province, as the Capital Iron and Steel Corporation did, and others may relocate to Beijing's exurbs, that is,

Table 12.1   Planned Spatial Components, Jing-Jin-Ji and Beijing

Jing-Jin-Ji Master Plan		Beijing Master Plan (2016–2035)	
Core (Beijing)		Core of Capital Functions	
		Beijing Urban Core	
		Beijing Capital Subcenter	
Three Axes	Beijing-Tangshan-Qinhuangdao Axis	Two Axes	Beijing Capital Subcenter
	Beijing-Baoding-Shijiazhuang Axis		Beijing-Xiongan New Area Axis
	Beijing-Tianjin Axis		
Four Districts	Central Core Function	Connections to Beijing	Beijing as the Core of Jing-Jin-Ji
	Eastern Coastal		
	Southern Functional Extension		Beijing-Xiongan Decentralization
	Northwestern Ecological Conservation		Ecological Conservation Zone
Multiple Urban Hubs in Hebei Province		Multiple Suburban Centers	

Source: "Urban Master Plan." July 12, 2019. eBeijing: The English web portal for the Beijing Municipal Government. http://www.ebeijing.gov.cn/feature_2/BeijingInvestmentGuide/BeijingProfile/t1593534.htm.

the metropolitan fringe areas under transition of suburbanization. In response to the central government's master plan for Jong-Jin-Ji, Beijing revised the focus of its 2016–2035 Master Plan as "one core, one main center, and one subcenter; two axes; multiple edge cities; and one zone" (Table 12.2). Execution of the Master Plan has been quickly reshaping the spatial patterns of Beijing's political, economic, and environmental operations.

Tongzhou: The Capital Subcenter as a Model City

An epic and evolving event is the relocation of the Beijing Municipal Government to Tongzhou, in the eastern suburbs. Beijing's historical layout, centered on the impassable royal compound, impeded traffic flows in the urban core. In modern times, especially during the PRC era, Beijing's urban core became overcrowded by the swelling central and local government bureaucracy. Until recently, Beijing's horizontal expansion, dubbed "making pancake," had been in the form of typical urban sprawl, chaotic spillover that lacks long-term planning and further exacerbates traffic congestion in the urban core. In the pre-reform era, the PRC government attempted to relieve overcrowding and traffic congestion by designating special zones of development. The western suburbs at the time became home of many central government agencies, the northwestern suburbs became a special zone for higher education, and new factories were located on the urban peripheries. These measures only provided temporary remedies and failed to cope with the onslaught of building boom and urban sprawl in the reform era.

In contrast, the ongoing process of decentralization is being led by leapfrogging; the new growth mainly takes place in suburban satellite centers that are interconnected by the new transportation infrastructure. The concept of satellite centers was introduced to Beijing's urban planning as early as 1958. In response to accelerated urban growth in the reform era, Beijing designated three specific "new cities" in its 2004 Master Plan. In 2005, the modified 2005–2020 Master Plan called for a shift of planned development from the west and northwest to the east and southeast of the city proper, and it designated Tongzhou, then the seat of Tongxian (County) as the "future subsidiary administrative center."

In 2012, the Beijing Municipal Government presented proposals for a capital subcenter in Tongzhou, where it would be relocated. In reality, the proposal had little chance of moving forward because of resistance from entrenched interests desiring to maintain the status quo. The Beijing Municipal Government had been centrally located in a huge compound

Table 12.2 Spatial Components of Beijing's 2016–2035 Master Plan

Name	Description	Major Users and Uses
Core (Capital Function Core)	East and West Districts; 92.5 square kilometers (35.7 square miles)	Functions of central government agencies; historical and cultural preservation zone
Main Center (Urban Core)	Six urban districts: East, West, Fengtai, Chaoyang, Haidian, and Shijingshan; 1,378 square kilometers (532 square miles)	Relocated activities and entities from the core in priority order: functions of central government agencies, creative and innovative activities, public and green space, supplemental public services, affordable housing and quality of life improvement, and infrastructure support
Subcenter (Capital Subcenter)	Tongzhou New City; 155 square kilometers (59.8 square miles)	Major edge city for relocated functions from the Core: administrative, business servicing, and recreational activities; inducing development in adjacent areas of Hebei Province
Two Axes	Central Axis (north–south) and its extension; Changan Avenue Axis (east–west) and its extension	Southward extension of Central Axis as engine for economic and ecological development of southern exurbs and connection with the new Daxing International Airport; eastward extension of Changan Avenue Axis as links with the Capital Subcenter and Tangshan–Qinhuangdao corridor
Multiple Edge Cities	Five edge cities: Shunyi, Daxing, Changping, Yizhuang, and Fangshan New Town	Edge cities in flatland areas as major receiving destinations of relocated functions and people from the Core; bases for high-tech and new industry connection with the rest of Jing-Jin-Ji megaregion; model development for urban-rural interface governance and new urban design
Zone (Ecological Conservation Zone)	Five mountainous districts (Mentougou, Pinggu, Huairou, Miyun, and Yanqing) and the hilly areas of the Changping and Fangshan Districts	Key mission: ecological security, safe water source, and "green lung" for the capital; ecological conservation and showcase of green economy

Source: Various Chinese media sources (in both Chinese and English).

that encompassed a princely mansion in the former Legation Quarter, within a stone's throw from Tiananmen Square. In 2014, however, the PRC government under President Xi began to press the Beijing Municipal Government to move to the proposed capital subcenter. Despite resistance and delay tactics from some Beijing officials, the central government prevailed.

In 2015, Beijing officially started drafting plans for construction in the capital subcenter, which was designated to be the administrative center of the Beijing Municipal Government, a major center of advanced business services, and a hub of cultural tourism and recreation. Construction proceeded quickly, and major government offices were completed by mid-2017. Government relocation began in late 2017, and the Beijing Municipal Government officially opened for business in Tongzhou in January 2019. It is anticipated that the municipal government could bring six hundred thousand to seven hundred thousand people, including government employees and their families, as well as many others, from the urban core to Tongzhou and its vicinities.

The capital subcenter is still under rapid and large-scale development. In 2019, a total of CNY 75 billion (over USD 11 billion) was to be invested in five major undertakings in Tongzhou, including (1) a full integration between local and metropolitan public transportation systems, including the largest underground transit hub in China; (2) inauguration of satellite campuses for higher education, medical services, and retirement communities; (3) ecological conservation through a nexus of waterways, wetlands, and greenbelts; (4) infrastructure development to facilitate the smart city[2] initiative; and (5) the induction of high-level business services and promotion of leisure-recreation industries ahead of the anticipated grand opening of nearby Universal Beijing Resort in 2021.

Tongzhou is designated to be a model new city. Upon completion, it will encompass an area of 155 square kilometers (60 square miles) with a projected population of about 1.3 million and a daily workforce between 600,000 and 800,000. Innovative components of the "livable city" are key to its design and planning. There is a so-called urban green lung at the city center, which is a green space of 11.2 square kilometers (4.3 square miles). It is at the intersection of a restored stretch of the Grand Canal, which will be an ecological conservation zone, and the East Sixth Ring Road, which goes through the Songzhuang Art Community, a center of the creative cultural industry. Government officials are targeting a 1:1.2 ratio between business and residential land use and a population density below 9,000 per square kilometer (3,500 per square mile). The government has also included plans to encourage shorter commutes or local residency for those who work at the subcenter.

The capital subcenter will be a major impetus for Beijing's functional realignment and decentralization. It will engender eastward growth along the Beijing-Tangshan-Qinhuangdao Corridor, the eastern axis of the two axes key to the development of Jing-Jin-Ji. Planning and development of the new city will be a testing case of concepts and planning for new urban designs that emphasize environmental sustainability and quality of life. It could be the model, if it succeeds, for the rest of China to emulate.

The Southern Frontiers for Beijing's Growth

The southern exurbs of Beijing have long been neglected by both the city government and the private sector for historical and environmental reasons. Some allege that the city missed the opportunity to develop the south by building the 2008 Summer Olympic Park in the northern suburbs. Beijing's spatial dynamics have changed in recent years, however, as new development concentrates in the southern and eastern suburbs. The central government's strategy for integrated Jing-Jin-Ji development provides definitive impetus for Beijing to expand southward and eastward, especially with the establishment of the Xiongan New Area (2017) to the south of Beijing.

Between 2010 and 2015, Beijing invested about CNY 700 billion (more than USD 100 billion) in its southern suburbs and exurbs. The new Jing-Jin-Ji initiative jump-started a new round of development in southern Beijing, the most important of which is the Beijing Daxing International Airport (PKX). Located near its southern border with Hebei Province, the new airport will help relieve the pressure on the Beijing Capital International Airport (PEK), which has already exceeded its designed capacity of ninety million annual passengers. More importantly, it will serve as the international air hub for Jing-Jin-Ji's southern flank, especially the Xiongan New Area. After four years of construction, PKX officially opened for business on September 25, 2019, with a projected annual passenger capacity of forty-five million by 2022, and seventy-two million by 2025. The long-term plan is to have seven runways and an annual passenger capacity of 100 million by 2040. The new airport has engendered concurrent infrastructure construction in the southern exurbs and adjacent areas in Hebei Province, which will culminate in a network of rail, light rail, subway, expressway, and highway connecting Beijing's urban core with its southern exurbs and the Xiongan New Area. The Beijing Daxing International Airport Express, a high-speed rail service between Beijing's urban core and PKX, covers the distance of 41 kilometers (25.5 miles) in nineteen minutes.

PKX is regarded as the new southern anchor of Beijing's extended central axis and connector with Hebei, which is flanked by the Beijing-Tianjin Corridor to the east and the Beijing-Shijiazhuang-Baoding Corridor to the

Beijing Daxing International Airport (PKX) is located 46 kilometers (29 miles) to the south of Tiananmen Square. Opened in late September 2019, it is the second international airport in Beijing and will be able to handle 45 million passengers by 2021. (Hurry/Dreamstime.com)

BEIJING'S TWIN AIRPORTS

Beijing Capital International Airport (PEK) is one of the largest airports in the world in terms of the yearly volume of passengers, second only to Hartsfield-Jackson International Airport in Atlanta, Georgia. Designed to have a capacity for sixty million passengers a year, it served ninety-seven million in 2017 and became severely bottlenecked. A second international airport, Beijing Daxing International Airport (PKX), opened to the public on September 26, 2019. Located in the southern suburbs of the Beijing metro area and near the border with Hebei Province, the new airport will have a capacity of seventy-two million passengers by 2025 that will eventually increase to one hundred million. It will help relieve the pressure on Beijing Capital International Airport and serve both Beijing and the Xiongan New Area.

west. A special investment zone, about 150 square kilometers (58 square miles), has been established at the new airport, two-thirds of which is in Hebei Province. Two specialized development zones have been planned between the two corridors, a scientific research and innovation zone and a Yongding River cultural activity zone, which includes the Marco Polo

Bridge. The current phase of development (2018–2020) is centered on building basic public services and extensive transit networks that integrate railroad, highway, and subway lines and connect Beijing's urban core with not only the southern suburbs and PKX but also the Xiongan New Area. Emphasis is also placed on environmental improvement, including wastewater and solid waste treatment facilities, an expansive forest park, wetland expansions, and cultural tourism. New enterprise zones and a series of regulatory policies appear to engender a domino effect in channeling traditional manufacturing firms and wholesale businesses from the urban core.

As planned expansions unfold to the east and south, businesses and other institutions in the categories of noncapital functions are encouraged or forced to depart Beijing, or at least move out of the capital's urban core. Beijing authorities have tightened business license application and renewal for small retailers and wholesalers as a way to discourage potential newcomers and push out the existing ones. Wholesalers, once representing a booming business sector in Beijing, were among the first to make the exodus. A milestone of Beijing's efforts in forcing out wholesalers was the shuttering of the Dongding Clothing Wholesale Mart, the largest of its kind in northern China. Neighboring the Peking Zoo, a major tourist attraction in Beijing, the wholesale market attracted an average of one hundred thousand customers every day and, for years, had been a major culprit of the traffic quagmire and failing public safety for zoo visitors. The nightmarish situation came to an end on November 30, 2017, when the market was closed for good. The vacated site will soon become the main center of a national innovation demonstration zone for financial technology.

By early 2019, Beijing had accumulatively dispersed over 2,600 manufacturing facilities, 260 wholesalers, and over 100 logistics and distribution centers from the urban core. Most of these businesses have relocated to Hebei Province. In 2018 alone, more than 650 manufacturing firms left the urban core, most of which were heavy polluting manufacturers in machinery, chemical, metal works, packaging, and building materials. Beijing's goal for 2019 is to disperse another 300 manufacturing facilities and sixty-six wholesale markets or logistics centers and to reclaim 4,000 hectares (9,880 acres) of public land.

Many health care and education institutions have either relocated to the suburbs or opened substantial suburban branches to accommodate decentralized population and businesses. Tiantan Hospital, which is renowned for its expertise in neurosurgery and had been inside the Temple of Heaven (Tiantan) since 1956, moved to a site on the South Fourth Ring Road in 2018. Other major teaching hospitals (3A hospitals) have opened suburban campuses, including the Soviet-built Friendship Hospital, the

Beijing Children's Hospital, and the Beijing Hospital of Chinese Medicine. At the same time, the government tries to improve access by expanding transportation infrastructure to connect the new campuses with suburban communities.

BEIJING IN THE TWENTY-FIRST CENTURY

Beijing is poised to continue drastic transformations as it enters the third decade of the twenty-first century. As it consolidates and strengthens the four capital functions laid out by the central government, Beijing will continue to disperse activities of noncapital functions out of the urban core and, as a result, experience profound changes in economic structure, employment, demographic characteristics, land use, and landscape. Beijing may start to appear and feel quite differently in the ensuing decades from its recent past.

Beijing will continue to be one of the top cities in China and will increasingly stand out as a prominent world city as it realigns its national and global roles and focuses on its best endowed prospects. A report by PricewaterhouseCoopers (PwC), "Chinese Cities of Opportunity 2019," rated Beijing as the most developed city in China, edging out Shanghai (Table 12.3). Beijing leads the country in areas directly influenced by the capital functions: its political dominance directly translates into economic clout, and as the cultural center, it is endorsed by unparalleled human resources and capital for innovations.

It has been proven futile to try to predict the future of China since the country embarked on unprecedented growth and change in the reform era four decades ago. For Beijing, however, the future is now. A profound transformation for the capital has been set in motion through direct, even heavy-handed, intervention by the central government. Beijing's reaffirmed role as the national capital, with its four identified capital functions, will transcend in every aspect of the city's urban development, providing opportunities and challenges to the economy, the environment, traditional and popular cultures, and the overall quality of life. The most far-reaching changes are undoubtedly in the economic and environmental arenas as well as the emergence of a megaregion in northern China.

The Capital Economy and the New Economy

As the national political center, Beijing continues to enjoy the unmatched advantage of attracting the executive branches of large corporations, as it is critical for them to have direct access to the top decision makers of China.

Table 12.3 Ranking of Leading Cities in Ten Dimensions*

Dimensions of Observation	Beijing's Ranking	Shanghai's Ranking	Guangzhou's Ranking	Shenzhen's Ranking	Top-Ranked City
Intellectual capital and innovation	1	2	6	13	Beijing
Technical maturity	3	5	2	1	Shenzhen
Major regional cities	2	1	4	6	Shanghai
Health, safety, and public security	4	2	5	6	Hong Kong
Transportation and urban planning	10	23	4	5	Zhuhai
Sustainable development and natural environment	7	8	9	2	Haikou
Culture and quality of life	15	4	25	20	Macao
Economic clout	1	4	8	3	Beijing
Cost	32	34	35	36	Baoding
Ease of doing business	10	5	7	6	Hong Kong
Total City Score	**1,329**	**1,328**	**1,251**	**1,248**	**n/a**

Source: "Chinese Cities of Opportunities, 2019." PricewaterhouseCoopers and China Development Research Foundation. https://www.pwccn.com/en/research-and-insights/chinese-cities-of-opportunities-2019-report.pdf.

* End of 2017 data.

Half of the 112 Mainland Chinese corporations on the 2019 Fortune Global 500, the world's five hundred largest corporations by annual revenue, are headquartered in Beijing. China's state-owned economy is the top reason for Beijing's draw of corporate headquarters. Three Chinese corporations in the top ten of the Fortune list, State Grid, Sinopec Group, and China National Petroleum, are state-owned enterprises under respective central government ministries. It is logical, even mandatory, for these corporations to be headquartered in Beijing because they are the business extensions of the central government bureaucracy. The same conclusion is true of the other six Chinese corporations, four of which are state-owned banks, in the top fifty of the 2019 Fortune Global 500. Beijing's political clout not only maintains but also grows its capital "headquarter economy," which is represented by the large concentration of corporate headquarters and high-level financial and business services.

Beijing will continue to be a leading incubator of the new economy as it gravitates further toward R & D and creative cultural activities fueled by domestic and global venture capital investment and the brain power from vibrant communities of artistic creation, higher education, and academics. In 2018 alone, Beijing oversaw the birth of twenty-five thousand new government-certified high and new technology enterprises (HNTE), which was a 25 percent increase over 2017 and equal to an average of almost two hundred HNTE startups per day. Beijing topped China in HNTE-related venture capital investment in 2018, accommodating eighty, or about half, of China's unicorns, those privately held companies with estimated market value exceeding USD 1 billion. In 2018, the new economy, represented by technology, information, and financial services, counted for about a third of Beijing's total economic output, with double-digit percentage increases in the electronic engineering, pharmaceutical, and high-tech manufacturing (AI, self-driving autos, etc.) subsectors.

Policy makers and academics share the consensus that Beijing must phase out traditional economic sectors to make space for the new economy. This consensus, however, is akin to social Darwinism because it blatantly discards the workers and their families associated with these economic sectors, who were dubbed as "low-end population." As Beijing thrives on the headquarter economy and new and high technology sectors, traditional manufacturing and wholesale activities are being channeled to Hebei Province. Many migrant workers have started to depart Beijing, either following their employers or being forced out as they are confronted with dwindling job opportunities and untenable living conditions in the city. Beijing's 2015 permanent non-household registered population, which mostly consists of migrant workers, had a menial increase of 0.5 percent over 2014 and has had a decrease every year since then. As a result, Beijing now suffers from a labor shortage in the low-wage service sector, which has turned into a jump in labor costs and declining accessibility to local residents.

Clean Air for Beijing? Progress in Environmental Quality

After repeated attacks of hellish smog on Beijing's air quality, quality of life, and psyche, Beijing authorities began to implement comprehensive measures to combat a wide range of environmental problems under pressure and with support from the central government. There are signs of environmental improvement as integrated development in the Jing-Jin-Ji megaregion continues to drive businesses considered nonessential to the capital away from Beijing's urban core. Air quality in Beijing and its vicinity has markedly improved as a result of more stringent and region-wide enforcement of national emission standards and a strong push for energy conversion from coal to natural gas. In 2018, Beijing's coal consumption decreased to four million tons, and 60 percent of the one hundred thousand annual new motor vehicle permits were slated for clean fuel cars.

A report by United Nations Environmental Programme (UNEP) found that, between 2013 and 2017, various air pollutants in Beijing proper had decreased by 25–83 percent, with PM2.5 falling by 35 percent in Beijing proper and by 25 percent in surrounding areas.[3] Official records show that Beijing's PM2.5 level fell another 12.1 percent in 2018. The number of heavy pollution days (AQI > 200), fifteen, was nine fewer than in 2017, and there was no heavy polluting period longer than three consecutive days. For the first eight months of 2019, Beijing's average PM2.5 level was forty-two micrograms per cubic meter and twenty-three micrograms per cubic meter in August—the lowest monthly level since 2013. Air quality improvement continues to experience great fluctuations. In late November, 2019, for example, northern China was blanketed by a heavy smog, with Beijing's PM2.5 reaching an unhealthy level of 161 µg/m³ by the night of November 22. Regional temperature inversion, dense fog and high humidity provided the environmental conditions that trapped air pollutants; emissions from industries, automobiles, and heating-related coal burning, however, were the major sources for the smog. The campaign to achieve sustainable air quality improvement still has a long way to go.

Beijing has also made progress in water conservation by using a portion of the water it received from the south–north diversion project to replenish its reservoirs and groundwater table. From 1998 to 2014, Beijing's ground table decreased 12.83 meters (42 feet). Beijing began to reverse the trend with both conservation efforts and water from the south–north diversion project. The largest reservoir for Beijing, the Miyun Reservoir, reached its highest storage capacity in more than two decades at

2.67 billion cubic meters by mid-2019, in comparison to the one billion cubic meters in 2015. Between 2016 and 2019, the water table in Beijing's flatland rose by 2.72 meters (8.9 feet). Beijing's sewage treatment rate has reached 93.4 percent, comparable to that of cities in developed economies.

Beijing is also undertaking projects to improve the quality, quantity, and access of urban green space. The Beijing Municipal Government has proposed to provide green space access of fewer than 500 meters (1,640 feet) to 80 percent of Beijing residents by 2020. While disproportionately affecting low-income groups, government-sanctioned demolition of illegally constructed structures has reclaimed plenty of public space in the crowded urban core for environmental improvement. In 2018 alone, Beijing reclaimed more than 6,800 hectares (16,800 acres) of squatted land, 1,680 hectares (4,100 acres) of which were transformed into public green space. Beijing is carrying out plans to reforest the city, returning it to "a city of trees" through reforestation and new suburban forest parks.

Construction started in 2019 on two parks, each about 4 to 4.5 acres, at where the central axis intersects with former Inner City walls, one on the north side and one on the south side. There will be a large forest and wetland park (250 acres) between the South Fourth and Fifth Ring Roads along the central axis. The first phase of the park started in March 2019, and when completed, the park will have a total of 2,600 acres of restored woodland and marshland, providing residents and visitors with leisure and recreational space on the site of former royal gardens and hunting grounds. Beijing's tree coverage now exceeds 40 percent due to successful reforestation.

Solid waste has reached crisis levels for large Chinese cities, which are responding with drastic measures to curtail waste generation. Beijing has experimented with garbage sorting with only limited success due to a lack of public awareness and material incentives. In July 2019, following Shanghai's implementation of a strict garbage classification system, Beijing initiated its own heightened waste disposal reduction program, including banning disposable utensils in all government agencies; compulsory waste sorting in hospitals, schools, hotels, office buildings, and large commercial facilities; and implementing pilot programs for household waste sorting at 224 subdistricts and promoting waste sorting in 500 villages. While new incinerators are being built, the goal of the new program is to significantly boost recycling and composting and to eventually approach zero waste generation. The authorities have also started providing incentives for sorting household waste. Residents receive free waste-sorting bags and register the amount of their sorted waste; in return, they receive credits that can be exchanged for daily necessities. All of this can be done by using smartphone scanning apps.

Beijing is building new public services while revamping existing ones with a focus on seniors and accessibility. Some of the most prestigious institutions in education and health care are moving to the suburbs, following and also encouraging the outbound migration of the household registered population. Short-distance and private automobile travel, a major culprit of air pollution, may decrease as a network of neighborhood convenience stores emerges, complementing the rapidly growing e-commerce-based express delivery system for just about any goods and services.

After enduring decades of neglect, Beijing's cultural and historical heritage may finally benefit from concerted conservation efforts, which is integral to the capital's function as the national cultural center. More financial resources are now available for historical preservation projects from both the government and the private sector. Improved air quality will reduce acid rain that has taken a toll on the white marble that was used extensively for historical landmarks. At the same time, the ethos of postreform China are being amplified by new landmarks in Beijing, the country's political center and international showcase. In its "2019 Report on the Works of the Beijing Municipal Government," the authorities revealed eight new landmarks for Beijing that encompass all the major endeavors that Beijing has been taking on to confront urban ills, improve livability, and carry out the capital functions (Table 12.4).

Beijing in the Jing-Jin-Ji Megaregion

With the announcement of long-term plans for the Xiongan New Area in 2017, the PRC government's new strategy for Jing-Jin-Ji began to unfold. The Tongzhou capital subcenter and Xiongan New Area have become Beijing's two wings of development and the growth poles of the Jing-Jin-Ji megaregion. While the Tongzhou capital subcenter has become the new seat of the Beijing Municipal Government, the Xiongan New Area will become a major development zone for manufacturing, wholesale, and education, new or relocated from Beijing. Billed as "the city of the future," the Xiongan New Area may be the PRC government's answer to megacity ills. The jury is still out, though, as to whether its design and governance can stimulate major economic growth in northern China and prevent the environmental and economic problems that traditional industries can inflict on cities and regions.

The Xiongan New Area is a centerpiece of the new Jing-Jin-Ji development strategy. With the new spatial and sectoral pattern shaping up, Jing-Jin-Ji is designed to become a low-density, ecofriendly, highly networked and new technology-driven megaregion. Emerging megaregions are based on complementary relationships through which more balanced regional

Table 12.4   The Eight New Landmarks of Beijing, 2019

Landmark	Description
"Huitian" Area	The largest planned suburban bedroom community with 800,000 residents and the epitome of poor planning and lack of sustainability. Complete overhaul with public services and transit linkage; the location for the first exclusive, barrier-free bicycle lane in China (4 miles long, 20 feet wide, speed limit 12 miles/hour)
Capital Subcenter	Beijing's new town, seat of the Beijing Municipal Government, and a model city for livability and sustainability
Daxing International Airport	The symbol of coordinated regional development in northern China and the twin of Beijing Capital International Airport that will serve the southern flank of the Jing-Jin-Ji megaregion
Wangfujing Pedestrian Shopping Street	Upscale boutique shopping district and a tourist attraction with its central location and legendary history
Central Axis	The epitome of Beijing's historical and political supremacy; continued work for property vacation and historical restoration along the 4.8-mile axis
Zhengyangmen– Yongdingmen Pedestrian Way	The 2-mile-long walkway as an extension of the central axis; focus on historical excavation and restoration of Beijing's folklore and life of the urban poor
Nanyuan Forest Park	Major ecological restoration and reforestation and the largest forest park (2,640 acres planned area) in southern Beijing
Capital Steel Relic Park	Multiuse complex converted from a former steel plant site; a major site for the 2022 Winter Olympics; a model for redevelopment of old industrial areas

Source: "2019 Report on the Works of the Beijing Municipal Government" (in Chinese). http://bj.people.com.cn/n2/2019/0123/c82837-32563414.html.

development can be achieved and megacity ills can be better mitigated. The PRC government has launched a plan to designate nineteen supercity clusters, or megaregions, for coordinated regional development.[4] Within each supercity cluster, development will be streamlined to overcome political and bureaucratic barriers.[5] China's megaregions are different from their Western counterparts, first, for their extremely large size, with some exceeding one hundred million in population. Second but more importantly, the government, rather than the market, plays a key role in planning, regulating, and implementing the development agendas of these megaregions.

The Jing-Jin-Ji megaregion is the second-largest of the nineteen super-city clusters in China. When fully integrated, it will have a population of more than one hundred million. It lags behind the Yangzi River Delta and Greater Bay Area anchored by Hong Kong, Shenzhen, and Guangzhou in economic output, productivity, and, particularly, regional economic integration. On the other hand, Jing-Jin-Ji's uneven development provides opportunities for economic integration with strong complementarity between Beijing and Tianjin, the two leading urban centers, and Hebei Province. The strategy is to convert complementarity into transferability by breaking down administrative barriers, dismantling entrenched local interests, and enhancing connectivity through regional infrastructure building.

Hebei's economy will benefit from the infusion of businesses and investment relocating from Beijing, and Beijing will trim down from a do-it-all megacity to one specializing in capital functions. Preliminary implementation of the new strategy has already generated more than CNY 70 billion (USD 12 billion) of investment from Beijing to Hebei between 2015 and 2018. In addition, joint legislative processes have been on track to pass regional environmental regulations and laws. The future of the Xiongan New Area and Jing-Jin-Ji is not all rosy, however, as progress appears to have stalled lately and skeptics have begun to argue that the lack of location and environmental advantages would make sustainable development difficult under market-driven conditions. Nonetheless, Beijing's decentralization proceeds as planned, and the city's transformation presses on.

In the fall of 2019, the Beijing Municipal Government proudly displayed the city's achievements as part of the celebration of the PRC's seventieth anniversary: Beijing ranked number one in business environment among the twenty-two major Chinese cities surveyed in 2018; it has the largest number of headquarters of Fortune Global 500 among all cities in the world; its per capita income has reached the level of developed countries; the new Beijing Daxing International Airport, along with Beijing Capital International Airport, will make Beijing the top city in the world in terms of passenger capacity in civil aviation; and the main event facilities of the 2022 Winter Olympics will all qualify for zero emission of carbon dioxide. The list goes on and glosses over ongoing megacity ills and tough challenges. After the pomp and circumstance, however, hard work will have to continue because Beijing and China cannot afford to fail.

Some may argue that Beijing has never succeeded or even qualified to be "the model of all places." At the same time, no one can deny that Beijing is the prime representative of China's joys and sorrows, triumphs and defeats, and promises and challenges. Beijing must continue to improve its living environment while developing a new economy grounded in sustained innovation and creativity. Sprouting skyscrapers and strangulating motorways have blemished the city that had situated so harmoniously in the Bay of Beijing (Peking), but they have not irreversibly damaged it. There is reason for confidence in China's collective wisdom and the local community's ceaseless efforts in striking a balance between its historical and cultural heritage and vibrant and reinvented present. Failure to do so would be an immeasurable loss to China and humanity.

MUSINGS ABOUT BEIJING

In the sweltering heat of August, seemingly endless streams of humanity fill the plaza made known to the world in 1989 as the site of the Tiananmen Square Massacre. The air is heavy and thick with the haze that earned Beijing a high rank on the list of cities with the world's worst air quality. The majority of foreign visitors appear to be from Asian countries, and although Western tourists are noticeable, the city's reputation for smog has been known to divert many prospective travelers from Europe and North America. Domestic tourists also make their mark. Only rarely able to afford luxury Buicks and arriving more often by bus than any other form of transport are large numbers of Chinese, mostly from adjacent provinces.

While a number of provincials find themselves attracted to shopping perhaps as much as, if not more than, touring iconic sites, others devote themselves to visiting family members and friends who have moved to China's cultural capital in search of economic opportunities unavailable in their hometowns. By and large much less educated than typical natives of the city, migrants from the provinces have found low-paying employment that Beijingers normally find both objectionable and necessary, for service in restaurants is a must, as is the disposal of waste. Yet, notwithstanding this symbiotic relationship, it seems to be a norm for the more cosmopolitan city natives to scorn unsophisticated rustics, who are perceived as being uncouth and poorly schooled peasants motivated largely by economic gain and unappreciative of the city's character and ambience.

Indeed, despite the congestion and pollution that characterize the city as well as the horror of Tiananmen Square's tragic history, great reverence for Beijing is felt by its native born. This topophilia is not only deeply rooted in the Great Wall, the Forbidden City, and the Temple of Heaven, it is sparked by a sense of place created by the neighborhoods, parks, and childhood memories that form a common identity among those raised in the global city. Worldliness is an attribute shared among the educated, and Beijing schools are considered among the country's best.

For sure, the urbane Beijinger is a marked contrast to the naïve rural migrant, and this prompts one to recognize that a rural-urban divide exists in

China that may not be so much unlike that in the United States. Given that, the question must be raised that although a centrally administered municipality is in place, what impact upon Beijing politics will this disharmony have in the future?

—*M.S. DeVivo*

NOTES

1. "Megaregions," America 2050, accessed September 23, 2019, http://www.america2050.org/content/megaregions.html.

2. "What Is a Smart City?" Cisco, accessed September 23, 2019, https://www.cisco.com/c/en/us/solutions/industries/smart-connected-communities/what-is-a-smart-city.html.

3. UN Environment, *A Review of 20 Years' Air Pollution Control in Beijing* (Nairobi, Kenya: United Nations Environment Programme, 2019), https://wedocs.unep.org/handle/20.500.11822/27645.

4. Mark Preen, "China's City Clusters: The Plan to Develop 19 Super-Regions," China Briefing, August 14, 2018, https://www.china-briefing.com/news/chinas-city-clusters-plan-to-transform-into-19-super-regions.

5. "A Tale of 19 Mega-Cities," *The Economist*, June 23, 2018, https://www.economist.com/china/2018/06/23/china-is-trying-to-turn-itself-into-a-country-of-19-super-regions.

Bibliography

Acharya, Shrawan. "Urban Development in Post-Reform China: Insights from Beijing." *Norsk Geografisk Tidsskrift-norwegian Journal of Geography* 59 (2005): 228–236. https://doi.org/10.1080/00291 950500228303.

Aisin-Gioro, Puyi. *From Emperor to Citizen: The Autobiography of Aisin-Gioro Pu Yi.* Translated by William John Francis Jenner. Beijing: Foreign Languages Press, 1989.

Allen, Bradley G. "Thresholds and Stages: Beijing's Central Political Space." Master's thesis, Savannah College of Art and Design, 2011. https://doi.org/10.18130/V3T67G.

Barmé, Geremie R. "Zhu Qiqian's Silver Shovel." *China Heritage Quarterly* 14 (June 2008). http://www.chinaheritagequarterly.org/features.php ?searchterm=014_zhuQiqian.inc&issue=014.

Brace, T. "Popular Music in Contemporary Beijing: Modernism and Cultural Identity." *Asian Music* 22, no. 2 (1991): 43–66. https://doi.org /10.2307/834306.

Bruno, Debra. "Beijing's Famed Street-Food Scene Struggles to Survive." Citylab, June 26, 2014. https://www.citylab.com/life/2014/06/beiji ngs-famed-street-food-scene-struggles-to-survive/373484.

Chang, Sen-dou. "Beijing: Perspectives on Preservation, Environment, and Development." *Cities* 15, no. 1 (1998): 13–25. https://doi.org/10.1016 /S0264-2751(97)10003-8.

Chen, Caroline. "Dancing in the Streets of Beijing: Improvised Uses within the Urban System." In *Insurgent Public Space: Guerrilla Urbanism and the Remaking of Contemporary Cities,* edited by Jeffrey Hou, 21–25. London: Routledge, 2010. https://bcourses.berkeley.edu/files /71853103/download?download_frd=1.

Chen, Chundi. "Planning Urban Nature: Urban Green Space Planning in Post-1949 China: Beijing as a Representative Case Study." PhD diss.,

Lincoln University, 2013. https://pdfs.semanticscholar.org/e78c/d6
6a627335d263b7209f8eaf1c9fee5beddf.pdf.

Chen, Xiaofei. "A Comparative Study of Supergrid and Superblock Urban Structure in China and Japan—Rethinking the Chinese Super-blocks: Learning from Japanese Experience." PhD diss., University of Sydney, 2017.

Chen, Xiaoming. "Community and Policing Strategies: A Chinese Approach to Crime Control." *Policing and Society* 12, no. 1 (2002): 1–13. https://doi.org/10.1080/10439460290006646.

Chinese Academy of Social Sciences (CASS). *Concise Historical Atlas of China*. Beijing: China Cartographic Publishing House, 1985.

Clark, Matthew Corbin. "Birth of a Beijing Music Scene." *PBS Frontline*, February 13, 2003. https://www.pbs.org/wgbh/pages/frontline/shows /red/sonic.

Cyr, Isabelle Marie. "Living in Beijing: A Suburban Topography." *Modu Magazine: A Tale of Urban China*, February 28, 2018. https://www .modumag.com/focus/living-in-beijing-a-suburban-topography.

Dai, Yanqiu Autumn. "City Art Guide: Beijing." *The Artling*, February 15, 2019. https://theartling.com/en/artzine/city-art-guides/beijing.

De Kloet, Jeroen. "Popular Music and Youth in Urban China: The Dakou Generation." *The China Quarterly* 183 (2005): 609–626. http:// www.jstor.org/stable/20192511.

Dong, Madeleine Yue. *Republican Beijing: The City and Its Histories*. Berkeley: University of California Press, 2003.

Dryburgh, Marjorie. "Living on the Edge: Welfare and the Urban Poor in 1930s Beijing." *Social History* 41, no. 1 (January 2016): 14–33. https://doi.org/10.1080/03071022.2015.1108708.

Fan, Ka-wai. "Climate Change and Chinese History: A Review of Trends, Topics, and Methods." *WIREs Climate Change* 6, no. 2 (March/ April 2015): 225–238. https://doi.org/10.1002/wcc.331.

Fang, Jin-Qi, and Guo Liu. "Relationship between Climatic Change and the Nomadic Southward Migrations in Eastern Asia during Historical Times." *Climatic Change* 22, no. 2 (October 1992): 151–168. https://doi.org/10.1007/BF00142964.

Feola, Josh. "Beijing's Do Hits Label Is Forging China's New Club Sound." Bandcamp Daily, March 29, 2017. https://daily.bandcamp.com/2017 /03/29/do-hits-label-profile.

French, Paul. *Midnight in Peking: How the Murder of a Young English-woman Haunted the Last Days of Old China*. New York: Penguin Books, 2012.

Gajer, Steven. "Deconstructing the Superblock: Universal Solutions vs. Cultural Specificity in Chinese Urban Planning." Master's thesis, Carleton University, 2015. https://doi.org/10.22215/etd/2015-10889.

Galloway, Colin. "Beijing: How Should China Handle Redevelopment of a Historical Hutongs?" Urban Land, May 29, 2018. https://urbanland .uli.org/economy-markets-trends/beijings-historic-hutongs-china -handle-redevelopment-historical-icon.

Gamble, Sidney D., J. Liang, and H. Wang. *How Chinese Families Live in Peiping: A Study of the Income and Expenditure of 283 Chinese Families Receiving from $8 to $550 Silver per Month*. New York: Funk & Wagnalls Company, 1933.

Gao, Yang. "Inventing the 'Authentic' Self: American Television and Chinese Audiences in Global Beijing." *Media, Culture and Society* 38, no. 8 (November 2016): 1201–1217. https://doi.org/10.1177/0163443 716635870.

Gao, Yuan, and Peter Newman. "Beijing's Peak Car Transition: Hope for Emerging Cities in the 1.5 °C Agenda." *Urban Planning* 3, no. 2 (2018): 82–93. https://doi.org/10.17645/up.v3i2.1246.

Gaubatz, Piper. "Changing Beijing." *Geographical Review* 85, no. 1 (January 1995): 79–96. https://doi.org/10.2307/215557.

Gaubatz, Piper. "China's Urban Transformation: Patterns and Processes of Morphological Change in Beijing, Shanghai and Guangzhou." *Urban Studies* 36, no. 9 (August 1999): 1495–1521. https://doi.org/10.1080 /0042098992890.

Geil, William Edgar. *Eighteen Capitals of China*. Philadelphia: J. B. Lippincott Company, 1911. https://archive.org/details/eighteencapitals00geiliala /page/n10.

Geiss, James. "Beijing under the Ming (1368–1644)." PhD diss., Princeton University, 1979.

Gohel, Sajjan M. "The 'Seventh Stage' of Terrorism in China." *CTC Sentinel* 7, no. 11 (November/December 2014): 16–19. https://ctc.usma .edu/the-seventh-stage-of-terrorism-in-china.

Graziani, Thomas. "Study of 151 Chinese Unicorns Shows Beijing #1 City for Startups." WalktheChat, April 30, 2018. https://walkthechat .com/study-151-chinese-unicorns-shows-beijing-1-city-startups.

Gu, Chaolin, Xiaohui Yuan, and Jing Guo. "China's Master Planning System in Transition: Case Study of Beijing." 46th ISOCARP Congress 2010. http://www.isocarp.net/Data/case_studies/1657.pdf.

Han, Lijian, Weiqi Zhou, Steward T. A. Pickett, Weifeng Li, and Yuguo Qian. "Multicontaminant Air Pollution in Chinese Cities." *Bulletin of the World Health Organization* 96 (2018): 233–242E. http://dx .doi.org/10.2471/BLT.17.195560.

Hancock, William, and Paula Jin. "Why You Need to Start Paying Attention to Beijing's Indie Rock Scene." *Waytogo by Smile Magazine*, January 18, 2018. https://waytogo.cebupacificair.com/beijing-indie -rock.

Hinsch, Bret. "Climate Change and History of China." *Journal of Asian History* 22, no. 2 (1988): 131–159. http://www.jstor.org/stable/41930720.

Hou, Eve. "Nine Dragons, One River: The Role of Institutions in Developing Water Pricing Policy in Beijing, PRC." Master's thesis, University of British Columbia, 2001. http://dx.doi.org/10.14288/1.0099535.

Hou, Renzhi. *A Historical Geography of Peiping.* New York: Foreign Language Teaching and Research Publishing Co., Ltd., and Springer-Verlag Berlin Heidelberg, 2014.

Hou, Renzhi. "The Transformation of the Old City of Beijing, China—A Concrete Manifestation of New China's Cultural Reconstruction." In *Symposium on Chinese Historical Geography*, 31–48. New York: Foreign Language Teaching and Research Publishing Co., Ltd., and Springer-Verlag Berlin Heidelberg, 2014.

Hou, Renzhi. *The Works of Hou Renzhi.* Beijing: Peking University Press, 1998.

Hu, Xiao. "Preserving the Old Beijing: The First Conflict between Chinese Architects and the Communist Government in the 1950s." Paper presented at the First Annual James A. Rawley Graduate Conference in the Humanities, Lincoln, Nebraska, April 8, 2006. http://digitalcommons.unl.edu/historyrawleyconference/8.

Johnson, Ian. "A Big New Airport Shows China's Strengths (and Weaknesses)." *New York Times*, November 24, 2018. https://www.nytimes.com/2018/11/24/world/asia/china-beijing-daxing-airport.html.

Kan, Har Ye, Ann Forsyth, and Peter Rowe. "Redesigning China's Superblock Neighbourhoods: Policies, Opportunities and Challenges." *Journal of Urban Design* 22, no. 6 (June 2017): 757–777. https://doi.org/10.1080/13574809.2017.1337493.

Layton, Kelly. "Beijing, the City Made Manifest." *China Heritage Quarterly* 14 (June 2008). http://www.chinaheritagequarterly.org/articles.php?searchterm=014_cityMadeManifest.inc&issue=014.

Lee, Nelson K. "How Is a Political Public Space Made?—The Birth of Tiananmen Square and the May Fourth Movement." *Political Geography* 28 (2009): 32–43. https://doi.org/10.1016/j.polgeo.2008.05.003.

Li, Lillian, Alison Dray-Novey, and Haili Kong. *Beijing: From Imperial Capital to Olympic City.* New York: Palgrave Macmillan, 2007.

Li, Tiankui, Yi Liu, Chaoran Wang, Gustaf Olsson, Zishu Wang, and Hao Wang. "Decentralization of the Non-Capital Functions of Beijing: Industrial Relocation and Its Environmental Effects." *Journal of Cleaner Production* 224 (July 1, 2019): 545–556. https://doi.org/10.1016/j.jclepro.2019.03.247.

Li, Tongtong, Qi Wang, and Zheng Xie. "Disaster Response Knowledge and Its Social Determinants: A Cross-Sectional Study in Beijing, China." *PLoS/ONE*, March 26, 2019. https://doi.org/10.1371/journal.pone.0214367.

Li, Xiaopeng, Jing Han, Shuxin Fan, Peiyao Hao, and Li Dong. "Assessing the Effects of Landscape Characteristics on the Thermal Environment of Open Spaces in Residential Areas of Beijing, China." *Landscape and Ecological Engineering* 14, no. 1 (2018): 79–90. https://doi.org/10.1007/s11355-017-0326-x.

Li, Ying. "Beijing's Forgotten Missionary Schools: A History of Protestant-Run Places of Learning in China's Capital." *Global Times*, September 8, 2014. https://www.globaltimes.cn/content/880417.shtml.

Liu, Ts'ui-Jung. "A Retrospection of Climate Changes and Their Impacts in Chinese History." In *Nature, Environment and Culture in East Asia*, edited by Carmen Meinert, 107–136. Leiden: Brill, 2013.

Lü, Yongqiang, Xinqi Zheng, Lin Zhou, and Lulu Zhang. "Decentralization and Polycentricity: Spatial Changes of Employment in Beijing Metropolitan Area, China." *Sustainability* 9, no. 10 (October 2017): 1880–1896. https://doi.org/10.3390/su9101880.

Ma, Jing, Chunjiang Li, Mei-Po Kwan, and Yanwei Chai. "A Multilevel Analysis of Perceived Noise Pollution, Geographic Contexts and Mental Health in Beijing." *International Journal of Environmental Research and Public Health* 15, no. 7 (2018): 1479. https://doi.org/10.3390/ijerph15071479.

Man, Bosat. "Backhill/Peking/Beijing." *Sino-Platonic Papers* 19 (June 1990): 1–6. http://sino-platonic.org/complete/spp019_peking_beijing.pdf.

Marvin, Carolyn. "'All under Heaven'—Megaspace in Beijing." In *Owning the Olympics*, edited by M. E. Price and D. Dayan, 229–259. Ann Arbor: University of Michigan Press. https://doi.org/10.3998/nmw.5646196.0001.001.

Mattone, James. "How Luckin Coffee Is about to Beat Starbucks at Its Own Game in China." Thinknum Media. Accessed September 23, 2019. https://media.thinknum.com/articles/luckin-coffee-challenges-starbucks-in-asia.

McDonell, Stephen. "A Woman's Murder in Peking and a Literary Feud." BBC, January 8, 2019. https://www.bbc.com/news/world-asia-china-46450210.

Meyer, Jeffrey F. *The Dragons of Tiananmen: Beijing as a Sacred City.* Columbia: University of South Carolina Press, 1991.

Moch, Jonathan M., Eleni Dovrou, Loretta J. Mickley, Frank N. Keutsch, Yuan Cheng, Daniel J. Jacob, Jingkun Jiang, Meng Li, J. William Munger, Xiaohui Qiao, et al. "Contribution of Hydroxymethane Sulfonate to Ambient Particulate Matter: A Potential Explanation for High Particulate Sulfur during Severe Winter Haze in Beijing." *Geophysical Research Letters* 45, no. 21 (November 2018): 11, 969–911, 979. https://doi.org/10.1029/2018GL079309.

Murphy, Dawn. "China's Approach to International Terrorism." United States Institute of Peace, October 2, 2017. https://www.usip.org/publications/2017/10/chinas-approach-international-terrorism.

Naquin, Susan. *Peking: Temples and City Life, 1400–1900.* Berkeley: University of California Press, 2000.

Pei, Qing. "Conquest of Beijing: Hidden Contributions of Climate Change to the Tumu Crisis, 1449–1450." *Environment & Society Portal, Arcadia* 12 (Autumn 2016). https://doi.org/10.5282/rcc/7639.

Pei, Qing, and D. D. Zhang. "Long-Term Relationship between Climate Change and Nomadic Migration in Historical China." *Ecology and Society* 19, no. 2 (2014): 68. http://dx.doi.org/10.5751/ES-06528-190268.

Potter, Philip B. K. "Terrorism in China: Growing Threats with Global Implications." *Strategic Studies Quarterly* 7, no. 4 (Winter 2013): 70–92. https://www.airuniversity.af.edu/Portals/10/SSQ/documents/Volume-07_Issue-4/2013winter-Potter.pdf.

Preen, Mark. "China's City Clusters: The Plan to Develop 19 Super-Regions." China Briefing, August 14, 2018. https://www.china-briefing.com/news/chinas-city-clusters-plan-to-transform-into-19-super-regions.

PricewaterhouseCoopers and China Development Research Foundation. "Chinese Cities of Opportunity 2019." Accessed September 23, 2019. https://www.pwccn.com/en/research-and-insights/chinese-cities-of-opportunities-2019-report.html.

Qiao, Zhi, Guangjin Tian, Lixiao Zhang, and Xinliang Xu. "Influences of Urban Expansion on Urban Heat Island in Beijing during 1989–2010." *Advances in Meteorology* 2014 (2014), Article ID 187169, 11 pages. https://doi.org/10.1155/2014/187169.

Qiu, Shiyong, and Ying Wang. "Toward Car-Free Cities: Beijing Seeks an Inroad to Sustainable Transport." TheCityFix. November 30, 2017. https://thecityfix.com/blog/toward-car-free-cities-beijing-seeks-an-inroad-to-sustainable-transport-shiyong-qiu-ying-wang.

Quaedackers, Esther. "A Little Big History of Tiananmen." In *Evolution: A Big History Perspective*, edited by L. E. Grinin, A. V. Korotayev, and B. H. Rodrigue, 269–280. Volgograd, Russia: Uchitel Publishing House, 2011.

Ratchnevsky, Paul. *Genghis Khan: His Life and Legacy.* New York: Wiley-Blackwell, 1993.

Schwartz, James D. "Photos: China's History of Bicycles." *The Urban Country* (blog). Accessed September 23, 2019. http://www.theurbancountry.com/2013/02/photos-chinas-history-of-bicycles.html.

Shang, Qian. "Underground Space: A View for the Conservation of Beijing Old City." *Procedia Engineering* 165 (2016): 265–276. https://doi.org/10.1016/j.proeng.2016.11.799.

Sheppard, Graeme. *A Death in Peking: Who Killed Pamela Werner?* Hong Kong: Earnshaw Books, 2018.

Shi, Mingzheng. "Beijing Transforms: Urban Infrastructure, Public Works, and Social Change in the Chinese Capital, 1900–1928." PhD diss., Columbia University, 1993.

Shin, Hyun Bang. "Urban Conservation and Revalorisation of Dilapidated Historic Quarters: The Case of Nanluoguxiang in Beijing." *Cities* 27, Suppl. 1 (June 2010): S43–S54. https://doi.org/10.1016/j.cities.2010.03.006.

Sim, Timothy, and Jun Lei Yu. "Natural Hazards Governance in China." *Natural Hazard Science*, August 28, 2018. https://doi.org/10.1093/acrefore/9780199389407.013.239.

Simon, Lydia Noelle. "'Cultural Creative Industry Parks' and Chinese Contemporary Art—A Comparative Study of Beijing's 798 Arts District and Songzhuang Artist Village." Master's thesis, Ohio State University, 2017. https://etd.ohiolink.edu/!etd.send_file?accession=osu149265536987791&disposition=inline.

Siren, Osvald. *The Walls and Gates of Peking*. London: John Lane, The Bodley Head Limited, 1924.

Sit, Victor F. S. "Soviet Influence on Urban Planning in Beijing, 1949–1991." *The Town Planning Review* 67, no. 4 (1996): 457–484. http://www.jstor.org/stable/40113418.

Song, Weijie. "Mapping Modern Beijing: A Literary and Cultural Topography, 1900s–1950s." PhD diss., Columbia University, 2006.

Steinhardt, S. Nancy. *Chinese Imperial City Planning*. Honolulu: University of Hawaii Press, 1999.

Strand, David. *Rickshaw Beijing: City People and Politics in the 1920s*. Berkeley: University of California Press, 1993.

Su, Y., L. Liu, X. Q. Fang, and Y. N. Ma. "The Relationship between Climate Change and Wars Waged between Nomadic and Farming Groups from the Western Han Dynasty to the Tang Dynasty Period." *Climate of the Past* 12 (January 2016): 137–150. https://doi.org/10.5194/cp-12-137-2016.

Sun, Emma. "New Beijing Mag Missionary Goes Deep on LGBTQ+ Culture in China." RADII, January 16, 2019. https://radiichina.com/new-beijing-mag-missionary-goes-deep-on-lgbtq-culture-in-china.

Sundby, Jon. "Bike Boom to Bike Bust: Learning from China to Get the Most out of Dockless Bikes." Frontier Group, March 8, 2019. https://frontiergroup.org/blogs/blog/fg/bike-boom-bike-bust-learning-china-get-most-out-dockless-bikes.

Tan, L., Y. Cai, Z. An, L. Yi, H. Zhang, and S. Qin. "Climate Patterns in North Central China during the Last 1800 Years and Their Possible Driving Force." *Climate of the Past* 7 (July 2011): 685–692. https://doi.org/10.5194/cp-7-685-2011.

Tanner, Murray Scot, with James Bellacqua. *China's Response to Terrorism.* Report sponsored by the U.S.-China Economic and Security Review Commission (USCC), Arlington, VA: CNA Analysis & Solutions, 2016. https://www.uscc.gov/sites/default/files/Research/Chinas%20Response%20to%20Terrorism_CNA061616.pdf.

Teo, Esther. "Chaoyang's Citizen Crime-Busters." *The Straits Times*, July 18, 2015. https://www.straitstimes.com/asia/chaoyangs-citizen-crime-busters.

Thornton, Patricia. "From Liberating Production to Unleashing Consumption: Mapping Landscapes of Power in Beijing." *Political Geography* 29, no. 6 (August 2010): 302–310. https://doi.org/10.1016/j.polgeo.2010.06.001.

Tung, Anthony M. "Erasing Old Beijing." World Monument Fund, Fall 2003. https://www.wmf.org/sites/default/files/article/pdfs/pg_38-45_hutongs.pdf.

Twitchett, Denis, and John K. Fairbank, eds. *The Cambridge History of China.* Vol. 12, *Republican China, 1912–1949, Part 1.* Cambridge, UK: Cambridge University Press, 1983. https://assets.cambridge.org/97805212/35419/frontmatter/9780521235419_frontmatter.pdf.

UN Environment. *A Review of 20 Years' Air Pollution Control in Beijing.* Nairobi, Kenya: United Nations Environment Programme, 2019. https://wedocs.unep.org/handle/20.500.11822/27645.

Wang, Jun. *Beijing Record: A Physical and Political History of Planning Modern Beijing.* Singapore: World Scientific Publishing Co., 2011.

Wang, Ying, Shiyong Qiu, and Ting Zhao. "Fewer Emissions, Better Life." World Resources Institute/Ross Center, May 2018. https://wrirosscities.org/research/publication/fewer-emissions-better-life-beijing-low-emission-zone-final-report.

Watts, Jonathan. "China: The Air Pollution Capital of the World." *The Lancet* 366, no. 9499 (November 19, 2005): 1761–1762. https://doi.org/10.1016/S0140-6736(05)67711-2.

Weston, Timothy B. *The Power of Position: Beijing University, Intellectuals, and Chinese Political Culture, 1898–1929.* Berkeley: University of California Press, 2004.

Willis, Bailey, Eliot Blackwelder, and R. H. Sargent. *Research in China.* Washington, DC: Carnegie Institution of Washington, 1907.

Wong, Frank Ka-Ho. "Xiong'an New Area: President Xi's Dream City." China Briefing, March 26, 2019. https://www.china-briefing.com/news/xiongan-new-area-beijing-tianjin-hebei.

Wright, Arthur F. "The Cosmology of the Chinese City." In *The City in Late Imperial China*, edited by G. William Skinner, 33–73. Stanford, CA: Stanford University Press, 1977.

Wright, Arthur F. "Symbolism and Function: Reflections on Changan and Other Great Cities." *The Journal of Asian Studies* 24, no. 4 (1965): 667–679. https://doi.org/10.2307/2051112.

Wu, Hung. *Remaking Beijing: Tiananmen Square and the Creation of a Political Space*. Chicago: University of Chicago Press, 2005.

Wu, Liangyong. "Conservation and Development in the Historic City of Beijing." *Ekistics* 64, no. 385/386/387 (1997): 240–246. http://www.jstor.org/stable/43623260.

Xia, Ming. "Organizational Formations of Organized Crime in China: Perspectives from the State, Markets, and Networks." *Journal of Contemporary China* 17, no. 54 (December 2007): 1–23. https://doi.org/10.1080/10670560701693039.

Xu, Yamin. "Wicked Citizens and the Social Origins of China's Modern Authoritarian State: Civil Strife and Political Control in Republican Beiping, 1928–1937." PhD diss., University of California, 2002.

Yan, J., Q. Ge, H. Liu, J. Zheng, and H. Fu. "Reconstruction of Sub-Decadal Winter Half-Year Temperature during 1651–2010 for the North China Plain Using Records of Frost Date." *Atmospheric and Climate Sciences* 4, no. 2 (April 2014): 211–218. https://doi.org/10.4236/acs.2014.42024.

Yang, Jiawen, Ge Song, and Jian Lin. "Measuring Spatial Structure of China's Mega-Regions." *Lincoln Institute of Land Policy Working Papers*, April 2013. https://www.lincolninst.edu/publications/working-papers/measuring-spatial-structure-chinas-mega-regions.

Yang, Tongya. "Morphological Transformation of the Old City of Beijing after 1949." Semantic Scholar, 2004. http://discovery.ucl.ac.uk/4114/1/4114.pdf.

Zhang, Da-Lin, Yonghui Lin, Ping Zhao, Xiaoding Yu, Songqiu Wang, Hongwen Kang, and Yihui Ding. "The Beijing Extreme Rainfall of 21 July 2012: 'Right Results' But for Wrong Reasons." *Geophysical Research Letters* 40, no. 7 (April 2013): 1426–1431. https://doi.org/10.1002/grl.50304.

Zhang, Jiwei, L. G. Tang, X. Q. Xiao, H. Zhou, and Z. Q. Zhang. "The Emergency Management Experience of Beijing 2008 Olympic Games." In *2010 IEEE International Conference on Emergency Management and Management Sciences*, 535–537. Beijing: IEEE, 2010. https://doi.org/10.1109/ICEMMS.2010.5563382.

Zhang, Xiaoli, and Jiyuan Hu. "Edge City and Its Formation and Growth Mechanism in China: Case Study of Yizhuang New Town, Beijing." Paper presented at the 48th ISOCARP Congress, Perm, Russia,

September 10–13, 2012. http://www.isocarp.net/Data/case_studies/2175.pdf.

Zhong, Lena Y. "Community Policing in China: Old Wine in New Bottles." *Police Practice and Research* 10, no. 2 (April 2009): 157–169. https://doi.org/10.1080/15614260802264594.

Zhu, Jianfei. *Chinese Spatial Strategies: Imperial Beijing, 1420–1911.* London: RoutledgeCurzon, 2003.

Zhu, Kezhen (Chu, K. Z.). "A Preliminary Study on the Climatic Fluctuations during the Last 5000 Years in China." *Scientia Sinica (Series A)* 16 (1973): 226–256.

Zou, Hui. *Jesuit Garden in Beijing and Early Modern Chinese Culture.* West Lafayette, IN: Purdue University Press, 2011.

Zuo, Junjie, Huili Gong, Beibei Chen, Kaisi Liu, Chaofan Zhou, and Yinghai Ke. "Time-Series Evolution Patterns of Land Subsidence in the Eastern Beijing Plain, China." *Remote Sensing* 11, no. 5 (2019): 539. https://doi.org/10.3390/rs11050539.

Index

About the Author

Qian Guo is an associate professor in the Department of Geography and Environment at San Francisco State University. He teaches courses in urban and regional geography and geopolitics. His research interests are in sustainable development and China's western frontiers. He is a native of Beijing.